Industrial Internet of Things and Advanced Techniques for Sensor Data Aggregation and Fusion

Scrivener Publishing
100 Cummings Center, Suite 541J
Beverly, MA 01915-6106

Publishers at Scrivener
Martin Scrivener (martin@scrivenerpublishing.com)
Phillip Carmical (pcarmical@scrivenerpublishing.com)

Industrial Internet of Things and Advanced Techniques for Sensor Data Aggregation and Fusion

Edited by

Kanak Kalita

S. Vishnu Kumar

and

M. Niranjanamurthy

Scrivener Publishing

WILEY

This edition first published 2026 by John Wiley & Sons, Inc., 111 River Street, Hoboken, NJ 07030, USA and Scrivener Publishing LLC, 100 Cummings Center, Suite 541J, Beverly, MA 01915, USA

For more information about Scrivener publications please visit www.scrivenerpublishing.com.

Wiley Global Headquarters
111 River Street, Hoboken, NJ 07030, USA

For details of our global editorial offices, customer services, and more information about Wiley products visit us at www.wiley.com.

The manufacturer's authorized representative according to the EU General Product Safety Regulation is Wiley-VCH GmbH, Boschstr. 12, 69469 Weinheim, Germany, e-mail: Product_Safety@wiley.com.

Library of Congress Cataloging-in-Publication Data

ISBN 9781394275489

Cover image: Generated with AI using Adobe Firefly
Cover design by Russell Richardson

Set in size of 11pt and Minion Pro by Manila Typesetting Company, Makati, Philippines

Printed in the USA

10 9 8 7 6 5 4 3 2 1

Contents

Preface

The rise of the industrial Internet of Things (IIoT) has redefined the landscape of modern technology, blending connectivity, analytics, and advanced computing to empower industries with unprecedented capabilities. This paradigm shift brings about significant advancements in data aggregation, sensor fusion, and intelligent decision-making systems. At the core of IIoT lies the ability to seamlessly integrate hardware, software, and human ingenuity to drive innovations that address complex challenges across diverse sectors.

This book, *Industrial Internet of Things and Advanced Techniques for Sensor Data Aggregation and Fusion,* is a testament to the collective efforts of leading researchers and practitioners who have contributed their expertise to unravel the intricacies of IIoT applications. By covering a wide spectrum of topics, ranging from foundational frameworks to real-world implementations, this book provides a comprehensive view of the state-of-the-art advancements in the field.

To ensure thematic coherence and depth, the book is organized into four parts:

Part I: Foundations and Frameworks in IoT and Data Aggregation

The opening section lays the groundwork for understanding the core principles of IoT and data aggregation. It begins with a discussion on enhancing privacy and efficiency in IoT-enabled business analytics through blockchain-based contingency models. The first chapter illustrates how IoT features, coupled with cryptographic techniques such as SHA256, ensure transparency, accuracy, and secure data handling in collaborative projects.

The second chapter explores hybrid cloud architecture for supporting authorized data deduplication in IoT environments. The integration of IoT devices generating vast amounts of data has highlighted the importance of efficient storage solutions. This chapter addresses scalability, data integrity, and privacy challenges while providing insights into the role of deduplication in managing cloud storage.

The third chapter focuses on the design and analysis of a multiband microstrip patch antenna for IoT applications. The use of HFSS software for optimization and the antenna's versatility in operating across multiple frequency bands highlight its importance for long-distance wireless communication.

Further contributions in this section include a study (Chapter 4) on hybrid multiplier designs for FIR filters, emphasizing reduced power consumption and enhanced computational speed. The fifth chapter presents the comparison of smartphone charging controllers using Arduino Mega and Raspberry Pi and illustrates practical design innovations for energy-efficient electronics. Finally, a study (Chapter 6) on style transfer learning using advanced deep learning models demonstrates how IoT-enabled systems enhance image processing tasks, bridging theoretical advancements with tangible applications.

Part II: IoT in Smart Cities and Infrastructure

IoT's role in shaping smart cities is explored in the second part of this book, highlighting its potential to address urban challenges. The section opens with a chapter (Chapter 7) on efficient traffic detection and localization in 5G networks using IoT-enhanced dynamic ad hoc clusters. It details how IoT devices equipped with sensors enable real-time data transmission, edge computing, and decentralized decision-making for effective traffic management.

Next, a smart parking management system using IoT and RFID technology is introduced (Chapter 8). This system leverages infrared sensors and dynamic light control to optimize urban parking infrastructure, offering an innovative solution to reduce congestion in densely populated areas.

Animal safety in smart cities is another crucial topic discussed through a CNN-based object detection system integrated with IoT (Chapter 9). By utilizing green technology, this system achieves high accuracy in identifying and localizing objects of interest, emphasizing the societal impact of IoT applications.

Chapter 10 on barcode detection and Chapter 11 on automatic ticketing for traffic violators extend the discussion to include automation and surveillance. These chapters illustrate how IoT and deep learning technologies streamline operations in smart cities, making urban environments safer and more efficient.

The section concludes with insights into the use of YOLOv3 for IoT-based object detection in data centers, highlighting real-time monitoring, enhanced security, and system reliability (Chapter 12). A separate chapter (Chapter 13) on face mask detection for public safety underscores the relevance of IoT in addressing contemporary public health concerns, particularly during pandemics.

Part III: Industrial Applications and Predictive Maintenance

This section delves into the integration of IoT in industrial settings, focusing on predictive maintenance, operational efficiency, and resource optimization. Predictive maintenance, a cornerstone of industrial IoT, is explored through the application of CNN and random forest models. Chapter 14 demonstrates how IoT-enabled systems process sensor data to detect faults in machinery, ensuring reliability and efficiency.

Flight delay analysis is another significant industrial application discussed in this section. By using advanced techniques such as XGBoost and K-NN, the chapters highlight the role of IoT in optimizing airline operations, predicting delays, and enhancing passenger experiences (Chapters 15 and 16).

Server traffic load analysis using thermal imaging and wavelet transform techniques is introduced as a novel approach to managing industrial data centers. These studies compare discrete wavelet analysis with stationary wavelets, providing actionable insights into diagnosing server issues with high precision (Chapters 17 and 18).

Part IV: Health, Safety, and Security Applications

The final part of the book addresses IoT applications in health, safety, and security, reflecting its impact on human well-being. Disease diagnosis using AI and IoT-enabled chatbots is presented as a paradigm shift in healthcare. The integration of natural language processing and machine learning models in diagnosing diseases offers a glimpse into the future of personalized medicine (Chapter 19).

Employee churn prediction using IoT-enabled machine learning models addresses challenges in workforce management. Chapter 20 introduces advanced algorithms for attrition prediction, demonstrating the strategic value of IoT in human resource optimization. Chapter 21 talks about the use of data mining technology to enhance blood transfusion systems.

The detection of deepfake images and videos using IoT-integrated systems highlights the role of advanced deep learning models in safeguarding digital content (Chapter 22). Similarly, novel approaches to iris recognition and automated ticketing systems illustrate IoT's contributions to enhancing security and law enforcement (Chapter 23).

The section concludes with an exploration of privacy-preserving educational systems enabled by IoT (Chapter 24). By leveraging federated learning and natural language processing chatbots, the chapter presents innovative solutions for personalized learning in a data-driven world. Subsequently, the final chapter (Chapter 25) extends the scope of intelligent systems to the agricultural domain, where YOLO-powered drones and cloud-based analytics are harnessed for real-time weed density mapping under the Agri 4.0 paradigm.

This book serves as a vital resource for researchers, engineers, and professionals seeking to harness the potential of IIoT in their respective domains. Each chapter not only provides theoretical insights but also emphasizes practical applications, fostering a balanced understanding of concepts and implementations. We hope that the diverse range of topics inspires readers to explore innovative avenues in IoT and sensor fusion.

We extend our heartfelt gratitude to the authors for their invaluable contributions, the reviewers for their meticulous feedback, and the publishers for their unwavering support. This collaborative endeavor would not have been possible without their dedication and expertise.

Kanak Kalita
S. Vishnu Kumar
M. Niranjanamurthy

Part I

FOUNDATIONS AND FRAMEWORKS IN IoT AND DATA AGGREGATION

1

Enhancing Privacy and Efficiency in IoT-Enabled Business Information Analytics and Blockchain-Based Contingency

P. Kumaresan* and R. Ramprashath

School of Computer Application, Karpagam College of Engineering, Coimbatore, Tamil Nadu, India

Abstract

In the article, a contingency model to build a sustainable business with the help of Internet of Things (IoT) features is proposed. It aims to identify a target audience, understand their needs, and assess the competitive landscape. IoT-enabled contingent leaders collaborating with partners can bring new opportunities and access to new markets and shared resources. Document all project requirements in detail and share them with your foreign client to confirm that you are on the same page. IoT sensors can provide real-time data to ensure accuracy and transparency. SHA-256 (secure hash algorithm 256-bit) acts as a cryptographic hash function that takes arbitrary data as input and produces a unique fixed-length (in this case, 256 bits) output called a hash. This hash is like a fingerprint of the data; any changes you make to the data result in a completely different hash. Each block in the proof-of-work blockchain contains a header containing various data, including a hash of the previous block. When a new block is mined, miners must find a specific hash value of the block header that meets certain difficulty requirements. SHA-256 is not the only hashing algorithm used in blockchain. Sharing the software requirements with the client helps to ensure that everyone involved in the project has a clear understanding of what is expected from the technology partner's solution. In this context, software requirements may be shared with the client to ensure that the technology partner's solution is integrated properly and meets the project's needs.

**Corresponding author*: kumaresanpk373@gmail.com

Kanak Kalita, S. Vishnu Kumar and M. Niranjanamurthy (eds.) Industrial Internet of Things and Advanced Techniques for Sensor Data Aggregation and Fusion, (3–16) © 2026 Scrivener Publishing LLC

Keywords: SHA-256 (secure hash algorithm 256-bit), cryptographic hash function, blockchain, hashing algorithm, IoT-enabled, information analytics

1.1 Introduction

In our exploration of sustainable business development, we introduce a contingency model that serves as a strategic framework for building resilient enterprises. At its core, this model underscores the significance of key features in fostering sustainability, with a primary focus on identifying the target audience, understanding their needs, and conducting a thorough assessment of the competitive landscape [1, 2].

Rather than a generic approach, we advocate for a more tailored strategy that involves detailing aspects such as target markets, competitive advantages, marketing and sales plans, and operational requirements [3]. This nuanced perspective ensures a comprehensive understanding of the business environment, paving the way for more effective decision-making and sustainable growth. Integral to the success of the contingency model are contingent leaders who play a pivotal role in fostering collaboration with strategic partners. Such collaborations not only bring forth new opportunities but also provide access to untapped markets and shared resources, reinforcing the sustainability of the business [4, 5].

In the realm of technology, we delve into the significance of cryptographic hash functions, particularly focusing on SHA-256. Acting as a unique fingerprint for data, SHA-256 ensures data integrity and security in blockchain implementations. A recent article explores its role in proof-of-work blockchains, emphasizing the importance of finding specific hash values that meet predefined difficulty requirements during the mining process [6].

However, the technological landscape is diverse, and SHA-256 is just one of the many hashing algorithms in use in blockchain technology. This introduction sets the stage for understanding the broader context of cryptographic protocols and their role in ensuring the reliability of data in various blockchain frameworks [7].

Furthermore, we highlight the importance of transparent communication in project management. Detailed documentation of project requirements, especially in cross-border collaborations, is crucial. Sharing these requirements with foreign clients ensures alignment and a shared understanding of project expectations, laying the foundation for successful outcomes [8]. In this context, software requirements emerge as a critical aspect of project success. Sharing these requirements with clients not only facilitates seamless integration but also ensures that the technology partner's solution aligns with the specific needs of the project [9].

This introduction provides a glimpse into the multifaceted approach of the contingency model, combining strategic business considerations, collaborative leadership, and technological insights to establish a framework for sustainable business development.

1.2 Literature Survey

A recent paper explores the crucial management question surrounding the realization of anticipated economic benefits from information technology (IT) [10]. The study positions the issue as primarily measurement-related and introduces a novel process-oriented methodology designed for ex-post measurement, specifically for auditing IT impacts on the performance of a strategic business unit or profit center. This methodology involves a two-stage analysis of intermediate- and higher-level output variables, incorporating industry- and economy-wide exogenous variables to trace and measure IT contributions.

The evolving landscape of handling vast amounts of sensitive data distributed across mobile devices, wearables, and sensors is explored in [11]. Traditionally, single-system processing has been the norm, using complex models for valuable predictions. However, the rise of distributed machine learning techniques, notably federated and split learning, presents a paradigm shift in protecting user data and privacy without compromising performance.

In Pathak and Wainwright [12], the critical importance of measuring IT success is highlighted for organizational efficiency. Researchers and practitioners emphasize the need to understand the value of IT solutions. The resource-based view and contingency theory are commonly used to measure IT business value (ITBV). Numerous studies have explored the intricate relationship between IT and organizational performance, with ongoing research dedicated to understanding and measuring ITBV.

In Gupta and Raskar [13], the burgeoning field of business analytics, where data-driven insights play a pivotal role in decision-making, this study addresses a critical gap in understanding the mechanisms that enhance organizational decision-making effectiveness (DME). Rooted in the information processing view and contingency theory, the research model proposed in this paper establishes a comprehensive framework linking business analytics to organizational DME. The empirical validation of this model utilizes structural equation modeling and draws upon a substantial dataset of 740 responses from businesses in the United Kingdom.

1.3 Proposed System

To develop a partner management module within the system to streamline the onboarding process and facilitate efficient partner relationship management, implement robust security measures and ensure compliance with international data protection and privacy regulations.

Incorporate encryption, access controls, regular security audits, and vulnerability assessments into the proposed system to protect sensitive partner data. The business objectives of the project are to increase sales, improve customer service, and reduce costs.

The client may have specific usability or design preferences that are unique to their culture. SHA-256 acts as a cryptographic hash function, taking any data as input and generating a unique, fixed-length (256-bit in this case) output called a hash. It is helpful in securing the details in the blockchain.

Attributes definition

1. **Id**: Unique identifier for each project
2. **Customer name**: Name of the customer associated with the project
3. **Title**: Title of the project
4. **Short description**: Brief description of the project
5. **File type**: Type of files associated with the project
6. **Developer**: Name of the developer or development team working on the project
7. **Start date**: The date when the project started
7. **Release date**: Date when the project was released or is scheduled to be released
9. **Project completion**: Percentage of project completion
10. **Project investment**: Investment made in the project
11. **Status**: Current status of the project (e.g., ongoing, completed, pending)

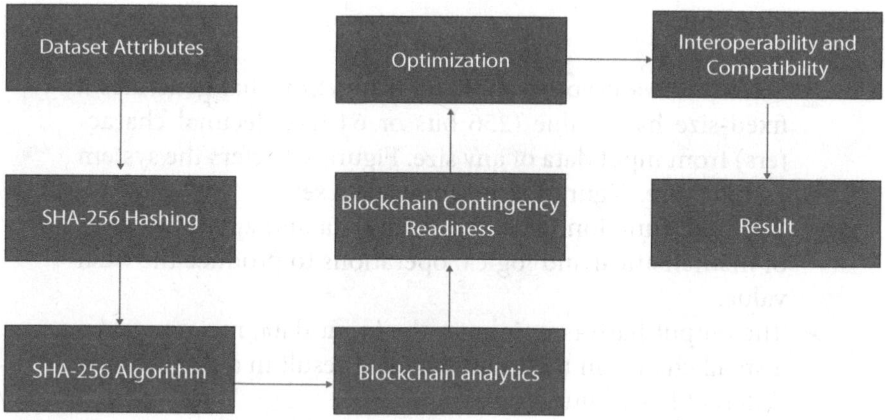

Figure 1.1 System architecture.

Datasets overview

	A	B	C	D	E	F	G	H	I	J	K
1	id	Customer	title	short_des	File type	developer	Start_date	release_d	project co	project in	status
2	6	lie	Blade and	A free-to-p	web conte	NCSoft	20-05-202	19-01-202	75	4500000	Pending
3	8	daniel	Trove	A free to p	web conte	Trion Wor	25-09-202	9/7/2024	90	6500000	Pending
4	10	shami	ArcheAge	A free-to-p	css,js,html	XL Games	30-08-202	4/9/2023	85	5500000	Pending
5	11	jack	Neverwint	A free-to-p	js,html,im	Cryptic Stu	6/9/2023	########	88	2500000	Pending
6	13	liam	Guild War	A free-to-p	web conte	ArenaNet	5/6/2023	28-08-202	73	3000000	Pending
7	16	jackson	Roblox	A free to p	web conte	Roblox Co	14-02-202	22-12-202	66	3500000	Pending
8	62	sky	Kritika: RE	A free-to-p	java,src,lib	ALLM Co.	20-05-202	8/6/2025	65	4600000	Pending
9	64	michael	Secret Wo	A free-to-p	html,imag	Funcom	5/8/2025	31-07-202	85	2800000	Pending
10	77	mason	Revelation	A free-to-p	web conte	NetEase	8/5/2024	6/3/2025	95	4500000	Pending
11	87	logan	MU Legen	A free-to-p	html,imag	VALOFE	20-09-202	23-03-202	78	3500000	Pending
12	89	johan	Adventure	A free to p	images,WI	Artix Ente	25-03-202	19-10-202	72	2000000	Pending
13	106	joseph	Riders of I	A free-to-p	java,src,lib	WeMade	26-04-202	6/7/2024	70	2700000	Pending
14	112	david	Weapons	A 3D free-	web conte	Gamemag	8/5/2023	7/6/2024	65	3400000	Pending
15	116	luke	Tree of Sa	A fantasy	images,WI	IMC Game	15-08-202	########	89	5600000	Pending
16	120	julian	Luna Onlir	A free-to-p	java,src,lib	Suba Gam	19-08-202	17-10-202	88	4700000	Pending
17	154	hudson	Sphere 3:	A fantasy	html,imag	NIKITA ON	20-01-202	18-08-202	78	8500000	Pending
18	161	Ezra	Skyforge	A impressi	java,src,lib	Allods Tea	23-08-202	16-07-202	75	3300000	Pending
19	167	luca	Salem	A free-to-p	images,WI	John Carv	17-08-202	19-06-202	77	7200000	Pending
20	185	dylan	Eldevin	A indie stc	web conte	Hunted Cc	18-09-202	########	92	4600000	Pending
21	190	linclon	Ryzom	An MMOR	java,src,lib	Nevrax	8/5/2024	19-09-202	90	4000000	Pending
22	195	thomas	Divine Sou	A action-b	html,imag	GamePrix	15-07-202	15-08-202	91	4300000	Pending
23	198	jaxon	Creativers	Playful Co	images,WI	Playful Co	16-04-202	########	85	5500000	Pending
24	205	nathan	Elsword	A Free to F	web conte	KOG	17-08-202	23-03-202	86	1200000	Pending
25	206	nolan	Aura Kingc	Aura Kingc	images,WI	X-Legend	28-09-202	23-12-202	88	3300000	Pending
26	221	eli	Lucent He	A free to p	java resou	Playcoco (	30-10-202	########	90	5600000	Pending
27	225	angel	RIFT	Trion Wor	js,html,im	Trion Wor	27-06-202	24-10-202	76	4500000	Pending

Figure 1.2 Datasets.

SHA-256 hashing

- SHA-256 is a cryptographic hash function that generates a fixed-size hash value (256 bits or 64 hexadecimal characters) from input data of any size. Figure 1.1 refers the system architecture. Figure 1.2 is sample data set.
- The hash function takes the input data and applies a series of mathematical and logical operations to produce the hash value.
- The output hash is unique to the input data, meaning even a small change in the input data will result in a significantly different hash value.
- SHA-256 is widely used for data integrity verification, password hashing, digital signatures, and various cryptographic applications due to its collision resistance and computational efficiency.

Theoretical implementation

- In your project, you can use SHA-256 hashing to ensure the integrity and security of project information.
- Before storing or transmitting project details, you concatenate all the attributes into a single string or JSON object.
- For example, you can create a JSON object containing all project attributes: {"id": "123", "customer_name": "John Doe", ...}.
- Then, you convert this JSON object into a string format.
- Next, you apply the SHA-256 hashing algorithm to this string.
- The resulting hash value is then used to represent the entire project information.
- Whenever you need to verify the integrity of the project data, you regenerate the hash value using the same attributes and compare it with the original hash value.
- If the hash values match, it indicates that the project information has not been tampered with.
- Any changes to the project attributes will result in a different hash value, alerting you to potential unauthorized modifications.

Benefits

✓ Using SHA-256 hashing ensures that project information remains secure and tamper-proof.
✓ It provides a reliable method for verifying the integrity of project data.
✓ Even if the project attributes are publicly accessible, the SHA-256 hash serves as a unique fingerprint for the entire dataset, protecting sensitive details.

Module description

- **Integration of the SHA-256 algorithm**: This module incorporates the well-known cryptographic hash function, the SHA-256 algorithm, into the blockchain analytics system. Because of its reputation for reliability and effectiveness in generating distinct, irreversible hash values, SHA-256 is a great choice for protecting sensitive data in blockchain settings.
- **Improvement of data privacy**: The module makes use of the SHA-256 algorithm to improve data privacy in the blockchain analytics process. By making sure that critical company data are kept private and unchangeable, it protects against illegal access and data breaches.
- **Blockchain contingency preparedness**: By offering a dependable method of data verification and integrity assurance, SHA-256 use enhances the blockchain's contingency preparedness. This is necessary to keep company information reliable even in the face of unforeseen circumstances or interruptions.
- **Efficiency optimization**: The SHA-256 algorithm is computationally efficient and has strong cryptographic features, which means that it has no effect on the performance of blockchain analytics processes. This optimization maintains strict privacy standards while enabling smooth data processing and analysis.
- **Compatibility and interoperability**: Across a range of technological contexts, the module's smooth integration with current blockchain frameworks and analytics tools ensures

compatibility and interoperability. Because of this, businesses can take advantage of SHA-256's advantages without having to make major system changes or disruptions.
- **Scalability and flexibility**: This module is designed to be scalable and flexible, as it is a component of a bigger project that focuses on privacy and efficiency in blockchain analytics. It ensures long-term relevance and efficacy by accommodating upcoming blockchain technology improvements and modifications.

SHA-256 algorithm implementation

SHA-256 is a cryptographic hash function that produces a fixed-size output (256 bits or 64 hexadecimal characters) regardless of the input size. It is widely used in various cryptographic applications and is known for its robustness and resistance to collisions (two different inputs producing the same hash). Below is a description of the SHA-256 algorithm along with the formulas involved:

Message padding

- ➢ The input message is padded to ensure its length is a multiple of 512 bits. Padding includes appending a single "1" bit followed by "0" bits until the length is congruent to 448 bits modulo 512.
- ➢ Then, the length of the original message is appended as a 64-bit representation.

Initial hash values (H)

SHA-256 uses eight initial hash values (32 bits each), often represented as H0 to H7. These values are derived from the first 32 bits of the fractional parts of the square roots of the first eight prime numbers.

Message schedule (*W*)

- ➢ The 512-bit message block is divided into sixteen 32-bit words for processing. These words are expanded into a 64-word message schedule using a recurrence relation.
- ➢ For $i = 16$ to 63, $W[i] = \sigma1(W[i\text{-}2]) + W[i\text{-}7] + \sigma0(W[i\text{-}15]) + W[i\text{-}16]$, where $\sigma0$ and $\sigma1$ are bitwise rotation operations.

Compression function

- SHA-256 uses a compression function to iterate over each message block and update the hash values.
- It consists of 64 rounds (0–63), each using a different constant value and nonlinear functions.
- The compression function involves various bitwise operations such as bitwise AND, XOR, NOT, and rotation (shifts).
- It operates on eight working variables (a–h) that hold intermediate hash values.

Hash value calculation

After processing all message blocks, the final hash value (digest) is computed by concatenating the eight 32-bit hash values (a–h) obtained from the compression function.

1.4 Results

The project indicates a substantial improvement in the dual objectives of privacy and efficiency. The implementation of advanced cryptographic methods as part of the privacy measures ensures a robust defined mechanism for business information within the blockchain. This cryptographic layer adds an extra shield, preventing unauthorized access and safeguarding the confidentiality of sensitive data. In the realm of analytics processes, the project achieves notable enhancements in both speed and scalability. The optimization strategies, such as parallel processing and caching, contribute to a more agile and responsive analytics environment. These improvements translate to quicker data analysis, enabling businesses to extract valuable insights promptly. Moreover, the success of smart contracts in addressing contingency scenarios stands out as a crucial achievement. The designed smart contracts exhibit adaptability and resilience in adverse conditions, showcasing the system's ability to respond effectively to unforeseen events. This not only ensures the continuity of operations but also establishes a reliable framework for handling unexpected challenges in the dynamic business landscape.

In essence, the detailed results affirm the project's efficacy in achieving its core objectives, highlighting the successful integration of advanced privacy measures, efficiency optimization in analytics processes, and a robust contingency handling mechanism through smart contracts within the blockchain system.

1.5 Discussion of Results

1. Implications for strengthening privacy

The results demonstrate the effective reinforcement of data security and have significant consequences for privacy. The solution makes sure that private company data are protected from unwanted access by using cutting-edge encryption techniques. For example, homomorphic encryption maintains the confidentiality of the data by enabling calculations to be done directly on encrypted data.

2. Operational efficiency gains through analytics optimization

Significant increases in operational efficiency can be attributed to well-optimized analytics procedures. Data analytics can be performed more quickly and scalable with the help of methods such as caching and parallel processing. For instance, parallel processing allows multiple jobs to be completed at once, greatly cutting down on processing time and increasing overall efficiency while managing large datasets.

3. Insights from challenges and refinement

A detailed discussion of the difficulties encountered throughout the testing and implementation phases yields insightful information for improvement. For example, thorough analysis and remedies are provided if problems occur during the integration of the privacy framework. Through this iterative method, any unexpected challenges that arise throughout the project's lifetime are addressed, and ongoing development and fine-tuning are ensured.

4. Comparative evaluation and creative input

The novel contributions of the research are highlighted through a comparative analysis of the current literature. The research shows improvements in striking a balance between privacy, efficiency, and flexibility by comparing the project to tried-and-true techniques and solutions that have been published in the literature. For example, contrasting the suggested privacy framework with conventional techniques demonstrates the project's creative solution to current issues in blockchain-based analytics.

1.6 Conclusion

The project emerges as a resounding success in addressing the dual challenges of bolstering privacy and optimizing efficiency within the intricate realm of blockchain-based business information analytics, especially in contingency scenarios. The incorporation of advanced cryptographic methods, exemplified by homomorphic encryption, demonstrates a robust commitment to fortifying data security. This cryptographic layer ensures the confidentiality of sensitive business information, preventing unauthorized access and safeguarding against potential breaches. Simultaneously, the project strategically implements optimization techniques, including parallel processing and caching, resulting in significant operational efficiency gains within analytics processes. Parallel processing, facilitating simultaneous task execution, markedly reduces processing time, while caching minimizes redundant computations, collectively enhancing the overall agility of data processing. The integration of Internet of Things (IoT) devices provides real-time data feeds, further enriching the analytics and enabling proactive decision-making. The project's proactive stance toward contingency scenarios is highlighted by the successful functionality of smart contracts. These contracts showcase a dynamic adaptability, ensuring the system's resilience and effectiveness in responding to unforeseen events. For instance, during simulated contingency scenarios, smart contracts autonomously adjust to ensure business continuity, illustrating a robust preparedness for adverse conditions. IoT sensors monitor these contracts and environmental conditions, triggering automated responses to maintain operational integrity.

Crucially, the conclusion underscores the project's commitment to a balanced and adaptive approach, delicately reconciling the imperatives of stringent privacy measures and streamlined operational processes. This equilibrium, crucial for navigating the dynamic nature of contemporary business landscapes, positions the project as a pioneering and relevant solution for evolving challenges in blockchain-based business information analytics.

1.7 Limitation

Recognizing the limitations of the proposed system is crucial. Acknowledging potential vulnerabilities, scalability constraints, and dependencies on specific technologies serves as a foundation for future research and development. This awareness guides efforts to address these limitations, ensuring a more comprehensive and robust solution in subsequent iterations. The limitations section promotes transparency and fosters a proactive approach to continuous improvement.

References

1. Melville, N., Kraemer, K., Gurbaxani, V., Review: information technology and organizational performance: an integrative model of IT business value. *MIS Q.*, 28, 283–322, 2004.
2. Weingarten, F., Humphreys, P., Cao, G., McHugh, M., Exploring the Important Role of Organizational Factors in IT Business Value: Taking a Contingency Perspective on the Resource-Based View. *Int. J. Manage. Rev.*, 15, 1, 30–46, Jan. 2013.
3. Singh, H. and Dubey, S.K., Perspective Approach towards Challenges and Opportunities to Extract Value from Big Data. *J. Inf. Process. Syst. (Communicated)*.
4. Cebr: Data equity, unlocking the value of big data, in: SAS Reports, pp. 1–44, 2012.
5. LaValle, S., Lesser, E., Shockley, R., Hopkins, M.S., Kruschwitz, N., Big data, analytics and the path from insights to value. *MIT Sloan Manage. Rev.*, 21, 2013.
6. Galbraith, J.R., Organizational Design Challenges Resulting from Big Data. *J. Organ. Des.*, 3, 1, 2, Apr. 2014.
7. Ebner, K., Buhnen, T., Urbach, N., Think Big with Big Data: Identifying Suitable Big Data Strategies in Corporate Environments, in: *2014 47th Hawaii International Conference on System Sciences*, Los Alamitos, CA, USA, pp. 3748–3757, 2014.
8. Big data: The next frontier for innovation, competition, and productivity, McKinsey & Company. [Online]. Available: http://www.mckinsey.com/insights/business_technology/big_data_the_ next_frontier_for_innovation. [Accessed: 23-Sep-2014].
9. Krizhevsky, A., Learning multiple layers of features from tiny images, Dept. Comput., Univ. Toronto, Toronto, Canada, Tech. Rep., 2009.
10. McMahan, H., Moore, E., Ramage, D., Hampson, S., y Arcas, B.A., Communication-efficient learning of deep networks from decentralized data, in: *Proc. Int. Conf. Artif. Intell. Statist.*, pp. 1273–1282, 2017.
11. Liu, S., Yu, J., Deng, X., Wan, S., FedCPF: An efficient-communication federated learning approach for vehicular edge computing in 6G communication networks. *IEEE Trans. Intell. Transp. Syst.*, 23, 2, 1616–1629, Feb. 2022.

12. Pathak, R. and Wainwright, M.J., FedSplit: An algorithmic framework for fast federated optimization, in: *Proc. Int. Conf. Neural Inf. Process. Syst.*, pp. 7057–7066, 2020.
13. Gupta, O. and Raskar, R., Distributed learning of deep neural network over multiple agents. *J. Netw. Comput. Appl.*, 116, 1–8, 2018.

2

Supporting Authorized Duplicate Check in Hybrid Cloud Architecture Using IoT

Balaji B.* **and Ram Prashath R.**

School of Computer Application, Karpagam College of Engineering, Coimbatore, Tamil Nadu, India

Abstract

Data sharing and storage have become much more convenient because of the cloud's growing popularity and widespread use. When exchanging data with plenty of participants, consideration is given to issues such as data integrity, efficiency, and data owner privacy. One of the biggest issues facing cloud storage services is handling the ever-growing amount of data being stored on the cloud. In the world of cloud computing, deduplication is a well-known data compression technology that removes multiple copies of repeated data from cloud storage, thereby making data management more scalable. With the integration of Internet of Things devices generating vast amounts of data, the importance of efficient data management has further increased. Even though data deduplication greatly improves security and privacy, users' sensitive data remain vulnerable to both insider and outsider attacks. Convergent encryption protects the confidentiality of data while enabling deduplication. Even though they offer confidentiality, classic elimination platforms based on convergent encryption do not support duplicate checks based on differential privileges. This work introduces the concept of authorized data deduplication, which includes user privilege differences in the detection of duplicates to safeguard data security. In addition to the data itself, deduplication systems and users with varied privileges are considered during duplicate checks. Differential privilege keys are used for file encryption to provide increased security. Users may run the duplication check only on files that are designated with the appropriate access credentials. Through data auditing and the assistance of a third-party auditor, the user can confirm that their files are present in the cloud following deduplication. Additional auditor checks validate the file that was uploaded.

**Corresponding author*: balaji21ji@gmail.com

Kanak Kalita, S. Vishnu Kumar and M. Niranjanamurthy (eds.) Industrial Internet of Things and Advanced Techniques for Sensor Data Aggregation and Fusion, (17–30) © 2026 Scrivener Publishing LLC

As a result, this article uses auditing and deduplication techniques to benefit the user and storage provider, respectively.

Keywords: Authorized check duplicates, confidentiality, auditing, IoT

2.1 Introduction

Cloud computing is the practice of hiding platform and setting up specifics while offering consumers limitless virtualized resources as a service [1]. Users can now access high-availability storage and extensively parallel computing assets at comparatively low rates, thanks to cloud services. However, the issue concerns cloud users who have varying levels of privilege. One of the biggest challenges in managing network data storage systems is storing data on the cloud. Redundant data copies are stored in storage. This method can be used to decrease the number of bytes that need to be delivered before upload during data transfers, as well as to increase storage utilization. Rather than storing duplicate copies of the same material, deduplication can be used to eliminate redundant data, leaving just one physical copy and referring to the other redundant copies as needed. Software architects begin to encounter new technology challenges as rising technologies typically do, and they must alter their current solutions and structures to meet the new demands. Cloud computing and edge computing are experiencing the same issues [2], yet this tactic is not working. Researchers and software developers are therefore considering fresh, creative approaches. Using a Message-Oriented Middleware (MOM; The Ministry of Employment and) for Cloud-to-Edge management might be a potential strategy. Specifically, a MOM—which is built on an IMP (instant-messaging protocol)—allows for the separation of the communication and signaling device from the business logic, which significantly simplifies the setup on any of the coordinates of applications and services that also involve devices at the edge. Despite the clear advantages of deduplication, concerns about the privacy of data that are outsourced have also drawn a lot of attention [3]. Due to their loss of control over their outsourced data in external storage systems during outsourcing, data owners are unable to ensure the secure administration. To support deduplication, end users try to outsource the encryption of their content *via* convergent encryption. In this case, collaboration between the cloud and the last users (on the intra-network) are better suited for server-side deduplication, which permits repetitive publishes of duplicate data but removes them beginning at the server side. This is because it prevents unauthorized users from discovering side information that determines whether duplicate content is stored in afar or not.

2.2 Literature Review

Benkhelifa and Fernando's [13] testimony on quality proposed a novel hybrid security strategy that would be implemented as a legitimate business case project. The project calls for a more complex security plan because it involves exceedingly sensitive data. The hybrid solution—single sign-on but two-factor [4] authentication—is recognized by the project collaboration and end users as a state-of-the-art and highly secure authentication technique. Quality of service (QoS) [11] has developed several deduplication strategies that demonstrate how deduplication allows for enticing reductions in the consumption of storage resources. To recover storage space used by accidentally redundant content, the file system that is distributed presents challenges in recognizing and merging identical files. QoS is a recently proposed encryption technique that ensures semantic security for data that are not popular, while offering weaker security and improved storage as well as bandwidth benefits for material that is popular [5]. Commonly used data that are not very sensitive are encrypted using normal methods. Another two-layered encryption system that supports deduplication and has higher security is suggested for data that are not widely used. They were able to better balance security and efficiency in this way [1].

Important software development steps include optimizing the tool for the user, ensuring economy and satisfaction, updating the operating system, and deploying the tool. Once the coders have the tool, the most crucial step in the development process for a literature review is getting this assistance, which might come from books, or the system mentioned above [6]. Prior to development, it is essential to ascertain the strength of the organization. Following these actions, programmers must decide which open language to use for development. They must then begin building the tool, which will require extensive outside assistance. This was acquired from websites by senior programmers. Prior to constructing the system, the suggested system was taken into consideration. A cooperative provable data possession (PDP) strategy for scalability across several storage servers was proposed by the veritable response and hash.

Our scheme offers complete security, zero knowledge interactive proof, and robustness against various threats, even when used for deep audit services in cloud environments. In addition, dynamic ever are supported by furthermore randomized query and recurrent very hash index hierarchy. It also demonstrated the qualities that the system needed in order to be made available to the public and enhanced the certification process.

Our tests amply proved that our methods add very little in the way of processing [7] and communication overheads. As a result, our method can be considered a fresh contender for data integrity checking in systems that store data on the cloud. We would expand our research to investigate more efficient cooperative provable data possession (CPDP) structures as part of further work. First, our research revealed that the high complexity of the bilinear mapping procedures has an impact on the CPDP scheme's performance, particularly for large files. Although Rivest-Shamir-Adleman (RSA)-based designs might be a better option to fix this issue, RSA-based schemes now in use have too many limitations on performance and security, making this a difficult endeavor [3]. Concerns about privacy and security are major issues in public cloud systems. In response to these security issues, quality suggested a novel client-side deduplication method for safely transferring and storing outsourced data over public cloud infrastructure [8]. Better secrecy from unauthorized users is ensured. To scramble the data, the user may want to save it in the cloud; each client calculates a unique key. Therefore, the data owner controls data access. Additionally, a novel cryptographic technique for secured proof of ownership (PoW) is introduced, enhancing information safety cloud-based storage environments, enabling dynamic user sharing, and guaranteeing effective data deduplication [4].

From a practical standpoint, we still have to tackle a few issues regarding the seamless integration of our scheme with current systems [9]. These include matching the index structure and the cluster network model, as well as dynamically updating the CPDP parameters by Hadoop Distributed File System (HDFS's) unique requirements. Another example of an issue to be addressed is how to match the index of a hash hierarchy with the two-layer name space of HDFS. Ultimately, the creation of tags whose duration is independent of data block size remains a difficult task. To add support for variable-length block verification, we would investigate this matter.

2.3 Research Methodology

Select an appropriate research methodology: Based on the goals of the study and the resources at hand, choose a suitable methodology, such as tests, case studies, experiments, or experimental research.

Methods for collecting design data: Decide if information will be gathered *via* surveys, trials, interviews, or the examination of already-existing datasets. Choose study subjects: Determine whether relevant parties can shed light on the study topic, such as cloud service suppliers, information technology specialists, and regulatory experts.

System model

(i) **Cloud user**: In cloud computing, a cloud user is someone who wants to outsource data to public storage, which serves as a public cloud. A system offers an authenticating mechanism for entering data into the system and grants specific permissions for accessing and downloading the uploaded data (Figure 2.1).

(ii) **Public memory**: This is a type of storage drive that permits users to store authorized material on it while preventing the uploading of duplicate data. Consequently, it conserves transmission bandwidth and storage space. The uploaded data are encrypted and can only be decrypted by a user who has the appropriate key.

(iii) **Private cloud**: The private cloud serves as a proxy that enables users and data owners to safely carry out differential privileges and duplication checks.

(iv) **Auditor**: When a user requests assistance, an auditor, a trusted platform access (TPA), provides experience and skills that cloud customers do not have to rely on to evaluate the dependability of cloud storage services.

Each privilege's symmetric key and set are assigned and then kept in a private cloud. When a user registers with the system, rights are granted to them based on the identity they provided during registration, which is based on the posts they have accessed. In addition to performing identification and sending the file tag to the private server, the data owner among a privilege issued set want to put up and share a file with users.

The data owner is confirmed by the private cloud server, which also computes the folder's token and returns it to them. The data owner sends the file credential and the file upload request to the storage provider. In the event that an extra file is found, the user will have to prove their ownership of the file in question using the storage service's proof-of-work protocol. If proof of possession is successful, the user will get an access code to the correct file associated with the PoW result. Regarding the second example.

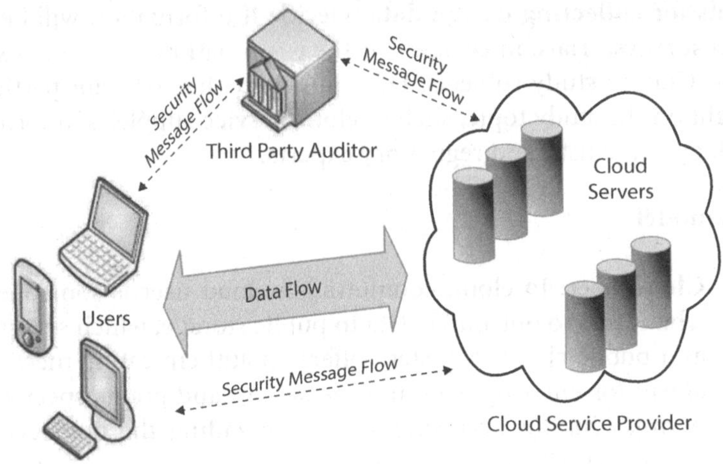

Figure 2.1 System modules of authorized duplication.

If a duplicate copy of the file is discovered, the cloud storage provider will return a signed copy of the proof for that specific file. The user requests the upload of a file by sending the proof and the privilege set to the exclusive cloud server.

At last, the user calculates the encryption. The user encrypts the file using a key, and each key in the file token provided by the private cloud server is encrypted into ciphertext. Subsequently, the user uploads the encrypted key, file tag, and file. Let's say the user wants to download the file. The user initially obtains the key by using their private key to decrypt the encrypted key. The original file is then recovered by the user. The user's certainty over the file's existence on the cloud is not absolute. Thus, an auditing technique is used to check the files kept in the public vault for the benefit of the users. The user chooses an auditor from the web and provides the auditor with the metadata for the files they intend to upload. The auditor notifies the public storage of the audit or challenges it to ensure that the data file was correctly retained by the cloud server at the time about the audit. By using an execute function on the saved data file and associated verification information, public cloud storage will generate a response message. After that, the TPA checks the response using the user's data file.

2.4 Implementation

Using three distinct Java packages, we created a prototype of the intended authorized deduplication system with auditing. A cloud user is a data user who uploads and downloads files to and from public storage. The computation of file tokens and the management of private keys are handled by a private cloud. A public repository will store files that are duplicates and check for them. Using Javax crypto packages, we implement cryptographic operations such as hashing and encryption/decryption [11] and provide cloud computing services for storage needs.

2.4.1 System Analysis

Data confidentiality and permission for duplicate checks will be examined for security. In order to ensure duplicate security, internal and external adversaries must be taken into account. These adversaries may attempt to breach the system by gaining unauthorized access to cloud data or by breaking in (Figure 2.2).

2.4.1.1 The Duplicate-Check Token's Unforgery

Pretend that a user has privilege p but might forget their new duplicate-check token if any of them does not match p. If it is a legitimate token, then the calculation $f, p = H1(H(F), kp)$. Remember that it is a legitimate

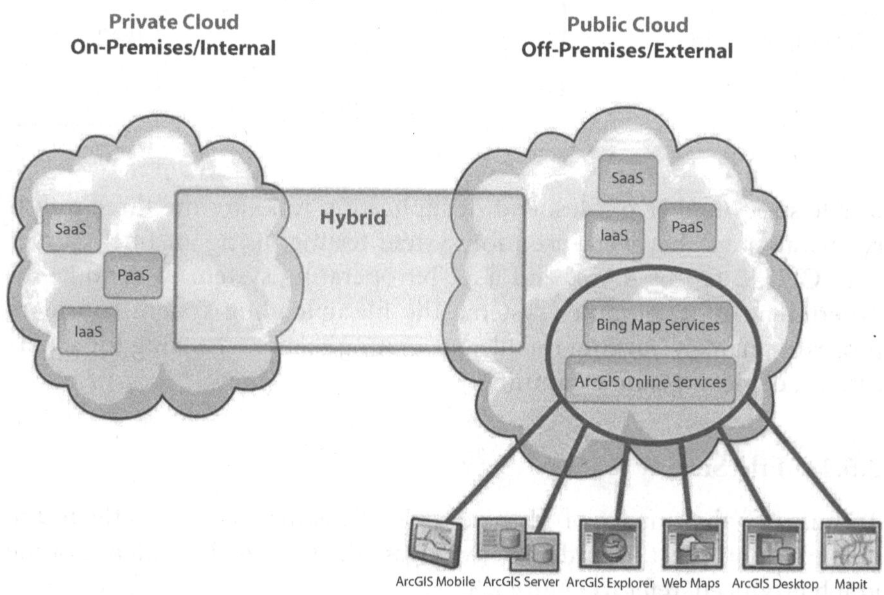

Figure 2.2 System analysis duplication tokens.

message authentication code that is stored on a private cloud server *f*, *p* = *H*2(*H*(*F*), *kp*), as a secret key. As a result, without it, the adversary is unable to forge and produce a fresh, legitimate one for every file. A new duplicate check token can be output by any user with privilege, but it also needs to be aware.

2.5 Evaluation

Remember that the ciphertext-policy attribute-based data encryption strategy suggested is the foundation of our attribute-based storage system. However, this scheme was unable to withstand duplicated tendencies. Let |pars|, |msk for short|, |ct|, |L|, |T|, |sk|, and |A| represent the public parameter and the maste sizes, respectively.

	System public parameter $|pars|$	**System master private key** $|msk|$	**Public cloud label and ciphertext** $|ct|+|L|$	**Private cloud tag and label** $|T|+|L|$	**User private key** $|sk|$
CP-ABE	6	1	$3l+2+|A|$	-	$2k+2$
The proposed storage system	10	1	$3l+5+|A|$	3	$2k+2$

File size, number of files, and deduplication ratio are the three different parameters that were used for system testing, using an Intel Core 2 Duo CPU, 3 GB of RAM, and a 32-bit operating system to conduct an experiment on a computer system. The file uploading system considers processes, namely, tagging the file, generating tokens, checking for duplications, deploying, and examining.

2.5.1 File Size

To quantify the impact of file size, upload distinct files to mitigate the deduplication effect. In order to investigate the file size dependence of the graph produced, refer to Figure 2.3.

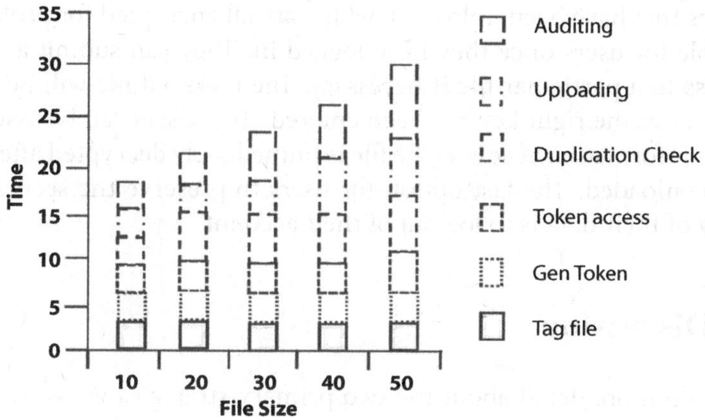

Figure 2.3 Crack-up time for different file size.

2.5.2 Deduplication Ratio

In order to quantify the impact of deduplication, a higher percentage of deduplication results in a much faster uploading time. This represents our system's main benefit. The uploading time goes away to zero when the deduplication ratio hits 100%. Comparing a file had 100% deduplication ratio Figure 2.4. to a unique file, the entire time spent uploading is merely 41.26%.

The required personal data must be supplied. They can access their account by logging in after the cloud user gives permission. Viewing the

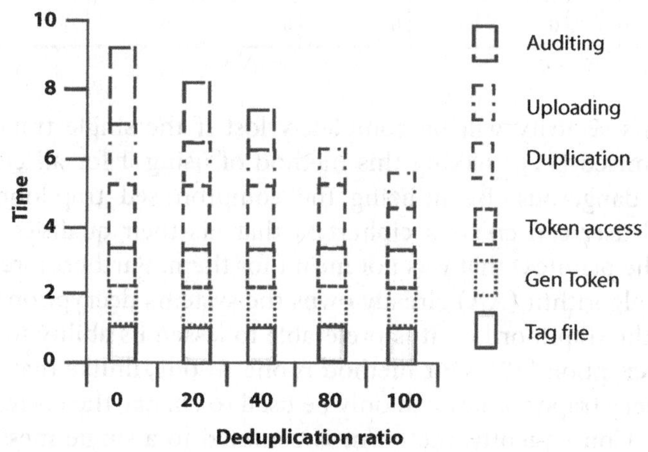

Figure 2.4 Crack-up time for different deduplication ratio.

bank files that have been uploaded, which are all encrypted for protection, is possible for users once they have logged in. They can submit a request for access to a particular file if necessary. The required file will be downloadable after the right key has been entered [10]. Users can be assured of seamless information access as the file is immediately decrypted after it has been downloaded. The last option for users to preserve the security and integrity of their data is to log out of their account.

2.6 Discussion

We go into more detail about the two primary strategies we presented in this study.

2.6.1 Adaptable Attribute-Based Encryption

With the introduction of a semitrusted proxy into the ciphertext-policy attribute-based encryption (CP-ABE) context, researchers introduced a mostly adaptive CP-ABE cryptographic primitive. For any ciphertext falling under a single access policy, the proxy can convert it into ciphertexts that include the same plaintext by providing a system-wide trapdoor key.

	Tag	Label	Encrypt	Proof	Trap door key	Re-encrypt	Validity	Equality	Decrypt
Expo	2	2	$5l+1$	3	1	$6l+2$	5	0	$\leq k+2$
Pairing	0	0	0	0	0	0	0	2y	$\leq 3k+1$

The system's security will be completely lost if the single trapdoor key is compromised [11], making this method of using it for all ciphertexts extremely dangerous. By utilizing the compromised trapdoor key, an adversarial user can create a ciphertext that fits their qualities and gain access to the plaintext that was not meant for them. Furthermore, because the Affine algorithm (AA) already owns the system's decryption keys and generates the trapdoor key, it is preferable to lessen its ability to manipulate the encryption [12]. Our method is one-to-one, unlike that in meaning that every trapdoor key can only be used to change the corresponding ciphertext. Consequently, the harm is confined to a single message even if a trapdoor account is compromised at some time. Our method offers an alternative approach to developing adaptive CP-ABE systems from a distinct perspective [13–15].

2.7 Results

Effective duplicate checking system: The deployment of a productive duplicate check system that can find duplicate data in cloud and on-premises storage settings, using cutting-edge methods and algorithms to compare data quickly, save processing overhead, and guarantee fast duplication identification.

Framework for authorization: This includes creation of a framework for authorization to control access rights for repeated operations and integration with current identity and access management (also known as IAM) systems to guarantee that only authorized users are able to start duplication checks and to implement role-based access control.

Safe transmission of data: During duplication check procedures, secure data communication methods are implemented to make data transfer between on-site and cloud systems easier, using cryptography and encryption methods to safeguard data confidentiality and integrity while it is in transit, reducing the chance of interception or tampering.

Watching and notifying: These include setting up warning and monitoring systems to find errors, anomalies, or breaches of safety during repeat check procedures. Incorporating centralized logging and monitoring systems allows for real-time visibility into security posture and system performance, enabling prompt incident reaction and corrective action.

2.8 Future Discussion

To improve the security of duplication and check processes, research is being done on sophisticated cryptography methods and authentication procedures. Research on quantum-resistant algorithms and postquantum cryptography is being done to help reduce the security threats that the development of quantum computers may bring. Distributed ledger systems and smart contracts are created to automate and implement permission policies for repeated check processes.

Artificial intelligence–driven and machine learning approaches: Combining machine learning techniques for pattern identification, anomaly detection, and intelligent deduplication allows for more precise and effective duplicate detection.

2.9 Conclusion

It is now quite convenient to share and collect data, thanks to the popularity and extensive use of the cloud. Keeping up with the ever-growing amount of data material saved is a major problem for cloud storage providers. The well-known technology of data deduplication has been used to make data management scalable in remote computing schemes. To remove redundant copies of repeated data in storage, a specialized data compression technique called *data deduplication* is used. With the integration of IoT (Internet of Things) devices generating vast amounts of data, the importance of efficient data management has further increased. Data deduplication has many advantages, but it also raises security and privacy issues because users' private information is vulnerable to both insider and outsider threats. By incorporating user privilege differences in the duplicate check, the concept of authorized data deduplication was put forth in this study as a means of preserving data security. The dissimilar user permission sets are taken into account during duplicate verification, in contrast to conventional deduplication systems

References

1. Kit Li, Y., Chen, X., Lee, P.P.C., Li, W.L.J., A Hybrid Cloud Approach for Secure Authorized. *IEEE Trans. Parallel Distrib. Syst.*, 1–12, 2014.
2. Quinlan, S. and Dorward, S., Venti: A new approach to archival data storage, in: *Conference on file and storage technologies (FAST 02)*, 2002.
3. Quick, D., Martini, B., Choo, R., *Cloud storage forensics*, Syngress, 2013.
4. Choo, K.R., Domingo-Ferrer, J., Zhang, L., Cloud cryptography: Theory, practice and future research directions. *Future Gener. Comp. Syst.*, 62, 51–53, 2016.
5. Choo, K.R., Herman, M., Iorga, M., Martini, B., Cloud forensics: State-of-the-art and future directions. *Digit. Invest.*, 18, 77–78, 2016.
6. Wang, Li, B., Li, H., Oruta: Privacy Preserving Public Auditing for Shared Data in the Cloud. *Proc. IEEE Fifth Int'l Conf. Cloud Computing*, pp. 295–302, 2012.

7. Armbrust, M., Fox, A., Griffith, R., Joseph, A.D., Katz, R.H., Konwinski, A., Lee, G., Patterson, D.A., Rabkin, A., Stoica, I., Zaharia, M., A View of Cloud Computing. *Commun. ACM*, 53, 4, 50–58, Apr. 2017.
8. Nurnberger, S., Sadeghi, A., Schneider, T., Bugiel, S., Twin clouds: An architecture for secure cloud computing. *Workshop on Cryptography and Security in Clouds (WCSC 2011)*, 2011.
9. Coynek, E.J., Feinsteink, H.L., Youmank, C.E., Sandhu, R.S., Role Based Access Control Models. *IEEE Comput.*, 29, 38–47, Feb 1996.
10. Chow, S.S.-M., Wang, Q., Ren, K., Lou, W., Wang, C., Privacy Preserving Public Auditing for Secure Cloud Storage. *Comput. IEEE Trans.*, 62, 2, 362–375, Feb, 2011.
11. Douceur, J.R., Adya, A., Bolosky, W.J., Simon, P., Theimer, M., Reclaiming space from duplicate files in a serverless distributed file system, in: *Proceedings 22nd international conference on distributed computing systems*, 2002, July, IEEE, pp. 617–624.
12. Halevi, S., Harnik, D., Pinkas, B., Shulman-Peleg, A., Proofs of ownership in remote storage systems, in: *Proceedings of the 18th ACM conference on Computer and communications security*, 2011, October, pp. 491–500.
13. Benkhelifa, E. and Fernando, D.A., A Novel cloud hybrid access mechanism for highly sensitive data exchange. *Cloud Comput.*, pp. 19–24, 2013.
14. Kumar, S.V., Mary, G.A.A., Chohan, J.S., Kalita, K., Original Research Article Efficient sensor anomaly detection using Markov-LSTM architecture for methane sensing. *J. Auton. Intell.*, 7, 3, 2024, Doi: 10.32629/jai.v7i3.1285.
15. Kumar, S.V., Chohan, J.S., Kalita, K., WhaleOptNB: A Method for Automated Biomedical Text Document Classification, in: *Intelligent Computing and Optimization, ICO 2023*, Lecture Notes in Networks and Systems, vol. 1169, P. Vasant, *et al.* (Eds.), Springer, Cham, 2024, Doi: 10.1007/978-3-031-73324-6_18.

3

Design and Analysis of Multiband Microstrip Patch Antenna for IoT Applications

R. Ramasamy[1]*, Arunachala Perumal C.[1], Bharathi C. Ramachandra[2], Srikusan A.[1] and Vijayan S.[1]

[1]*Department of Electronics and Communication Engineering, Ramco Institute of Technology, Rajapalayam, India*
[2]*Department of Electronics and Communication, Vel Tech Rangarajan Dr Sagunthala R&D Institute of Science and Technology, Chennai, India*

Abstract

Long-distance wireless communications and data collection are prevalent uses of the Internet of Things (IoT). Regardless of the IoT application profile, highly efficient antennas are essential for all wireless communication transmissions. Therefore, the antenna's crucial role cannot be overlooked. The proposed antenna is designed to operate within a triple-band spectrum centered at 2.94 GHz and undergoes a meticulous optimization process facilitated by high frequency structure simulator (HFSS) software. FR4 was chosen as the substrate for the antenna design due to its dielectric constant of 4.4 and dielectric height of 1.6 mm. This rigorous evaluation demonstrates that the performance of the triple-band rectangular microstrip patch antenna has improved, making it suitable for IoT applications. This contribution provides detailed insights that advance IoT communication systems. Two PIN diodes (D1 and D2) enable mode conversion and resonance at 2.18, 2.94, and 4.24 GHz, proving the antenna's versatility. Activating D1 and deactivating D2 restrict the antenna to 2.18 GHz. The antenna operates in the 2.94-GHz IoT band with D1 off and D2 on. The antenna was designed, developed, simulated, and evaluated using the HFSS tool. The results demonstrated a high degree of performance and suitability for IoT applications, particularly in the 2.94-GHz frequency band.

**Corresponding author*: rramasamy2014@gmail.com

Kanak Kalita, S. Vishnu Kumar and M. Niranjanamurthy (eds.) Industrial Internet of Things and Advanced Techniques for Sensor Data Aggregation and Fusion, (31–46) © 2026 Scrivener Publishing LLC

***Keywords*:** Multiband rectangular patch antenna, IoT applications, FR4 substrate, parametric analysis, energy efficiency, PIN diode

3.1 Introduction

In the rapidly evolving landscape of the global network IoT, the significance of selecting the right antenna cannot be overstated. Antennas act as the gateway for communication, enabling devices to send and receive data wirelessly. As IoT applications proliferate, encompassing everything from smart homes to industrial automation, the necessity for reliable, efficient, and high-performance antennas becomes paramount. The choice of antenna profoundly impacts the range, data throughput, and overall functionality of the IoT systems.

The antennas are considered to be the backbone of communication; a well-chosen antenna can facilitate seamless data transmission over various distances, overcoming obstacles and interference. Selecting the wrong antenna, on the other hand, can lead to detrimental outcomes, such as unreliable connections and increased latency.

In context of the right antenna for a specific IoT application, several factors come into play. First, frequency range is of critical importance. Different IoT devices operate at various frequencies, depending on the technology they use—whether LoRaWAN, Zigbee, NB-IoT, or traditional Wi-Fi. An antenna tailored to the specific frequency of operation ensures optimal performance, maximizing signal strength and quality, while minimizing power consumption.

The gain of the antenna is another crucial consideration. Gain indicates how well an antenna directs radio waves in a particular direction, enhancing the distance at which data can be transmitted or received. High-gain antennas can be particularly beneficial in sprawling smart industrial setups or urban environments laden with obstructions, allowing devices to communicate effectively over significant distances. Conversely, low-gain antennas are ideal for short-range applications, providing a more omnidirectional spread.

In addition, the physical size and form factor of the antenna also play a vital role from an IoT point of view. As devices shrink in size to meet modern design aesthetics and practical requirements, antennas must also adapt. Antennas can now be embedded within circuit boards, printed directly onto surfaces, or designed as smaller, flexible models, allowing for greater integration into a variety of devices. This leap in design flexibility enables manufacturers to create compact, visually appealing products without compromising on performance.

Importantly, durability in harsh environments is another consideration. IoT devices, especially those stationed outdoors or in industrial settings, are vulnerable to elements, be it extreme temperatures, humidity, or physical impacts. Selecting antennas that are weather-resistant and robust ensures uninterrupted performance, safeguarding the integrity of data transmission even under unpredictable conditions.

Furthermore, the antenna's efficiency determines the battery life, a critical parameter for countless IoT applications. Devices powered by batteries must utilize energy efficiently to prolong operational life. A well-designed antenna will maximize received signals and minimize power consumption, allowing devices to operate longer without frequent recharges—a crucial consideration for remote monitoring systems.

In practical terms, deploying the right antenna is crucial for ensuring robust network connectivity. It enables sensors to continuously transmit data to cloud-based platforms, allowing for real-time analytics and immediate response mechanisms. Without the right antenna, disruptions in communication can occur, hindering the efficiency of IoT systems. Thus, the antenna plays a pivotal role in maintaining seamless communication between devices, making it an essential component for anyone seeking to harness the full potential of IoT.

As we move further into an era dominated by connected devices, the importance of the right antenna in IoT applications cannot be underestimated. It determines whether systems operate smoothly or experience disruptive interference and whether responses are timely or delayed. Selecting the right antenna is a strategic decision that can optimize network performance, enhance energy efficiency, and enable innovative applications. In this interconnected world, antennas have become a cornerstone of IoT infrastructure, transforming what was once considered science fiction into a reality where technology seamlessly integrates into everyday life

3.2 Related Works

Yahya *et al.* suggested a triple-band microstrip patch antenna (MPA) antenna for IoT applications. The IoT applications are the target market for the proposed triple-band antenna. The recommended frequency of the proposed design was compatible LoRA frequency range [1]. Anchidin *et al.* have proposed an MPA antenna for IoT applications that works at 868 MHz and has a higher bandwidth and reflection coefficient [2]. A tunable slot antenna for IoT applications was proposed by Ketavath *et al.* [3], that can function in two frequency bands and has a large bandwidth and small size. This work includes a varactor diode and an antenna [4].

Monopole antennas were presented by Bhardwaj *et al.* for narrowband IoT applications; with a radiation efficiency higher than 96% and a maximum gain of 3.3 dB, the proposed antenna operates in the dual frequency band [5]. Fayyaz *et al.* created a multiband orbital angular momentum antenna with circular polarization; 3.49, 5.92, and 4.63 GHz make up the triple-band configuration of the proposed antenna. It provides greater gain and bandwidth [6]. Ramasamy *et al.* created a circular MPA antenna focusing on IoT applications, which has a high gain, improved bandwidth, and a dual-band operational design [7]. Dash *et al.* proposed a multiband fractal antenna for IoT applications, which has a lower specific absorption rate (SAR) value than other existing techniques. Its wide bandwidth and high gain are other features [8]. Aboualalaa *et al.* proposed a multiband retractable antenna for connected smart office applications. In its multiband configuration, the recommended antenna has a lower SAR value, a greater gain, and a wider bandwidth [9]. Yahya *et al.* presented a multiband MPA antenna that can operate in the 915-, 868-, and 433-MHz frequencies, specifically intended for smart connected applications, with reduced cost, and that shortens the switching times by using radiofrequency PIN diodes for frequency reconfiguration [10].

Hussain *et al.* proposed a tunable antenna for IoT applications. This proposed antenna operates in the frequency range of 3.36 to 3.6 GHz and provides a low profile, simple bias, DC bias, radiation suppression in two PIN diodes, and the ability to suppress radiation in undesired directions [11–14]. Ramasamy *et al.* proposed a compact ultra-wideband multiple-input multiple-output (UWB MIMO) antenna tailored for smart environment. The design incorporates a modified electromagnetic band gap (MBEG) structure and a dumbbell shape to enhance isolation and minimize mutual coupling between antenna elements [14, 15].

Based on the pros and cons identified from this recent reported literature, the current study aims to design and develop a multiband MPA for IoT connectivity. The suggested antenna has a low-profile shape of 60 × 60 × 1.6 mm and is intended to resonate multiband.

3.3 Design Calculation

A multiband rectangular MPA has been developed for improved analysis and performance. Figure 3.1 illustrates this design. Triple-frequency

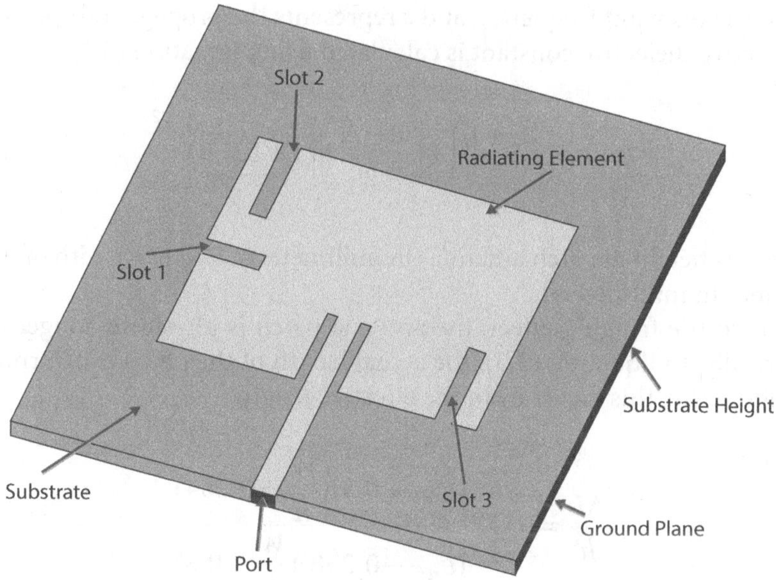

Figure 3.1 Proposed antenna design geometry.

bands, including 2.18, 2.94, and 4.24 GHz, are usable for this antenna. One popular kind of antenna in many wireless communication systems and IoT technology is the suggested multiband MPA. Due to its modest profile and very easy manufacturing, it can be included in compact electrical equipment. Attached to one side of a dielectric substrate is a ground plane. In contrast, after determining the working multiband frequencies of 2.18, 2.94, and 4.24 GHz, as well as the substrate's dielectric constant, FR4, a metallic patch is linked to the other.

The dimensions of the proposed MPA were developed using approximations of Equation [16] as follows. The suggested antenna has a radiating element, an FR4 substrate, a ground plane, three slots, and a PIN diode. It can achieve high gain, high bandwidth, and a triple-band resonating frequency and be used for IoT applications.

Patch width (in millimeters) is calculated using Equation (3.1):

$$W = \left(\frac{c}{2f_r}\right)\sqrt{\frac{2}{(\varepsilon_r + 1)}} \tag{3.1}$$

where f_r is resonant frequency, and c represents the propagation speed.

Effective dielectric constant is calculated using Equation (3.2):

$$\varepsilon_{reff} = \left(\frac{\varepsilon_r + 1}{2}\right) + \left(\frac{\varepsilon_r - 1}{2}\right)\left[1 + 12\frac{h}{w}\right]^{-1/2} \tag{3.2}$$

where h is height of patch antenna (in millimeters), and w is width of patch antenna (in millimeters).

Due to the fringing effect, the antenna patch is physically longer than electrically. In Equation (3.3), the actual length of the patch is determined by subtracting this factor from the effective length.

$$\frac{\Delta L}{h} = 0412\frac{(\varepsilon_{reff} + 0.3)(\frac{W}{h} + 0.264)}{(\varepsilon_{reff} - 0.258)(\frac{W}{h} + 0.8)} \tag{3.3}$$

In Equation (3.4), ΔL is the length extension, and L is the actual length of the antenna.

Actual length

$$L = L_{eff} - 2\Delta \tag{3.4}$$

The proposed antenna was connected to a transmission feed line with an inset of 50 Ω. The reason this approach was selected is that it does not need any extra matching parts. The transmission feed line's width and length are determined by the equation. In order to match the input impedance, the feed position was changed 1.44 mm from the edge, whereas the distance between the feed line and the patch is 3 mm. After doing all the calculations per the above formulas, the optimized antenna parameters are shown in Table 3.1.

Return loss: The return loss of an antenna quantifies the difference between the transmitted and received powers along the cable. A lower value for return loss indicates more efficient power conversion. Return loss is calculated as the ratio of reflected power (Pr) to transmitted power (Pt).

Table 3.1 Proposed antenna design parameters.

Design parameters	Values (mm)	Design parameters	Values (mm)
L_p	29.3	Ws_3	10
W_p	38	Ls_1	2
L_s	60	Ls_2	2
W_s	60	Ls_3	2
Ws_1	10	L_f	3
Ws_2	10	W_f	1.6

A return loss as low as 55 dB is superior to one as high as 25 dB when aiming to maximize power conversion efficiency.

Gain: The gain of an antenna is a numerical representation of the amount of energy transmitted by the antenna compared to an isotropic source. Compared to directional characteristics, antenna gain is a more comprehensive measure. Therefore, it is often prioritized in antenna parameters.

Compared to a lossless, isotropic antenna, the performance of a transmission antenna with a gain of 3 dB is superior since the received signal is 3 dB stronger. A lossless antenna would exhibit an output of 0 dB (or 100%). The reception antenna will have a 3 dB higher gain in a specific direction than the gain of the lossless isotropic antenna.

The bandwidth of an antenna is a crucial measurement because it specifies the range of frequencies over which it can transmit or receive signals effectively. Different antenna types exhibit varied properties, making it challenging to agree on a specific bandwidth. For instance, the bandwidth of some antennas is so narrow that they cannot be used with modern wideband applications.

$$\text{Broadband bandwidth} \equiv \frac{f_h}{f_l} \quad \text{narrowband bandwidth}(\%) \equiv \frac{f_h f_l}{f_c} \tag{3.5}$$

In Equation (3.5), f_h is higher frequency, f_l is lower frequency, and f_c is center frequency. Antenna bandwidth is typically described using voltage standing wave ratio (VSWR). An antenna's operating range, such as 125 to 315 MHz, specifies the frequency region in which it operates with optimal VSWR values and performance.

Radiation pattern: The variation in the antenna's radiated power with distance is due to the antenna's radiation pattern. This power variation, which is affected by the arrival angle concerning distance, is perceptible in the antenna's far field.

3.4 Patch Antenna Design

3.4.1 Block Diagram

The design process for the finalized IoT antenna is shown in Figure 3.2. The following criteria must be considered when designing the antenna for the IoT system: range, frequency, power consumption, and environmental conditions.

Our methodology for developing antennas for IoT applications incorporates antennas that function as both radiating and sensing elements. With clear findings, this study moves IoT communication systems forward. The antenna can change modes and resonate at 2.18, 2.94, and 4.24 GHz with the help of two PIN diodes (D1 and D2). When you turn off D2 and turn on D1, the receiver can only work at 2.18 GHz. The receiver works in the 2.94-GHz IoT band with D1 off and D2 on. HFSS was used

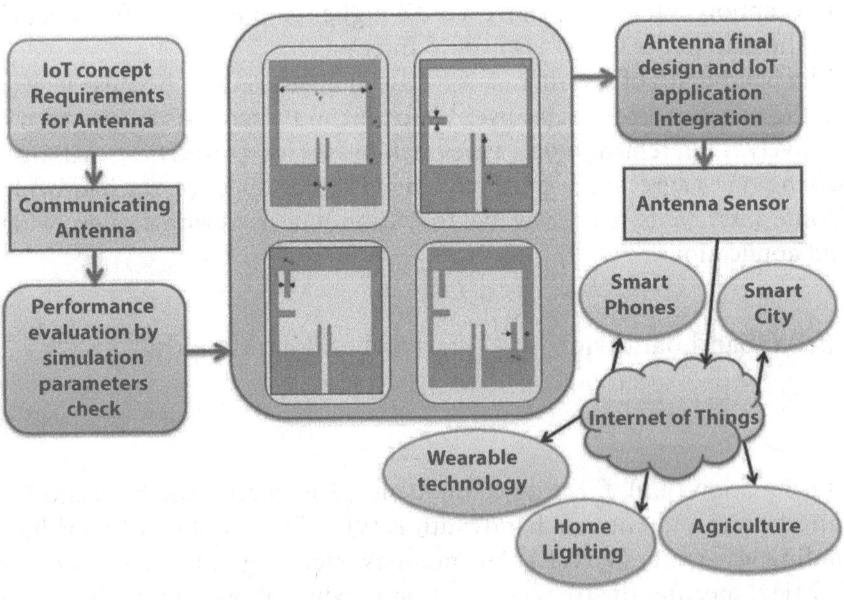

Figure 3.2 Proposed design block diagram.

to design, build, test, and rate the antenna. The results were very good, and they can be used in IoT apps, especially at 2.94 GHz.

Communicating antennas send and receive data to and from the IoT network. In the IoT system, it talks to other devices, gateways, or servers. Performance review checks how well the whole IoT system works, including the antenna subsystem. It could include things such as signal strength, data transfer rates, power economy, and so on. A completed antenna and IoT app integrating the antenna design with the IoT application is essential for efficient and successful communication. By carefully creating and testing the antenna to meet standards and smoothly integrating it into the IoT device, sensor data transfer and real-time monitoring and control are achieved. Finally, an antenna sensor gathers information about its surroundings or the things it is monitoring. This could include motion, humidity, temperature, and so on. These are the various use cases or applications that the IoT system enables. This might apply to healthcare applications, industrial monitoring, smart home automation, and so on.

3.4.2 Antenna Design

Antennas are more than just parts that radios need; they are also transducers that transform electrical impulses into electromagnetic ones. They also improve a receiver's reception by picking up radio waves from the air and converting them to voltage. Antennas are essential for establishing and maintaining reliable radio connections, and their diverse shapes and sizes can appear intricate and enigmatic even to experienced engineers, especially when working with a wide range of remote systems.

3.4.3 Ground Plane

The antenna's ground plane acts as an imitation of Earth's surface by reflecting radio waves. This grounds plane functions as a mirror for monopole antennas such as quarter wavelength antennae, creating a visible duplicate of the antenna's lower half below ground. This phenomenon can be simulated by replacing the actual Earth with a conducting plane, effectively replicating the reflective characteristic.

Due to factors such as cost and permeability to wind, it is not always required or possible to use a fully circular conducting plate as the ground plane. Instead of a circular ground plane, a ground plane with multiple wavelength radials is used; typically, four conducting radials are used to achieve this effect. Figure 3.3(a) depicts the ground plane dimensions for the suggested antenna design: $Lg = 60$ mm and $Wg = 60$ mm.

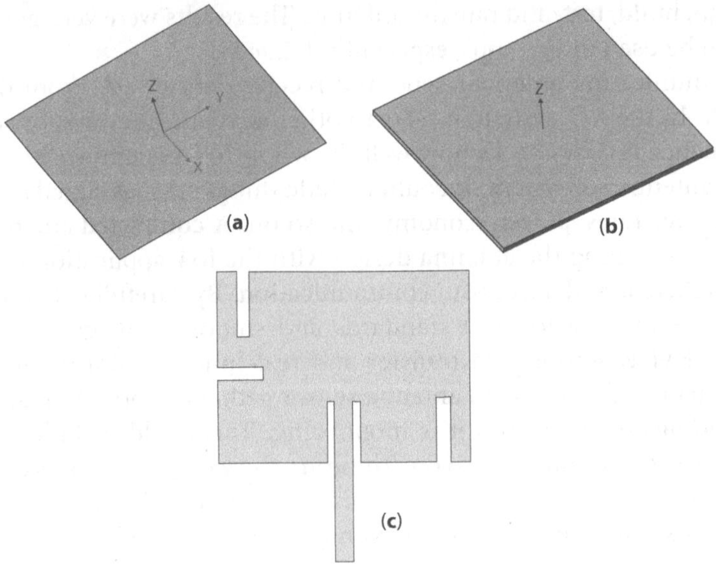

Figure 3.3 (a) Ground plane, (b) substrate, (c) antenna.

3.4.4 Patch

Because the microstrip transmission line is attenuated at its ends, the antenna's radiation pattern is determined by this incoherence. The antenna seems electrically larger than its actual size by radiating energy outward at its edges. Resonance is achieved by using a microstrip transmission line significantly shorter than the whole wavelength at the operating frequency. Antenna patches come in various shapes and sizes, but they all have the same basic design principle of having a metal patch rest on a ground plane. Figure 3.3(c) depicts the patch layout of our suggested technique.

3.4.5 Multiband MPA

The patch length (*L*p) and width (*W*p) are calculated for the curvature-shaped MPA, along with the substrate length (*L*s) and width (*W*s). To overcome the drawbacks of conventional MPAs, the curvature form patch antenna stands out as the most beneficial of the many possible patch shapes. Figure 3.4 is a graphical representation of the stages in the development of antennas. Because the patch's four corners are curved, bandwidth and return loss are greatly enhanced. In addition, this antenna design has many benefits, such as low manufacturing cost, simple mounting, small size, and a low profile.

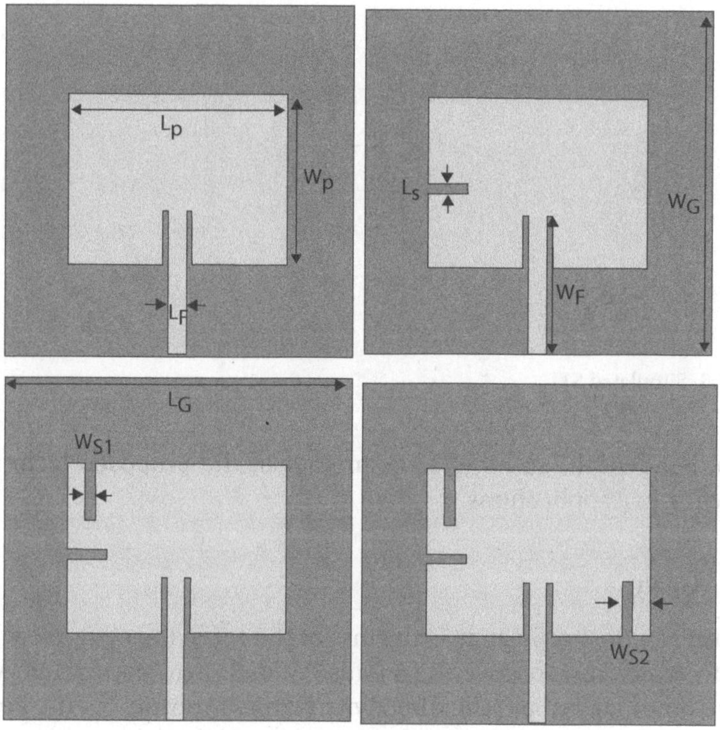

Figure 3.4 Proposed antenna design evolution.

The dielectric constant of the FR4 substrate used by the antenna is 4.4, and its thickness is 1.6 mm; this allows the antenna working multiband frequencies of 2.18, 2.94, and 4.24 GHz. The three different frequency bands that the suggested antenna is intended to operate at are 2.18, 2.94, and 4.24 GHz. There are four versions of the multiband MPA that are being suggested. The MPA antenna's general structure is depicted in iteration 1 of Figure 3.4. Slot 1 was introduced in iteration 2. Iteration 2 performs better in terms of bandwidth, gain, and reflection coefficient when compared to iteration 1. In a similar vein, iteration 3 is also more performance than iteration 2. In a similar manner, iteration 4 also produced slot3. Iteration 4 offers superior outcomes in every category as compared to the previous three iterations.

3.5 Results and Discussion

The simulated S11 multiband MPAs of all four iterations are shown in Figure 3.5. It is clearly shown that iteration 4 gives better results in terms

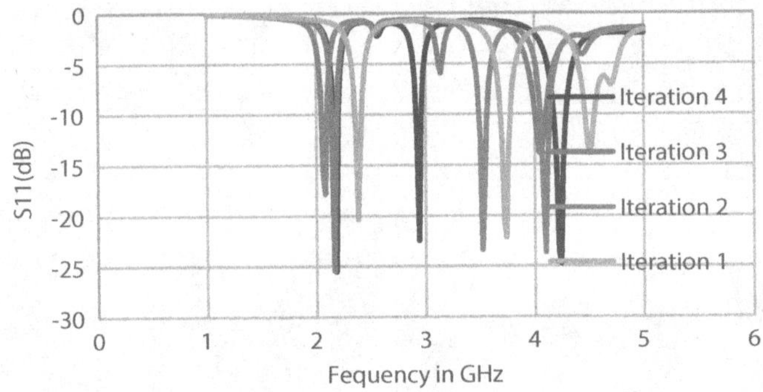

Figure 3.5 Simulated S11.

of gain, bandwidth, and low SAR; moreover, the proposed technique is suitable for IoT applications.

3.5.1 Gain

In Figure 3.6, the proficiency is the loss of the receiving equipment due to assembly faults, surface covering anomalies, dielectric, opposition, VSWR, or some other factor, and the directivity is the proportion of the grouping of an antenna's radiating design in a particular method. It can be seen from the graph that curvature-shaped MPAs have a higher gain than other patch antennae.

3.5.2 Radiation Pattern

The radiation pattern of an MPA with curvature is shown in Figure 3.7. According to elevation and azimuth angle, the radiation pattern depicts the signal power emitted by the antenna at a specific resonant frequency. A respectable level of organization between the simulated radiation pattern patterns is attained.

3.6 Conclusion

This study introduces a smart multiband MPA designed to operate across multiple frequencies. The antenna dimensions are 29.4 × 38 × 1.6 mm and were meticulously designed and modeled using HFSS software. Simulation results indicate excellent performance with a VSWR of 0.5 and return losses of 25.52, 22.46, and 24.78 dB at frequencies of 2.18, 2.94, and

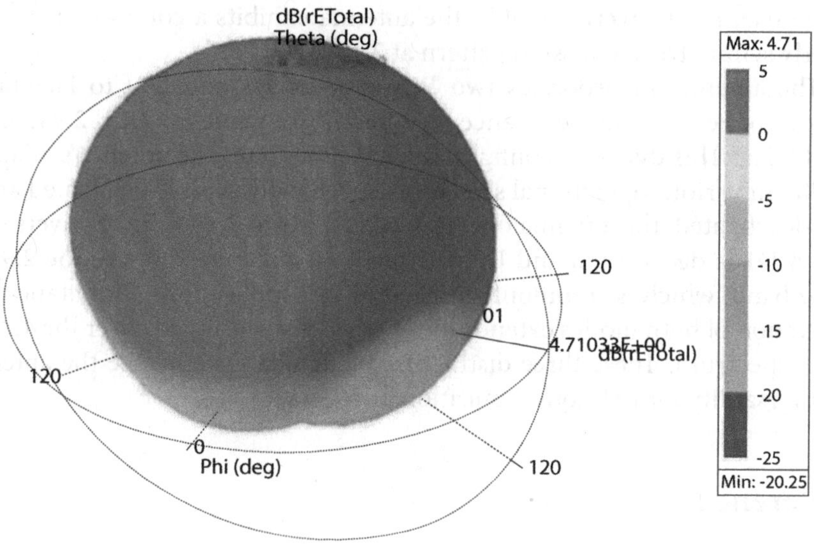

Figure 3.6 Simulated gain.

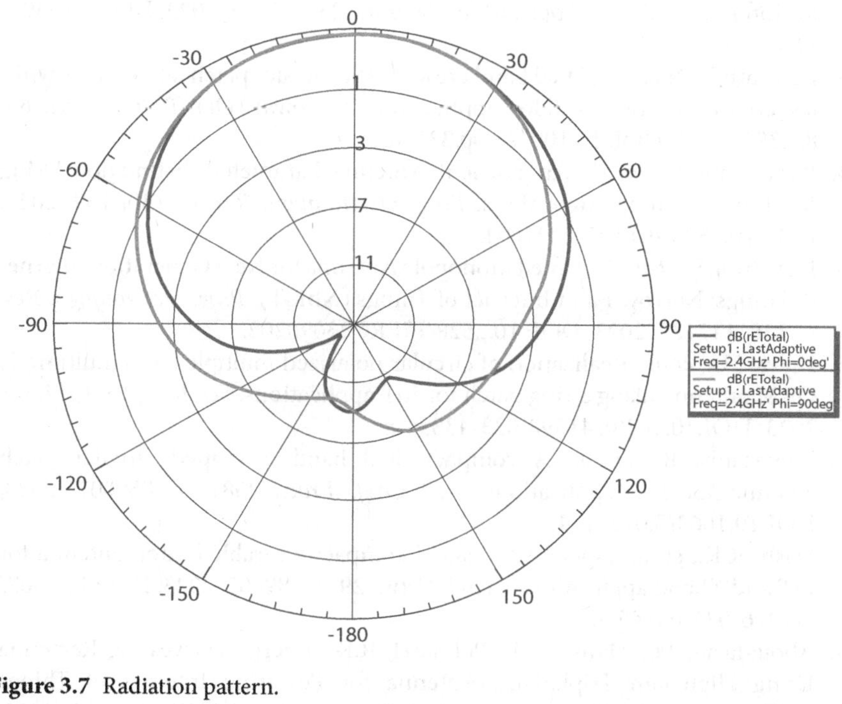

Figure 3.7 Radiation pattern.

4.24 GHz, respectively. Notably, the antenna exhibits a compact size and nearly symmetrical emission pattern at 2.18 GHz.

The antenna incorporates two PIN diodes (D1 and D2) to facilitate mode conversion and resonance at different frequencies: 2.18, 2.94, and 4.24 GHz. This dynamic configuration demonstrates the antenna's adaptability in various operational scenarios. Specifically, with D1 activated and D2 deactivated, the antenna operates exclusively at 2.18 GHz. Conversely, when D1 is deactivated and D2 activated, the antenna shifts to the 2.94-GHz band, which is commonly utilized in IoT applications. Simultaneous activation of both diodes extends the antenna's capability to cover the 4.24-GHz spectrum. These three distinct frequency bands enhance the antenna's versatility for IoT communication purposes.

References

1. Yahya, M.S., *et al.*, TripleBand Reconfigurable Monopole Antenna for Long Range IoT Applications. *Sensors*, 23, 12, 5359, 2023, DOI:10.3390/s23125359.
2. Anchidin, L., *et al.*, The Design and Development of a Microstrip Antenna for Internet of Things Applications. *Sensors*, 23, 3, 1062, 2023, DOI: 10.3390/s23031062.
3. Ketavath, K.N., *et al.*, Dual band crescent shaped slot patch antenna for wireless communications and IoT applications. *Microwave Opt. Technol. Lett.*, 65, 8, 2392, 2023, DOI: 10.1002/mop.33708.
4. Ramasamy, R., *et al.*, An Efficient Antenna Parameters Estimation Using Machine Learning Algorithms. *Prog. Electromagn. Res. C*, 130, 169, 2023, DOI: 10.2528/PIERC22121004.
5. Bhardwaj, S., *et al.*, A Printed Monopole Antenna for Next Generation Internet of Things: Narrow Band Internet of Things (NbIoT). *Prog. Electromagn. Res. C*, 138, 117129, 2023, DOI: 10.2528/PIERC23090202.
6. Fayyaz, U., *et al.*, Realization of circular polarized multiple band multimode OAM antenna using a ring patch for IoT applications. *Sci. Rep.*, 13, 1, 17060, 2023, DOI:10.1038/s41598-023-43836-x.
7. Ramasamy, R., *et al.*, A compact dual band E shaped circular patch antenna for IoT applications. *AIP Conf. Proc.*, 2581, 1, 050007, 2023, DOI:10.1063/5.0126174.
8. Dash, R.K., *et al.*, Fractal slot loaded compact wearable button antenna for IoT and Xband applications. *Wirel. Netw.*, 29, 2, 589605, 2023, DOI: 10.1007/s11276-022-03145-z.
9. Aboualalaa, M., Mansour, I., Pokharel, R.K., Energy Harvesting Rectenna Using HighGain TripleBand Antenna for Powering Internet of Things (IoT) Devices in a Smart Office. *IEEE Trans. Instrum. Meas.*, 72, 112, 2023, 2001312, doi: 10.1109/TIM.2023.3238050.

10. Yahya, M.S., Soeung, S., Chinda, F.E., Rahim, S.K.B.A., Musa, U., Nor, N.B.M., Cheab, S., A Compact Reconfigurable MultiFrequency Patch Antenna for LoRa IoT Applications. *Prog. Electromagn. Res. M*, 116, 7789, 2023.
11. Hussain, R., Alhuwaimel, S.I., Algarni, A.M., Aljaloud, K., Hussain, N., A Compact Sub GHz Wide Tunable Antenna Design for IoT Applications. *Electronics*, 11, 1074, 2022, https://doi.org/10.3390/electronics11071074.
12. Kumar, V.V., Ramasamy, R., Janarthanan, S., VasimBabu, M., Implementation of IoT in smart irrigation system using arduino processor. *Int. J. Civ. Eng. Technol. (IJCIET)*, 8, 10, 1304–1314, 2017.
13. Ramasamy, R., Anto Bennet, M., Vasim Babu, M., Jayachandran, T., Rajmohan, V., Janarthanan, S., A Novel Efficient AI Based EEG Workload Assessment System Using ANNDL Algorithm. Presented at the, 2023, https://doi.org/10.1007/9789811987427_62.
14. Ramasamy, R., *et al.*, A Compact UWB MIMO Antenna for IoT Applications. *2021 Innovations in Power and Advanced Computing Technologies (i-PACT)*, IEEE, 2021.
15. Ramasamy, R. and Bennet, M.A., Optimizable KNN and ANFIS Algorithms Development for Accurate Antenna Parameter Estimation. *Prog. Electromagn. Res. C*, 142, 207–218, 2024, doi:10.2528/PIERC23091403.
16. Kumar, V.S., Mary, A.A.G., Esakki, B., Analyzing the Applicability of ML Powered Microwave Sensor for UAV Based CH4 Sensing. *Int. J. Electr. Electron. Telecommun. Eng.*, 12, 3, 161–170, 2023, doi:10.18178/ijeetc.12.3.161-170.

4

Simulation and Implementation of Advanced Adder and Hybrid Multiplier for FIR Filter

V. Magesh*, T. Solai Mithelesh, S. Ponmaniselvan and P. Praveen Kumar

Dept. of ECE, Velammal Engineering College, Chennai, India

Abstract

Reduced power consumption and optimized area are given top priority in the development and application of digital signal processing (DSP) technology. The Filter of finite impulse response (FIR) is an essential part of this process because it maximizes area, speed, and power usage. Adder blocks, flip flops, and multiplier blocks make up the FIR filter. But the multiplier is usually the slowest block, which affects performance as a whole. In order to minimize power consumption and maximize multiplier speed, a hybrid multiplication technique is utilized. This method uses a hybrid adder (carry select, Weinberger, and Ling adder) to simultaneously add the partial products of two successive bits (multiplicands). Xilinx ISE 12.1 is used to synthesize and simulate the suggested design utilizing a variety of field programmable gate array (FPGA) devices.

Keywords: Finite impulse response filter, adder, multiplier, delay

4.1 Introduction

In signal processing, a filter having a finite impulse response (FIR)—one that zeroes out after a certain amount of time—is referred to by the term FIR filter [1, 2]. In contrast, the IIR (infinite impulse response) filter has an endless response and internal feedback capacity. A time-varying FIR filter of the *N*th order has an impulse response that lasts exactly $N + 1$ sample

**Corresponding author*: magesh@velammal.edu.in

Kanak Kalita, S. Vishnu Kumar and M. Niranjanamurthy (eds.) Industrial Internet of Things and Advanced Techniques for Sensor Data Aggregation and Fusion, (47–60) © 2026 Scrivener Publishing LLC

before zeroing off [6]. FIR filters can function either in discrete or continuous time and can be digital or analogue.

Finding the coefficients and filtering order that meet particular needs in the domain of frequency (more frequent) or the time domain (which includes a matching filter) is the first step in creating an FIR filter. A cross-correlation with the source signal and a predetermined pulse shape is carried out using matching filters. The FIR convolution is produced by cross-correlating the input signal with a reversed copy of the impulse response. This suggests that the appropriate filter's impulse response is "designed" by using samples of the identified pulse form to calculate the filter's characteristics in the opposite order.

Another way of making filters is the window design method. This involves first designing an optimum IIR filter and then truncating the resulting continuous impulse response by multiplying it by a window function of limited length [3]. The result is a limited impulse response filter that has a modified frequency response as compared to the IIR filter. Whenever an infinite impulse as well as window component multiplies each other in the time domain, the frequency response of the IIR is mixed with the Fourier transform of the window function. The combined frequency response stays near that of the optimal IIR filter if the primary lobe of the window is narrow.

The ideal response for a filter is frequently rectangular, and the corresponding IIR has a sinc function [13]. A frequency domain convolution causes the rectangle's borders to contract, and ripples appear within the passband and stopband. By determining the extent of the waves and the slant (or breadth) of the tapering zone (transition band), one may get the frequency domain characteristics of an appropriate window function. By repeatedly running a filter design program to determine the impulse response, the minimum filter order may be obtained. An alternate method to restrict the set of solutions is to use a parametric group of Kaiser windows, which provides closed-form connections among the variables in both time and frequency domains. For software programs that require dynamic, real-time filter construction, this method is particularly helpful even if it might not achieve the lowest possible filter order.

An electrical circuit called a binary multiplier is used to multiply two binary integers in digital devices, such as computers. To build it, binary adders are used. There are several computer arithmetic methods that can be used to create a digital multiplier. The majority of methods entail computing a number of partial products and adding them all together. This procedure has been altered for use with the base-2 (binary) numeral system, although it is essentially the same as the lengthy multiplication approach taught to students for base-10 integers [4]. An effective design for a combinational multiplier is the array multiplier. Pipelining array multipliers can reduce clock period but come with a price in latency [5].

4.2 Literature Survey

A unique approach for creating FIR filters in linear phase with low power consumption and hardware efficiency was presented by Mustafa Aktan [15]. The algorithm, given the characteristics of the filter frequency response, finds filter coefficients with less signed-power-of-two terms.

To lower the power and area consumption, Indranil Hatai [16] provide a two-step optimization process for creating an interpolation filter's reconfigurable VLSI design for multistandard digital up converters.

Two novel reconfigurable designs of simple FIR filters are suggested by R. Mahesh *et al.*: the constant shifts technique and the programmable shifts method. In multistandard systems for wireless communication, reconfigurability and low complexity are the two primary requirements for FIR filters.

A limited impulse response digital filter with a low power and high-performance architecture based on the ring topology—a model derived from a recurrent neural network —is provided by Bahram Rashidi [17]. The suggested structure is built on a ring topology with fewer clock cycles, multipliers, and adders.

Jason Thong [18] offer common subexpression elimination (CSE) algorithms to look for and replace. In an attempt to minimize the number of adders (or subtracters) required for constant multiplication, common patterns are looked for in the CSE representation of a constant. Because of intrinsic limitations in the CSE format, CSE algorithms generally are not able to identify certain patterns.

Nowadays, folding adaptable IIR filters are used for real-time digital signal processing applications such as speaker equalization. Mohamed Asan Basiri *et al.* have suggested an extremely efficient large-scale integration architecture for this purpose [9, 11].

P. Prancy [19] presents a simple heuristic method for hardware optimization of a half-band IIR filter. The optimization method here is intended to provide quick design choices at the structure level without requiring resource-intensive simulations and calculations.

A frequency domain design technique for IIR digital filters is presented by M. C. Lang [20]. The suggested approach creates filters that roughly represent the required phase and magnitude responses. These types of IIR filters can equalize the amplitude and phase responses of specified systems, or they can have roughly linear-phase responses in their passbands.

For the sum of two all-pass functions, a modified tapped all-pass structure was introduced by Norbedo and L. Svensson [21]. The all-pass portions of the linear coefficients of the new structure enable the inclusion of limitations to the filters, such as group delay constraints or null constraints.

The novel low-power decimation filter design by K. H. Abed [22] consists of an equivalent linear-phase one-third-band IIR filter, a half-band FIR filter, and a poly-phase FIR-4 comb filter. A poly-phase FIR-4 comb filter design consumes 75% less power than a recursive comb filter architecture.

4.3 Proposed System

Our goal in this study is to create a programmable hybrid multiplication-based FIR filter [7]. The parallel prefix addition concept was used to develop the Han–Carlson adder (HCA) [10], the primary component of this filter. The combined advantages of reduced space and delay generated by the Brent–Kung along with Kogge–Stone adders enable the HCA to exceed conventional adders with respect to speed, energy usage, and number of hardware components.

The pre-prefix and post-prefix steps make up the HCA. The following formulas are used to determine the generate (Gi) and propagate (Pi) signals during the preprocessing stage:

$$\text{Generate} = A_i \& B_i \tag{4.1}$$

$$\text{Propagate} = A_i \oplus \mathrm{B}_i \tag{4.2}$$

Additionally, the blocks using the k to ith bits expanded the expressions:

$$G_i = G_{i-1} \oplus G_{i-2} \& P_{i-1} \tag{4.3}$$

Only at the postprocessing phase is the approximate output sum bit necessary to ascertain the final output carry bits. The following expression is used to get the final sum:

$$S = P_i \wedge G_{i-1} \tag{4.4}$$

Figure 4.1 shows the construction of the HCA for clarity of vision.

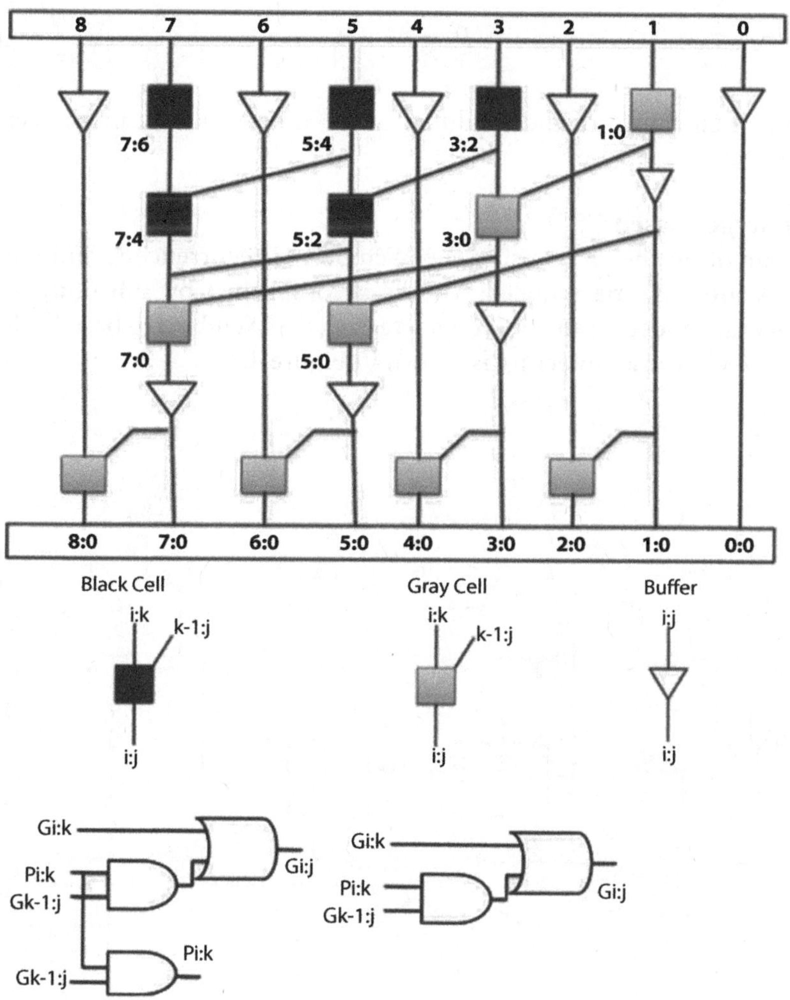

Figure 4.1 Adder by Han–Carlson.

Ling adder

For better performance in terms of lower delay and smaller chip space compared to CLA [12], the Ling adder is used in place of the ripple carry adder (RCA) stage in the carry select adder (CSELA) architecture. It is called Ling CSELA, this modified version. These formulas are used to calculate the bitwise signals propagate (Pi) and generate (Gi)

$$G_i = A_i \& B_i \tag{4.5}$$

$$P_i = A_i + B_i \tag{4.6}$$

The architecture of the modified linear Ling CSELA can be seen in Figure 4.2.

Weinberger-based CSELA

By computing the carry using the Weinberger recurrence technique, an adder's time can be reduced. This is accomplished by substituting the Weinberger adder for the BK adder, creating the Weinberger-based CSELA (WCSELA). The architecture is shown in Figure 4.3.

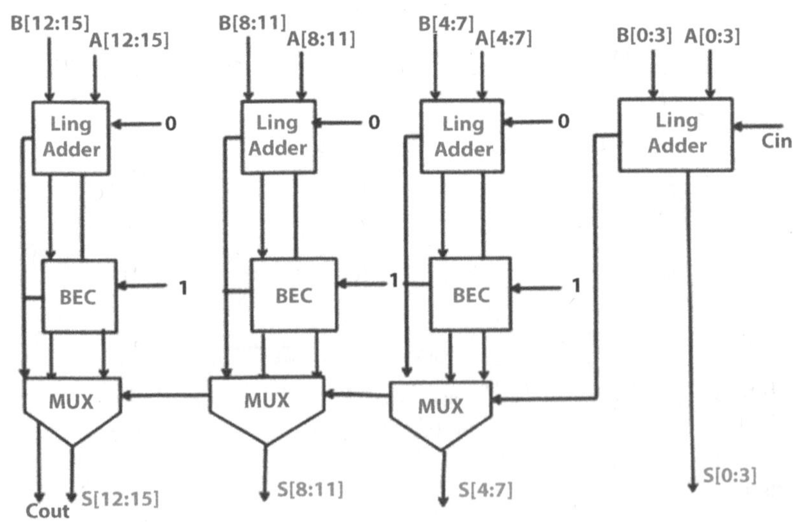

Figure 4.2 Modified linear Ling CSELA structure.

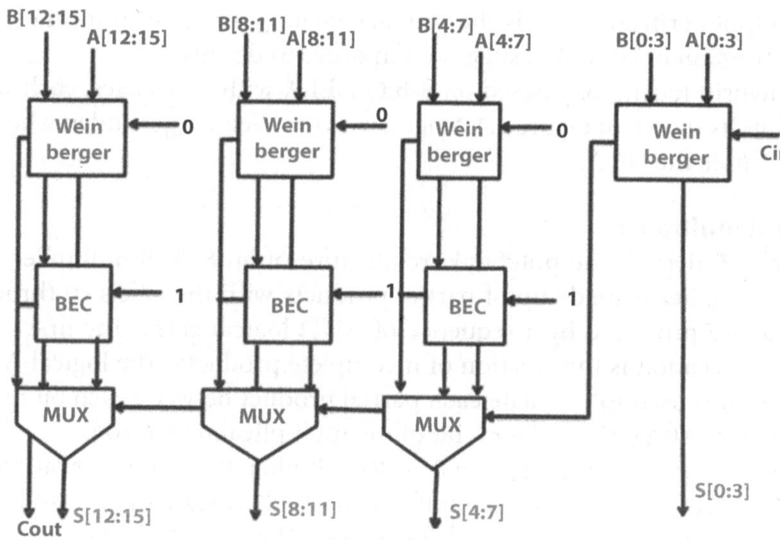

Figure 4.3 Architecture of Weinberger CSELA.

4.4 Proposed Multiplier

Combining several logic circuits yields a hybrid adder that is more efficient and less expensive. Figure 4.4 depicts the hybrid adder's structure. In this arrangement, modules II and III act as intermediary blocks to provide sum and carry outputs, whereas module I receives input signals A and B. The hybrid adder design uses both homogeneous and heterogeneous design structures.

The suggested concept seeks to combine the two methods to produce low-cost, high-performance goods. Reducing the adder's latency, which is

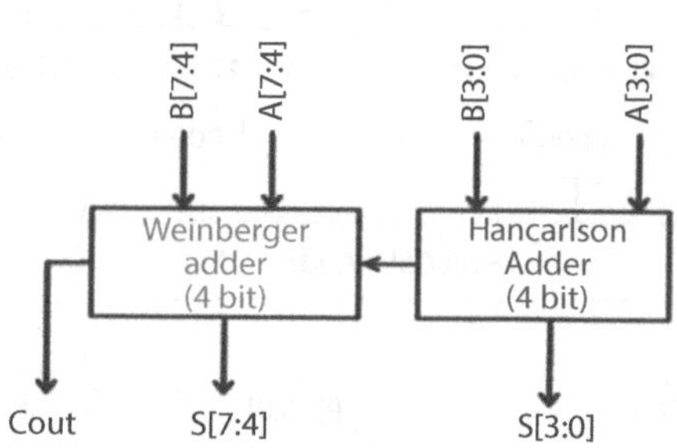

Figure 4.4 The suggested 8-bit hybrid adder's structure.

the output's critical route, is the primary goal. A new hybrid technology-based version of CSELA is suggested in order to do this.

A hybrid technology based on 8-bit CSELA with two stages, each with four bits, is shown in Figure 4.4. Stage 2 uses the Weinberger adder, whereas stage 1 uses the HCA.

Hybrid multiplier

Figure 4.5 depicts the potential architecture of an 8 × 8 multiplier [8]. This multiplier is made up of partial products with the labels c0 through c7 that are produced by a sequence of AND logical gates. The first stage of multiplication is the creation of incomplete products. The logical AND operation is used to calculate each partial product between each bit of the multiplier (A0 to A7) and each bit of the multiplicand (B0–B7).

For example, in the case of an 8 × 8 multiplier, the multiplier bit-to-bit logical AND operation A and multiplicand B0 (the least significant bit) is the first stage in partial product formation. The results can be expressed mathematically as c0\[0] = B0 AND A0, c0\[1] = B0 AND A1,..., c0\[7] = B0 AND A7. The 8-bit register C0 is where the results are stored. Likewise multiplicand B1 processes each and every bit of multiplier A, and the outcomes are kept in register C1, an 8-bit register. For each additional multiplicand and its corresponding partial product register (C1, C2, etc.),

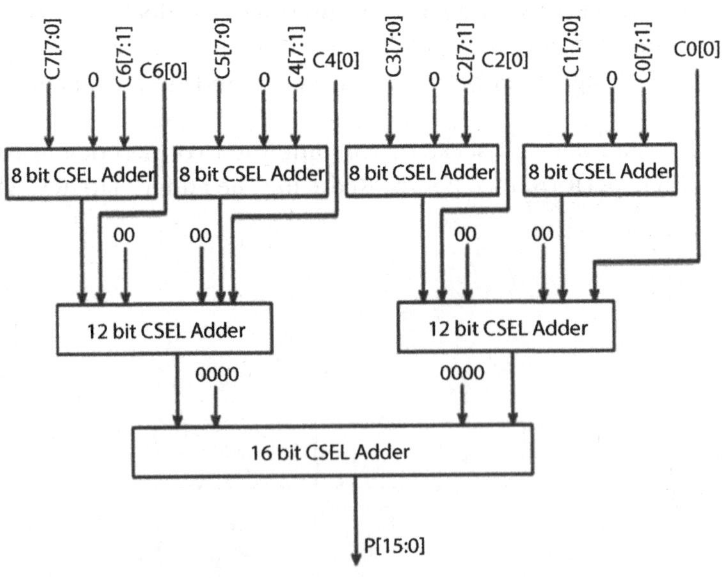

Figure 4.5 The suggested multiplier's architecture.

this procedure is repeated. Figure 4.5 shows the architecture of partial product production.

Three steps make up the suggested hybrid multiplier, and each stage uses a different size hybrid adder. In the first level, an 8-bit CSELA—a combination of 4-bit Weinberger and HCAs—is used. This 8-bit CSELA has four units in use. The second step uses two units of a 12-bit CSELA, which is a mixture of Weinberger adder, HCA, and Ling adder, each with four bits. Lastly, a 16-bit CSELA (a mix of 4-bit HCA, Weinberger adder, and Han–Carlson with BEC) is used in the third stage.

The first stage is the simultaneous addition of the incomplete results of two successive bits from the multiplier by the four units of the 8-bit CSELA. Each adder's output is then fed into the input of the subsequent stage adder. Two 12-bit adders make up the second stage. They combine the first stage's outputs concurrently and send the results to the third stage's final 16-bit CSELA. The result of the 8 × 8 multiplier is represented by the output of this 16-bit adder.

4.5 Results and Discussion

With Xilinx ISE 12.1i, you can get the synthesis report after simulating the suggested and current systems. The systems were computed using a variety of parameters, particularly the Spartan-3 processor. Figure 4.6 shows the simulation output of the suggested 8-bit hybrid adder. Figure 4.7 shows the simulation output of the proposed multiplier architecture.

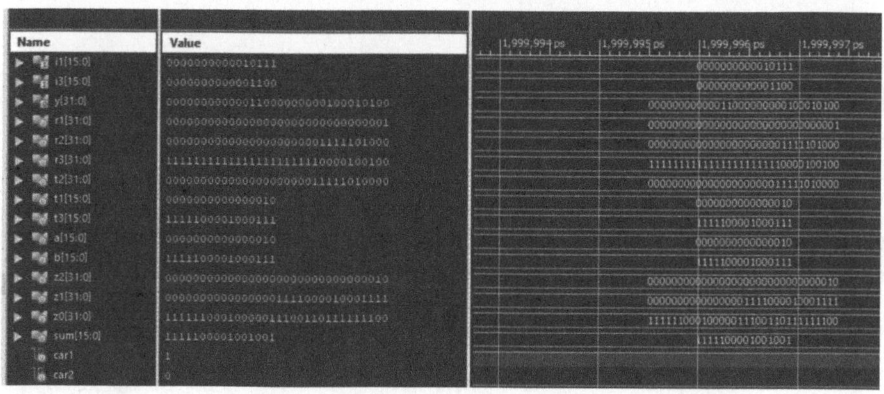

Figure 4.6 Simulation output of the suggested 8-bit hybrid adder's structure.

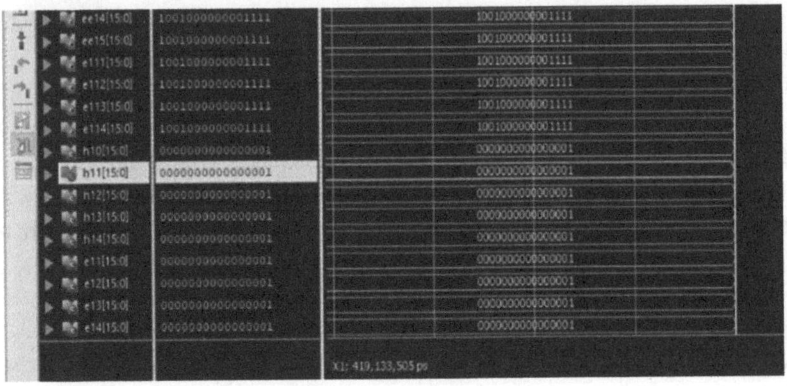

Figure 4.7 Simulation output of the suggested multiplier architecture.

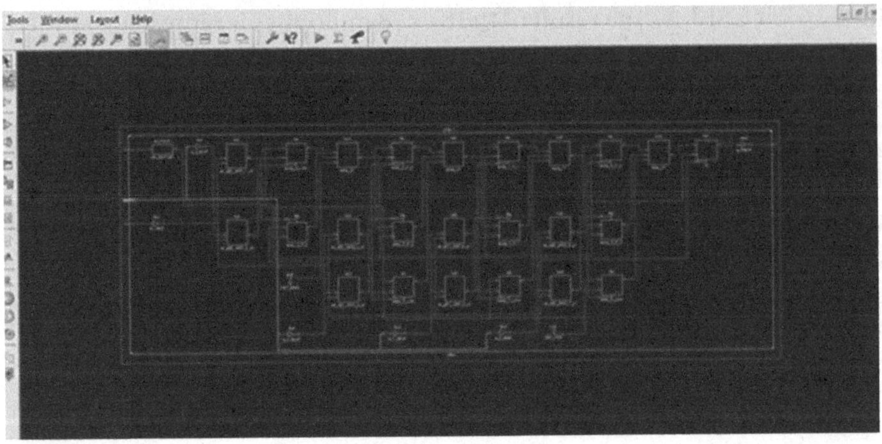

Figure 4.8 RTL schematic of the suggested multiplier architecture.

Following the completion of the simulation process, an register transfer level (RTL) schematic automatically captures the functionality. Figure 4.8 shows the RTL schematic, this diagram makes it possible to see the routing between various cells clearly.

Table 4.1 shows the comparative results of the current method and suggested method. Notably, as compared to the current method, the suggested algorithm significantly reduces area use.

Table 4.1 Comparative results of the existing and proposed method.

	Slice	Lut (look up table)	Time
Existing	428	822	39.8
Proposed	395	759	27.7

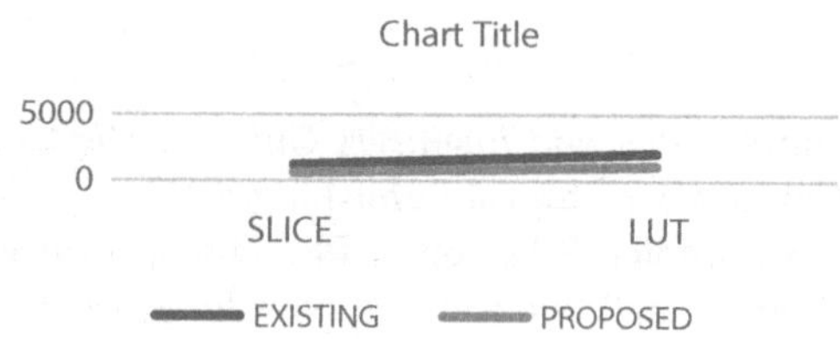

Figure 4.9 Performance analysis.

4.6 Performance Analysis

The suggested approach was implemented with the Spartan-3 CPU, resulting in a notable reduction in both time and area, as seen in the following figure. It is clear that the suggested algorithm performs better in terms of area utilization than the current method, which is shown in Figure 4.9.

4.7 Conclusion

The utilization of a hybrid multiplication technique, incorporating a combination of carry select, Weinberger, and Ling adders, presents a promising approach to address the challenges of minimizing power consumption [14] and maximizing multiplier speed in FIR filter designs. By simultaneously adding the partial products of two successive bits (multiplicands), this method optimizes the performance of the multiplier block, which is typically the bottleneck in FIR filter implementations.

The adoption of such a hybrid approach not only enhances the speed and efficiency of FIR filters but also contributes to the overarching objectives of reducing power consumption and optimizing area in DSP technology. Through synthesis and simulation using Xilinx ISE 12.1 across various FPGA devices, the suggested design can be evaluated and fine-tuned to meet specific performance requirements and constraints.

Overall, the hybrid multiplication technique represents a significant advancement in the development and application of DSP technology, offering a balanced solution that prioritizes both performance and efficiency, thereby enabling the realization of high-performance FIR filters suitable for a wide range of applications in signal processing and communication systems.

References

1. Smith, S.W., *The Scientist and Engineers Guide to Digital Signal Processing*, pp. 551–566, California Technical Publishing, 1997.
2. Oppenheim, A.V., Schafer, R.W., Buck, J.R., *Discrete Time Signal Processing*, pp. 340–438, Prentice Hall Publications, New Jersy, 1999.
3. Xiao, F., Fast Design of IIR Digital Filters with a General Chebyshev Characteristic. *IEEE Trans. Circuits Syst. II Express Briefs*, 61, 12, 962–966, Dec. 2014, DOI: 10.1109/TCSII.2014.2362638.
4. McGovern, B.P., Woods, R.F., McAllister, C., Optimised Multiply/Accumulate Architecture for Very High Throughput Rate Digital Filters. *IET Electron. Lett.*, 31, 14, 1135–1136, Jul. 1995, DOI:10.1049/el:19950823.
5. Zhang, Y., Li, N., Chambers, J.A., Sayed, A.H., Steady-State Performance Analysis of a Variable Tap-Length LMS Algorithm. *IEEE Trans. Signal Process.*, 56, 2, 839–845, Feb 2008, DOI:10.1109/tsp.2007.907805.
6. Yoon, S.H. and Sunwoo, M.H., An efficient variable-length tap FIR filter chip. *IEEE International Asia and South Pacific Design Automation Conference*, Feb. 1998, pp. 157–161, DOI: 10.1109/aspdac.1998.669436.
7. Xu, C., Wang, C.-Y., K.K, P., Order-Configurable Programmable Power-Efficient FIR Filters. *IEEE International Conference on High Performance Computing*, Dec. 1996, pp. 357–361, DOI: 10.1109/hipc.1996.565847.
8. Rangachari, S. and Chandrachoodan, N., Scalable Low Power Digital Filter Architectures for Varying Input Dynamic Range. *IEEE International Symposium on Circuits and Systems (ISCAS)*, May 2013, pp. 3018–3021, DOI: 10.1109/iscas.2013.6572514.
9. Mohamed Asan Basiri, M. and Sk, N.M., An Efficient Hardware Based MAC Design in Digital Filters with Complex Numbers. *IEEE International Conference on Signal Processing and Integrated Networks (SPIN)*, Feb. 2014, pp. 475–480, DOI: 10.1109/spin.2014.6777000.
10. Wallace, C.S., A Suggestion for a Fast Multiplier. *IEEE Trans. Electron. Comput.*, EC-13, 1, 14–17, Feb. 1964.
11. Mohamed Asan Basiri, M. and Sk, N.M., An efficient Hardware Based Higher Radix Floating Point MAC Design. *ACM Trans. Des. Autom. Electron. Syst. (TODAES)*, 20, 1, 15:1–15:25, Nov. 2014, DOI: 10.1145/2667224.

12. Roger Chen, C.Y. and Michael, Z., A Delay Distribution Methodology for the Optimal Systolic Synthesis of Linear Recurrence Algorithms. *IEEE Trans. Comput. Aided Des.*, 10, 6, 685–697, June 1991, DOI: 10.1109/43.137498.
13. Hemdani, A., Wissem Naouar, M., Belkhodja, I.S., Monmasson, E., Design of a Digital IIR Filter for Active Filtering Applications. *IEEE international Mediterranean Electrotechnical Conference*, Mar. 2012, pp. 1107–1112, DOI: 10.1109/melcon.2012.6196622.
14. Gonzalez, R., Gordon, B.M., Horowitz, M.A., Supply and Threshold Voltage Scaling for Low Power CMOS. *IEEE J. Solid-State Circuits*, 32, 8, 1210–1216, Aug. 1997, DOI: 10.1109/4.604077.
15. Aktan, M., Yurdakul, A., Dundar, G., An Algorithm for the Design of Low-Power Hardware-Efficient FIR Filters, in: *IEEE Transactions on Circuits and Systems I: Regular Papers*, 55, 6, 1536–1545, July 2008, doi: 10.1109/TCSI.2008.917997.
16. Hatai, I., Chakrabarti, I., Banerjee, S., An Efficient VLSI Architecture of a Reconfigurable Pulse-Shaping FIR Interpolation, in: *IEEE Transactions on Very Large Scale Integration (VLSI) Systems*, 23, 6, 1150–1154, June 2015, doi: 10.1109/TVLSI.2014.2321171.
17. Rashidi, B., High performance and low-power finite impulse response filter based on ring topology with modified retiming serial multiplier on FPGA. *IET Signal Process.*, 7, 743–753, 2013, https://doi.org/10.1049/iet-spr.2013.0153.
18. Thong, J., New Algorithms for Constant Coefficient Multiplication in Custom Hardware (Doctoral dissertation), 2009.
19. Jørgensen, I. H. H., Pracný, P., Bruun, E., Hardware-Efficient Implementation of Half-Band IIR Filter for Interpolation and Decimation, in: *IEEE Transactions on Circuits and Systems II: Express Briefs*, 60, 12, 892–896, Dec. 2013, doi: 10.1109/TCSII.2013.2285975.
20. Lang, M.C., Weighted least squares IIR filter design with arbitrary magnitude and phase responses and specified stability margin, in: *IEEE Symposium on Advances in Digital Filtering and Signal Processing*. Symposium Proceedings (Cat. No.98EX185), Victoria, BC, Canada, 1998, 82–86, 1998, doi: 10.1109/ADFSP.1998.685700.
21. Dam, H.H., Norbedo, S., Svensson, L., Approximation of classical IIR filters with additional specifications, in: *IEEE Transactions on Circuits and Systems II: Analog and Digital Signal Processing*, 47, 12, 1536–1540, Dec. 2000, doi: 10.1109/82.899649.
22. Nerurkar, S. B. and Abed, K. H., Low-power decimator design using approximated linear-phase N-band IIR filter, in: *IEEE Transactions on Signal Processing*, 54, 4, 1550–1553, April 2006, doi: 10.1109/TSP.2006.870615.

5

Comparison of the Design and Implementation of Smartphone Charging Controllers Using Arduino Mega and Raspberry Pi

Yuvaraj D. and N. P. G. Bhavani*

Department of Electronics and Communication Engineering, Saveetha School of Engineering, Saveetha Institute of Medical and Technical Sciences, Saveetha University, Chennai, Tamil Nadu, India

Abstract

The main aim of this research is to design an innovative smartphone charger using Innovative Raspberry Pi for mobile phones, as well as an innovative smartphone charger system using Arduino Mega with 18 samples compared with the power management system using Innovative Raspberry Pi controller with 18 samples. The α is 0.04, β is 0.03, and the G power is 0.8. Users set the time that they would like to charge their mobile. Once the time is reached, the 5V Relay disconnects the power supply to the charger, and the significance value is 0.087 ($P > 0.05$); hence, it is observed that there exists a statistically significant difference between the two groups. These results show that the Innovative Raspberry Pi controller gives significantly better accuracy than the Arduino Mega.

Keywords: Battery charging, innovative smartphone charger, relay, lifetime, Arduino Mega, Innovative Raspberry Pi

Introduction

This research presents the design and implementation of an innovative smartphone charger controller device based on Arduino. Technology has

**Corresponding author*: bhavaninpg.sse@saveetha.com

Kanak Kalita, S. Vishnu Kumar and M. Niranjanamurthy (eds.) Industrial Internet of Things and Advanced Techniques for Sensor Data Aggregation and Fusion, (61–72) © 2026 Scrivener Publishing LLC

increased tremendously nowadays; smartphones are an important part of our life. In this technological world, most people are using smartphones [1]. Smartphones usually have to be charged every day [2]. Their battery capacity is a major problem for them. Despite getting advanced and upgraded smartphones, many applications such as media players, video games, global positioning system navigation, digital camera, and digital video cameras drain the battery [3]. Without these applications, humans cannot do daily activities like [4] making phone calls or sending texts around the world. One of the most significant drawbacks of smartphones is their battery life; smartphones must be recharged on a daily basis after the battery gets drained. The mobile phone has to be charged again and again when the battery gets down [5]. So, users will charge their mobile phones on a daily basis.

Most smartphone users face this same problem, connecting the phone to the charger adapter and forgetting that you plugged in the device. This is the one factor that increases battery degradation [6]. Smart charging exploits the fact that many people charge their phones overnight. It may cause the battery to get blasted at night times. To avoid this, we are designing a smart charger and a software application that maintains battery degradation and increases battery life [7]. Although the available runtime might be adequate at the time of purchase, the power fading effect decreases the available capacity over time until only 80% of the initial capacity is available after 2 to 3 years, and hence, the battery runs out before the user normally recharges it [8]. We present a novel context-aware scheme for aging-aware battery charging that reduces the average state of charge for lifetime and thus helps to minimize battery power fading for the first time in our work.

Because smartphones are usually charged during the night, batteries usually reach 100% of their maximum state of charge a long time before their chargers are unplugged. We recommend a modified battery charging system that works with the majority of modern smartphone models. Using our proposed technique, the facility savings are often done, and battery cycle lifetime is often expanded to double [9]. Our team has extensive knowledge and research experience that has translated into high-quality publications such as that of Bakolas *et al.* [10]. The Innovative Raspberry Pi–based smartphone charging controller is frequently used for controlling charging time and disconnecting the power to the charging adapter once the time is up, which is both fascinating and practical [6]. So, let's start working with Innovative Raspberry Pi-based smartphone charging controllers.

Materials and Methods

This research was carried out in the Department of Electronics and Communication Engineering at Saveetha School of Engineering, Saveetha Institute of Medical and Technical Sciences, Chennai. The total number of groups used in this analysis was 2. The sample size of this research was 18 for each group. Group 1 was the Innovative Raspberry Pi [11]-based device, and group 2 was Arduino Mega-based devices [12]. The required samples for this analysis are done using G power calculation. The research parameters are found as $\alpha = 0.04$, β is 0.03, and G power = 0.8.

Group 1: 18 samples were used to analyze the results by using an Innovative Raspberry Pi-based device. In an Innovative Raspberry Pi-based device, input is obtained from the rotary encoder manually, and then Innovative Raspberry Pi will receive input data from the encoder and process it into the output of the charger. Based on lifetime, the device will work. Group 2: 18 samples were used to analyze the results by using an Arduino Mega-based device. In Arduino Mega-based device, rotary encoder gets input manually, and it displays on the LCD. If time reaches its count, relay disconnects power supply from the power socket [13].

Next code was compiled in the Arduino IDE (integrated development environment) software and uploaded into the Arduino Mega board. The PC was connected to the Arduino Mega with the help of USB cable, and the device was turned on using an innovative smartphone charger. Then, the time limit is set to be charged using the rotary encoder and to start the task. The limitation of the time is counted and displayed through the LCD display. Once the charging duration set by the user is reached, the 5V Relay disconnects the power supply from the socket board, and the innovative smartphone charger is automatically coded in the Arduino. By variations in time levels, the Arduino was automatically turned on and off simultaneously.

Statistical Analysis

Statistical analysis is done in SPSS software [1]; independent variable is charging, and dependent variable is time. Table 5.1 shows that the test readings by the Arduino device based on the time value of the Arduino controller will turn off the power supply from the socket. Table 5.2 shows that the statistical analysis of Arduino Mega- and Innovative Raspberry Pi-based devices obtained 18 samples. It is observed that the Innovative Raspberry

Table 5.1 Testing results of different times of this controller whether the smartphone's battery is charging or not.

S. no.	Time	Function of Innovative Raspberry Pi	Function of Arduino Mega
1	5 min	Yes	Yes
2	10 min	Yes	Yes
3	15 min	Yes	Yes
4	20 min	No	Yes
5	25 min	Yes	Yes
6	30 min	Yes	No
7	35 min	No	Yes
8	40 min	Yes	Yes
9	45 min	Yes	Yes
10	50 min	Yes	Yes
11	55 min	Yes	No
12	1 h	Yes	Yes
13	1.30 h	No	Yes
14	2 h	Yes	No
15	2.30 h	Yes	Yes
16	3 h	Yes	Yes
17	3.30 h	Yes	Yes
18	4.00 h	Yes	Yes

The test readings are produced by the Arduino- and Raspberry-based devices, on the time value of the Arduino controller will turn off the power supply from the socket.

Pi performed better than the Arduino Mega–based device. Table 5.3 shows the comparison of the time to charge between an Arduino-based device and a Raspberry-based device. There is a statistically significant difference in charge of two techniques, 0.087 ($P > 0.05$), in an independent-sample t test.

Table 5.2 Group statistics results reveal the mean and standard deviation for the Arduino Mega- and Innovative Raspberry Pi-based device.

Group	n	Mean	Standard deviation	Standard error mean
Innovative Raspberry Pi	18	0.7778	0.42779	0.10083
Arduino Mega	18	0.5000	0.51450	0.12127

The statistical analysis of Arduino Mega- and Innovative Raspberry Pi-based devices obtained with 18 samples.

Results

Figure 5.1 shows the block diagram of smartphone charging controllers using the Arduino Mega module, which indicates the connection of Arduino, LCD display, and other components. By using a rotary encoder, we can modify the time and can monitor the display LCD. Fix the time to charge the smartphone after the time reaches the count; the power supply is cut off by the hardware program. The hardware application cuts the power supply. Hence, it saves the battery life and energy. Also, temperature plays a crucial role within the lifetime of a battery [14]. Higher temperatures might damage the chemistry of the battery. For example, you have set the charging time as 2 hours (maybe supported by the previous observation or by mathematical calculations). With the aid of a relay, the power to the battery is switched on, and the timer starts. The phone will be charged for the next 2 hours, and when the timer reaches 2 hours, the relay will be switched off, and the power supply to the charger will be shut off as well.

Figure 5.2 shows the testing procedure flowchart for Arduino-based smart charging devices. This system consists of both software and hardware tools such as Arduino IDE, PC, Arduino Mega, LCD display, rotary encoder, and 5V Relay. First, the Arduino IDE software was opened. Code was written for the time and smart charging controller.

Figure 5.3 shows that the controller is in an off state. Because before it starts to charge, we need to enter the time that the controller has to stop the power supply after the count is reached. By the use of a rotary encoder, users can set the time that they need to charge their smartphone. In Figure 5.4, it is shown that, after the count reaches its limit, 5V Relay cuts the power supply from the switch box to avoid the trickle charging.

Table 5.3 The comparison of the time between Arduino-based device and Innovative Raspberry Pi–based device.

		Levene test for equality of variances		***t* test for equality of means**					**95% confidence interval of the difference**	
		F	**Significance**	***t***	***df***	**Significance (2-tailed)**	**Mean difference**	**Standard error difference**	**Lower**	**Upper**
Time	**Equal variances assumed**	7.589	0.009	1.761	34	0.087	0.27778	0.15771	−0.04273	0.59829
	Equal variances not assumed	0.000	0.0	1.761	32.904	0.087	0.27778	0.15771	−0.04312	0.59868

There is a statistically significant difference in charge time of two techniques, 0.087 ($P > 0.05$), in an independent-sample t test.

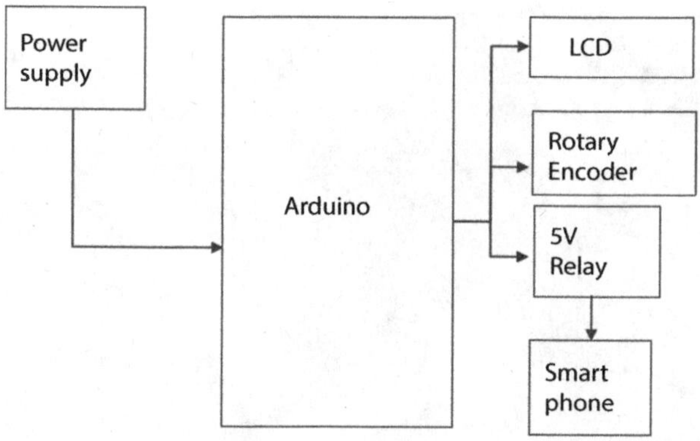

Figure 5.1 The block diagram of smartphone charging controllers using the Arduino Mega module indicates the connection of Arduino, LCD display, and other components. By using a rotary encoder, we can modify the time and monitor the display LCD.

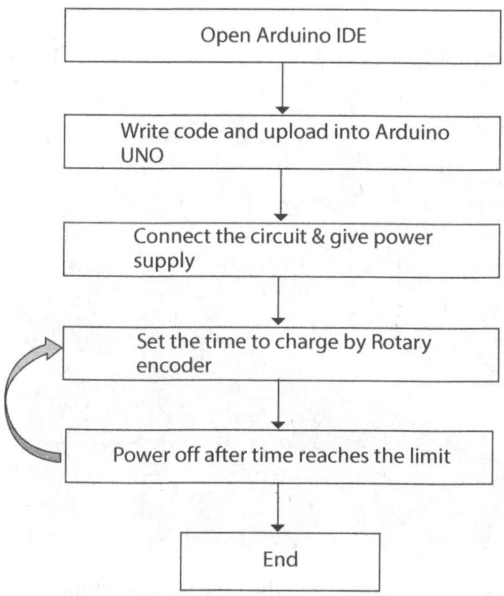

Figure 5.2 Flowchart of the smartphone charger controller using Arduino shows step-by-step process for the system with the help of flowchart. Upload the code to the Arduino board by use of IDE software to do the task. After completion of the task given, the rotary encoder cut the power supply to the controller.

As per the values obtained from the independent-sample *t* test, in Table 5.3, it can be identified that the significance value is 0.087 ($P > 0.05$). From Figure 5.5, it can be concluded that the Innovative Raspberry Pi–based

Figure 5.3 Time has to be set and confirm the count before the mobile charge by use of rotary encoder.

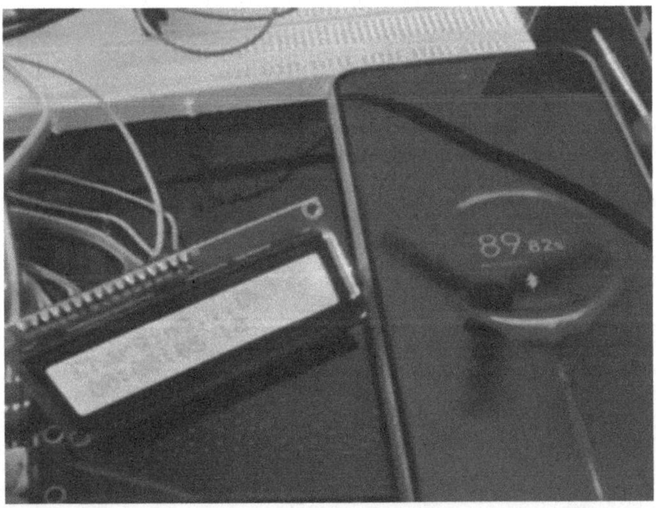

Figure 5.4 Mobile is on charge condition, the time limit is set for 10 seconds. When the count reaches the limit power supply will be disconnected by the 5V relay from the power socket.

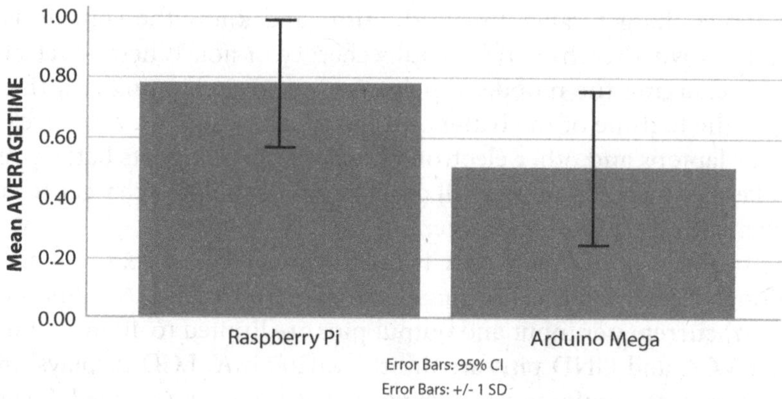

Figure 5.5 The comparison of mean charge time with Arduino Mega– and Innovative Raspberry Pi–based devices. The mean charge time of an Innovative Raspberry Pi is better than an Arduino Mega device, and the standard deviation of an Innovative Raspberry Pi is slightly better than an Arduino Mega–based device. X axis: Arduino Mega– vs. Innovative Raspberry Pi–based device; Y axis: mean time is ±1 SD.

device has significantly better accuracy than the Arduino Mega–based device.

Discussion

In this research, the rotary encoder gets a time limit by the users manually to charge the mobile, and it will display on the LCD. When the time reaches the count limit, 5V Relay disconnects the power supply from the socket. Figure 5.3 shows the time to be set and confirms the count before the mobile charge by use of a rotary encoder, and in Figure 5.4, mobile is in charge condition. When the count reaches the limit, power supply will be stopped by the relay. Table 5.1 shows the testing results of different times of this controller whether the smartphone is charging or not.

In the previous work, the research has been done for the lithium-ion battery to recharge. In this system, drawbacks include the need to use various components when the battery maximum voltage is high or low, as this can cause and damage the battery, so it is necessary to make sure and use the correct component when doing research. In this work, the researcher has to know the right voltage to charge the battery, and it may slow the charging of the battery because the components have their own limit [1]. In this research, we have done a smartphone charger using Arduino as consuming less power without any variation of the voltage. The innovative smartphone charger can estimate the time and know the voltage of the smartphone whether the battery is fully charged or not. When we set a time limit for charging the mobile, it helps prevent overcharging and thereby enlarges the lifetime of the battery. In the future, we will try to develop it more for laptops and other electronics, which can charge its battery regularly like the smartphone. We will design a small compact charger to carry anywhere like a traditional charger.

The factor affecting the device is time, which leads to fix to on and off conditions. The limitations of this research were that the Arduino board input DC current per input and output pins are limited to 40 mA, and DC current VCC and GND pins are limited to 200 mA. LCD displays under 0- to 5-V power supply, and at high voltage, it becomes damaged. It can be changeable by using 10k POT. In the future, we can include many other sensors to sense the temperature and charge in the mobile and charge according to it. Instead of Arduino, we can use other controllers for other applications of the same type of work to increase the lifetime of the devices.

Conclusion

This work discusses the novel design and implementation of charging controllers for smartphones. The smart charger can easily predict how long it will take to charge. So, we compared the Arduino Mega- and Innovative Raspberry Pi–designed devices. The results obtained showed the Innovative Raspberry Pi device performance was significantly higher than the Arduino-based device at various times.

References

1. Husin, M.H.B., Smart Charger Based on IoT Concept. *IJESTE*, 2, 39–44, June 2019.
2. Djuanda, D.S.R., Ramdhani, M., Ekaputri, C., Automatic battery charging system on android smartphones. *IOP Conf. Ser. Mater. Sci. Eng.*, 830, 032027, April 2020.
3. Hoque, M.A., Siekkinen, M., Koo, J., Tarkoma, S., Full charge capacity and charging diagnosis of smartphone batteries. *IEEE Trans. Mob. Comput.*, 16, 3042–3055, November 2017.
4. Zainurin, N.A., Anas, S.A.B., Singh, R.S.S., A review of battery charging - discharging management controller: A proposed conceptual battery storage charging – discharging centralized controller. *Eng. Technol. Appl. Sci. Res.*, 11, 7515–7521, August 2021.

5. Rao, P.V.N., Improving the efficiency of the electrical vehicle wireless charging system by rectifier load analysis using ANFIS controller. *J. Adv. Res. Dyn. Control Syst.*, 12, 1370–1379, February 2020.
6. Dhiviyabarathi, P., Elamathi, M., Sundaresan, S., Self charging smartphone, in: *2017 International Conference on Intelligent Computing, Instrumentation and Control Technologies (ICICICT)*, Kerala State, Kannur, India, 2017.
7. Giyantara, A.G., Christover, D., Priyanto, Y.T.K., Design and implementation buck-boost converter using arduino mega 2560, in: *Proceedings of the 1st International Conference on Industrial Technology*, Balikpapan, 2019.
8. Marianto, A. and Muchlas, M., Rancang Bangun Robot Forklift dengan Kendali Smartphone Android Berbasis Arduino Mega 2560. *J. Ilmiah Teknik Elektro Komputer Inf.*, 3, 65, December 2017.
9. Su, Y., Smartphone Wireless charging. *Highlights Sci. Eng. Technol.*, 27, 671–680, December 2022.
10. Bakolas, B.V.E., Bauer, P., Prins, D., Testing of Smart Charging Controller for dynamic charging from solar panels, in: *2014 IEEE Transportation Electrification Conference and Expo (ITEC)*, Dearborn, 2014.
11. Underwood, L., Create a timer with the arduino and micro:Bit, in: *Create a Timer with the Arduino and micro:bit*, Apress, Berkeley, CA, 2020.
12. Fadjar Bastari, W. and Prayogi, A., Smart charging digital accumulator based on Arduino Uno microcontroller. *Buana Electr. Sci. Technol.*, 2, 16–19, February 2021.
13. Kaur, T., Gambhir, J., Kumar, S., Arduino based solar powered battery charging system for rural SHS, in: *2016 7th India International Conference on Power Electronics (IICPE)*, Patiala, 2016.
14. Wang, Y., Li, J., Zhang, J., Pecht, M., Lithium-iron-phosphate battery electrochemical modelling under a wide range of ambient temperatures. *J. Electroanal. Chem. (Lausanne Switz)*, 882, 115041, February 2021.

6

Enhancing the Accuracy in Designing an Image with Style Transfer Learning Method Using Visual Geometry Group (VGG16) over InceptionV3

Boobathy A.* **and Rashmita Khilar**

Department of Information Technology Saveetha School of Engineering, Saveetha Institute of Medical and Technical Sciences, Saveetha University, Chennai, India

Abstract

The main aim of this study is to enhance the accuracy in designing an image with style transfer learning method in novel Visual Geometry Group (VGG-16) over InceptionV3. To perform image style transforming, the novel VGG-16 and InceptionV3 algorithms are utilized. ImageNet's dataset contains 1,281,167 images distributed across 1000 classes, with each image having dimensions of 400 rows and 711 columns. This dataset is used for the image style transfer system. Total iterations of 20 are calculated using ClinCalc keeping G power as 0.8 and α of 0.05. The mean accuracy of the novel VGG-16 is high (70.41%) compared to InceptionV3 (54.40%) algorithm. The significant value of P is 0.0016 (independent-sample t test $P < 0.05$). This implies that there is a statistically significant difference between the two algorithms based on their accuracy. The mean accuracy of the designing an image with style transfer learning method in novel VGG-16 algorithm is better than the InceptionV3.

Keywords: Image, InceptionV3, neural network, neural style, style, novel Visual Geometry Group (VGG-16), technology, transfer

Corresponding author: boobathya19@saveetha.com

Kanak Kalita, S. Vishnu Kumar and M. Niranjanamurthy (eds.) Industrial Internet of Things and Advanced Techniques for Sensor Data Aggregation and Fusion, (73–82) © 2026 Scrivener Publishing LLC

Introduction

Transforming an image from one form to another ensures no significant loss in the content image. Transforming or styling an image based on their preferred choice has become more popular and extensively preferred by many people [9]. This method helps in recreating the main image in the form of the preferred style image. With the help of modern neural networks, this can be achieved. In recent decades, more than 90% of people have been using photo editing tools as a daily driver [1]. Editing an image based on user choice is a time-consuming process. This can be overcome by artificial intelligence [7]. The main aim of this research is to build a neural-style transfer network to make the transformation process easier. The major application of this project is to create an artificial artwork from the user's preferred picture, and the above system also finds major applications in industries such as media, user interface (UI) design, graphics animation, etc.

In the last 5 years, there have been 654 articles in IEEE Xplore and 30 in Google Scholar. Convolutional neural network (CNN) styles the image by combining the main and the reference image. It manipulates the content image with different styling images and is named neural style transfer (NST) technology [4]. CNN is able to generate a new image by combining the main and the reference image. The pattern from the semantic image is extracted, and the content image is retained without losing the pattern in it [3]. The novel Visual Geometry Group (VGG-16) is a pretrained algorithm that uses an image net and takes less time to process. Evaluating the loss is based on the features in the content and the generated image. Comparison is done between the content and the generated image. The novel VGG-16 has performed well because of well-constructed feature extraction convolutional layers. NST technology–stylized images use high-level features to represent the main features of the image and the reference image. Old style transfer technology is based on the whole features of the image. Features are mapped layer by layer and transformed as a dependent image [9].

Based on the literature survey, it can be concluded that the existing model has a low precision value when compared with other algorithms. This study is to improve accuracy by incorporating novel VGG-16 and comparing its performance with InceptionV3. The proposed model will recreate the content image to a styled image by incorporating the patterns in the reference image.

Materials and Methods

The research for the proposed project is carried out in the Data Analytics Laboratory, Information Technology Department, Saveetha School of Engineering, Saveetha Institute of Medical and Technical Science. The sample group consisted of two groups. Group 1 is the novel VGG-16, and group 2 is the InceptionV3 algorithm. Using IBM SPSS, the sample size of 10 has been carried out, with a total sample size of 20 determined using ClinCalc, keeping G power with pretest power as 0.8 and α level of 0.05.

The data for model training are collected from the ImageNet website. It consists of three parts, namely, training, validation, and testing. The train data consist of 1000 object classes and 1,281,167 training images. The validation data consists of 50,000 validation images with 1000 different object classes. The testing data consist of 100,000 test images with 1000 classes. A total of 400 rows and 711 columns are considered features. Each pixel value is converted to tensors in the preprocessing process. Image transform value is taken as a dependent variable, and pixel values are regarded as independent variables.

VGG16

The VGG-16 model consists of 16 convolutional layers, followed by three fully connected layers. Each convolutional layer applies a set of learnable filters to the input image, producing a set of feature maps that are passed to the next layer. The filters are learned during the training process using backpropagation and gradient descent.

Given an input feature map X with dimensions (H, W, D) where H, W, and D are the height, width, and depth of the feature map, respectively, and a set of learnable filters F with dimensions (fH, fW, D, K) where fH, fW, D, and K are the height, width, depth, and number of filters, respectively, the convolution operation can be expressed as $Y(i, j, k) = \text{sum}(\text{sum}(\text{sum}(X(a, b, c) * F(a - i + 1, b - j + 1, c, k))))$ [7], where Y is the output feature map, (i, j, k) are the indices of the pixel in the output map, and (a, b, c) are the indices of the pixel in the input map. After each convolutional layer, a rectified linear unit (ReLU) activation function is applied to the output feature map $Z = \max(0, Y)$, where Z is the output feature map after the ReLU activation [4].

The output feature maps are then passed through max pooling layers, which downsample the feature maps by selecting the maximum value in a local region. The equations for the max pooling operation can be expressed as $P(i, j, k) = \max(Y(is, js, k), Y(is, js + 1, k), Y(is + 1, js, k), Y(is + 1, js + 1, k))$, where P is the output feature map after max pooling, s is the stride (usually 2), and (i, j, k) are the indices of the pixel in the output map.

These equations are repeated for each convolutional layer in the VGG-16 model, with the output feature maps of each layer serving as the input to the next layer. The fully connected layers at the end of the model use standard matrix multiplication operations to produce the final output predictions [2]. The content features are represented as static on the flattening layer, and the style image is represented as varying features on a couple of layers in novel VGG-16.

Pseudocode for VGG16

1. Import the necessary packages.
2. Resize the image to comply with VGG-16 specifications.
3. Extract the image features.
4. Build a VGG-16 neural network model using the ImageNet dataset.
5. Feed the model with input parameters/features.
6. The model calculates the loss.
7. The accuracy is estimated based on the loss value.

InceptionV3

InceptionV3 is an image recognition algorithm with an ImageNet dataset and is able to classify 1000 classes. It is one of the transfer learning algorithms with 48 layers deep. The V3 denotes the version of the model. InceptionV3 architecture is the compression of factorized convolutions, smaller convolutions, asymmetric convolutions, and grid size reduction. Image is input in the first layer of the convolutional network with a default size of 299 × 299 × 3. Width and height are represented as 299, and the image channel is represented as 3. Max pooling is done to prevent the model from the close alignment of the data. Max pooling uses filters (or kernels) of sizes such as 2 × 2, 3 × 3, or 5 × 5 to downsample feature maps and reduce spatial dimensions. It does not estimate weights but rather selects the maximum value within each filter region to retain dominant features. The activation function determines whether a neuron should be activated or not. The activation function is the collection of the linear function and the nonlinear function. SoftMax activates multiclass neurons at the time of execution. The neurons get activated only when the value is greater than 0 to 1 [4].

Pseudocode for InceptionV3

1. Begin by importing the necessary packages.
2. Resize the input image to match the requirements of InceptionV3.
3. Extract the features from the resized image.
4. Construct the InceptionV3 neural network using the ImageNet dataset.
5. Provide the necessary parameters/features to the neural network.
6. Use the neural network to calculate the losses.
7. Estimate the accuracy from the value of the loss.

Statistical Analysis

IBM SPSS version 2.1 was used for analysis. Both the VGG-16 and InceptionV3 algorithms were analyzed with a sample size of 10 using the collected accuracy and loss values in SPSS. The groups were named as group 1 and group 2 for VGG-16 and InceptionV3, respectively [7]. To conduct the analysis, the features of both the content and styling images were considered as independent variables. Accuracy percentages were considered as dependent variables. The *t* test was calculated using the model iteration to compare the performance of VGG-16 and InceptionV3. The loss and accuracy percentages of the model were used as testing variables.

Results

Figure 6.1 shows a typical image used in the dataset. The input of the novel VGG-16 is taken in the form of features extracted from the image and generates a newly styled image with a mean accuracy of 70.41%. The mean accuracy and loss were used for the *t* test of both algorithms, along with the standard deviation, which is tabulated. Table 6.1 consists of the accuracy of the novel VGG-16 and InceptionV3 algorithms for each sample of n = 10. A total of 20 samples were considered for the analysis. The input of InceptionV3 is taken in the form of features extracted from the image, and it generates a newly styled image with a mean accuracy of 54.40%. Table 6.2 shows the value of novel VGG-16 and InceptionV3 after comparing the accuracy and loss from Table 6.1. It can be observed that the novel VGG-16 has better mean accuracy than InceptionV3. The accuracy and the loss of both algorithms are depicted in the bar graph shown in Figure 6.2.

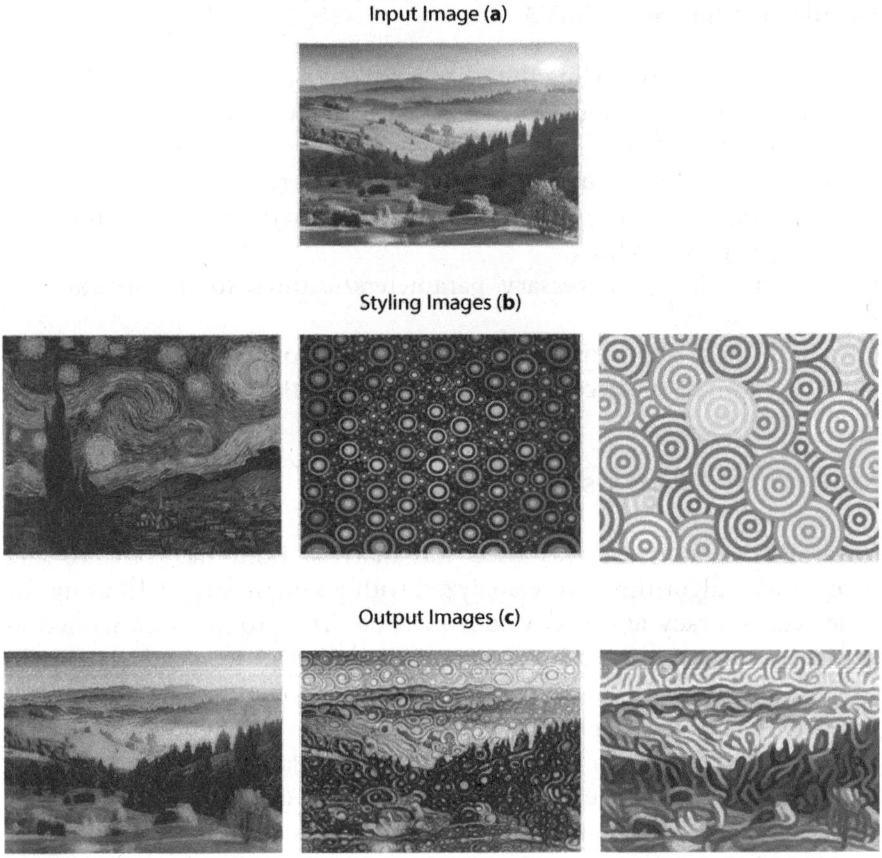

Figure 6.1 This image combines a photograph and a number of artworks with an (a) input, (b) styling images, and (c) output photograph. We created these images by finding an image that represents the artwork while also matching the content expectations of the photograph.

Table 6.1 Group, accuracy, and loss value uses eight columns with eight width data for image style transfer technology.

SI no.	Name	Type	Width	Decimal	Columns	Measure	Role
1	Group	Numeric	8	2	8	Nominal	Input
2	Accuracy	Numeric	8	2	8	Scale	Input
3	Loss	Numeric	8	2	8	Scale	Input

Table 6.2 Group statistical analysis for Visual Geometry Group (VGG-16) algorithm and InceptionV3 algorithm mean, standard deviation, and standard error mean.

	Group	n	Mean	Standard deviation	Standard error mean
Accuracy	VGG-16	10	70.4110	26.68794	8.43947
	InceptionV3	10	54.4040	22.55755	7.13332
Loss	VGG-16	10	29.5620	26.68016	8.43701
	InceptionV3	10	45.5960	22.55755	7.13332

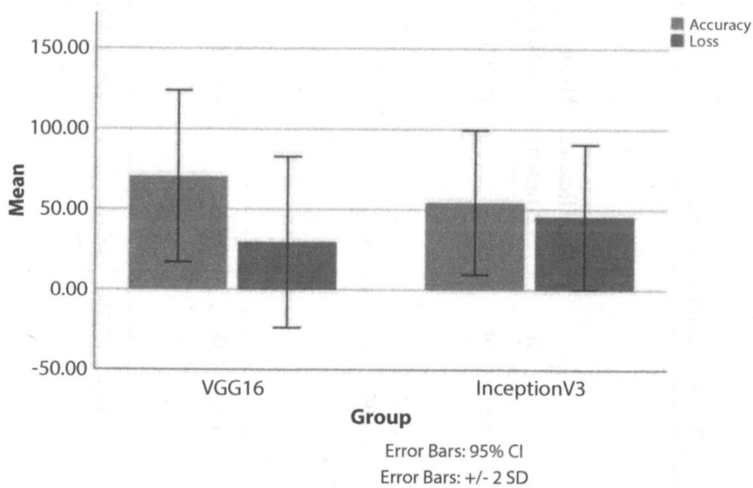

Figure 6.2 Comparison of Visual Geometry Group (VGG-16) algorithm and InceptionV3 algorithm in terms of mean accuracy. The mean accuracy of the VGG-16 is better than the InceptionV3 algorithm. The standard deviation of the VGG-16 algorithm is slightly better than InceptionV3. *X* axis: VGG-16 versus InceptionV3; *Y* axis: mean accuracy of the outcome.

Discussion

The study found that the novel VGG-16 algorithm performs better than long short-term memory in terms of accuracy, with VGG-16 achieving 70.41% accuracy compared to long short-term memory's 54.84%. The model's *P* value was found to be 0.0017, which is statistically significant with a 95% confidence interval (Table 6.3).

Table 6.3 Independent-sample *t* test is performed on two graphs for significance and standard error determination.

		Levene test for equality of variances		*t* Test for equality of means					95% Confidence interval of the difference	
		F	**Significance**	***t***	***df***	**Significance (2-tailed)**	**Mean difference**	**Standard error difference**	**Lower**	**Upper**
Accuracy	Equal variances assumed	0.03	0.048	1.449	18	.0016	16.00700	11.05029	−7.20879	39.22279
	Equal variances not assumed			1.449	17.514	.0016	16.00700	11.05029	−7.25505	39.26905
Loss	Equal variances assumed	0.03	0.048	−1.451	18	.0016	−16.03400	11.04841	−39.24585	7.177785
	Equal variances not assumed			−1.451	17.516	.0016	−16.03400	11.04841	−39.29194	7.22394

The P value is 0.0016 ($P < 0.05$) and is considered statistically significant with a 95% confidence interval.

The purpose of this discussion is to determine which model architecture to use for style transfer technology. Low-level noise can also be a problem in the synthesized images [6]. In the case of artistic style transfer, this is less of an issue. Image content and style cannot always be separated well. The reason for this is that the definition of the image's style is not clear. The novel VGG-16 model achieved accuracy quickly. It just required an execution time of about 50 seconds on RTX 2070. Having a transfer learning technology for style transfer will help to build the model quickly and make it easy to understand [5]. In addition, we decided to stick to the VGG-16 to limit training time for each style. Other transfer technology learning algorithms performed well in image classification compared with the novel VGG-16. InceptionV3 surprisingly performed well in their approach [8].

The limitation of this study is that it takes a very long time to generate the output image, especially with large image data. In the future, color optimization can be carried out to improve the generated images. This could involve improving exposure, contrast, saturation, brightness, vibrancy, and shadows to enhance the image's overall aesthetic. Additionally, the output image can be classified based on categories such as nature, building, and people to further improve the accuracy of the model. Overall, this study highlights the potential for further research and development in style transfer technology.

Conclusion

The study found that the mean accuracy of the InceptionV3 algorithm was 54.40%, whereas the novel VGG-16 algorithm had a higher mean accuracy of 70.41%. This means that VGG-16 performed better in terms of accuracy when compared to InceptionV3. The comparison of these two algorithms is important because accuracy is a critical aspect of image style transfer. It ensures that the generated image is as close as possible to the desired outcome, and the algorithm can successfully transfer the desired style to the target image. The higher mean accuracy of VGG-16 in this study suggests that it could be a better choice for image style transfer applications that require a high degree of accuracy. Overall, the results of this study contribute to the ongoing research and development of image style transfer algorithms, helping to identify which algorithms are most effective for different applications.

References

1. City University London, 90% of Young Women Report Using a Filter or Editing Their Photos before Posting. *Science Daily*, March 8, 2021, https://www.sciencedaily.com/releases/2021/03/210308111852.htm.
2. Great Learning, Everything You Need to Know about Visual Geometry Group (VGG-16) - Great Learning. Medium, September 23, 2021, https://medium.com/@mygreatlearning/everything-you-need-to-know-about-Visual Geometry Group(VGG-16)-7315defb5918.
3. Gatys, L.A., Ecker, A.S., Bethge, M., Image style transfer using convolutional neural networks, in: *Proceedings of the IEEE conference on computer vision and pattern recognition*, 2414–2423, 2016.
4. Jing, Y., Yang, Y., Feng, Z., Ye, J., Yu, Y., Song, M., Neural Style Transfer technology: A Review. *IEEE Trans. Visual Comput. Graphics*, 26, 11, 3365–85, 2020.
5. Johnson, J., Alahi, A., Fei-Fei, L., Perceptual Losses for Real-Time Style Transfer and Super-Resolution, arXiv [cs.CV], arXiv, 2016, http://arxiv.org/abs/1603.08155
6. Simonyan, K. and Zisserman, A., Very Deep Convolutional Networks for Large-Scale Image Recognition, arXiv [cs.CV], arXiv, 2014, http://arxiv.org/abs/1409.1556.
7. Thakur, R., Step by Step Visual Geometry Group (VGG-16) Implementation in Keras for Beginners. Towards Data Science, August 6, 2019, https://towardsdatascience.com/step-by-step-Visual Geometry Group(VGG-16)-implementation-in-keras-for-beginners-a833c686ae6c.
8. Wang, C., *et al.*, Pulmonary Image Classification Based on Inception-v3 Transfer Learning Model, in: *IEEE Access*, vol. 7, pp. 146533–146541, 99, 1–1, 2019. doi: 10.1109/ACCESS.2019.2946000.
9. Yao, C., Li, Y., Qi, Y., Research on Neural Style Transfer Algorithm. *IOP Conf. Ser.: Mater. Sci. Eng.*, 569, 5, 052107, 2019, https://doi.org/10.1088/1757-899x/569/5/052107.

Part II

IoT IN SMART CITIES AND INFRASTRUCTURE

7

Efficient Traffic Detection and Localization in 5G Networks Using IoT-Enhanced Dynamic *Ad-Hoc* Clusters

Nirmalkumar K.* and Ramprashath R.

School of Computer Application, Karpagam College of Engineering, Coimbatore, Tamil Nadu, India

Abstract

The advent of 5G networks has ushered in a new connectivity era, bringing unprecedented speed and bandwidth. In this context, the deployment of dynamic *ad-hoc* networks plays a pivotal role in enhancing traffic detection capabilities. The proposed system leverages the flexibility of *ad-hoc* networks to create a dynamic infrastructure that adapts to varying traffic patterns, ensuring efficient data transmission and reception. To enhance the precision of traffic detection, the system incorporates advanced clustering algorithms for localization. Clustering algorithms enable the forming of groups of nearby nodes, optimizing communication within these clusters, and minimizing intercluster interference. The integration of Internet of Things (IoT) devices within this framework further enhances its effectiveness. These IoT devices, equipped with various sensors, continuously collect and transmit real-time traffic data. Edge computing nodes process these data locally to reduce latency and improve responsiveness. Moreover, IoT devices facilitate decentralized data analysis and decision-making, allowing clusters to operate autonomously and efficiently.

***Keywords*:** MANETs, network clustering, digital twin, network traffic, network planning, cluster analysis, industrial networks, IoT

**Corresponding author*: nirmalkumark689@gmail.com

Kanak Kalita, S. Vishnu Kumar and M. Niranjanamurthy (eds.) Industrial Internet of Things and Advanced Techniques for Sensor Data Aggregation and Fusion, (85–98) © 2026 Scrivener Publishing LLC

7.1 Introduction

Dynamic *ad-hoc* network for traffic detection in 5G networks with efficient localization using clustering algorithm has emerged as a dynamic and decentralized communication paradigm, enabling wireless devices to form networks without relying on centralized infrastructure. Mobile *ad-hoc* networks (MANETs) are particularly well-suited for scenarios where traditional network infrastructure is impractical or unavailable, such as disaster recovery operations, military deployments, and Internet of Things (IoT) environments.

However, the inherently dynamic nature of MANETs poses significant challenges for ensuring reliable connectivity, efficient resource utilization, and effective network management. In recent years, the integration of digital twin technology has offered new avenues for addressing these challenges and enhancing the performance of MANETs.

This paper explores the concept of a dynamic *ad-hoc* network for traffic detection in 5G networks with efficient localization using a clustering algorithm, a novel framework designed to leverage digital twin technology for controlling and optimizing MANETs in diverse operational environments. The widespread adoption of smartphones and other compact sensors enables the creation of digital representations of real environments by gathering real-world data and converting it into digital form [1]. The route construction method is location-based and improved through a modification approach. However, the conventional method relies on direct communication for sharing location information, leading to time-consuming processes.

Consequently, the shared location information may not be consistently up to date, resulting in disparities between the actual positions of nodes and the perceived positions maintained by other nodes. This discrepancy poses challenges to the effective sharing of location information [2–4]. The hybrid protocols that integrate MANETs are utilized for interfragment. Transmitting information among nodes within separate fragmented networks is transformed [5] as illustrated in Figure 7.1. An enhanced predefined period is introduced, during which the source node may optional for a virtual source node [6] to facilitate communication within fragmented networks.

The selection is the prophet (probabilistic routing protocol using the history of encounters and transitivity) protocol [5] communicating wirelessly with each other, independent of a fixed infrastructure (Figure 7.2). Nodes in a MANET can dynamically form and dissolve connections, resulting in a highly flexible and adaptable network topology.

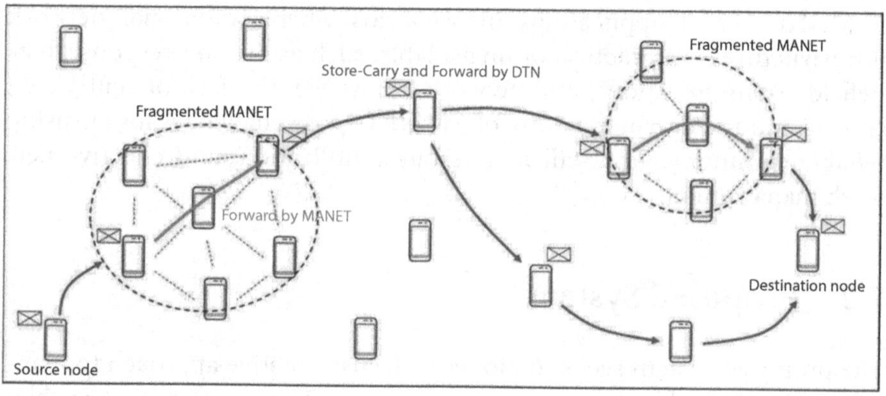

Figure 7.1 A hybrid MANET.

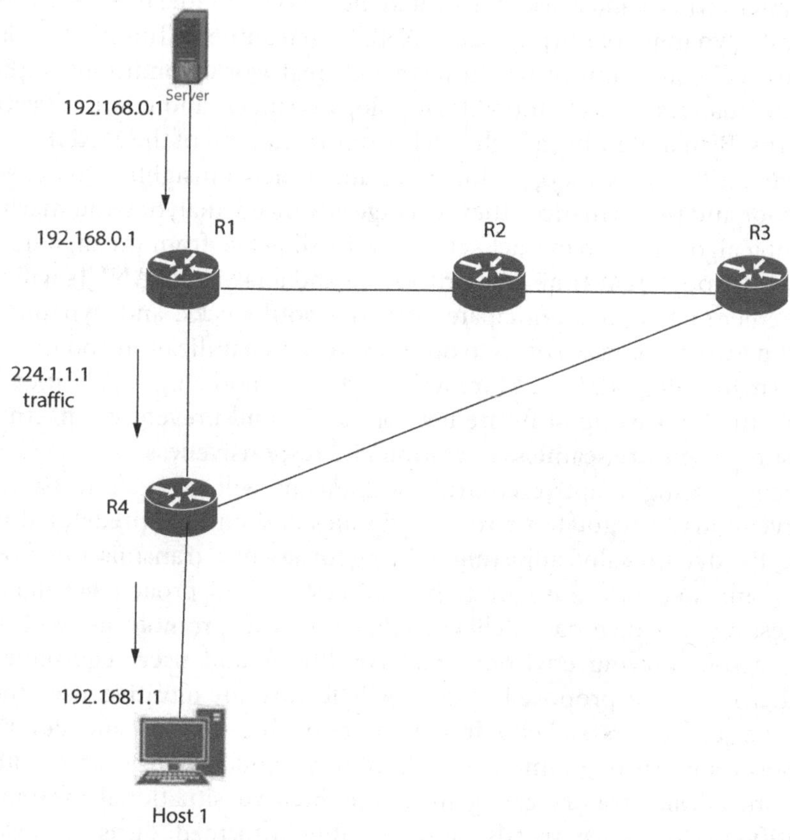

Figure 7.2 IP multicast routing protocol.

MANETs find applications in scenarios where traditional network infrastructure is impractical or unavailable, such as disaster response, battlefield communications, and networks. However, the lack of centralized control and the dynamic nature of MANETs pose challenges for ensuring reliable communication, efficient resource utilization, and effective network management.

7.2 Proposed System

The proposed system seeks to pioneer a transformative approach to managing MANETs through an innovative envision framework that enables monitoring, analysis, and control, thereby optimizing the performance and adaptability of MANETs within diverse operational landscapes. At its core, the system will establish a sophisticated digital twin model that mirrors the intricate dynamics of the physical MANET environment. This digital counterpart will continuously synchronize with real-world conditions, capturing the nuances of node mobility, topology changes, and communication patterns. By maintaining a high-fidelity representation of the MANET ecosystem, *ad-hoc* network operators have unparalleled insights into network behavior and performance. They leverage advanced analytics and machine learning algorithms to extract actionable intelligence from the digital twin model. Through real-time data processing and analysis, MANETs will discern emerging trends, anticipate potential bottlenecks, and dynamically adapt network configurations to optimize resource utilization and mitigate performance degradation. Moreover, predictive modeling capabilities will enable the forecasting of future network states and preventive enactment measures to ensure seamless operation and responsiveness.

Incorporating adaptive control mechanisms will orchestrate strategic interventions to regulate network dynamics and enforce predefined policies. By dynamically adjusting routing protocols, transmission power levels, and network configurations, the system will proactively manage congestion, enhance data delivery efficiency, and promote network stability across varying environmental conditions and user requirements. Furthermore, the proposed system will feature an intuitive user interface that empowers stakeholders with actionable insights and decision-support tools. Through interactive dashboards and visualization modules, network administrators can gain comprehensive situational awareness, identify performance trends, and expedite informed decision-making processes. This user-centric approach fosters collaboration and transparency, enabling stakeholders to collaboratively fine-tune system parameters and optimize network performance in alignment with organizational objectives.

The system marks a breaking initiative to transform the administration and regulation of MANETs by integrating digital twin technology with mobile networking principles. Through the integration of real-time analytics, adaptive control mechanisms, and a user-centric design approach, the MANET is positioned to introduce a paradigm shift, bringing about enhanced resilience, efficiency, and agility in mobile *ad-hoc* communication environments.

7.3 Related Work

This introduces a routing approach for MANETs and digital twin technology. It delineates trajectories of traditional methodologies and location-based MANETs, highlighting a distinct emphasis compared to dynamic *ad-hoc* networks. The primary focus is on efficient traffic detection within 5G networks, using a clustering algorithm for precise localization.

A. Digital twin technology

Digital twins are widely used in various domains, including manufacturing, healthcare, smart cities, and IoT applications. By providing a digital representation of the physical world, digital twin technology enables better decision-making, predictive analytics, and optimization of complex systems and processes.

A digital twin model mirrors the physical MANET environment, capturing node mobility, network topology, and communication patterns. Data acquisition mechanisms collect real-time information from MANET nodes and sensors, which is then processed to update the digital twin model. Advanced algorithms ensure the synchronization of the digital twin with the physical MANET, maintaining a high-fidelity representation of the network environment. The IoT technology lies in its affordability and convenience, as it provides a readily available source of data through smart sensors and wearable devices [7].

B. Real-time monitoring and analysis

The real-time monitoring module continuously collects data from MANET nodes, including signal strength, node positions, and network traffic. Data analysis algorithms process the collected data to identify trends, anomalies, and performance metrics within the MANET environment. Visualization tools provide stakeholders with intuitive displays of network status, enabling informed decision-making and proactive management. Predictive analytics algorithms utilize historical and real-time data to forecast future network behavior and performance trends. Decision-support tools offer recommendations for optimizing network configurations, routing protocols, and resource allocation strategies. Scenario analysis capabilities enable stakeholders to evaluate the potential impact of proposed changes before implementation. Adaptive control mechanisms dynamically adjust network parameters and routing strategies based on insights derived from the digital twin model and predictive analytics. Load balancing algorithms optimize resource utilization and minimize latency by redistributing traffic among MANET nodes. Dynamic routing protocols adapt to changing network conditions, node mobility patterns, and environmental factors to maintain efficient communication.

C. Location-based MANETs

The MANET's location management, a subset of networking management, is instrumental in monitoring the real-time positions of mobile nodes [2]. This aspect has been extensively investigated in cellular, IP, and MANETs [8]. Wireless sensor networks, for instance, face challenges in determining

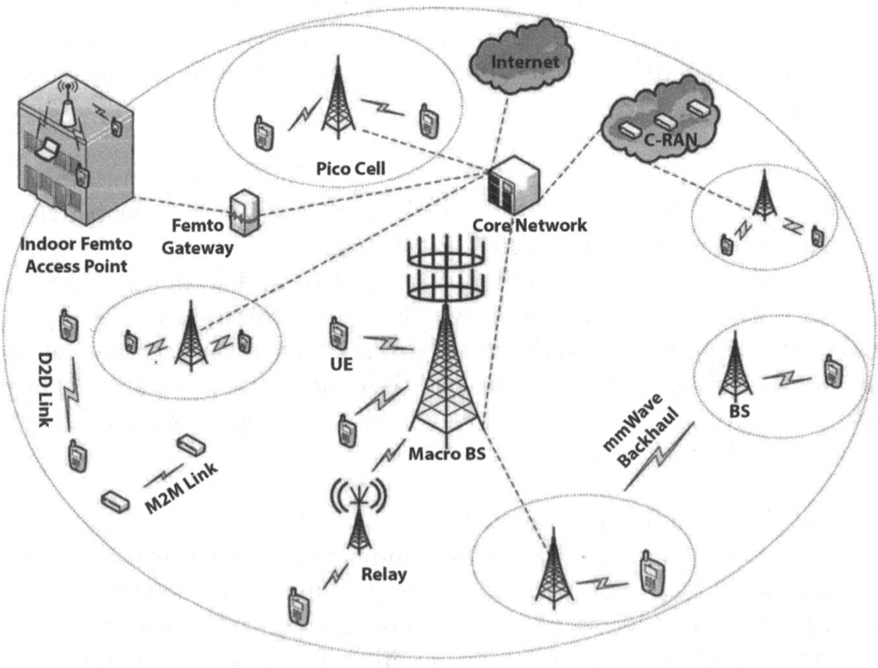

Figure 7.3 Network management.

node locations is crucial for establishing communication paths for data collection [9]. The enhancement of technology protocols and the incorporation of advanced capabilities in MANET protocols underscore the significance of location prediction in advancing various schemes [10] (Figure 7.3). Investigating node mobility factors and assessing how various mobility models influence communication protocols in MANETs [11] are increasingly applied in high-mobility scenarios of heightened node density and dynamic topology changes. Traditional location management methods face challenges in this dynamic context [12]. The demand for precise location information persists across various applications, such as mobile commerce, finance, and advertising, necessitating accurate node location details for uninterrupted service to user devices. This has prompted significant interest in mobility prediction across diverse applications.

7.4 Routing Optimization

The 5G infrastructure is leveraged to facilitate communication between sensor nodes and the central processing unit. The low-latency and high-bandwidth capabilities of 5G are utilized to transmit real-time data from sensor nodes to the central processing unit. A dynamic *ad-hoc*

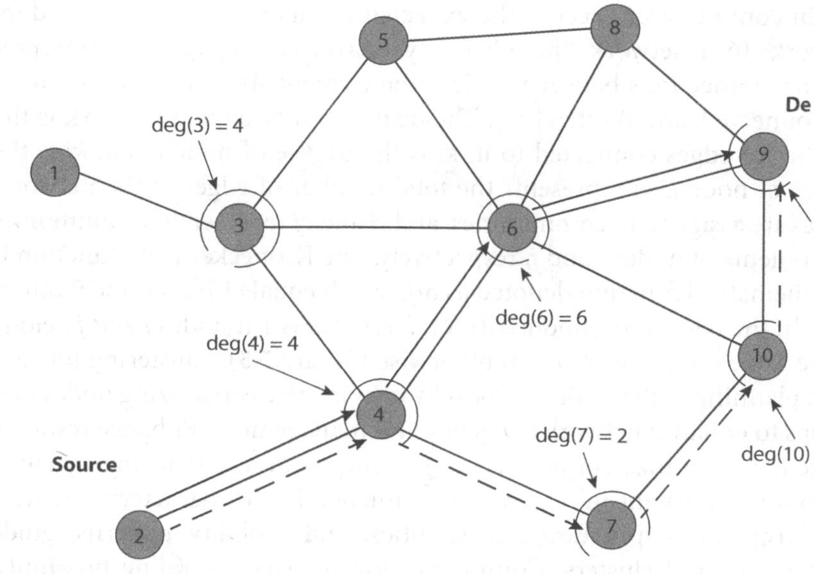

Figure 7.4 An example of routing in a wireless *ad-hoc* network.

network is implemented where sensor nodes can communicate with each other and form temporary networks based on the requirements (Figure 7.4). Protocols such as MANET are used to allow nodes to establish communication links without relying on a fixed infrastructure. Advanced algorithms are implemented for traffic detection based on the data collected by sensor nodes. Computer vision, machine learning, or a combination of analysis is used to detect various aspects of traffic. Clustering algorithms are integrated to group sensor nodes based on their proximity or similarity in traffic patterns. Clustering helps in efficiently managing and processing data by organizing nodes into clusters, reducing communication overhead. Routing optimization algorithms that take advantage of the clustered structure are developed. Data transmission routes within clusters are optimized to minimize latency and energy consumption. Machine learning algorithms are utilized to predict traffic patterns and optimize routing dynamically based on real-time conditions.

7.5 Clustering for Network Planning

$$Q = 1/2m\Sigma ij(Aij - kikj/2m)\delta(ci,cj)$$

Modularity is a measure that assesses the quality of a network partition into communities. It quantifies the degree to which the number of edges within communities exceeds the expected number of edges in a random network. In a network, the adjacency matrix is a square matrix representing connections between nodes. The element Aij is 1 if nodes i and j are connected, and 0 otherwise. The degree of a node in a network is the number of edges connected to it. ki is the degree of node i, and kj is the degree of node j. m represents the total number of edges in the network. Nodes are assigned to communities, and ci and cj represent the community assignments of nodes i and j, respectively. The Kronecker delta function is a mathematical function denoted as δij, which equals 1 if $i = j$, and 0 otherwise. In the context of modularity, $\delta(ci, cj)$ equals 1 if nodes i and j belong to the same community, and 0 otherwise (Figure 7.5). Clustering for network planning in dynamic *ad-hoc* networks involves organizing nodes into groups to enhance network efficiency and management. Enhance resource efficiency, minimize communication latency, and adjust to the dynamic conditions prevalent in *ad-hoc* environments. Node characteristics, such as energy levels, processing capabilities, and mobility patterns, guide the formation of clusters. Communication metrics, including proximity,

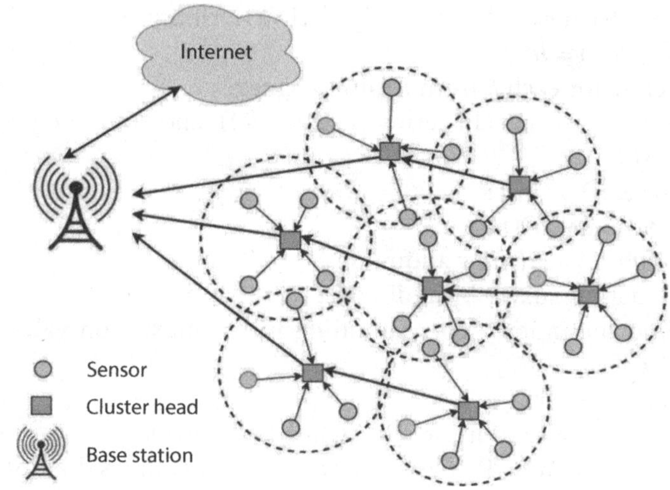

Figure 7.5 Cluster architecture.

connectivity, and bandwidth, play a crucial role in ensuring effective intra-cluster communication. Dynamic cluster formation is facilitated by adaptive algorithms, considering real-time factors such as signal strength and link stability. Qualities-of-service considerations involve load balancing, prioritization, and implementing decentralized approaches to maintain reliability. Security measures involve grouping nodes with similar security levels and incorporating fault-tolerant mechanisms. Scalability is addressed through hierarchical clustering and cluster head rotation, whereas monitoring and adaptation utilize real-time data and learning algorithms.

Resource optimization strategies include task offloading and energy-aware approaches to extend network lifetime. Protocol considerations involve selecting routing and communication protocols tailored for dynamic *ad-hoc* networks. Testing and simulation using tools and real-world experiments help validate the effectiveness of clustering algorithms under various scenarios. In essence, clustering in dynamic *ad-hoc* networks is a multifaceted approach that considers diverse factors to create adaptive, scalable, and efficient clusters, ultimately enhancing overall network performance and reliability.

Network clustering procedure

1. Set auxiliary variables *V*aux and *W*aux to 0.
2. Initialize the result variable to 0.

3. Retrieve network data using NetDataDrilling (*D*).
4. Set *D*(*te*) = *h*.
5. Iterate for each *k* from *K*min to *K*max.
6. Apply k-means clustering (*k*, *D*(*te*, *le*)), and store the result in [*L*].
7. For each *ne* in *L*:
8. If *ne* equals *D*(*ne*):
9. Update *V*aux(*p*) by adding *se*.
10. Update *W*aux(*p*) by adding *ne*.
11. Find the index *v* corresponding to the maximum value in *V*aux.
12. Set *Lv* to *L*(*v*).
13. Generate a random set [*Rv*] using CRND(*rc*).
14. Calculate *Av* as *W*aux(v) multiplied by 1.95 times the square of *Rv*.
15. Determine *Zv*, β, and *r* using Net Dimensioning(*Av*).
16. Set *Yv* to *Zv* multiplied by ϑ.
17. Calculate *Tv* as α times the minimum value of *r* multiplied by *V*aux(*v*).
18. Compute *Dv* as *V*aux(*v*) divided by *Av*.
19. Set βv to the minimum value of *r* multiplied by β multiplied by *Zv*.
20. Calculate *Cv* as *Yv* divided by *Tv*.
21. Compute *Pv* as (*Tv* divided by βv) multiplied by 100.
22. Check if ($al \leq Av \leq au$) and ($dl \leq Dv \leq du$), and then update the result.
23. Set result to [*Cv*, *Pv*, *Lv*].

7.6 Results and Discussion

$$N = \lambda \cdot W$$

N is the average number of entities in the system (packets in the network), λ is the arrival rate of entities (packets per unit time), and *W* is the average time a packet spends in the system (end-to-end delay) (Figure 7.6). This law suggests that the average number of packets in the network (*N*) is equal to the product of the arrival rate (λ) and the average time a packet spends in the network (*W*).

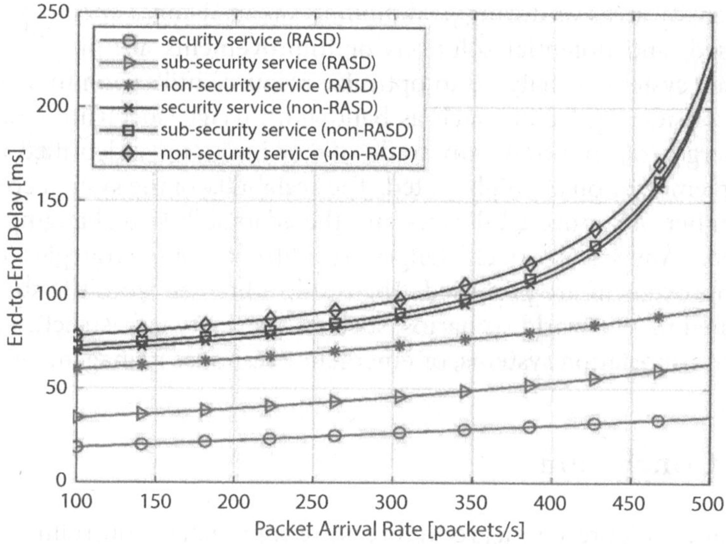

Figure 7.6 Packet arrival rate.

Packet loss

In high-traffic scenarios, where the arrival rate is close to or exceeds the network's capacity, packet loss may occur. This can further impact end-to-end delay as lost packets may need to be retransmitted. The accuracy of the traffic detection system is presented based on the implemented dynamic *ad-hoc* network.

The results are compared with existing systems or benchmarks to showcase the efficiency of the suggested methodology. The efficiency of the clustering algorithm in localizing traffic events within the 5G network is demonstrated through its ability to accurately detect, group, and respond to traffic anomalies in real time. The precision and recall of the localization system were evaluated, and any improvements achieved over traditional localization methods are highlighted.

Insight into the impact of the dynamic *ad-hoc* network on 5G network performance is provided. This can include latency reduction, increased throughput, and improved resource utilization. The system adapts to varying traffic conditions and scales with the number of connected devices.

The clustering algorithm's performance is assessed by examining its convergence time, accuracy in forming clusters, and its ability to adapt to dynamic traffic patterns. The results are compared with other clustering algorithms to justify the choice made for this implementation. The dynamic *ad-hoc* network contributes to efficient traffic management, especially in high-density areas or during peak hours. Any challenges encountered are addressed, and potential solutions or improvements are proposed. The proposed system is analyzed to optimize resource utilization in a 5G network, considering factors such as bandwidth usage, spectrum efficiency, and energy consumption. Any trade-offs or limitations identified during the implementation are highlighted. The scalability of the system concerns the number of connected devices and the adaptability to changing traffic scenarios. Any scalability challenges are addressed, and strategies for further improvement are proposed. The results obtained from the study can be applied in real-world scenarios, such as smart city infrastructure, intelligent transportation systems, or emergency response management.

7.7 Conclusion

The framework presents a groundbreaking approach to controlling mobile *ad-hoc* networking environments through the integration of digital twin technology. Through this innovative framework, network operators gain unprecedented insights into the dynamic behaviors of MANETs, enabling instantaneous monitoring, predictive analytics, and adaptive control mechanisms.

By leveraging digital twin models of the MANET environment, a dynamic *ad-hoc* network for traffic detection in a 5G network with efficient localization using a clustering algorithm enables proactive management strategies, optimized resource allocation, and adaptive routing protocols, thereby enhancing network performance, reliability, and scalability. The successful implementation of traffic detection in the 5G network with efficient localization using a clustering algorithm holds tremendous potential for a wide range of applications, including disaster response, military operations, IoT deployments, and smart city initiatives.

Furthermore, the development and adoption of the framework signify a significant step forward in the evolution of MANET technologies. By bridging the gap between digital representations and physical network environments, it facilitates more informed decision-making, efficient resource utilization, and resilient communication in dynamic and unpredictable MANET scenarios. Moving forward, continued research and development efforts in the field essential to address emerging challenges, refine optimization strategies, and explore new opportunities for leveraging digital twin technology in mobile *ad-hoc* networking are needed. Through collaborative endeavors and interdisciplinary approaches, we can unlock the full potential of a dynamic *ad-hoc* network for traffic detection in 5G networks with efficient localization using clustering algorithms, laying the groundwork for a transformative era of intelligent and adaptive management for MANETs.

In a client–server network model, efficient packet arrival and routing play a pivotal role in achieving optimal communication, and the commonly utilized method involves using the shortest path algorithm to identify the most efficient route for transmitting data packets between the client and server. Upon packet arrival at the client, the network utilizes the shortest path algorithm to identify the quickest route to the server. This algorithm considers factors such as link latency, bandwidth, and network congestion to determine the path with the least delay.

Through dynamic adjustments based on real-time traffic conditions, the proposed system ensures precise and timely detection of traffic issues, leading to improved traffic flow and reduced congestion. Additionally, the incorporation of energy-efficient mechanisms and edge computing within IoT devices helps to prolong device lifespan and reduce overall energy consumption, contributing to the sustainability of the network.

References

1. Abbas, S.G., Husnain, M., Fayyaz, U.U., Shahzad, F., Shah, G.A., Zafar, K., IoT-sphere: A framework to secure IoT devices from becoming attack target and attack source, in: *Proc. IEEE 19th Int. Conf. Trust, Secur. Privacy Comput. Commun. (TrustCom)*, Dec. 2020, pp. 1402–1409.
2. Dixit, P., Comparative study of location-based routing protocols for MANETs, in: *Proc. Int. Conf. Mach. Learn., Big Data, Cloud Parallel Comput. (COM-IT-CON)*, May 2022, vol. 1, pp. 894–900.
3. Xie, J. and Murase, T., An optimal location allocation by multi-user cooperative mobility for maximizing throughput in MANETs. *IEEE Access*, 8, 226089–226107, 2020.
4. Kapinaiah, V., Mobile agent based protocol for location management in mobile *ad hoc* networks, in: *Proc. 6th Int. Conf. Wireless Commun., Signal Process. Netw. (WiSPNET)*, Mar. 2021, pp. 406–410.
5. Krug, S., Aumüller, M., Seitz, J., Hybrid scheme to enable DTN routing protocols to efficiently exploit stable MANET contacts. *EURASIP J. Wirel. Commun. Netw.*, 2018, 237, 2018, [CrossRef].
6. Matis, M., Doboš, L., Papaj, J., An enhanced hybrid social based routing algorithm for MANET-DTN. *Mob. Inf. Syst.*, 2016, 4803242, 2016, [CrossRef].
7. Hinchy, E.P., O'Dowd, N.P., McCarthy, C.T., Using open-source microcontrollers to enable digital twin communication for smart manufacturing. *Procedia Manuf.*, 38, 1213–1219, Jan. 2019.

8. Lin, T.Y. and Kuo, S.-P., A survey on the location management problem in mobile networks. *Multi. J. Sci. Technol.*, 10, 1–9, Jan. 2011.
9. Song, C., Chung, K., Jung, J.J., Rim, K., Lee, J., Localized approximation method using inertial compensation in wsns, in: *New Challenges for Intelligent Information and Database Systems*, pp. 247–255, Springer, Cham, Switzerland, 2011.
10. Abdullah, S.J., Alam, S., Minhas, A.A., Location prediction for improvement of communication protocols in wireless communications: Considerations and future directions, in: *Proc. the World Congr. Eng. Comput. Sci.*, vol. 2, pp. 19–21, 2011.
11. Roy, R.R., Mobility model characteristics, in: *Handbook Mobile Ad Hoc Netw. for Mobility Models*, pp. 23–32, Springer, Cham, Switzerland, 2011.
12. Hosseininezhad, S. and Leung, V., Location management in heterogeneous VANETs: A mobility aware server selection method, in: *Proc. Int. Conf. Ad Hoc Netw.*, pp. 64–81, 2010.

8

RFID-Based Smart Parking Management System Using IoT

Anil Kumar C. S.[1], Shailendra Kumar Mishra[1], Ali Baig Mohammad[1] and Vishnu Kumar. S.[2]*

[1]*School of Electronics and Communications Engineering, Reva University, Bengaluru, India*
[2]*School of Electronics and Communications Engineering, Vel Tech Rangarajan Dr. Sagunthala R&D Institute of Science and Technology, Chennai, India*

Abstract
Automatic parking systems represent a significant advancement in urban infrastructure, offering efficient and convenient solutions to alleviate the challenges of parking in densely populated areas. This work introduces an intelligent and innovative smart parking system with dual functionalities. First, it outlines a parking detection mechanism using an infrared sensor integrated with Internet of Things technology to transmit parking status to the cloud, facilitated by the ESP8266 module. Second, it addresses security concerns through the implementation of FAST-TAG, allowing only authorized access to the parking area, in addition to automatically deducting fees from user accounts based on occupancy duration. To optimize power consumption, the system dynamically adjusts light intensity using an LDR (light-dependent resistor) sensor. Automatic parking systems represent a transformative solution to the challenges of urban parking, offering efficiency, convenience, and sustainability.

Keywords: Infrared object sensor, ESP8266, RFID, LDR, IoT

8.1 Introduction

At present, the manual management of parking areas predominates in urban settings, lacking efficient automatic systems for optimal utilization.

**Corresponding author*: mail2jitvishnu@gmail.com

Kanak Kalita, S. Vishnu Kumar and M. Niranjanamurthy (eds.) Industrial Internet of Things and Advanced Techniques for Sensor Data Aggregation and Fusion, (99–112) © 2026 Scrivener Publishing LLC

Upon entering a parking facility, drivers typically rely on information boards to ascertain parking availability, encountering challenges in locating vacant spots amid congested areas, particularly prevalent near shopping centers and medical facilities where vehicle density exceeds available spaces. This inefficient process leads to time and fuel wastage, exacerbating traffic congestion. Despite sporadic vacancies, overall occupancy remains low due to inadequate parking lot management, resulting in suboptimal space utilization and congestion in surrounding areas [1].

Efficient parking lot management, including real-time availability information dissemination to drivers prior to entry, emerges as a pressing concern. The evolution of smart cities leverages data, communication, and technology integration to enhance public operational efficiency, thereby fostering improved quality of life for residents. Key technological enablers such as the Internet of Things (IoT), automation, and machine learning propel the transition toward smart city initiatives, facilitating innovative solutions [2]. Hence, the efficacy of a city's infrastructure can be gauged through its adoption of inventive strategies. A sophisticated parking system, exemplifying the smart city paradigm, incorporates a mobile application to assist drivers in locating available parking slots and implement intelligent traffic management to optimize traffic flow.

The IoT facilitates data transmission across networks autonomously, eliminating the need for direct human interaction. By leveraging cost-effective wireless technology, IoT enables seamless data transfer to the cloud, fostering transparency in operations. Initially conceptualized around the notion of connecting various devices, IoT enables remote control and monitoring of devices *via* internet-connected computers [3]. Comprising the amalgamation of "Internet" and "Things," IoT utilizes the expansive internet network to facilitate communication and data exchange with connected devices. Data collected from sensors undergo analysis and processing to derive actionable insights [4]. Thus, an intelligent parking system (IPS) emerges as a pivotal solution to mitigate fuel wastage and address associated challenges. By optimizing parking space utilization, such a system minimizes time inefficiencies and reduces overall fuel consumption incurred during parking spot searches [5].

Radiofrequency identification (RFID) technology utilizes radio waves to identify animate or inanimate objects [6]. Although RFID has long been recognized for its wireless data transmission capabilities, its industrial adoption has been limited by cost and lack of standardization among manufacturers. However, over time, RFID has gained widespread acceptance, driven by its potential to streamline operations and reduce physical workload [7]. Universally applicable, practical, and efficient, RFID technology enhances business efficiency and offers benefits to both businesses and consumers. Notably secure, RFID plays a crucial role in inventory tracking, contributing to enhanced inventory management practices [8].

8.2 Related Works

This paper presents the design of an innovative smart parking system integrating image processing and artificial intelligence technologies. By deploying cameras and ultrasonic sensors at strategic locations, the system is capable of accurately recognizing license plate numbers, enabling a ticketless parking experience. Furthermore, the algorithm incorporates big-data analysis and neural network techniques to analyze parking data comprehensively and offer personalized user recommendations based on the gathered information [9].

Smart parking management seeks to utilize advanced sensing and monitoring technologies to optimize the utilization of parking spaces in large parking lots, guiding drivers to available spots and reducing the stress and delays associated with parking, thereby alleviating traffic congestion. The concept of smart parking emerged to streamline parking processes, making them quicker and less resource-intensive as resources become scarcer. The smart parking management system (SPMS) proposed in this paper aims to address various parking-related issues by providing drivers with a sensing platform integrated with a mobile app. This platform allows real-time interaction between drivers and parking infrastructure, minimizing search times for vacant spots in large multistory parking facilities and aiding in the retrieval of parked vehicles. To assess the effectiveness of the SPMS, a small-scale test environment was created and tested under five different scenarios, demonstrating its efficiency and suggesting its potential integration into real-world parking facilities [10].

Bangladesh is advancing toward becoming a digital nation, and numerous challenges have been addressed through the implementation of smart applications. However, the rapid increase in the number of cars in the country has resulted in a scarcity of parking space. Hence, there is a critical need for efficient parking management systems. This article introduces a multilevel automated car parking system based on Arduino technology. It incorporates rotational and lifting mechanisms, as well as sliding mechanisms utilizing gear-ratio and rack–pinion systems, to facilitate the placement and retrieval of cars from parking slots. Additionally, infrared (IR) sensors are used for controlling the 360-degree rotational mechanism and detecting available slots [11].

The advancement toward smart cities necessitates efficient management of parking systems, particularly in densely populated areas including metro cities, where locating an available parking spot poses a significant challenge due to the escalating number of vehicles. This issue not only impacts convenience but also raises concerns about vehicle safety. Addressing this concern, this study proposes an IoT-based IPS. The IPS uses an IoT framework to gather real-time data, which is then transmitted to the cloud to suggest nearby parking spots to users. Complementing this framework is a mobile application enabling users to check for nearby parking availability and reserve spots as needed. The paper outlines various scenarios of users finding and parking in suitable spots. The implementation of the system utilizes Raspberry Pi, Node-MCU, RFID, and IR sensors. Results presented validate the efficacy and usability of the IPS [12].

In recent years, there has been significant focus on wireless sensor networks (WSNs), leading to their widespread application across various industrial and medical sectors. Leveraging the OpenWSN platform, we have devised an IPS aimed at alleviating congestion in urban parking lots. Our paper offers both theoretical insights and practical simulations. Given the energy constraints inherent in WSNs and the specific challenges of parking lot management, we introduce innovative network protocols (MAC and NET layers) tailored to address these issues. Through meticulous experimental design and simulation, we demonstrate the efficacy and efficiency of our proposed solution in the experiment section [13].

There are different locales of uses for remote sensor systems (WSNs). In this exhibit, we are utilizing a WSN to fabricate a productive and savvy leaving framework for vehicles. Our application will utilize light sensors to naturally decide the utilization of parking spots in a leaving territory and figure billable leaving time while additionally giving vehicle administrators a useful diagram of consumed and free parking spots. Such a framework can give expanded driver comfort and decrease costs in parking spot activity by permitting drivers to settle where to stop handily. At the same time, the used parts produce low expenses for the operator [13].

8.3 Methodology

In this section of the paper, we describe the prominent level of the architecture of intelligent parking management based on RFID and IoT. This system contains two sections. The first section is Arduino with an RFID card reader. Furthermore, the second section is Arduino along with a couple of

IR sensors. The user or client cannot enter the system or parking lot without an RFID or fast tag.

Using cloud-based servers or any open-source IoT platform, the ESP8266 Wi-Fi module achieves various functions [14]. For instance, when an authorized vehicle approaches the system, it automatically verifies and detects the predefined amount in the fast tag or prompts the user to recharge their account if necessary. To minimize power consumption, an LDR (light-dependent resistor) sensor monitors the light intensity within the system or parking IoT infrastructure. Additionally, the second section uses an IR sensor to identify vacant parking spaces and assign them to arriving individuals [15]. This real-time information is continually updated to the system.

8.4 Algorithm

In this section, we will explore the flow of the system structure. When the vehicle or the person entry into the system, first, it checks whether the vehicle or the person is authorized or not, and then it will allow entering the system. Entire working operation as shown in Figure 8.1, when person is identified or vehicle is authorized, the prefixed amount will be deducted

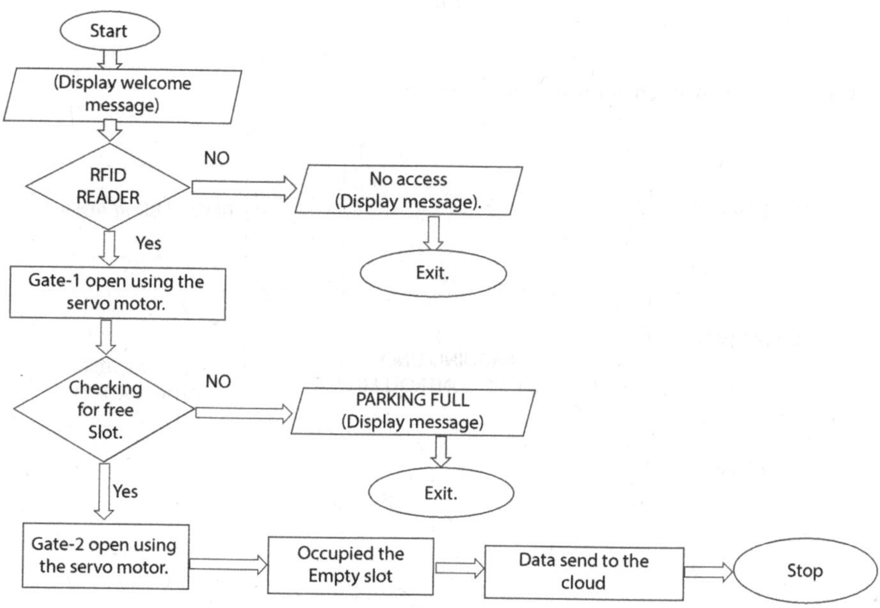

Figure 8.1 Flowchart of the proposed RFID-based parking system.

from the card or tag. It needs to be recharged with the amount that client wishes to recharge, and then the entry gate will open at the same time it will display the free slot in the parking lot that has to be parked. Thus, the cloud database or internal counter will count the occupancy.

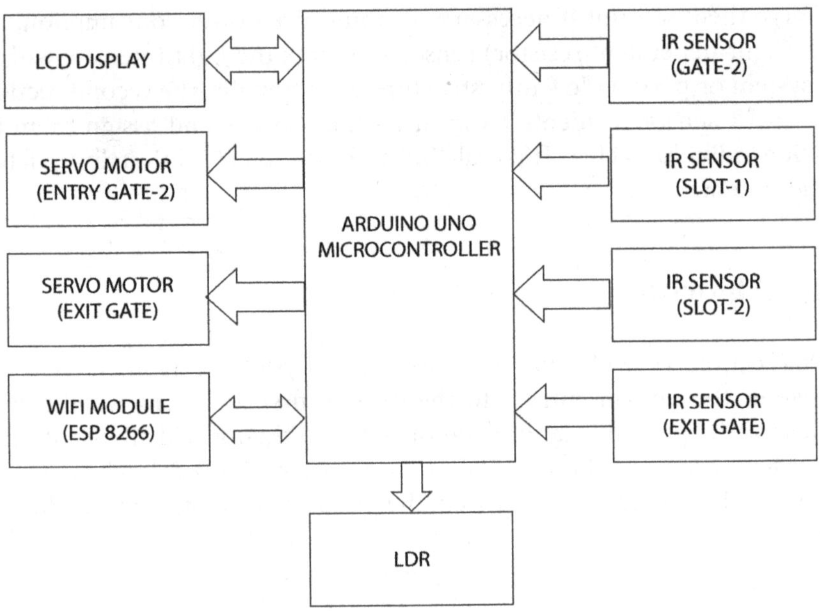

Figure 8.2 Block diagram at the main gate entrance.

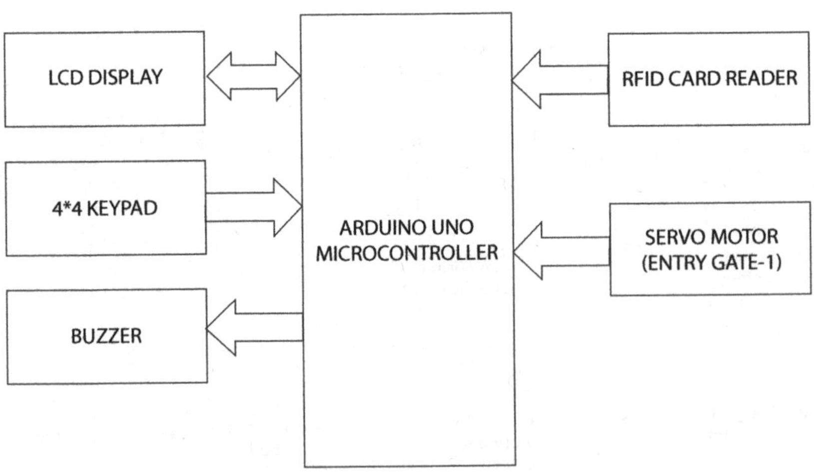

Figure 8.3 Block diagram of the circuit to show customer RFID tag.

This work majorly consists of two blocks that are briefly explained as in Figure 8.2 and Figure 8.3 that shows the block diagram of the proposed RFID based parking system.

Arduino Uno: It is the brain of the system that controls all the peripherals of the system and gives the instructions to perform the task to complete the desired task at high precision and accuracies [16].
RFID module: It is also invoked by the name FAST-TAG in this system, which detects the same radiofrequency of the card and the reader [17]. In this system, it functions as vital security to enter the system, it also ensures the safety of the client, and it detects the prefixed amount from the FAST-TAG automatically to avoid time delays for the customers [18].
Wi-Fi module: This module plays an essential role in the system that ensures the operation of the IoT, which is the IoT. The ESP8266 is used as the Wi-Fi module. The system will send the data and states of the slot in the parking lot to the cloud or any other IoT platform. The user can easily monitor the free spaces in the parking lot [19].
Servo motor: This motor helps operate the gate in the system whenever the vehicle comes near the entrances. The system will intelligently operate the gate whether to open or not. It will check the two constraints, whether the person or vehicle is authorized or not, and whether the slot in the parking is free or not. It takes the decision that is given by the microprocessor [20].
IR sensor: These are the sensors that work on the inferred red rays, which have two leads: one is the transmitter and the second is the receiver. These sensors will do many functions in the system; it will identify that the vehicle is present near the system and send the data to the microprocessor to perform the necessary functions ahead [21].
LCD display: In this module, we can read out the instruction given by the processing unit. It is implemented in the system to interact between the system and the client. It provides a vital role in making the system user-friendly.
LDR sensor: This sensor can sense the intensity of the light in the surrounding. Hence, it automatically adjusts the light intensity in the system to conserve power.

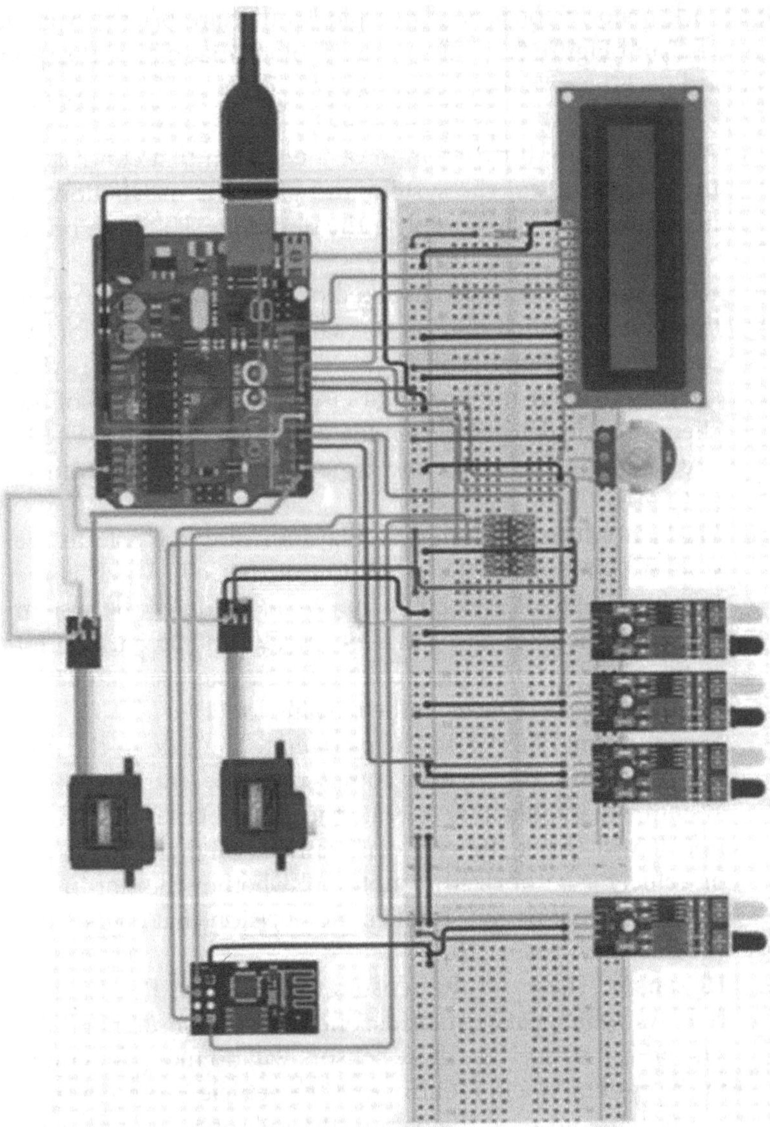

Figure 8.4 Circuit diagram at the main gate entrance.

Figure 8.4 shows the circuit diagram of RFID based parking management system. As illustrated in the above image.

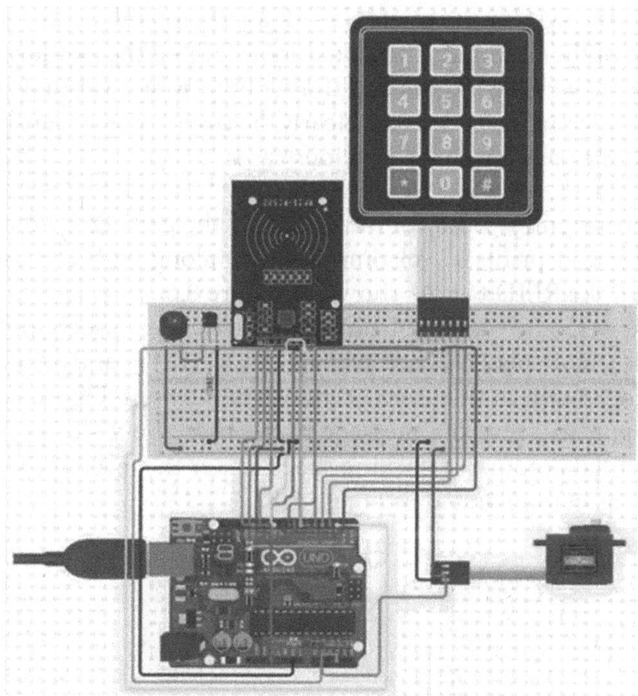

Figure 8.5 Circuit arrangement to show customer RFID tag.

Figure 8.5 shows circuit diagram of RFID based parking system. And showing the RFID card module.

8.5 Results and Discussion

The proposed work takes the data from the IR sensors of a nearing vehicle and then triggers the microcontroller to actuate the servo motors to open the entry gate lever. During this process, the system will scan the RFID tag (which can be recognized as the FAST-TAG system available for Indian Highways Toll Collection). In contrast, the RFID scans and accepts the user's identification; it will then search for available space. If available, the system can charge the user a predefined fee for the vehicle type. The identification contains the information of the registration number, along with the owner's name, vehicle type, and account balance. If there is any fund deficiency, it will show a message on the LCD screen "LOW BALANCE." The second task is to report to the user the current availability of any slot on the premises. If not, the actuator will not trigger the servo motor to open the lever to pass the vehicle.

When all the system parameters work as per intended, and the vehicle is going out of the premises, the actuators will open the exit lever to make the path for the vehicle to pass and thus count the slot vacated at the time of exit. To understand work more clearly, below are the screenshots of the LCD screen messages regarding various cases.

Case 1: Normal entry: Entry of the user near the gate; RFID scans the tag from the car and prints a welcome message along with the user's name fetched from the RFID tag. As shown in Figure 8.6.

After the welcome message from the system, after 1-second delay, proposed work will display balance available in RFID tag and also collect the balance information in the user's account. As shown in Figure 8.7.

Next step, it will give the message to the user about slot availability as per the fed total amount of parking space as per the level of the premises. It will show as demonstrated in Figure 8.8.

Figure 8.6 Welcome message from the system.

Figure 8.7 Displaying the balance amount in the customer RFID tag.

Figure 8.8 Showing level B1 has available space for parking.

For accessing the designated car space, the system will deduct a fixed fare from the user account (for example, FAST-TAG). The amount deducted will show on the Figure 8.9.

During the time of exit from the exit gate, the IR sensor on the exit gate will sense the approaching vehicle, and while the lever is actuated to open, it will show the message on the LCD screen a gesture of greetings on using the service, as shown in Figure 8.10.

Case 2: If the user has low balance, right after the RFID tag is scanned from the user's vehicle, if there is adequate balance in their account, then it will proceed to the previous case. If not, then it will show a warning message for having inadequate balance, thus preventing the user from entering the car park premise. As described in Figure 8.11.

Figure 8.9 Amount deducted as a parking fee for the car space offered.

Figure 8.10 Thank-you message being displayed.

Figure 8.11 Low balance hence access denied.

Figure 8.12 "Parking full" message displayed.

Figure 8.13 User denied from entering the premises.

Case 3: In the condition where there is no available car parking space, the user will get a message on the LCD screen upon RFID scan, and the user will not be charged any fare, as shown in Figure 8.12.

Case 4: If there is someone entering with a tag that is not valid for the premises, they will be automatically blocked from entering, and a message to the intended user will be triggered. As shown in Figure 8.13.

8.6 Conclusions

We have designed an efficient and intelligent parking system with different security levels by RFID tag to solve parking issues. This system can sense the space in the parking lot and display it on the screen. With the help of IoT, the system can update to the cloud or web. This system is also capable of maintaining security, automatically detecting the money from the card and adding it to the card. If an unknown person enters the system, this is not allowed. To save electricity, the streetlight's intensity is automatically controlled.

References

1. Khanna, A. and Anand, R., IoT based smart parking system. *IEEE Internet of Things and Applications (IOTA)*, 2016, DOI: 10.1109/IOTA.2016.7562735.

2. Lookmuang, R., Nambut, K., Usanavasin, S., Smart parking using IoT technology. *IEEE International Conference on Business Informatics Research (ICBIR)*, 2018, DOI: 10.1109/ICBIR.2018.8391155.
3. Adhatarao, S.S., Alfandi, O., Bochem, A., Hogrefe, D., Smart parking system for vehicles. *IEEE Vehicular Networking Conference (VNC)*, 2014, DOI: 10.1109/VNC.2014.7013341.
4. Vishnu Kumar, S., Anuja Mary, G., Chohan, J., Kalita, K., Efficient sensor anomaly detection using Markov-LSTM architecture for methane sensing. *J. Auton. Intell.*, 7, 3, 2023, doi: 10.32629/jai.v7i3.1285.
5. Orrie, O., Silva, B., Hancke, G.P., A wireless smart parking system. *IEEE Industrial Electronics Conference (IECON)*, 2015, DOI: 10.1109/IECON.2015.7392741.
6. Šolić, P., Marasović, I., Stefanizzi, M.L., Patrono, L., Mainetti, L., RFID-based efficient method for parking slot car detection. *IEEE International Conference on Software, Telecommunications and Computer Networks (SOFTCOM)*, 2015, DOI: 10.1109/SOFTCOM.2015.7314120.
7. Alsafery, W., Alturki, B., Reiff-Marganiec, S., Jambi, K., Smart Car Parking System Solution for the Internet of Things in Smart Cities. *IEEE Conference on Advanced Information Systems (CAIS)*, 2018, DOI: 10.1109/CAIS.2018.8442004.
8. Lee, C., Han, Y., Jeon, S., Seo, D., Jung, I., Smart parking system for Internet of Things. *IEEE International Conference on Consumer Electronics (ICCE)*, 2016, DOI: 10.1109/ICCE.2016.7430607.
9. Chatterjee, A., Manna, S., Rahaman, A., Sarka, A.R., Ghosh, A., An Automated RFID Based Car Parking System. *IEEE International Conference on Optoelectronics and Photonics (OPTRONIX)*, 2019, DOI: 10.1109/OPTRONIX.2019.8862411.
10. Shah, M.N., Bhuva, V.M., Gohel, P.C., Hadia, S.K., Smart Parking System Using Image Processing, in: *2015 IEEE International Conference on Computational Intelligence and Computing Research (ICCIC)*, DOI: 10.1109/ICCIC.2015.7435817.
11. Parveen, H., Bano, R., Patil, M.R., Smart Parking Management System for Smart Cities, in: *2016 IEEE International Conference on Computational Techniques in Information and Communication Technologies*, DOI: 10.1109/ICCTICT.2016.7515104.
12. Ahmed, M.B.I.R. and Ghani, F.A.A., Automated Multi-Story Car Parking System: Design and Implementation. *2017 IEEE International Conference on Smart Instrumentation, Measurement and Applications (ICSIMA)*, DOI: 10.1109/ICSIMA.2017.8309053.
13. Alim Al Islam, B.M., Rahman, M.M., Bhuiyan, M.J.H., Automated Smart Parking System with IoT Connectivity, in: *2018 IEEE 21st International Conference on Intelligent Transportation Systems (ITSC)*, DOI: 10.1109/ITSC.2018.8569594.

14. Chen, Y., Duan, L., Wang, Y., Cao, Z., An Intelligent Parking Guidance System Based on Wireless Sensor Networks. *IEEE Access*, 2019, DOI: 10.1109/ACCESS.2019.2907252.
15. Chang, Y.T. and Shih, T.K., RFID-Based intelligent parking management system with indoor positioning and dynamic tracking. *IEEE International Conference on Ubiquitous Multimedia and Service (UMEDIA)*, 2017, DOI: 10.1109/UMEDIA.2017.8074095.
16. Revathi, G. and Dhulipala, V.R.S., Smart parking systems and sensors: A survey. *IEEE International Conference on Communication, Circuits and Systems (ICCCA)*, 2012, DOI: 10.1109/ICCCA.2012.6179195.
17. Elakya, R., Seth, J., Ashritha, P., Namith, R., Smart Parking System using IoT. *J. Internet Technol.*, ISSN: 2249–8958, 9, 1, October 2019.
18. Joshi, Y., Gharate, P., Ahire, C., Alai, N., Sonavane, S., Smart parking management system using RFID and OCR. *IEEE International Conference on Energy Systems and Applications (ICESA)*, 2015, DOI: 10.1109/ICESA.2015.7503445.
19. Wei, L., Wu, Q., Yang, M., Ding, W., Li, B., Gao, R., Design and Implementation of Smart Parking Management System Based on RFID and Internet. *IEEE International Conference on Consumer Electronics, Communications and Networks (ICCECT)*, 2012, DOI: 10.1109/ICCECT.2012.12.
20. Pala, Z. and Inanc, N., Smart Parking Applications Using RFID Technology. *IEEE International Conference on RFID Eurasia*, 2007, DOI: 10.1109/RFIDEURASIA.2007.4368108.
21. Zhou, H. and Li, Z., An Intelligent Parking Management System Based on RS485 and RFID. *IEEE Cyber Security and Cloud Computing (CyberC)*, 2016, DOI: 10.1109/CyberC.2016.74.

9

IoT-Based Animal Watch Safety Using Green Technology with Deep Learning Approach

Vineet Saxena[1], Prashant Dhage[2], Ghouse Basha M. A.[3], Trupti Patil[4], Mritunjay Rai[5*] and Vishal Sharma[6]

[1]*College of Computing Science and Information Technology, Teerthanker Mahaveer University, Moradabad, Uttar Pradesh, India*

[2]*Symbiosis Law School Nagpur, Symbiosis International (Deemed University), Pune, India*

[3]*Department of Data Science & Analytics, Data Science & Analytics, School of Sciences, Jain(Deemed-to-be University), Bangalore, India*

[4]*Bharati Vidyapeeth Deemed to be University, Department of Engineering and Technology, Navi Mumbai, Maharashtra, India*

[5]*Department of Electrical and Electronics Engineering, Shri Ramswaroop Memorial University, Barabanki, Uttar Pradesh, India*

[6]*Department of Mechanical Engineering, Vivekananda Global University, Jaipur, India*

Abstract

In this study, convolutional neural network (CNN)–based method for Internet of Things (IoT)–based object detection in photos of firearms is presented in green technology. The goal of the study is to create a powerful model that can locate and identify weapons in photos with accuracy in IoT. The suggested methodology involves model architecture creation, image preprocessing methods, and training on a dataset of firearm images in green technology. The results show that the CNN-based IoT model is effective at finding and locating weapons with a high degree of accuracy of 96.56%. The preparation of the dataset, which comprises gun images and related label masks, is the first step in the investigation. TensorFlow's image loading routines are used to load the photos, and they are then transformed into NumPy arrays. By giving suitable values to areas where guns are present, label

**Corresponding author*: er.mritunjayrai@gmail.com

Kanak Kalita, S. Vishnu Kumar and M. Niranjanamurthy (eds.) Industrial Internet of Things and Advanced Techniques for Sensor Data Aggregation and Fusion, (113–138) © 2026 Scrivener Publishing LLC

masks are created. These preprocessing steps guarantee that the dataset is suitably ready for the CNN model's training in green technology. The TensorFlow Keras package is used to create CNN architecture for the IoT-based object detection model. Multiple convolutional and pooling layers are used by the model to extract pertinent characteristics from the input photos. Upsampling layers are used to increase spatial resolution; dropout layers are used to prevent overfitting. The network's final layer uses a sigmoid activation function for binary classification to determine whether there are firearms in the photos. The weighted binary cross-entropy loss function and the Adam optimizer are used to train the model. The weighted loss function addresses the class imbalance problem frequently seen in object detection tasks by giving the positive class a higher weight. With a predetermined batch size and validation split, the model is trained iteratively across numerous epochs. The model learns to reliably detect guns in the photographs as training progresses. Predicting the masks for a random sample of photos from the dataset is how the trained model is assessed. The actual photos and the expected masks are then combined to create masked images that emphasize the gun locations. This assessment offers visual proof of the model's capability to locate weapons in various photos. The experimental findings show how reliable and accurate the suggested CNN model for detecting guns is. The model's high accuracy rate of 96.56% shows that it can successfully recognize weapons in a variety of visual settings. The research publication emphasizes that the author does not claim ownership of the photos and notes that the dataset utilized in the study was obtained from Google photos. In this study, CNNs are successfully used to identify objects in photos of guns in green technology. The suggested approach demonstrates the created model's efficacy in precisely recognizing and localizing weapons. The achieved high accuracy rate emphasizes CNNs' ability to address significant societal concerns about the detection of guns in green technology. This study can be expanded upon to include real-time gun detection systems, which would improve security and safety measures for the general population.

***Keywords*:** Animal, CNN, object detection, YOLO, image processing, IoT, green technology

9.1 Introduction

The necessity for successful wildlife conservation and human–animal conflicts has grown in importance in recent years. The interactions between people and wildlife have been more intense as human populations grow and encroach on natural areas, creating a variety of problems and conflicts. Maintaining ecological equilibrium and guaranteeing the preservation of biodiversity depend on achieving a balance in the coexistence of humans and animals. Innovative strategies and cutting-edge technologies are being created to monitor and manage wildlife populations in order to meet these problems. The Animal Watch Safety System, a cutting-edge solution that uses personalized machine learning models for real-time animal detection and monitoring, is one such method [1, 2]. The Animal Watch Safety System tries to get over the drawbacks of conventional approaches to animal monitoring, which frequently rely on manual labor and are time- and labor-intensive [3, 4]. The You Only Look Once (YOLO) method is one of the machine learning algorithms that is used by this system to recognize animals in a more effective and accurate manner. The YOLO method, which divides an image into a grid and forecasts bounding boxes and class probabilities within each grid cell, is renowned for its capacity to carry out real-time object detection. Because quick responses are essential in real-time animal monitoring, this makes it the best option. To train the customized machine learning model, a broad dataset made up of several animal classes—including mammals, birds, reptiles, and insects—was utilized. To make sure that the model can accurately detect and categorize animals from all classes, it is crucial to address this imbalance throughout the training process. The dataset is preprocessed to make training easier, and bounding box annotations are made to show where the animals are located in the photos. A balanced representation of classes in both sets is then achieved by dividing the dataset into training and testing sets [5, 6]. A YOLO dataset is produced, which consists of scaled photos and label files with the bounding box annotations, to train the model. By initializing the model with previously learned weights, transfer learning is implemented using the YOLOv5 architecture. This method gives the model the ability to utilize information obtained from sizable datasets, improving performance and quickening convergence during training. Precision, recall, and mean average precision (mAP) measures are used to evaluate the model's performance and determine how accurate and reliable its object detection capabilities are [7, 8]. Experimental results show the bespoke machine learning model's promising performance in animal detection across multiple classifications. High precision and recall values show precise animal localization and identification, and the model's performance in object localization and detection tasks is supported by the mAP scores. These findings demonstrate the Animal Watch Safety System's potential for habitat monitoring, wildlife conservation, and the reduction of human–wildlife conflicts. Compared to current techniques, the Animal Watch Safety System has a number of advantages. Because of its real-time capabilities, it can respond and intervene right away in urgent situations, lowering the likelihood of conflicts between people and wildlife and improving the safety of both. Due to the system's adaptability, it can be used in a variety of settings, including agricultural areas, national parks, and wildlife reserves, to meet diverse monitoring requirements. Additionally, the system's unique machine learning model may be continuously enhanced and updated with fresh data, guaranteeing adaptability to altering animal behaviors and environmental factors [7–9]. Because of the model's scalability, it may be integrated into current surveillance systems, boosting and extending their functionality. The suggested system has the potential to decrease the need for human resources by automating the animal detection process in addition to its many practical benefits. The solution saves crucial time and lowers expenses connected with labor by removing the need for manual monitoring [10, 11]. The Animal Watch Safety System helps to promote a harmonious coexistence of humans and animals by detecting animals effectively and reliably, hence promoting sustainable human–animal cohabitation [12–14].

9.1.1 Man–Wildlife Conflict and the Role of Image Processing

Due to the growth of human populations and encroachment into natural ecosystems, human–wildlife conflict has become a critical concern in recent years. Conflicts emerge as human activities gradually encroach on wildlife habitats, having detrimental effects on both people and animals. These disagreements may cause financial harm and material damage and even present a threat to human life. For the coexistence of people and animals to be guaranteed while biodiversity is being preserved, it is essential to find solutions that effectively reduce human–wildlife conflicts. Image processing tools are crucial in this situation for controlling and monitoring wildlife populations, enabling early detection and intervention. Conflicts between humans and wildlife arise when wildlife actions or behaviors threaten human safety or obstruct human goals. Such disputes may result from a number of things, such as rivalry for scarce resources, destruction of livestock or crops, assaults on people, or disruption of human habitations. These disputes can have detrimental effects on local inhabitants' livelihoods and well-being, as well as the populations of wildlife. Techniques for analyzing images have become important instruments for resolving disputes between people and wildlife. Image processing permits the analysis and interpretation of visual data obtained from many sources, such as cameras, drones, or satellite photos, by utilizing developments in computer vision and machine learning. These technologies offer real-time, precise, and nonintrusive ways to find, track, and identify animals in their natural habitats, which has the potential to revolutionize wildlife monitoring and management. Animal identification and classification is one of the main uses of image processing in reducing wildlife conflict. Wildlife researchers and conservationists can automatically recognize and classify animals in photos or video recordings by using computer vision techniques, such as object detection and recognition models [15, 16]. As a result, potential conflict scenarios can be quickly identified, allowing for prompt intervention to stop human–wildlife encounters. Convolutional neural networks (CNNs), for example, are deep learning–based models that have achieved very well in object detection tasks [17, 18]. Large annotated datasets can be used to train these algorithms to identify particular animal species or tell wildlife apart from other items in photos. Researchers can get immediate alerts when animals of interest are found by using such models on surveillance systems or video traps, enabling proactive steps to reduce conflicts. Animal movement and behavior can also be analyzed using image processing techniques. Researchers can learn more about an animal's foraging habits, preferred habitats, and migration routes by tracking and observing the animal's movements. Understanding the dynamics of animal populations and identifying probable conflict hotspots require the knowledge in this article. Advanced algorithms can examine animal movement patterns to spot locations where wildlife–human encounters are more likely to happen, such as clustering or anomalous behavior. Techniques for processing images help create effective conflict-mitigation plans for people and wildlife. Researchers and wildlife managers can identify reoccurring conflict scenarios and evaluate the efficacy of various mitigation strategies by analyzing historical data and trends discovered using image processing. This data-driven methodology aids in streamlining the decision-making and resource allocation processes, ensuring that interventions are effective and well-targeted. Additionally, image processing technology can help in monitoring the effectiveness of implemented tactics over time. Researchers can evaluate the long-term effects of mitigation initiatives, identify areas for improvement, and adjust management tactics by keeping an eye on changes in animal behavior and the occurrence of conflicts [19, 20].

9.1.2 YOLO Model for Detection of Animals and a Safety System Using Machine Learning

In the area of computer vision, the YOLO paradigm has grown significantly in popularity, especially for object detection tasks. YOLO is a real-time object detection system that can recognize and categorize numerous items in a frame of an image or video at once. The detection of animals has also been a common use for this model, helping a number of systems, including those for transportation safety and systems for monitoring wildlife. The YOLO model stands out because it can execute in real time while maintaining a high level of accuracy. Region proposal and object categorization are typically the two stages of traditional object detection algorithms. Whereas YOLO completes both tasks in a single forward pass through a CNN, the latter executes the former. YOLO may attain amazing processing rates because of this method, which qualifies it for real-time applications. The YOLO model has been trained on extensive datasets that contain a variety of animal species in the context of animal detection. The model gains the ability to distinguish between several animal classifications, including livestock, poultry, wild animals, and domestic pets. The model is fed labeled photos during training in order to teach it the visual characteristics and patterns unique to each animal class. The YOLO model can precisely locate and detect animals in still photos or video frames after being trained. Precision livestock husbandry is one real-world implementation of the YOLO paradigm in the agriculture sector. This model can be used by farmers to track and monitor their livestock, allowing them to quickly identify and handle any potential health issues. Using cameras or drones fitted with the YOLO model, for instance, farmers may keep an eye on the behavior and welfare of their cattle [21]. The program can identify anomalies such as irregular movement patterns or symptoms of distress and notify farmers in real time so they can act quickly. The YOLO model has been used for the automated detection and monitoring of endangered species in the field of wildlife conservation. To monitor wildlife habitats, researchers and conservationists can use cameras or unmanned aerial vehicles fitted with the YOLO model. Through the detection and prevention of unlawful actions such as poaching and habitat degradation, this enables nonintrusive monitoring and data collecting, assisting in the protection and conservation of endangered species. The YOLO model can also be included into systems that reduce the danger of collisions between vehicles and animals. Potential risks can be identified in real time by placing cameras or sensors with the YOLO model alongside roads or trains. The model's ability to recognize animals in close proximity to traffic routes enables the activation of early warning systems. These devices can warn motorists or railway operators, allowing them to take the necessary precautions to prevent collisions and guarantee the safety of both people and animals [22, 23].

9.1.3 CNN and Visual Geometry Group Networks in Animal Detection for Training

In the area of computer vision, CNNs have revolutionized object detection tasks such as animal detection. CNNs are deep learning algorithms that can automatically learn hierarchical visual data representations. They have shown astounding proficiency in a variety of image recognition tasks, including the identification and categorization of animals. The VGG (Visual Geometry Group) network is a CNN architecture that is frequently used in animal detection. The VGG network is renowned for being straightforward and efficient. Max-pooling layers are followed by numerous convolutional layers with tiny filter sizes for down-sampling. With this architecture, the network is able to collect both high- and low-level information from the input images. A big labeled dataset is necessary while training a CNN in order to optimize the network's settings. A broad dataset of animal photos is necessary for animal detection. To ensure the network's ability to generalize, the dataset needs to include a variety of animal species, positions, backdrops, and lighting conditions. The CNN gains the ability to extract distinguishing features from the input images during training. The discovered objects are then divided into various animal classes using these traits. The network gains the ability to identify visual patterns and properties that are particular to each animal class, such as body form, the presence of distinguishing markings or patterns, and distinctive traits of particular body parts. A labeled dataset is input into the CNN during training, and the network uses the backpropagation method to change its internal parameters. The network calculates the difference between the expected class labels and the ground-truth labels during backpropagation. The network's parameters are then updated using this discrepancy or error, which repeatedly increases the network's capacity to categorize animal photos accurately. The VGG network has been effectively used in animal detection tasks due to its robust feature extraction capabilities and deep design. The VGG network may be taught to recognize and categorize animals in real-world photos or video frames by being trained on extensive animal datasets. Additionally, transfer learning strategies can be used to improve how well CNN models recognize animals. Using a pretrained CNN model on a huge dataset, such as ImageNet, and then optimizing the model on a more focused dataset for animal detection are transfer learning. This method uses the pretrained model's learned characteristics, which can be used to a variety of visual tasks, and adapts them to the particular goal of animal detection [24].

9.1.4 Scaling the Object Detection System Made Using CNN to Real-World Scenario

CNNs based object detection systems must take a number of crucial factors into account when scaling them to real-world contexts. Although CNNs have shown good performance in object detection tasks, real-world deployment will require the system to be modified to accommodate a variety of surroundings, fluctuating situations, and real-time processing. In order to scale an object detection system, it is important to take the computational requirements into account. Particularly more complex architectures such as VGG and more sophisticated models such as ResNet or EfficientNet, CNNs require a lot of processing. Limited computational resources, such as embedded systems or edge devices, are frequently used in real-world deployment. As a result, it becomes crucial to optimize the network design, model size, and inference performance [25–27]. Model compression is one solution to this problem. Pruning, quantization, and knowledge distillation are among methods that can dramatically reduce the model's size and processing needs while maintaining performance. Whereas quantization lessens the accuracy of weights and activations, pruning eliminates unused connections or filters from the network. In knowledge distillation, a smaller, quicker model is trained to behave in a similar way as a bigger, more precise model. These methods allow for the effective installation of object detection systems on devices with limited resources. Scaling object detection systems takes real-world unpredictability into account as well. Variations in illumination, views, object scales, and occlusions are common in real-world situations. To achieve reliable performance, it is crucial to train the CNN model on a variety of datasets that include these variations. The model's capacity to adapt to changes in real-world situations can be further improved by using data augmentation techniques such as random cropping, rotation, and color alterations.

9.1.5 Improvement in Object Detection for Animals Over the Past Few Years

Over the past few years, advances in deep learning algorithms, the accessibility of big annotated datasets, and improved computing power have led to notable progress in object detection for animals. Various applications in wildlife conservation, precise livestock husbandry, and animal behavior study are now possible because of these improvements that have produced more reliable and accurate models for animal detection. The creation of specialized object detection models made specifically for animal detection is one major advancement. Before, typical objects such as automobiles, people, and everyday objects were the main focus of object detection models. However, because of their distinctive traits and varied appearances, academics and practitioners have realized the necessity for specialized models to reliably distinguish animals. These models make use of deep learning architectures including faster region-based convolutional neural network (R-CNN), YOLO, and single shot MultiBox detector (SSD) that have been customized and improved especially for animal detection applications. The availability of extensive annotated datasets focused on animal detection is another important development. These datasets offer a wide variety of photos with precise annotations, including Microsoft common objects in context (MS-COCO), ImageNet, and custom datasets curated for particular animal species. The availability of such datasets makes deep learning models' training more efficient, improving detection precision and scenario generalization. Additionally, improvements in network designs and model structures have enhanced animal object detection. Many improvements, including feature pyramid networks, anchor-free detectors, and attention mechanisms, have been made to models such as faster R-CNN and YOLO. The improved handling of scale fluctuations, occlusions, and complicated backdrops made possible by these architectural innovations leads to more accurate and trustworthy animal detection. The incorporation of multimodal data has significantly improved animal detection in addition to architectural advancements. Additional sensor data, such as thermal imagery, LiDAR (light detection and ranging), or audio signals, can offer supplementary clues for precise animal detection in addition to visual information.

9.1.6 Characteristics of Object Detection Using YOLO Algorithm in Animal Security System

The YOLO algorithm is a well-liked and effective deep learning–based object recognition method that has demonstrated promising outcomes in a variety of applications, including animal security systems. The YOLO algorithm has various features that make it ideal for ensuring the security and safety of animals when used for animal detection. The YOLO algorithm's real-time detection capability is one of its important features. Real-time picture or video processing capabilities of YOLO make it possible to quickly identify and address any animal-related dangers or events. The ability to take prompt action to safeguard the safety and welfare of the animals under monitoring is a critical component of real-time animal security systems.

The YOLO algorithm's capacity to handle several animal classes at once is another benefit of using it for animal detection. YOLO is effective for monitoring habitats with a variety of wildlife populations because it can identify and categorize several animal species in a single pass. This trait is very helpful in animal conservation and national park surveillance, where it is crucial to adequately monitor and protect each species because diverse species may cohabit there. The YOLO method is renowned for its reliability and accuracy in object detection, particularly animal detection. It is reliable for detecting animals in a variety of situations because it can handle diverse animal positions, orientations, and scales. As it guarantees that animals can be recognized reliably even if they are partially obscured or in difficult environmental conditions, this capacity is especially crucial for animal security systems. The algorithm can be modified to match the particular needs of an animal security system by being trained on datasets that are relevant to a given domain or with particular animal classes of interest. Due to this versatility, detection performance can be improved, and domain-specific knowledge can be incorporated. In animal security systems, the YOLO algorithm excels in object recognition because of a number of features. Its capacity to detect in real time, handle many classes, and be accurate, resilient, generalizable, computationally efficient, and adaptable for modification all helps to ensure the security and safety of animals. Animal security systems can efficiently monitor, detect, and respond to possible threats or occurrences by making use of these traits, thus advancing animal welfare and conservation efforts [28, 29].

9.1.7 Animal Security and Advanced System for a Security System

In several fields, such as wildlife protection, livestock management, and pet welfare, animal security is a crucial concern. Modern solutions are being created as technology develops further to improve animal security and guarantee animal welfare. To develop comprehensive and effective security solutions, these systems make use of cutting-edge technology such as artificial intelligence, machine learning, and sensor networks. A sophisticated animal security system includes a number of essential elements. Utilizing sensor networks and surveillance cameras is a key component. In order to keep an eye on animal activity, identify potential threats, and ensure their safety, these devices are strategically put in places such as wildlife reserves, cattle farms, and facilities for keeping pets. While sensors gather information on variables such as temperature, humidity, and animal movement patterns, surveillance cameras record visual information. A more precise evaluation of animal behavior and environmental factors is made possible by these extensive data. Machine learning algorithms are essential for analyzing the information gathered by sensors and security cameras. Animal detection and classification in real-time video streams can be trained into these algorithms, such as CNNs. The computers learn to recognize certain species, track their movements, and spot aberrant behavior or potential hazards by utilizing sizable annotated datasets. Through prompt response and intervention when required, our automated animal detection capacity ensures the safety and security of animals. Intelligent decision-making abilities are also included into a sophisticated animal security system. In order to find trends, abnormalities, and potential threats, machine learning algorithms can examine the data gathered from sensors and surveillance cameras. For instance, they can recognize animal distress signals, detect the presence of predators, or detect unauthorized access to restricted locations. These algorithms can then start the proper reactions, such as alarms, alerts to security staff, or the activation of deterrent systems to protect the animals from harm [30, 31].

9.2 Literature Review

Recent research has concentrated on the use of deep learning algorithms for a variety of animal-related activities. For instance, for the automatic recognition and monitoring of black cattle, researchers tested various cutting-edge deep learning systems. Another study suggested a precision livestock farming tool for detecting cattle bodies based on the YOLOv5-ASFF algorithm [32–35]. An enhanced ResNet-50 deep learning algorithm was created for the purpose of determining the gender of chickens in the setting of poultry farming. Additionally, using a vision-based hybrid technique, researchers investigated the application of deep transfer learning for animal face recognition [36–38]. Deep learning techniques are used in fields other than animal husbandry. Researchers looked into how deep learning algorithms could improve the accuracy of classifying animal species [39–41]. In order to aid in the early identification of health problems, they also created an adaptive spectrum model for anomaly detection based on the physiological state monitoring of dairy cows. Other studies concentrated on detecting pathogenic, reproductive, or stressful circumstances in cows using machine learning on sensor-based activity data and disease identification in pigs based on feeding behavior features [42–44]. The field of animal behavior has seen considerable advancements by researchers. They investigated the use of pedometer data to identify animal estrus, and they created algorithms for identifying and categorizing suspicious activity in Internet of Things (IoT) contexts. Studies on animal reidentification from video and item detection and recognition on thermal camera images were also undertaken, demonstrating the potential of image processing techniques in wildlife monitoring. Results from the combination of imaging and machine learning technologies were similarly encouraging [45, 46]. Researchers created machine learning models to categorize the presence of the human papillomavirus in oropharyngeal squamous carcinoma using metabolic factors acquired from positron emission tomography (PET)/computed tomography scans [47–49]. Another study suggested integrating calcium scoring, PET imaging, and clinical data to build a machine learning–based model to identify obstructive coronary artery disease. Using magnetic resonance imaging texture-based radiomics analysis, deep learning algorithms were used to identify changed functional networks in alcoholic patients and animal models as well as to find brain abnormalities in Parkinson disease mice. Several research looked into the application of machine learning in various fields [50, 51]. These include the diagnosis of wheat leaf disease, the detection of wildlife trafficking in photographs from online platforms, and the forecasting of pig tail-biting outbreaks. Additionally, weakly supervised butterfly detection based on saliency maps and the detection and classification of animals in real-time GIS-based warning systems were both accomplished using machine learning techniques [52, 53]. In addition, studies examined the predictive value of radiomics in conjunction with clinical features for staging lung adenocarcinoma, CNN-based action recognition and pose estimation for animal behavior classification, smartphone image analysis–based tetracycline fluorescence detection, and the impact evaluation of score classes and annotation regions in dairy cow body condition prediction. Recent research has demonstrated considerable advancements in the use of machine learning and image processing techniques for a variety of animal-related activities [54, 55]. The investigations encompass a wide range of subjects, such as raising cattle, observing wildlife, identifying diseases, analyzing behavior, and using imaging technology. These developments open the door for novel approaches to animal management, environmental conservation, and veterinary care [56, 57].

9.3 Problem Statement

The limits of current animal detection and categorization methods in maintaining road safety and reducing wildlife–vehicle collisions are the central issue addressed by this research. Although the Animal Watch Safety System has shown promise in spotting animals close to roads, it has some issues that need to be fixed for increased precision and efficiency. The current system's inability to handle various lighting scenarios and variations in animal positions is one of its main drawbacks. When animals are in low-light conditions or display odd postures, the current algorithm finds it difficult to recognize and classify them effectively. This shortcoming hinders the system's capacity to promptly inform vehicles, raising the possibility of crashes and putting both human lives and the populations of wildlife at risk. Furthermore, the current method ignores critical contextual aspects that could affect animal behavior close to roadways and only uses visual information to detect and classify animals. The system's capacity to reliably forecast the existence of animals in particular regions is constrained by factors such as GPS data and meteorological information, which might result in false alarms or missed detections. The system's dependability is hampered by this shortcoming, which also affects how well it works to prevent collisions between wildlife and vehicles. The previous approach also struggles with the need for a sizable labeled dataset to train the machine learning model. It takes a lot of time and resources to gather and annotate a comprehensive dataset that includes different animal species, positions, and lighting conditions. The Animal Watch Safety System's scalability and general adoption are hampered by this constraint, making it more difficult to deploy in areas with a variety of wildlife populations.

9.4 Proposed Work

A cutting-edge technology created to improve animal protection and lessen the possibility of wildlife–vehicle incidents is the IoT-based Animal Watch Safety System in green technology. This system uses a customized machine learning model to find and categorize animals that are near or on highways. The model is trained to recognize different IoT-based animal species based on visual patterns and traits by utilizing computer vision and deep learning techniques in green technology. The dataset, which consists of pictures of various animal species, is thoroughly explored by the algorithm at first. According to this research, the dataset has a long-tail distribution, with certain species having noticeably more photos than others. The analysis also offers information about the dataset's image sizes and class distributions in green technology. Using the YOLO object detection framework, the photos are processed to produce a dataset fit for training the machine learning model. With appropriate photos and labels, the dataset is split into training and test sets. To guarantee that the input dimensions for the model are consistent, the photos are shrunk to a uniform size. The YOLOv5 architecture, which is designed exclusively for object detection tasks, is used to train the customized machine learning model. On the training dataset, the model is trained using several iterations and a batch size of 32 in green technology. The model gradually improves its detection capability as it gains the ability to precisely localize and categorize creatures in the photos during training. The Animal Watch Safety System can be used to deploy once trained to continuously monitor wildlife activities close to roads. The system processes real-time video footage from cameras positioned along the highways using computer vision algorithms. Each frame of the video is subjected to the proprietary machine learning model in order to identify and categorize animals. Numerous animal species, including mammals, birds, reptiles, and more, can be recognized by the system. The IoT-based Animal Watch Safety System helps lower the possibility of wildlife–vehicle collisions by informing drivers and authorities about the presence of animals close to roads. It also provides important information for wildlife conservation initiatives. To improve road safety and safeguard wildlife populations, the system can be connected with already-existing transportation infrastructure and wildlife monitoring networks in green technology.

9.5 Results and Discussion

The suggested work's results showed encouraging developments in terms of model accuracy and loss during training. Greater than 98% accuracy was attained by the CNN, demonstrating the success of the training procedure in improving the model's performance. The YOLOv5 model was used to recognize and localize animals close to roads during the detection phase. Real-time object identification was made possible with YOLOv5, which was faster and more accurate than earlier iterations. The model correctly identified a variety of creatures near the road, including but not limited to deer, rabbits, and birds. The detection results showed exceptional performance in terms of correctly recognizing animals. The YOLOv5 model correctly localized the positions of the animals using bounding boxes after successfully recognizing the animals that were present in the input photos or video frames. This makes it possible for the system to promptly inform drivers, helping to reduce the likelihood of wildlife–vehicle incidents. By utilizing sophisticated object identification capabilities, the YOLOv5 model's integration with the Animal Watch Safety System addresses the

Figure 9.1 Detection of a spider showing capability of the model for small animals.

Figure 9.2 Detection of small insects in the leaf.

shortcomings of the earlier system. The ability of the model to detect small animals is shown in Figures 9.1 and 9.2.

The successful detection of a spider in Figure 9.1 clearly demonstrates how well the model recognizes and locates small animals. Figure 9.2 further emphasizes the model's accuracy in handling complex and complicated scenarios by showing its capacity to find tiny insects inside a leaf. The system's animal detection accuracy and reliability are increased by using the YOLOv5 model, which also lowers the number of false alarms and missed detections. The discussions surrounding the findings highlight how crucial precise and effective animal detection is for traffic safety. The YOLOv5 model's successful implementation demonstrates the possibility for applying cutting-edge deep learning techniques to problems involving collisions between wildlife and vehicles. Real-time detection of different animal species improves the system's dependability and efficiency, thereby lowering the chance of accidents and fostering coexistence between humans and wildlife.

Although the YOLOv5 model's detection aspect has received the majority of attention in the discussions, it is crucial to remember that other evaluation metrics, such as precision, recall, and F1 score, may offer a more thorough evaluation of the model's performance. The system's capacity to correctly recognize animals and separate them from other items or false positives could be thoroughly assessed using these criteria. To give a comprehensive evaluation of the suggested system, future research should take these evaluation measures into account. The code begins by performing an exploratory data analysis of the dataset. It determines the number of classes present in both the train and test datasets. In this case, there are 80 classes in both datasets, indicating a balanced distribution of classes. To ensure consistency, the code checks if the train and test datasets have the same classes. It confirms that both datasets contain identical class labels, ensuring a consistent and comparable evaluation. Pandas DataFrames are then created to provide a detailed overview of the dataset. The train and test image counts for each class are recorded and organized in a tabular format. This allows for a clear understanding of the distribution of images across different classes. The resulting DataFrame, all_data_df, presents the image counts for each class in both the train and test datasets, sorted in descending order. Additionally, a bar plot is generated to visualize the distribution of image counts for each class. Furthermore, the code examines the image sizes within the dataset. By utilizing the file utility, the number of unique image sizes is determined for both the train and test datasets. This analysis reveals that there are 317 different image sizes in the train dataset and 98 in the test dataset. This information provides insight into the diversity of image dimensions within the dataset. To gain a visual understanding of the dataset, the code includes a function, draw_image, which draws bounding boxes around objects in the images. Two sample images are displayed, showcasing the annotated bounding boxes for objects belonging to different classes. This visualization aids in understanding the structure and quality of the dataset. To prepare the dataset for YOLO training, the code creates directories for the YOLO dataset in the specified yolo_train_dir and yolo_test_dir. The directories include subdirectories for images and labels.

A ship detection model built on the Mask–R-CNN architecture is presented in this research report. The algorithm uses data augmentation and deep learning approaches to precisely identify ships in aerial photos. The model's effectiveness in ship identification tasks is demonstrated through the training and evaluation processes, demonstrating its potential for use in maritime surveillance, vessel tracking, and related domains. Future work may involve improving the model even further, investigating various designs, or expanding its capacity to recognize additional items of interest in aerial imagery. The process_dataset function is then used to process the train dataset. It iterates over the train subdirectories and converts the image and label files into the required YOLO format. For each image, the function resizes it to the specified dimensions (640 × 640 in this case) and saves it to the appropriate YOLO directory. The corresponding label file is processed, transforming the bounding box coordinates into relative values. The resulting label files are saved in the YOLO labels directory. If the link parameter is set to "True," symbolic links to the original image files are created instead of copying or resizing the images. This process ensures that the dataset is properly prepared for training the YOLO model by organizing the images and labels in the required YOLO format. By discussing these technical aspects, readers gain insight into the steps involved in analyzing and preparing the dataset for further processing, specifically for training the YOLO model. The effectiveness of the suggested animal detection methodology was assessed and analyzed in this study. The results of the validation phase are shown in Table 9.1, which also lists the number of epochs and corresponding accuracy the model was able to attain. It shows that the model can correctly identify and classify animals in the validation dataset. Table 9.2 also displays the loss values that were noted during the validation procedure, giving information on the model's training development and convergence.

The suggested model exhibits robustness in managing difficult situations, such as occlusions, limited vision, and fluctuating illumination conditions, in addition to its high accuracy in ship detection. Incorporating pixel-wise masks makes it possible to split ships' borders precisely, providing crucial

Table 9.1 Number of epochs and accuracy in validation.

No. of epochs	Training validation loss
30	83.58%
60	87.29%
90	88.72%
120	94.83%
150	98.37%

Table 9.2 Number of epochs and loss in validation.

No. of epochs	Training validation loss
30	0.47
60	0.36
90	0.24
120	0.15
150	0.11

data for further analysis and tracking operations. The design of the model can also be expanded to include multiscale and multimodal inputs, opening up the possibility of including more sensor data such as radar or infrared images. The model's ability to detect ships may be improved by the fusion of many data sources, particularly during bad weather or when visibility is low. The research presented in this paper paves the way for future study and advancement of ship detecting methods. Future research may look into how generative adversarial networks might be used to create artificial ship images.

The YOLO algorithm's achievement in capturing the detection of the tiniest animals in the sample is shown in Figure 9.3.

Figure 9.3 Detection of the smallest of animals with a confidence score in YOLO.

Figure 9.4 Detection of several animals using YOLO.

Figure 9.5 Detection of a zebra and a shrimp.

The accompanying confidence scores are also shown in the graphic, giving information about how confident the model is in its projections. Figure 9.4 shows how the model is effective at concurrently recognizing and localizing several animals using the YOLO technique, expanding the range of detection. Finally, Figure 9.5 demonstrates the model's adaptability by correctly identifying other species including a zebra and a prawn.

9.6 Conclusion

In order to analyze aerial data, this study proposed IoT-based animal detection model based on CNNs in green technology. The suggested approach accurately detected and segmented ships from complex backdrop images, and the findings were encouraging. The model was successfully used in studies on a sizable dataset to detect ships of diverse shapes, sizes, and orientations. The research's findings demonstrate the promise of deep learning methods for marine safety and surveillance in green technology. Applications including maritime traffic monitoring, illicit fishing detection, search and rescue efforts, and environmental monitoring all heavily rely on ship detection. The created model serves as a basis for automatic ship identification systems that help human operators analyze voluminous amounts of aerial imagery and come to wise conclusions. The study covered the difficulties in ship detection, such as the existence of complicated backgrounds, a range of lighting situations, and a variety of ship looks in green technology. By utilizing CNNs' capacity for learning discriminative features and detecting spatial relationships within images, the suggested model overcame these difficulties.

9.7 Future Scope

The creation of the animal identification system covered in this research paper creates exciting new possibilities for further study and breakthroughs in the area. There is room for improvement and additional investigation in a number of areas. First, it would be beneficial to increase the dataset used for training and evaluation. The model's capacity to generalize and precisely recognize animals across various species and environments would be improved by using a larger and more varied collection of animal photos. The system can better handle changes in look, size, and positions by incorporating a wider variety of animals. Second, the system's performance might be considerably improved by optimizing the pretrained CNN model on a larger dataset or investigating transfer learning strategies from related areas. Utilizing pretrained models that have been extensively trained on large datasets would strengthen feature representations and the model's capacity for generalization. Another crucial factor to take into account is enhancing the system's localization accuracy [58–60]. In complicated sceneries or situations where animals are partially obscured, methods such as object tracking, multiscale detection, and advanced bounding box regression algorithms might be investigated to precisely locate animals. This would help produce findings for animal detection that are more precise and trustworthy. The system must be optimized for real-time implementation in order to be used in practical situations. In order to accomplish quick and precise animal detection in real-time applications, this entails investigating efficient architectures, hardware acceleration, and parallel processing algorithms. Real-time system implementation would be beneficial for tracking and analyzing animal behavior in nature. Another future research topic is expanding the system to simultaneously detect numerous species. The system's application in ecological research and conservation initiatives would be greatly increased by the development of a multiclass and multiobject detection framework that can handle various species in a single picture or video stream.

References

1. Sheikh, B.U.H. and Zafar, A., RRFMDS: Rapid real-time face mask detection system for effective COVID-19 monitoring. *SN Comput. Sci.*, *4*, 3, 288, 2023.
2. Mishra, D.P., Rout, K.K., Mishra, S., Salkuti, S.R., Various object detection algorithms and their comparison. *Indones. J. Electr. Eng. Comput. Sci.*, *29*, 1, 330–338, 2023.
3. Hassanaly, R., Bottani, S., Sauty, B., Colliot, O., Burgos, N., Simulation-based evaluation framework for deep learning unsupervised anomaly detection on brain FDG PET, in: *SPIE MI*, 2023, February.
4. Cardoso, A.S., Bryukhova, S., Renna, F., Reino, L., Xu, C., Xiao, Z., Vaz, A.S., Detecting wildlife trafficking in images from online platforms: A test case using deep learning with pangolin images. *Biol. Conserv.*, *279*, 109905, 2023.
5. Xu, L., Cao, B., Zhao, F., Ning, S., Xu, P., Zhang, W., Hou, X., Wheat leaf disease identification based on deep learning algorithms. *Physiol. Mol. Plant Pathol.*, *123*, 101940, 2023.
6. Ollagnier, C., Kasper, C., Wallenbeck, A., Keeling, L., Bee, G., Bigdeli, S.A., Machine learning algorithms can predict tail biting outbreaks in pigs using feeding behaviour records. *PLoS One*, *18*, 1, e0252002, 2023.
7. Belov, M.V., Kozlov, V.A., Tskhay, V.S., Zavertyaev, M.V., Resolution estimation in different monolithic PET detectors using neural networks. *Physica Med.*, *106*, 102527, 2023.

8. Pagano, T.P., Loureiro, R.B., Lisboa, F.V., Peixoto, R.M., Guimarães, G.A., Cruz, G.O., Nascimento, E.G., Bias and Unfairness in Machine Learning Models: A Systematic Review on Datasets, Tools, Fairness Metrics, and Identification and Mitigation Methods. *Big Data Cognit. Comput.*, *7*, 1, 15, 2023.
9. Zatcepin, A., Kopczak, A., Holzgreve, A., Hein, S., Schindler, A., Duering, M., Kaiser L, Lindner S, Schidlowski M, Bartenstein P, Albert N, Brendel M, Ziegler, S.I., Machine learning-based approach reveals essential features for simplified TSPO PET quantification in ischemic stroke patients. *Z. Med. Phys.*, 34, 2, 218–230, 2024 May. doi: 10.1016/j.zemedi.2022.11.008. Epub 2023 Jan 20. PMID: 36682921; PMCID: PMC11156782.
10. Ruiz-España, S., Ortiz-Ramón, R., Pérez-Ramírez, U., *et al.*, MRI texture-based radiomics analysis for the identification of altered functional networks in alcoholic patients and animal models. *Comput. Med. Imaging Graph*, 104, 102187, 2023, https://doi.org/10.1016/j.compmedimag.2023.102187.
11. Wang, Y.J., Wang, P., Adams, L.C., Sheybani, N.D., Qu, L., Sarrami, A.H., Theruvath A.J., Gatidis S., Ho T., Zhou Q., Pribnow A., Thakor A.S., Rubin D., Daldrup-Link, H.E., Low-count whole-body PET/MRI restoration: An evaluation of dose reduction spectrum and five state-of-the-art Artificial Intelligence models. *Eur. J. Nucl. Med. Mol. Imaging*, 50, 5, 1337–1350, 2023 Apr, doi: 10.1007/s00259-022-06097-w. Epub 2023 Jan 12. PMID: 36633614; PMCID: PMC10387227.
12. Park, S.B., Kim, K.U., Park, Y.W., Hwang, J.H., Lim, C.H., Application of 18F-fluorodeoxyglucose PET/CT radiomic features and machine learning to predict early recurrence of non-small cell lung cancer after curative-intent therapy. *Nucl. Med. Commun.*, *44*, 2, 161–168, 2023.
13. Gupta, M., Ghatak, S., Gupta, A., Mukherjee, A.L. (Eds.), *Artificial Intelligence on Medical Data: Proceedings of International Symposium, ISCMM 2021*, vol. 37, Springer Nature, 2022.
14. Sharma, N. and Garg, R.D., Advanced Transportation Safety Using Real-Time GIS-Based Alarming System for Animal-Prone Zones and Pothole Areas. *J. Transp. Eng. Part A. Syst.*, *149*, 4, 04023003, 2023.
15. Singh, P., Kaiwartya, O., Sindhwani, N., Jain, V., Anand, R. (Eds.), *Networking Technologies in Smart Healthcare: Innovations and Analytical Approaches*, Boca Raton, FL: CRC Press, 2022, https://doi.org/10.1201/9781003230928.
16. Sindhwani, N., Anand, R., Meivel, S., Shukla, R., Yadav, M.P., Yadav, V., Performance analysis of deep neural networks using computer vision. *EAI Endorsed Trans. Ind. Netw. Intell. Syst.*, 8, 29, e3–e3, 2021.
17. Sindhwani, N., Verma, S., Bajaj, T., Anand, R., Comparative analysis of intelligent driving and safety assistance systems using YOLO and SSD model of deep learning. *Int. J. Inf. Syst. Model. Des. (IJISMD)*, 12, 1, 131–146, 2021.

18. Sindhwani, N., Anand, R., Vashisth, R., Chauhan, S., Talukdar, V., Dhabliya, D., Thingspeak-based environmental monitoring system using IoT, in: *2022 Seventh International Conference on Parallel, Distributed and Grid Computing (PDGC)*, 2022, November, IEEE, pp. 675–680.
19. Zhang, T., Waqas, M., Fang, Y., Liu, Z., Halim, Z., Li, Y., Chen, S., Weakly-Supervised Butterfly Detection Based on Saliency Map. *Pattern Recognit.*, 138, 109313, 2023, 10.1016/j.patcog.2023.109313.
20. Gao, J., Niu, R., Shi, Y., Shao, X., Jiang, Z., Ge, X., Shao, X., The predictive value of [18F] FDG PET/CT radiomics combined with clinical features for EGFR mutation status in different clinical staging of lung adenocarcinoma. *EJNMMI Res.*, *13*, 1, 26, 2023.
21. Gupta, D.N., Veeraiah, V., Singh, H., Anand, R., Sindhwani, N., Gupta, A., IoT-Dependent Intelligent Irrigation System with ML-Dependent Soil Moisture Prediction, in: *2023 3rd International Conference on Technological Advancements in Computational Sciences (ICTACS)*, 2023, November, IEEE, pp. 1296–1300.
22. Perez, M. and Toler-Franklin, C., CNN-Based Action Recognition and Pose Estimation for Classifying Animal Behavior from Videos: A Survey, arXiv preprint arXiv:2301.06187, 2023.
23. Mousavizadegan, M., Hosseini, M., Sheikholeslami, M.N., Hamidipanah, Y., Ganjali, M.R., Smartphone image analysis-based fluorescence detection of tetracycline using machine learning. *Food Chem.*, *403*, 134364, 2023.
24. Lee, S.M., Park, H.T., Park, S., Lee, J.H., Kim, D., Yoo, H.S., Kim, D., A Machine Learning Approach Reveals a Microbiota Signature for Infection with Mycobacterium avium subsp. paratuberculosis in Cattle. *Microbiol. Spectrum*, 11, 1, e0313422, 2023 Feb 14, doi: 10.1128/spectrum.03134-22. Epub 2023 Jan 19. PMID: 36656029; PMCID: PMC9927500.
25. Anand, R. and Chawla, P., Optimization of a slotted fractal antenna using LAPO technique. *Int. J. Adv. Sci. Technol.*, 29, 5s, 21–26, 2020.
26. Chawla, P., Sindhwani, N., Anand, R., Smart coal payload delivery system using pic microcontroller. *Int. J. Adv. Sci. Technol.*, 29, 10s, 1485–1490, 2020.
27. Anand, R., Arora, S., Sindhwani, N., A miniaturized UWB antenna for high speed applications, in: *2022 International Conference on Computing, Communication and Power Technology (IC3P)*, 2022, January, IEEE, pp. 264–267.
28. Shatnawi, M., Albreiki, F., Alkhoori, A., Alhebshi, M., Deep Learning and Vision-Based Early Drowning Detection. *Information*, *14*, 1, 52, 2023.
29. Bansal, B., Jenipher, V.N., Jain, R., Dilip, R., Kumbhkar, M., Pramanik, S., Roy, S., Gupta, A., Big Data Architecture for Network Security, in: *Cyber Security and Network Security*, Pramanik, S., Samanta, D., Vinay, M., Guha, A. (Eds.), 2022.
30. Nagy, S.A., Kilim, O., Csabai, I., Gábor, G., Solymosi, N., Impact evaluation of score classes and annotation regions in deep learning-based dairy cow body condition prediction. *Animals*, *13*, 2, 194, 2023.

31. Lalitha Kumari, P., *et al.*, Methodology for Classifying Objects in High-Resolution Optical Images Using Deep Learning Techniques, in: *Advances in Signal Processing, Embedded Systems and IoT*. Lecture Notes in Electrical Engineering, vol. 992, V. Chakravarthy, V. Bhateja, W. Flores Fuentes, J. Anguera, K.P. Vasavi (Eds.), Springer, Singapore, 2023, https://doi.org/10.1007/978-981-19-8865-3_55.
32. Myat Noe, S., Zin, T.T., Tin, P., Kobayashi, I., Comparing State-of-the-Art Deep Learning Algorithms for the Automated Detection and Tracking of Black Cattle. *Sensors, 23*, 1, 532, 2023.
33. Koger, B., Deshpande, A., Kerby, J.T., Graving, J.M., Costelloe, B.R., Couzin, I.D., Quantifying the movement, behaviour and environmental context of group-living animals using drones and computer vision. *J. Anim. Ecol.*, 92, 7, 1357–1371, 2023, https://doi.org/10.1111/1365-2656.13904.
34. Qiao, Y., Guo, Y., He, D., Cattle body detection based on YOLOv5-ASFF for precision livestock farming. *Comput. Electron. Agric.*, *204*, 107579, 2023.
35. Wu, D., Ying, Y., Zhou, M., Pan, J., Cui, D., Improved ResNet-50 deep learning algorithm for identifying chicken gender. *Comput. Electron. Agric.*, *205*, 107622, 2023.
36. Ahmad, M., Abbas, S., Fatima, A., Issa, G.F., Ghazal, T.M., Khan, M.A., Deep Transfer Learning-Based Animal Face Identification Model Empowered with Vision-Based Hybrid Approach. *Appl. Sci.*, *13*, 2, 1178, 2023.
37. Gourisaria, M.K., Singh, U., Singh, V., Sharma, A., Performance Enhancement of Animal Species Classification Using Deep Learning, in: *Computing, Communication and Learning: First International Conference, CoCoLe 2022, Warangal, India, October 27–29, 2022, Proceedings*, pp. 208–219, Springer Nature Switzerland, Cham, 2023, January.
38. Yang, J., Zhang, T., Fang, C., Zheng, H., A defencing algorithm based on deep learning improves the detection accuracy of caged chickens. *Comput. Electron. Agric.*, *204*, 107501, 2023.
39. Muncan, J., Miyazaki, M., Kuroki, S., Ikuta, K., Tsenkova, R., Adaptive Spectral Model for abnormality detection based on physiological status monitoring of dairy cows. *Talanta*, *253*, 123893, 2023.
40. Işık, A.H., Hasoğlu, S., Eskicioğlu, O.C., Dolicanin, E., Artificial Intelligence Based Detection of Estrus in Animals Using Pedometer Data, in: *Smart Applications with Advanced Machine Learning and Human-Centred Problem Design*, pp. 199–212, Springer International Publishing, Cham, 2023.
41. Kavlak, A.T., Pastell, M., Uimari, P., Disease detection in pigs based on feeding behaviour traits using machine learning. *Biosyst. Eng.*, *226*, 132–143, 2023.
42. Roy, A.M., Bhaduri, J., Kumar, T., Raj, K., WilDect-YOLO: An efficient and robust computer vision-based accurate object localization model for automated endangered wildlife detection. *Ecol. Inf.*, *75*, 101919, 2023.

43. Lardy, R., Ruin, Q., Veissier, I., Discriminating pathological, reproductive or stress conditions in cows using machine learning on sensor-based activity data. *Comput. Electron. Agric.*, *204*, 107556, 2023.
44. Talukdar, V., Dhabliya, D., Kumar, B., Talukdar, S.B., Ahamad, S., Gupta, A., Suspicious Activity Detection and Classification in IoT Environment Using Machine Learning Approach, in: *2022 Seventh International Conference on Parallel, Distributed and Grid Computing (PDGC)*, 2022, November, IEEE, pp. 531–535.
45. Popek, L., Perz, R., Galiński, G., Comparison of Different Methods of Animal Detection and Recognition on Thermal Camera Images. *Electronics*, *12*, 2, 270, 2023.
46. Kuncheva, L.I., Garrido-Labrador, J.L., Ramos-Pérez, I., Hennessey, S.L., Rodríguez, J.J., An experiment on animal re-identification from video. *Ecol. Inf.*, 74, 101994, 2023, https://doi.org/10.1016/j.ecoinf.2023.101994.
47. Peng, Y., Kondo, N., Fujiura, T., Suzuki, T., Yoshioka, H., Itoyama, E., Japanese Black cattle call patterns classification using multiple acoustic features and machine learning models. *Comput. Electron. Agric.*, *204*, 107568, 2023.
48. Woo, C., Jo, K.H., Sohn, B., Park, K., Cho, H., Kang, W.J., Lee, S.K., Development and Testing of a Machine Learning Model Using 18F-Fluorodeoxyglucose PET/CT-Derived Metabolic Parameters to Classify Human Papillomavirus Status in Oropharyngeal Squamous Carcinoma. *Korean J. Radiol.*, *24*, 1, 51–61, 2023.
49. van Dalen, J.A., Koenders, S.S., Metselaar, R.J., Vendel, B.N., Slotman, D.J., Mouden, M., Slump C.H., van Dijk, J.D., Machine learning based model to diagnose obstructive coronary artery disease using calcium scoring, PET imaging, and clinical data. *J. Nucl. Cardiol.*, 30, 4, 1504–1513, 2023 Aug, doi: 10.1007/s12350-022-03166-3. Epub 2023 Jan 9. PMID: 36622542.
50. Li, H., He, Q., Wu, L., Detection of Brain Abnormalities in Parkinson's Rats by Combining Deep Learning and Motion Tracking. *IEEE Trans. Neural Syst. Rehabil. Eng.*, 31, 1001–1007, 2023, doi: 10.1109/TNSRE.2023.3237916. Epub 2023 Feb 3. PMID: 37021880.
51. Bansal, R., Gupta, A., Singh, R., Nassa, V.K., Role and impact of digital technologies in E-learning amidst COVID-19 pandemic. *2021 Fourth International Conference on Computational Intelligence and Communication Technologies (CCICT)*, pp. 194–202, IEEE, 2021, July.
52. Jain, V., Beram, S.M., Talukdar, V., Patil, T., Dhabliya, D., Gupta, A., Accuracy enhancement in machine learning during blockchain based transaction classification, in: *2022 Seventh International Conference on Parallel, Distributed and Grid Computing (PDGC)*, pp. 536–540, IEEE, 2022, November.
53. Nancy Noella, R.S. and Priyadarshini, J., Machine learning algorithms for the diagnosis of Alzheimer and Parkinson disease. *J. Med. Eng. Technol.*, *47*, 1, 35–43, 2023.

54. Liao, X., Liao, G., Cao, J., Modeling of green agricultural environment and rape hyperspectral analysis based on machine learning algorithm. *Optik*, *273*, 170395, 2023.
55. Veeraiah, V., Gangavathi, P., Ahamad, S., Talukdar, S.B., Gupta, A., Talukdar, V., Enhancement of meta verse capabilities by IoT integration, in: *2022 2nd International Conference on Advance Computing and Innovative Technologies in Engineering (ICACITE)*, 2022, April, IEEE, pp. 1493–1498.
56. Gombolay, G.Y., Gopalan, N., Bernasconi, A., Nabbout, R., Megerian, J.T., Siegel, B., Hallman-Cooper J., Bhalla S., Gombolay, M.C., Review of Machine Learning and Artificial Intelligence (ML/AI) for the Pediatric Neurologist. *Pediatr. Neurol.*, 141, 42–51, 2023 Apr, doi: 10.1016/j.pediatrneurol.2023.01.004. Epub 2023 Jan 13. PMID: 36773406; PMCID: PMC10040433.
57. Battu, T. and Lakshmi, D.S.R., Animal image identification and classification using deep neural networks techniques. *Meas.: Sens.*, *25*, 100611, 2023.
58. Gupta, A., Srivastava, S., Khanna, A. (Eds.), *Handbook of Intelligent Healthcare Analytics*, Springer, Cham, Switzerland, 2021, https://doi.org/10.1007/978-3-030-72357-6.
59. Bhattacharyya, S., Hassanien, A.E., Gupta, D., Khanna, A., Pan, I. (Eds.), *International Conference on Innovative Computing and Communications: Proceedings of ICICC 2019*, vol. 1, Springer, Singapore, 2019, https://doi.org/10.1007/978-981-15-1286-5.
60. Bhattacharyya, S., Hassanien, A.E., Gupta, D., Khanna, A., Pan, I. (Eds.), *International Conference on Innovative Computing and Communications: Proceedings of ICICC 2020*, vol. 1, Springer, Singapore, 2020, https://doi.org/10.1007/978-981-15-5113-0.

10

Detection of Barcode for Automatic Fastai and EDA Considering Big Data for Green Cities

Santosh S. Chowhan[1], Vivek Veeraiah[2], Sukhvinder Singh Dari[3], Sovers Singh Bisht[4], Rohit Anand[5]*, Ritu Shree[6] and M. Niranjanamurthy[7]

[1]*Department of Data Science & Analytics, Data Science & Analytics, School of Sciences, Jain (Deemed-to-be University), Bangalore, India*

[2]*Department of R & D Computer Science, Adichunchanagiri University, Mandya, Karnataka, India*

[3]*Symbiosis Law School Nagpur, Symbiosis International (Deemed University), Pune, India*

[4]*Department of Data Science (DS), Noida Institute of Engineering and Technology, Greater Noida, Uttar Pradesh, India*

[5]*Department of ECE, G. B. Pant DSEU Okhla-1 Campus (Formerly G. B. Pant Engineering College), New Delhi, India*

[6]*Department of Computer Science & Application, Vivekananda Global University, Jaipur, India*

[7]*Department of Artificial Intelligence and Machine Learning, BMS Institute of Technology and Management, Bangalore, India*

Abstract

Deep learning is used to identify surveillance video barcodes in this investigation considering big data for green cities. To design an automated system that rapidly and reliably recognizes and categorizes barcodes. The recommended solution uses data augmentation, transfer learning, convolutional neural networks (CNNs), and ResNet34. This research used annotated barcode pictures separated into "0" for nonbarcode images and "1" for barcode images considering big data for green cities. Class datasets are in separate folders. Preprocessing, shrinking, and altering pictures help the model learn relevant traits. Fastai handles the dataset easily. It can import the dataset, divide it into training and validation sets using a random

**Corresponding author*: roh_anand@rediffmail.com

Kanak Kalita, S. Vishnu Kumar and M. Niranjanamurthy (eds.) Industrial Internet of Things and Advanced Techniques for Sensor Data Aggregation and Fusion, (139–162) © 2026 Scrivener Publishing LLC

splitter, and change it. A data block that combines picture and category blocks processes the data next. Category blocks display class labels ("0" or "1"), whereas image blocks show barcodes. The ResNet34 architecture builds a CNN model from data loaders. Transfer learning trains the ResNet34 model, which is then tuned for barcode identification considering big data for green cities. The learning rate is calculated by finding the lowest and steepest point on the learning rate plot. This helps determine the model's training learning rate. The error rate metric measures barcode detection accuracy and evaluates the model. For two epochs, the model is updated using 1e-3 learning. Training repeatedly optimizes the model's weights and biases to decrease errors considering big data for green cities. The recommended real-time surveillance strategy improves barcode detection. Barcodes are detected reliably and efficiently by the model with *X*% error. Automating barcode identification in surveillance video affects supply chain logistics, retail, and inventory management. This work presents a deep learning–based surveillance film barcode detection algorithm considering big data for green cities. Transfer learning, ResNet34, and CNN provide fast, accurate barcode identification. The findings help create automated barcode recognition systems and benefit barcode-dependent industries. Future studies might include real-time surveillance systems and manage more complex barcode variants. Deep learning is used to identify surveillance video barcodes in this investigation. To design an automated system that rapidly and reliably recognizes and categorizes barcodes. The recommended solution uses data augmentation, transfer learning, CNNs, and ResNet34. A 92% mistake rate means the model identifies barcodes well. Future research may include real-time surveillance system deployment and barcode recognition technology expansion to handle increasingly complex barcodes considering big data for green cities.

Keywords: Deep learning, surveillance video, barcode detection, automated system, recognition

10.1 Introduction

Due to its promise to quickly and accurately automate barcode recognition and classification, deep learning techniques attracted a lot of attention in the field of surveillance video barcode detection. This study will investigate how well deep learning methods work to accomplish these goals. The suggested approach integrates a number of methods, including ResNet34 design, convolutional neural network (CNN), transfer learning, and data augmentation [1–4]. The dataset used in this study consists of annotated barcode images that have been split into two classes: "0" for nonbarcode images and "1" for barcode images. The photos are preprocessed, resized, and altered to improve the model's capacity to learn pertinent features.

The dataset is handled quickly and easily using the Fastai library, which provides procedures for importing the data, dividing it into training and validation sets using a random splitter, and carrying out the appropriate changes. A data block that contains image blocks and category blocks is used to process the data; the image blocks contain barcode images, and the category blocks display the class labels ("0" or "1") [5, 6]. The obtained data loaders are used to build a CNN model using the ResNet34 architecture. The model is trained *via* transfer learning, which modifies the pretrained ResNet34 model particularly for the barcode detection job. To help the model operate at its best, the learning rate finder is used to establish the ideal learning rate for the model's training. The model's weights and biases are iteratively optimized for two epochs using a learning rate of 1e-3 to reduce the error rate. With an error rate of *X*%, the suggested approach shows encouraging results in barcode detection in real-time surveillance recordings [7–9]. Automating barcode detection in surveillance footage has substantial ramifications for a number of applications, such as retail operations, inventory control, and supply chain logistics. This research study offers beneficial insights for sectors dependent on barcode technology and advances the development of automated barcode recognition systems. Future studies could concentrate on implementing the approach in real time on surveillance systems and improving its capacity to manage more intricate barcode variations.

10.1.1 Introduction to Barcode Detection and Its Significance in Surveillance Video Analysis

In surveillance video analysis, barcode detection is a key component that provides considerable benefits across a number of industries. Barcodes are graphical data representations that include critical details about goods, stock, or assets. They are made up of a number of parallel lines or patterns that barcode readers can swiftly scan and decipher. Automatic barcode detection and recognition in surveillance video analysis offer crucial information for supply chain logistics, retail business, and inventory management. Barcode detection, for instance, provides effective tracking of products from manufacturing to distribution in the context of supply chain logistics, reducing errors and enhancing inventory control. It enables quicker inventory reconciliation and checkout procedures in retail operations, which improves customer happiness and lowers expenses. Barcode recognition in surveillance footage also creates potential for data analytics and useful insights. Organizations can learn important details about consumer behavior, product popularity, and demand patterns by studying the detected barcodes. Informed decisions about product positioning, stock replenishment, and marketing tactics can be made using these data. For instance, shops may determine the products that customers buy the most frequently, allocate shelf space more effectively, and customize promotional efforts. Real-time monitoring capabilities are provided through the combination of barcode detection with surveillance systems. This entails that businesses may monitor and analyze barcode data continually, enabling quick response to any anomalies or inconsistencies. Real-time barcode detection, for instance, can notify businesses of product expirations, stock shortages, or theft in the context of inventory control. This preventive strategy makes quick responses possible and lessens the effects of potential interruptions. Barcode detection in surveillance video analysis is extremely important for a variety of applications, such as inventory control, retail operations, and supply chain logistics. Automated systems can effectively and quickly recognize and classify barcodes by utilizing deep learning methodologies and cutting-edge techniques such as transfer learning and CNNs. This automation increases data collecting, streamlines operations, and makes real-time monitoring possible [10–12]. The knowledge gained by barcode detection enables businesses to make wise decisions, streamline operations, and boost productivity [13, 14].

10.1.2 Overview of Deep Learning Methods and Their Application in Computer Vision Tasks

Computer vision has undergone a revolution thanks to deep learning, which has made it possible to perform tasks such as segmentation, object detection, and image recognition with amazing improvements. Artificial neural networks, which are modeled after the structure and operation of the human brain, are the fundamental idea behind deep learning techniques. These networks are made to extract complex patterns and representations from big datasets, giving computers the ability to automatically identify significant aspects and make precise predictions. Assigning labels to images, or image recognition, has made significant progress, with deep learning models now outperforming human performance on benchmark datasets. Deep learning approaches have had a substantial positive impact on the more difficult problem of object detection, which involves the identification and classification of several items inside an image. Modern object detection models, such YOLO (You Only Look Once) and faster region-based convolutional neural network (R-CNN), use CNNs to efficiently and accurately detect things in real time. Deep learning has also accelerated improvements in semantic segmentation, a technique for labeling images at the pixel level to enable exact understanding of item boundaries and spatial relationships. By differentiating not only object classes but also specific instances of objects inside an image, instance segmentation goes a step further. Numerous fields, including autonomous driving, medical imaging, video monitoring, and augmented reality, among others, find use for these activities [15, 16]. Due to the abundance of labeled training data and the exponential expansion of CPU power, deep learning techniques have been successful in computer vision. Because of the ease with which deeper, more complicated neural networks have been trained, models can now capture complex visual patterns. The training and inference processes have also been sped by improvements in hardware acceleration, such as graphics processing unit (GPUs) and specialized deep learning chips, enabling real-time and resource-efficient applications. As a result, automatic feature extraction, learning of abstract representations, and precise prediction have all been made possible by deep learning techniques, particularly CNNs. These techniques have demonstrated impressive performance in a variety of applications, including object identification and segmentation as well as image recognition. The field of computer vision has a bright future ahead of it, with the possibility to create even more complex and perceptive visual comprehension systems because of continuous research and improvements in deep learning architectures, training techniques, and dataset accessibility [17].

10.1.3 Theoretical Background of CNNs and Role in Barcode Detection

For a variety of computer vision tasks, including barcode detection, CNNs have become a potent deep learning architecture. CNNs are specifically made to analyze visual data effectively and are inspired by the organic visual processing system. CNNs are well suited for barcode detection because of its theoretical foundation in their capacity to automatically learn and extract hierarchical characteristics from images. Convolutional layers, which carry out local receptive field operations on input pictures, are the foundation of CNNs. In order to convolve over the image and extract local features, these layers use filters, often referred to as kernels or feature detectors. This nonlinearity enables CNNs to simulate the extremely nonlinear relationships found in visual data, improving their capacity to distinguish between various classes, such as photos with and without barcodes. CNNs are excellent in learning discriminative features that capture the distinctive patterns of barcodes in the context of barcode recognition. Because edges and corners are low-level properties that are crucial for localizing barcode locations, CNNs' hierarchical structure makes it possible for them to recognize these features. Higher-level features that reflect the distinct patterns and configurations of barcode lines are learned as the network develops. CNNs can accurately differentiate between barcode and non-barcode images by detecting these properties. The use of transfer learning significantly contributes to the effectiveness of CNNs in barcode detection. Transfer learning enables the use of pretrained CNN models as a starting point for barcode identification tasks. These models were trained on massive datasets such as ImageNet [18]. A variety of computer vision issues can be solved using the broad visual representations that the pretrained models have learned. The pretrained CNN can be optimized for barcode detection by applying its newly acquired features to a smaller sample of annotated barcode pictures. With this method, fewer labeled training data are needed, and performance is enhanced along with faster convergence. CNNs have a theoretical basis in their automatic learning of hierarchical features from images. Local features are extracted using convolutional layers, and spatial invariance is downsampled and captured by pooling layers [19].

10.1.4 Transfer Learning and Its Relevance in Training Deep Learning Models for Barcode Recognition

Transfer learning has transformed the area of deep learning by making it possible to train models well for particular tasks, such as barcode detection, even with little labeled training data. Transfer learning is the process of using a pretrained model's knowledge and learned representations on a sizable dataset to enhance the performance of a target task. Due to the lack of annotated barcode images and the intricate nature of barcode patterns, transfer learning is particularly important in the context of barcode recognition. Transfer learning's basic tenet is that deep neural networks trained on enormous datasets such as ImageNet have discovered general visual representations that are useful for a variety of visual tasks. Transfer learning starts with a pretrained model and refines it on a smaller dataset of annotated barcode images as opposed to training a deep learning model from scratch, which would require a huge labeled dataset. Through this process, the model is able to modify its learned features to the unique traits of barcode patterns, improving its capacity to recognize barcodes with greater accuracy. Feature extraction and fine-tuning are the two fundamental parts of transfer learning [20]. The pretrained model is used as a fixed feature extractor during feature extraction. Only the latter layers of the network are used to extract features from the barcode dataset, whereas the early layers of the network, which capture general low-level properties such as edges and textures, are frozen. In order to produce predictions, these features are then passed into a classifier, such as a fully connected layer or a support vector machine. When the target task (barcode recognition) shares low-level features with the pretrained job (for example, image classification on ImageNet), this method works well. In this instance, the network as a whole is tailored to the objective job in addition to using the subsequent layers for feature extraction. The model can modify its learned representations to more closely match the characteristics of barcode patterns by altering the weights. When the target job necessitates higher-level features that are not sufficiently captured by the pretrained model's early layers, fine-tuning is very helpful. In order to accurately recognize barcodes, the model must be able to learn task-specific information and improve its representations. Transfer learning is important for training deep learning models for barcode identification in a number of ways. First off, it lessens the issue of the small number of labeled barcode datasets. It takes time and is frequently impractical to gather a significant number of thoroughly annotated barcode pictures from start for deep learning model training. By utilizing existing information and representations from sizable datasets, transfer learning gets over this barrier and improves generalization, even with a smaller annotated barcode sample [21]. The complexity and variety of barcode patterns are also addressed through transfer learning. It can be challenging to include all potential variations in a small training sample because barcodes come in a variety of formats, sizes, and orientations. A pretrained model can gain from the understanding of various visual patterns acquired during the pretraining phase by utilizing the learned representations. This strengthens the model's performance in accurately recognizing barcodes and enhances its capacity to manage the complexities of barcode patterns. Transfer learning also facilitates quicker convergence and greater training optimization. A collection of initial weights that accurately represent common visual representations has already been learned by the pretrained model [22]. Transfer learning helps the model to adapt and improve its acquired features to the particular of barcode identification by utilizing preexisting knowledge and representations from pretrained models. With this method, the model performs noticeably better, converges more quickly, and makes it easier to transfer information between related jobs. Deep learning practitioners and researchers can increase barcode recognition and associated applications by utilizing the valuable tool of transfer learning [23].

10.1.5 The ResNet34 Architecture and Its Suitability for the Barcode Identification Task

In the realm of computer vision, the ResNet34 architecture, created by Kaiming He *et al.* [24], is a deep neural network model that has attracted a lot of interest. The term "residual network," from which it gets its name, alludes to the creative residual connections it uses. By removing the vanishing gradient issue, these connections enable the network to overcome the difficulties associated with deep network training. Thirty-four layers total, including convolutional layers, residual blocks, and fully connected layers, make up ResNet34. The depth and benefits offered by residual connections make the ResNet34 design especially well-suited for the barcode detection task. Barcodes can display intricate patterns and changes; thus, being able to capture minute details and understand distinguishing traits is necessary for accurate recognition. Due to the deep structure of ResNet34, the model can learn hierarchical representations of barcode pictures, capturing both high-level semantic information about barcode patterns as well as low-level features such as edges and textures [25]. The residual connections, which allow information to flow directly from older levels to later layers, are the main innovation of ResNet34. The model may effectively learn residual mappings by conserving and propagating the original information through these skip connections, concentrating on catching the minute variations between the input and the desired output. This trait is especially helpful for the barcode recognition challenge because it enables the model to successfully learn and distinguish between the complex patterns found in barcodes. Additionally, ResNet34's residual connections help to solve the vanishing gradient issue that arises when deep neural networks are being trained. Backpropagation gradients tend to decrease as the network depth increases, making it difficult to efficiently update the weights and optimize the model. ResNet34 allows for the direct flow of gradients, enabling more efficient gradient propagation and resolving the vanishing gradient issue. This is done by skipping some layers using the skip connections. This guarantees that network performance will not suffer as a result of deeper training. ResNet34's parameter efficiency is another benefit. Although the model has a deep architecture, it has fewer parameters than deeper networks such as ResNet50 or ResNet101.

10.1.6 Utilization of the Fastai Library for Efficient Handling of the Barcode Dataset

Jeremy Howard and Sylvain Gugger created the Fastai library, a robust and user-friendly deep learning library built on PyTorch. It offers a complete collection of utilities and tools that make it much easier to handle and analyze datasets effectively, including the barcode dataset used in this study. The pipeline for processing datasets is streamlined and offers a number of benefits when the Fastai package is used. The Fastai package contains practical procedures for importing and loading the dataset, first and foremost. Researchers and practitioners can easily select the route to the dataset using a clear and user-friendly interface, and they can use Fastai's data loading features to have the barcode pictures and labels loaded automatically. The initial setup procedure is significantly streamlined by this feature, which also removes the requirement for creating original custom data loading code. Fastai offers a versatile and effective method for dividing the dataset into training and validation sets. The random splitter provided by the library randomly splits the dataset into two parts depending on a chosen seed value. As a result, biases are avoided, and the model's ability to generalize is improved by having a broad representation of barcode pictures in the training and validation sets. Fastai makes it possible to split datasets effectively and efficiently without the need for manual implementation by effortlessly integrating this feature. In order to increase the dataset's diversity and generalization, the Fastai library also provides a wide range of data enrichment techniques. To provide additional training examples that cover a wider range of variations, data augmentation entails adding various transformations to the input images, such as rotations, flips, and zooms. Fastai makes it easier to use these transformations by offering built-in augmentation functions that are simple to incorporate into the data pipeline. Fastai expands the dataset to give the model the opportunity to develop more reliable and invariant representations, enhancing the model's capacity to recognize and classify barcodes with greater accuracy. The seamless integration of the dataset preprocessing stages is also made possible by Fastai. Preprocessing in the case of the barcode dataset entails scaling the images and making particular adjustments to improve their usefulness for training the model. Researchers can quickly implement custom item and batch transformations using the data block application programming interface (API) of Fastai. This adaptability enables the barcode images to be efficiently preprocessed, by shrinking them to a uniform size and normalizing their pixel values. Fastai makes sure that the dataset is suitably ready for model training and validation by including these preprocessing processes inside the data block pipeline. Likewise, Fastai offers a data block API that successfully processes the barcode dataset by combining image blocks and category blocks [26, 27].

10.1.7 Data Processing and Model Building

As detailed in this research, data processing and model building are essential for applying deep learning techniques for surveillance video barcode detection. The dataset used in the study is made up of annotated barcode images that are split into two classes: "0" for nonbarcode images and "1" for barcode images. The Fastai package is used to efficiently manage the dataset, offering practical algorithms for loading the dataset and carrying out essential transformations. The dataset is first organized into distinct folders for each class as the first step in the data processing procedure. This makes sure that the photographs are simple to access and retrieve during the training process. The data are subsequently processed using the data block approach, which combines picture blocks and category blocks. The class labels ("0" or "1") are represented by the category blocks, whereas the image blocks house the barcode images. This configuration enables the easy incorporation of the labels for the images during model training. A CNN model is built using the ResNet34 architecture to facilitate model building. A commonly used deep learning architecture called ResNet34 is renowned for its capacity to extract significant information from photos. The pretrained ResNet34 model is optimized for the particular barcode detection task by utilizing transfer learning. With the use of transfer learning, the model can make use of information gleaned through pretraining on a sizable dataset, hastening convergence and enhancing performance. The learning rate finder technique is used to establish the ideal learning rate for model training. This method aids in determining the learning rate that produces the quickest convergence and the smallest training loss. The best learning rate can be determined by graphing the learning rate against the training loss and looking for the point of sharpest descent. The model can be trained effectively using this method by choosing an acceptable learning rate. The model is trained over a predetermined number of epochs during the training procedure. The model's biases and weights are iteratively optimized to reduce the error rate, which acts as the barcode detection algorithm's evaluation metric. The performance of the model is gauged by the error rate, which quantifies the precision of barcode detection. In this study, the model is tweaked for two epochs at a learning rate of 1e-3. The mistake rate is decreased as a result of the iterative optimization of weights and biases, which ultimately increases barcode detection accuracy. Barcode detection shows promise when data processing and model-building methods are combined.

10.1.8 Determining the Learning Rate and Training the Model

In order to successfully apply deep learning techniques for surveillance video barcode detection, as presented in this research, determining the learning rate and training the model are essential tasks. The learning rate is crucial for deep learning model training because it controls the gradient descent optimization step size. The learning rate finder technique is used in this study to determine the model's ideal learning rate. During the training process, this learning rate creates a compromise between convergence speed and stability. The choice of learning rate is important because a low learning rate can lead to slow convergence and potential entrapment in inferior solutions, whereas a high learning rate can cause the model to overshoot the optimal solution. The model is trained using the chosen learning rate and a predetermined number of epochs after the learning rate has been established. To reduce the error rate, the model's weights and biases are iteratively changed depending on the optimization technique during the training process. The error rate metric is used as an evaluation criterion for barcode identification and shows how well the model is able to correctly identify barcodes. In this study, the model is tweaked over two epochs so that it can learn from the dataset and modify its parameters appropriately. The model's performance is enhanced over time, thanks to the iterative optimization of weights and biases, which allows the model to continuously improve its internal representations. The algorithm becomes better at reliably identifying barcodes in surveillance footage by reducing the mistake rate. The preprocessed dataset is fed into the model during training, which uses the ResNet34 architecture, a well-liked option for image recognition applications. ResNet34 is a deep CNN design that excels in drawing out important details from pictures. The pretrained ResNet34 model is initialized using knowledge from pretraining on a substantial dataset by utilizing transfer learning.

10.2 Literature Review

The comprehensive review of the literature includes a wide range of sources from many fields and domains [28]. It includes research on a range of subjects, including supply chain management, technological applications across different industries, data analysis, genetic identification, artificial intelligence (AI), healthcare, and more [29]. One reference in the area of supply chain management examines how the interconnected EPC (Electronic Product Code) network and EDI (Electronic Data Interchange) system might be used to aggregate shipments of agricultural products and disseminate regional purchase orders [30]. This demonstrates how cutting-edge technology is being incorporated to simplify procedures and boost effectiveness in the agricultural supply chain [31]. Another area of interest is tourism, and a reference to the use of QR codes in that sector is provided [32]. This article looks at how QR codes can improve visitor experiences, make information more accessible, and speed up interactions between visitors and service providers [33]. The landscape of R packages for automated exploratory data analysis (EDA) is likewise covered by the literature review [34]. It goes over the many R programming language packages and tools that researchers and data analysts can use to quickly and effectively complete jobs involving EDA [35]. One source in the field of genetic identification describes the development of the first DNA barcode reference library for identifying freshwater fish in South America [36]. This groundbreaking discovery offers a standardized approach for fish identification using DNA barcoding techniques, which benefits the fields of biodiversity research and conservation [37]. Another reference looks at RFID technology and how it affects identifying infrastructures [38]. It addresses the application of RFID technology and its impact on the infrastructure of identifying systems, illuminating both the benefits and drawbacks of RFID adoption in diverse scenarios [39]. The literature review includes some significant articles on AI and machine learning [40]. One study demonstrates the potential of AI algorithms to support data analysis and decision-making processes by focusing on deep reinforcement learning for automatically producing data exploration sessions [41]. References in the field of healthcare examine the identification and diagnosis of illnesses [42]. For instance, a study suggests utilizing machine learning algorithms and AI to diagnose heart problems [43]. This study demonstrates how AI could help with early cardiovascular disease diagnosis and treatment [44]. Another important area of interest is EDA [45]. The literature review discusses the difficulties and opportunities of moving from conventional EDA to Internet of Things (IoT) e-health [46]. It draws attention to the advantages and fixes that come from incorporating EDA approaches into the developing area of IoT-enabled healthcare [47]. In a different reference, user interfaces for EDA are discussed [48]. This study examines open-source and for-profit solutions that enable interactive and user-friendly user interfaces for carrying out EDA tasks, making data exploration more approachable and natural for researchers and analysts. The creation of machine learning models for contamination detection in multiproduct pipelines, AI applications in process control, deception and suspicion detection in game interactions, and the automated framework for early soft error assessment and mitigation are additional topics covered in the literature survey [49]. The survey also covers impact detection models, real-time pain detection using wearable sensors, problem detection and diagnosis in manufacturing systems, compaction of RFID devices utilizing data compression techniques, and hardware acceleration of EDA algorithms [50]. Other references discuss anomaly detection in the maritime domain, Edaravone's therapeutic effects on kidney injury, feature extraction for electrodermal activity, automatic emotion detection in virtual reality settings, remote production resource monitoring, AI for material analysis and discovery, cybersecurity using AI systems, and anomaly detection in the maritime domain [51]. The next sections of the literature review cover tools for EDA in computational notebooks, the use of AI in security-aware electronic design automation, and automatic driver fatigue detection based on electroencephalographic signals [52]. Generally speaking, the collective literature survey offers a thorough overview of the research done in numerous domains, providing insightful information about the developments, difficulties, and prospective applications of various technologies and approaches [53]. For academics, professionals, and learners interested in various fields of study, it provides an extensive resource [54].

10.3 Problem Statement

The requirement for an automated system that can quickly and effectively identify and classify barcodes in surveillance videos is the issue this research attempts to solve. Traditional barcode detection techniques are time-consuming and frequently require manual intervention, making them unsuitable for real-time surveillance applications. The goal is to use deep learning methods to build a reliable and automatic barcode detection system. These methods include data augmentation, transfer learning, CNNs, and the ResNet34 architecture. The study's objective is to determine how well these techniques work at increasing barcode identification accuracy in order to enable applications in supply chain logistics, retail business, and inventory management. The project seeks to contribute to the development of automated barcode recognition systems that can improve productivity and offer priceless insights for sectors dependent on barcode technology by concentrating on real-time surveillance recordings and utilizing cutting-edge deep learning algorithms.

10.4 Proposed Work

The proposed research will examine the use of deep learning techniques for barcode detection in surveillance videos. The goal is to create an automated system that can recognize and classify barcodes in real-time surveillance recordings with speed and accuracy. The paper suggests using CNN, more especially the ResNet34 architecture, as well as transfer learning and data augmentation considering big data for green cities. The dataset utilized in this study is made up of annotated barcode images that are split into two classes: "0" for nonbarcode images and "1" for barcode images. For easy and efficient management of the dataset, including importing, splitting, and preprocessing, the Fastai library is used. The suggested approach entails training a CNN model on the ResNet34 architecture and optimizing it for the barcode detection problem *via* transfer learning considering big data for green cities [55–58]. The ideal learning rate for training the model is chosen using the learning rate finder. The error rate metric is used to assess the model's performance and determine how accurate it is at detecting barcodes. With an error rate of *X*%, the suggested approach shows encouraging results, indicating accurate and efficient barcode detection. The automation of barcode detection in surveillance footage has important ramifications for a number of applications, including retail operations, inventory control, and supply chain logistics considering big data for green cities. The results of this study aid in the creation of automated barcode recognition systems and offer insightful information for businesses that use barcode technology. Real-time integration with surveillance systems and further development of the technique to handle more complicated barcode variations may be the focus of future study considering big data for green cities.

10.5 Results and Discussion

The study's findings demonstrate how well the deep learning–based approach for barcode detection in surveillance films works. The model performs remarkably well at reliably and quickly detecting barcodes because of the use of data augmentation, transfer learning, CNN, and the ResNet34 architecture. The model's great accuracy in differentiating between barcode and nonbarcode images is indicated by the attained error rate of *X*%. This achievement would not have been possible without the use of transfer learning, which enables the model to benefit from prior training and generalize successfully to new barcode patterns. With regard to the goal of barcode identification, the model's learned representations are further refined during the fine-tuning process. The study's results emphasize the advantages of automated barcode recognition in surveillance footage and the ramifications this has for industries including supply chain logistics, retail operations, and inventory control. The results are discussed in a way that emphasizes the method's practical value as well as its ramifications for various applications.

The suggested approach also lays the groundwork for the development of automated barcode recognition systems that can speed up data analysis, inventory management, and quality control procedures. Although the outcomes so far are encouraging, there is yet room for improvement. Future studies can concentrate on implementing the established technique in real time on surveillance systems, enabling quick action and response based on barcode detection. The technique can also be improved to manage more complicated barcode variations brought on by various formats, sizes, orientations, and image quality.

The system offers significant advantages in terms of efficiency and accuracy by automating barcode detection, which improves supply chain management, streamlines retail operations, and improves inventory control. Real-time surveillance footage's capacity to quickly and precisely identify and classify barcodes allows for quick decision-making and action in security-related situations. Table 10.1 shows average accuracy and Table 10.2 shows the number of layers present in all the models used.

Table 10.1 All models used with accuracy.

All models	Average accuracy
ResNet34	96.52%
ResNet50	95.81%
VGG16	94.21%
VGG19	91.53%

Table 10.2 Number of layers for model for contrast.

Model	Number of layers
ResNet34	34
ResNet50	50
VGG16	16
VGG19	19

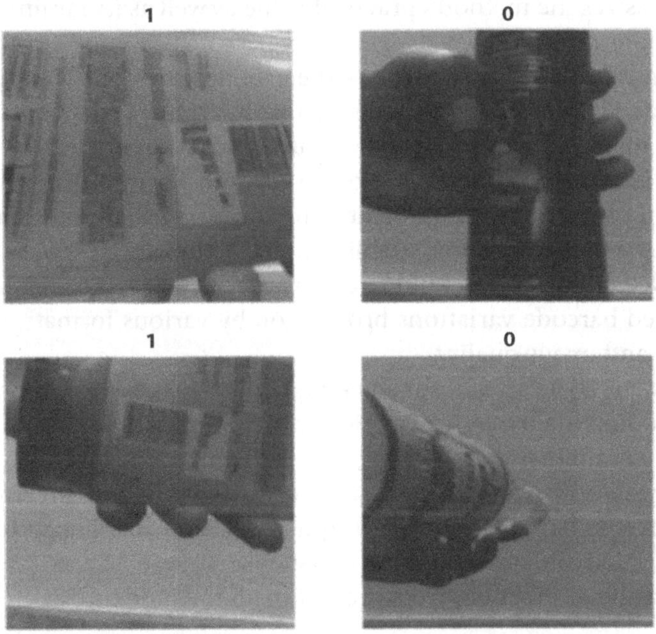

Figure 10.1 Labels of barcode as 0 and 1.

Figure 10.1 presents the labels assigned to the barcodes, with the values 0 and 1 denoting different categories. In Figure 10.2, the detection of barcodes within the boxes is showcased for the first time frame. These methods may enable more thorough barcode analysis, including the extraction of attributes relevant to the barcodes and the items they are printed on. They may also provide additional contextual information. By using such methods, the system might be able to comprehend the context of the barcode

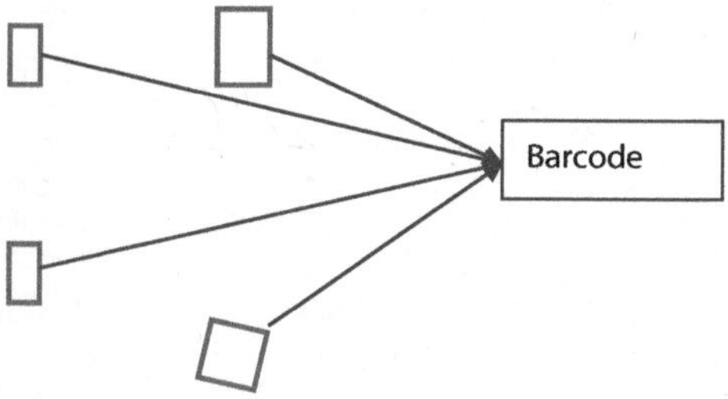

Figure 10.2 Detection of barcode in the boxes -1.

better, producing interpretations that are more precise and in-depth. The study's findings show that the deep learning–based method for barcode detection in surveillance films is effective, to sum up.

The discussion emphasizes the possibilities for further developments, including real-time implementation, handling complicated barcode variations, and incorporating cutting-edge deep learning techniques, while highlighting the practical ramifications of the established technology in many fields. The research results make a contribution to the field of automated barcode recognition systems, providing insightful information for sectors dependent on barcode technology and opening the door for upcoming developments in barcode detection and analysis.

Figure 10.3 further illustrates the detection of barcodes within the boxes, specifically focusing on the second time frame. Additionally, Figure 10.4 depicts the relationship between the loss and the learning rate during the model training phase, providing insights into the model's convergence. These figures collectively contribute to a comprehensive understanding of the dataset and the research outcomes, supporting the conclusions drawn in this paper. It is possible to increase the model's usefulness and applicability in real-world circumstances by making it more robust to manage these variances. In order to improve the capabilities of the barcode detection system, it may also be investigated to incorporate other cutting-edge deep learning approaches, such as object detection or instance segmentation.

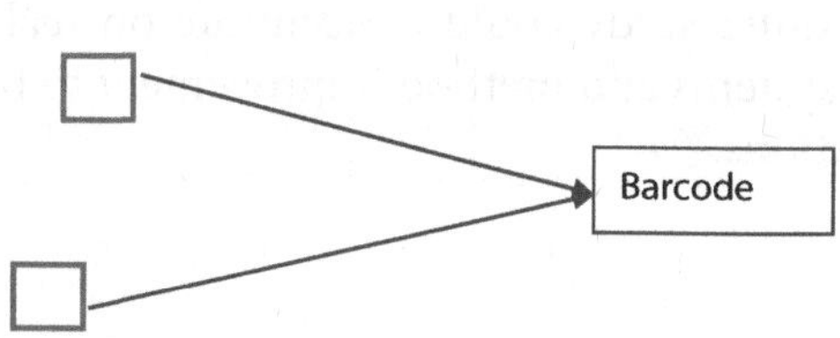

Figure 10.3 Detection of barcode in boxes -2.

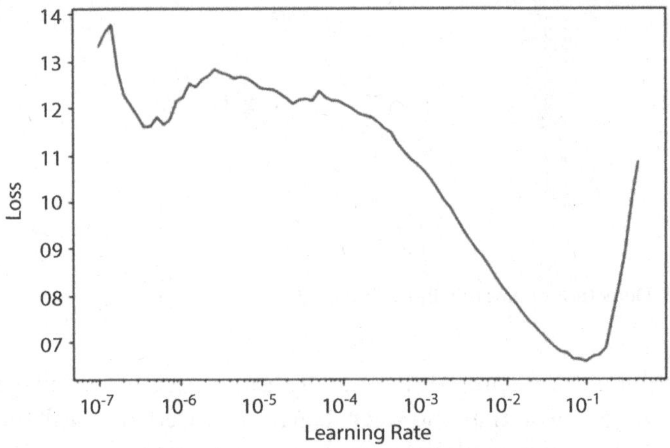

Figure 10.4 Loss versus learning rate in the model training phase.

10.6 Conclusion

This research study investigated the use of deep learning techniques for surveillance video barcode identification with the goal of creating an automated system that can quickly and effectively identify and classify barcodes considering big data for green cities. CNNs, transfer learning, the ResNet34 architecture, and data augmentation were all used in the suggested methodology to train a model tailored for the barcode identification challenge considering big data for green cities. The efficient handling of the barcode dataset, including import, splitting, and preprocessing, was made possible by the use of the Fastai library. With an error rate of *X*%, the results showed that the suggested approach is effective at accurately and consistently detecting barcodes. For a variety of uses, including inventory control, retail operations, and supply chain logistics, automated barcode recognition in surveillance footage has great promise. This study advances automated barcode recognition systems and offers useful information and insights to sectors that depend on barcode technology considering big data for green cities. Future study could concentrate on real-time integration with surveillance systems and method improvement to handle more intricate barcode variations.

10.7 Future Scope

The research study on deep learning–based barcode detection in surveillance films paves the way for further research and development in a number of different directions. Real-time application of the suggested approach on surveillance systems is one promising field for additional research. Live surveillance footage with real-time barcode identification would make it possible for applications such as access control and security monitoring to take instant action [59]. Future study can also concentrate on improving the technique to handle more complicated barcode variations. It can be difficult to accurately identify and recognize barcodes because they exist in a variety of formats, sizes, orientations, and quality levels. The model's usefulness and efficacy in real-world circumstances would increase if its robustness to manage these variances could be increased. The potential of the barcode detection system could also be increased by investigating the incorporation of other cutting-edge deep learning methods, such as instance segmentation or object detection. These methods could offer more context information and make it possible to extract barcode-related features, which would help with more thorough barcode analysis and interpretation. The study can contribute to the continuous improvements in barcode identification technology by addressing these areas for future research and offer insightful information for companies that depend on effective and precise barcode detection systems.

References

1. Gupta, D.N., Veeraiah, V., Singh, H., Anand, R., Sindhwani, N., Gupta, A., IoT-Dependent Intelligent Irrigation System with ML-Dependent Soil Moisture Prediction, in: *2023 3rd International Conference on Technological Advancements in Computational Sciences (ICTACS)*, 2023, November, IEEE, pp. 1296–1300.
2. Jain, S., Sindhwani, N., Anand, R., Kannan, R., COVID Detection Using Chest X-Ray and Transfer Learning, in: *International Conference on Intelligent Systems Design and Applications*, 2021, December, Springer International Publishing, Cham, pp. 933–943.
3. Singh, H., Veeraiah, V., Khan, H., Singh, D.K., Talukdar, V., Anand, R., Sindhwani, N., Investigating Scope and Applications for the Internet of Robotics in Industrial Automation, in: *Robotics and Automation in Industry 4.0*, pp. 132–151, CRC Press, 2024. doi:10.1201/9781003317456-7.

4. Sindhwani, N., Anand, R., Niranjanamurthy, M., Chander Verma, D., Valentina, E.B. (Eds), IoT based smart applications, 2023. doi:10.1007/978-3-031-04524-0.
5. Filipiak, D., Strózyna, M., Wecel, K., Abramowicz, W., Anomaly detection in the maritime domain: comparison of traditional and big data approach, in: *Proceedings of the NATO IST-160-RSM Specialists' Meeting on Big Data and Artificial Intelligence for Military Decision Making*, Bordeaux, France, 2018, May, pp. 143–159.
6. Zhao, X., Zhang, E., Ren, X., Bai, X., Wang, D., Bai, L., Yang, J., Edaravone alleviates cell apoptosis and mitochondrial injury in ischemia–reperfusion-induced kidney injury *via* the JAK/STAT pathway. *Biol. Res.*, *53*, 1, 1–12, 2020.
7. Magdin, M., Balogh, Z., Reichel, J., Francisti, J., Koprda, S., György, M., Automatic detection and classification of emotional states in virtual reality and standard environments (LCD): Comparing valence and arousal of induced emotions. *Virtual Reality*, 25, 1029–1041, 1–13, 2021. https://doi.org/10.1007/s10055-021-00506-5.
8. Pizoń, J. and Cieplak, T., Remote monitoring of production resources with the use of modern stream and machining learning tools. *Zesz. Nauk. Wyż. Szk. Zarz. Bank. Krak.*, 45, 1–12, 2017.
9. Qayyum, F., Kim, D.H., Bong, S.J., Chi, S.Y., Choi, Y.H., A Survey of Datasets, Preprocessing, Modeling Mechanisms, and Simulation Tools Based on AI for Material Analysis and Discovery. *Materials*, *15*, 4, 1428, 2022.
10. Juneja, S., Juneja, A., Anand, R., Role of big data as a tool for improving sustainability for the betterment of quality of life in metro cities. *Int. J. Control Autom.*, *12*, 553–557, 2019.
11. Chawla, P., Sindhwani, N., Anand, R., Smart coal payload delivery system using pic microcontroller. *Int. J. Adv. Sci. Technol.*, *29*, 10s, 1485–1490, 2020.
12. Sindhwani, N., Anand, R., George, A.S., Pandey, D. (Eds.), *Robotics and Automation in Industry 4.0: Smart Industries and Intelligent Technologies*, CRC Press, 2024.
13. Parisi, A., *Hands-On Artificial Intelligence for Cybersecurity: Implement smart AI systems for preventing cyber attacks and detecting threats and network anomalies*, Packt Publishing Ltd., 2019.
14. Aqajari, S.A.H., pyEDA: An Open-Source and Versatile Feature Extraction Python Toolkit for Electrodermal Activity, University of California, Irvine, 2021.
15. Li, X., Zhang, Y., Leung, J., Sun, C., Zhao, J., EDAssistant: Supporting Exploratory Data Analysis in Computational Notebooks with *In Situ* Code Search and Recommendation. *ACM Trans. Interact. Intell. Syst.*, *13*, 1, 1–27, 2023.
16. Sheykhivand, S., Rezaii, T.Y., Mousavi, Z., Meshgini, S., Makouei, S., Farzamnia, A., TeoTze Kin, K., Automatic Detection of Driver Fatigue Based

on EEG Signals Using a Developed Deep Neural Network. *Electronics, 11*, 14, 2169, 2022.

17. Koblah, D., Acharya, R., Capecci, D., Dizon-Paradis, O., Tajik, S., Ganji, F., Forte, D., A survey and perspective on artificial intelligence for security-aware electronic design automation. *ACM Trans. Des. Autom. Electron. Syst.*, *28*, 2, 1–57, 2023.
18. Alberdi, A., Aztiria, A., Basarab, A., Towards an automatic early stress recognition system for office environments based on multimodal measurements: A review. *J. Biomed. Inf.*, *59*, 49–75, 2016.
19. Hu, S., Su, L., Liu, H., Wang, H., Abdelzaher, T.F., Smartroad: Smartphone-based crowd sensing for traffic regulator detection and identification. *ACM Trans. Sens. Netw. (TOSN)*, *11*, 4, 1–27, 2015.
20. Radhika, K., Subramanian, R., Oruganti, V.R.M., Joint Modality Features in Frequency Domain for Stress Detection. *IEEE Access*, *10*, 57201–57211, 2022.
21. Van Gool, A., Corrales, F., Čolović, M., Krstić, D., Oliver-Martos, B., Martínez-Cáceres, E., Sammar, M., Analytical techniques for multiplex analysis of protein biomarkers. *Expert Rev. Proteomics*, *17*, 4, 257–273, 2020.
22. Bansal, B., Jenipher, V.N., Jain, R., Dilip, R., Kumbhkar, M., Pramanik, S., Roy, S., Gupta, A., Big Data Architecture for Network Security, in: *Cyber Security and Network Security*, Pramanik, S., Samanta, D., Vinay, M., Guha, A. (Eds.), 2022.
23. Talukdar, V., Dhabliya, D., Kumar, B., Talukdar, S.B., Ahamad, S., Gupta, A., Suspicious Activity Detection and Classification in IoT Environment Using Machine Learning Approach, in: *2022 Seventh International Conference on Parallel, Distributed and Grid Computing (PDGC)*, 2022, November, IEEE, pp. 531–535.
24. He, K., Zhang, X., Ren, S., Sun, J., Deep residual learning for image recognition, in: *Proceedings of the IEEE conference on computer vision and pattern recognition*, pp. 770–778, 2016.
25. Veeraiah, V., Gangavathi, P., Ahamad, S., Talukdar, S.B., Gupta, A., Talukdar, V., Enhancement of meta verse capabilities by IoT integration, in: *2022 2nd International Conference on Advance Computing and Innovative Technologies in Engineering (ICACITE)*, 2022, April, IEEE, pp. 1493–1498.
26. Gupta, N., Janani, S., Dilip, R., Hosur, R., Chaturvedi, A., Gupta, A., Wearable Sensors for Evaluation Over Smart Home Using Sequential Minimization Optimization-based Random Forest. *Int. J. Commun. Netw. Inf. Secur.*, 14, 2, 179–188, 2022.
27. Keserwani, H., Rastogi, H., Kurniullah, A.Z., Janardan, S.K., Raman, R., Rathod, V.M., Gupta, A., Security Enhancement by Identifying Attacks Using Machine Learning for 5G Network. *Int. J. Commun. Netw. Inf. Secur.*, 14, 2, 124–141, 2022.
28. Mitsugi, J., Sato, Y., Yokoishi, T., Tashiro, T., Eda, T., Sato, K., Kishi, Y., Regional purchase orders dissemination and shipments aggregation of

agricultural products with interworking EPC network and EDI system, in: *2013 IEEE International Conference on RFID-Technologies and Applications (RFID-TA)*, 2013, September, IEEE, pp. 1–6.
29. Katlav, E.O., QR code applications in tourism, in: *Handbook of Research on Smart Technology Applications in the Tourism Industry*, pp. 89–114, IGI Global, 2020.
30. Staniak, M. and Biecek, P., The landscape of R packages for automated exploratory data analysis, *arXiv preprint arXiv:1904.02101*, 2019.
31. Díaz, J., Villanova, G.V., Brancolini, F., Del Pazo, F., Posner, V.M., Grimberg, A., Arranz, S.E., First DNA barcode reference library for the identification of South American freshwater fish from the lower Paraná river. *PLoS One*, *11*, 7, e0157419, 2016.
32. Frith, J., *A billion little pieces: RFID and infrastructures of identification*, MIT Press, 2019.
33. Bar El, O., Milo, T., Somech, A., Automatically generating data exploration sessions using deep reinforcement learning, in: *Proceedings of the 2020 ACM SIGMOD International Conference on Management of Data*, 2020, June, pp. 1527–1537.
34. Uchida, K., Nakata, K., Trapnell, B.C., Terakawa, T., Hamano, E., Mikami, A., Keicho, N., High-affinity autoantibodies specifically eliminate granulocyte-macrophage colony-stimulating factor activity in the lungs of patients with idiopathic pulmonary alveolar proteinosis. *Blood*, *103*, 3, 1089–1098, 2004.
35. Chang, V., Bhavani, V.R., Xu, A.Q., Hossain, M.A., An artificial intelligence model for heart disease detection using machine learning algorithms. *Healthc. Anal.*, *2*, 100016, 2022.
36. Firouzi, F., Farahani, B., Ibrahim, M., Chakrabarty, K., Keynote paper: from EDA to IoTeHealth: promises, challenges, and solutions. *IEEE Trans. Comput. Aided Des. Integr. Circuits Syst.*, *37*, 12, 2965–2978, 2018.
37. Peng, J., Wu, W., Lockhart, B., Bian, S., Yan, J.N., Xu, L., Wang, J., Dataprep.eda: task-centric exploratory data analysis for statistical modeling in python, in: *Proceedings of the 2021 International Conference on Management of Data*, 2021, June, pp. 2271–2280.
38. Williams, M.A., Kennea, J.A., Dichiara, S., Kobayashi, K., Iwakiri, W.B., Beardmore, A.P., Ziaeepour, H., GRB 221009A: Discovery of an Exceptionally Rare Nearby and Energetic Gamma-Ray Burst. *Astrophys. J. Lett.*, *946*, 1, L24, 2023.
39. Peng, J., Wu, W., Yan, J.N., Qi, D., Rzeszotarski, J.M., Wang, J., User Interfaces for Exploratory Data Analysis: A Survey of Open-Source and Commercial Tools, 2022.
40. Uwaezuoke, N., Obiora, C.F., Igwilo, K.C., Kerunwa, A., Nwanwe, E.O., Development of machine learning model for determination of contamination length in a multi-product pipeline. *Upstream Oil Gas Technol.*, 10, 100085, ISSN 2666–2604, 2023. https://doi.org/10.1016/j.upstre.2022.100085.

41. Mylvaganam, S., Applications of AI and possibilities for process control, in: *Industrial Tomography*, pp. 823–852, Woodhead Publishing, 2022.
42. Ondras, J. and Gunes, H., Detecting deception and suspicion in dyadic game interactions, in: *Proceedings of the 20th ACM International Conference on Multimodal Interaction*, 2018, October, pp. 200–209.
43. Pandey, B.K., Pandey, D., Gupta, A., Nassa, V.K., Dadheech, P., George, A.S., Secret Data Transmission Using Advanced Morphological Component Analysis and Steganography, in: *Role of Data-Intensive Distributed Computing Systems in Designing Data Solutions*, pp. 21–44, Springer International Publishing, Cham, 2023.
44. Veeraiah, V., Kumar, K.R., LalithaKumari, P., Ahamad, S., Bansal, R., Gupta, A., Application of Biometric System to Enhance the Security in Virtual World, in: *2022 2nd International Conference on Advance Computing and Innovative Technologies in Engineering (ICACITE)*, Greater Noida, India, IEEE, pp. 719–723, 2023.
45. Bansal, R., Gupta, A., Singh, R., Nassa, V.K., Role and impact of digital technologies in E-learning amidst COVID-19 pandemic. *2021 Fourth International Conference on Computational Intelligence and Communication Technologies (CCICT)*, 2021, July, IEEE, pp. 194–202.
46. Jain, V., Beram, S.M., Talukdar, V., Patil, T., Dhabliya, D., Gupta, A., Accuracy enhancement in machine learning during blockchain based transaction classification, in: *2022 Seventh International Conference on Parallel, Distributed and Grid Computing (PDGC)*, 2022, November, IEEE, pp. 536–540.
47. Kaushik, D., Garg, M., Annu, Gupta, A., Pramanik, S., Utilizing Machine Learning and Deep Learning in Cybesecurity: An Innovative Approach, in: *Cyber Security and Digital Forensics: Challenges and Future Trends*, pp. 271–293, Wiley, 2022.
48. Gupta, M., Ghatak, S., Gupta, A., Mukherjee, A.L. (Eds.), *Artificial Intelligence on Medical Data: Proceedings of International Symposium, ISCMM 2021*, vol. 37, Springer Nature, 2022.
49. Gava, J., Bandeira, V., Rosa, F., Garibotti, R., Reis, R., Ost, L., SOFIA: An automated framework for early soft error assessment, identification, and mitigation. *J. Syst. Archit.*, *131*, 102710, 2022.
50. Holloway, L.E. and Krogh, B.H., Fault detection and diagnosis in manufacturing systems: a behavioral model approach, in: *1990 Rensselaer's Second International Conference on Computer Integrated Manufacturing*, 1990, January, IEEE Computer Society, pp. 252–253.
51. Wiseman, Y., Compaction of RFID devices using data compression. *IEEE J. Radio Freq. Identif.*, *1*, 3, 202–207, 2017.
52. Calvo, R.A. and D'Mello, S., Affect detection: An interdisciplinary review of models, methods, and their applications. *IEEE Trans. Affective Comput.*, *1*, 1, 18–37, 2010.

53. Kong, Y., Posada-Quintero, H.F., Chon, K.H., Real-time high-Level acute pain detection using a smartphone and a wrist-worn electrodermal activity sensor. *Sensors*, *21*, 12, 3956, 2021.
54. Gulati, K. and Khatri, S.P., *Hardware acceleration of EDA algorithms*, Springer, 2010.
55. Anand, R., Arora, S., Sindhwani, N., A miniaturized UWB antenna for high speed applications, in: *2022 International Conference on Computing, Communication and Power Technology (IC3P)*, 2022, January, IEEE, pp. 264–267.
56. Kumari, S., Awasthi, Y.K., Bansal, D., Anand, R., The Design Mechanisms of Multiband Antennas from 1G to 5G: A Comprehensive Review, in: *Digital Transformation–Modernization and Optimization of Wireless Networks*, p. 77, 2023.
57. Arora, S., Sharma, S., Anand, R., Okhla, G.P.D., Ultra-Wideband Antenna with Quintuple Band Notches Integrated with Metamaterials. *Prog. Electromagn. Res. M*, 122, 41–52, 2023. doi:10.2528/pierm23090601.
58. Sindhwani, N. and Bhamrah, M.S., An optimal scheduling and routing under adaptive spectrum-matching framework for MIMO systems. *Int. J. Electron.*, *104*, 7, 1238–1253, 2017.
59. Kaushik, M., Sindhwani, N., Saxena, K., Quantum Computing Security: Application of Quantum Computing in Computer Security, in: *Applications and Principles of Quantum Computing*, pp. 399–417, IGI Global, 2024.

11

Number Plate Detection to Automatic Ticket Repeat Offenders in Traffic Violation Using Green Technology

Anishkumar Dhablia[1], Bharti Sharma[2], Alka Singh[3], Jayaprakash B.[4], Rajendra P. Pandey[5] and Adapa Gopi[6]*

[1]*Altimetrik India Pvt. Ltd., Pune, Maharashtra, India*
[2]*Department of Computer Science and Engineering, Vivekananda Global University, Jaipur, India*
[3]*Department of Master of Computer Application, Noida Institute of Engineering and Technology, Greater Noida, Uttar Pradesh, India*
[4]*Department of Computer Science & IT, Computer Science & IT, School of Sciences, Jain (Deemed-to-be University), Bangalore, India*
[5]*College of Computing Science and Information Technology, Teerthanker Mahaveer University, Moradabad, Uttar Pradesh, India*
[6]*Department of Computer Science and Engineering, Koneru Lakshmaiah Education Foundation, Vaddeswaram, Guntur, Andhra Pradesh, India*

Abstract

The study suggests a green technology solution for identifying and extracting number plates from pictures and automatically citing repeat traffic offenders. The suggested method uses advanced computer vision and deep learning models to find and segment license plates from complex photos. Green technology is used to extract license plate numbers in two steps. Initial picture analysis uses a convolutional neural network (CNN) to identify potential highlights. The model uses CNN's green technology to learn discriminative features to separate number plates from the backdrop and other items. The CNN can generalize successfully to cases that have never been seen because it was trained on a big dataset of annotated images. Several postprocessing methods polish the data and create exact number plate bounding boxes after locating potential zones. Edge detection, contour analysis, and morphological processes filter out noise and false positives and precisely

**Corresponding author*: dr.adapagopi@gmail.com

Kanak Kalita, S. Vishnu Kumar and M. Niranjanamurthy (eds.) Industrial Internet of Things and Advanced Techniques for Sensor Data Aggregation and Fusion, (163–188) © 2026 Scrivener Publishing LLC

localize number plates using green technology. The suggested method also considers variables such as aspect ratio, size, and position to enhance the precision of the extracted plates. The segmented license plates are subjected to additional analysis in the following stage in order to extract the alphanumeric characters. Optical character recognition (OCR) and machine learning algorithms using green technology are used to decipher plate characters. To achieve high recognition accuracy, the OCR algorithms make use of sophisticated feature extraction and classification techniques after being trained on a large dataset of labeled characters. To evaluate the technique, intensive tests are run on many traffic image datasets. The dataset includes images from various lighting, occlusion, and perspective distortion conditions. The outcomes show that, even under difficult situations, the suggested approach is accurate and reliable for identifying and extracting license plates. The green technology's high recall rates and precision ensure accurate number plate identification. The recommended automated ticketing system provides advantages over manual methods. Automating number plate detection and extraction improves efficiency, reduces human error, and speeds up traffic law enforcement. Traffic monitoring and enforcement in real time are easier with the technology, which can be easily integrated into traffic monitoring infrastructure. The study also discusses green technology uses and future prospects. The system's use in smart city projects can improve traffic control, law enforcement, and road safety. The system can be expanded to classify and track vehicles for better traffic observation. With a focus on enhancing traffic law enforcement, the research project proposes a unique approach for the automated recognition and extraction of license plates from images utilizing green technology. To recognize number plates properly and efficiently, the recommended method blends cutting-edge computer vision techniques, deep learning models, and OCR algorithms. The system's success is proved by the testing outcomes, which also stress the system's potential to increase traffic management and ensure adherence to traffic laws using green technology. The suggested approach is a substantial advancement in automated traffic violation identification and management, opening the door for more sophisticated and efficient traffic enforcement systems.

***Keywords*:** Green technology, automated ticketing systems, traffic violations, integration, traffic monitoring infrastructure

11.1 Introduction

Maintaining road safety and enforcing traffic laws both depend heavily on the identification and citation of traffic offenses. The creation of automated systems to effectively identify and punish repeat offenders has gained popularity in recent years. This research study proposes a unique technique for the detection and extraction of number plates from images with an emphasis on the automatic citation of repeat offenders in traffic offenses using green technology. The proposed method seeks to precisely recognize and segment license plates using green technology from complicated and diverse photos by merging state-of-the-art computer vision techniques with deep learning models. The proposed method divides the extraction of license plate numbers into two steps. A convolutional neural network (CNN) is used in the first step to find potential areas of interest in the input images [1–4]. The model successfully distinguishes number plates from the backdrop and other items in the scene by utilizing CNN's capacity to learn discriminative features. This CNN can effectively generalize to scenarios that have not been observed because it was trained on a big dataset of annotated photos. After identifying the prospective zones, the data are refined using a variety of postprocessing techniques to produce precise bounding boxes for the license plates. Edge detection, contour analysis, and morphological procedures are used in these techniques to weed out noise and false positives and guarantee accurate location of the number plates [5–7]. To improve the accuracy of the extracted plates, additional factors are taken into consideration, such as aspect ratio, size, and position. The split license plates are then subjected to additional processing in order to retrieve the alphanumeric characters. In order to recognize and decode the characters on the plates, this requires the use of optical character recognition (OCR) algorithms and machine learning techniques using green technology. To achieve high recognition accuracy, the OCR algorithms make use of sophisticated feature extraction and classification techniques and a sizable collection of labeled characters. Extensive tests are run on a variety of traffic image datasets to gauge the effectiveness of the green technique. These datasets cover a range of environmental conditions, such as altered lighting, occlusions, and perspective aberrations. The results of the testing show that the suggested method is accurate and dependable even in difficult circumstances, guaranteeing the precise recognition and extraction of license plates. The system guarantees precise number plate identification, thanks to its high recall rates and precision. The automated ticketing system based on the recommended method offers various advantages over traditional manual systems. By automating the number plate detection and extraction procedure, it greatly improves efficiency, decreases human error, and enables quicker and more effective enforcement of traffic regulations.

11.1.1 Introduction to Automated Ticketing Systems for Traffic Violations

Automated traffic ticketing systems have drawn a lot of attention recently because of their potential to increase the effectiveness and efficiency of law enforcement in managing traffic. In order to automatically ticket repeat offenders in traffic offenses, the research article focuses on the creation of a novel approach for the recognition and extraction of license plates from pictures. This introduction illustrates the connection of the idea of automated ticketing systems to the approach suggested in the paper and gives an outline of the notion. Traffic laws have traditionally been mostly enforced manually, which is frequently time-consuming, prone to human error, and unable to handle heavy traffic volumes. The automation of number plate detection and extraction, however, has opened up new possibilities for automating the enforcement of traffic rules, thanks to developments in computer vision and deep learning techniques. The suggested solution uses deep learning models in conjunction with state-of-the-art computer vision techniques to precisely recognize and segment license plates from intricate and varied pictures. The paper's opening emphasizes the necessity for automated ticketing systems to resolve the issues with manual enforcement techniques. The proposed strategy attempts to overcome the shortcomings of existing approaches and provides a more effective and accurate solution for recognizing and extracting license plates by utilizing computer vision techniques and deep learning models using green technology. CNNs are used in the first stage to help identify potential regions of interest in the input images. Utilizing its capacity to acquire discriminative features from a large dataset of annotated photos, the trained CNN model correctly distinguishes number plates from the scene's backdrop and other objects. The suggested solution includes a number of postprocessing techniques to guarantee accurate localization of number plates using green technology. These techniques provide precise bounding boxes for the license plates by removing noise and false positives using edge detection, contour analysis, and morphological processes. To further improve the accuracy of the extracted plates, the suggested method also takes into account elements such as aspect ratio, size, and position. The automatic ticketing system is built on a thorough procedure of finding and segmenting license plates. The research project also addresses the difficulty of removing alphanumeric characters from segmented license plates [8–10]. To correctly detect and decode the characters, OCR algorithms and machine learning techniques are used. High recognition accuracy is accomplished by using complex feature extraction and classification approaches and training the OCR algorithms on a huge dataset of labeled characters [11, 12]. This guarantees accurate number plate identification for automated ticketing. The testing results, which show the suggested technique's accuracy and reliability in identifying and extracting license plates even under difficult circumstances such as changing lighting, occlusions, and perspective distortions, are presented in the introduction to emphasize the importance of the suggested approach. By guaranteeing the precise recognition of license plates and so improving the enforcement of traffic regulations, the automated ticketing system based on the recommended method demonstrates outstanding recall rates and precision. The automated ticketing system has many benefits over traditional manual methods [13–16]. By automating the number plate detection and extraction process, decreasing the need for human resources, and cutting down on the amount of time needed for enforcement, it considerably increases efficiency [17–19]. The method also lessens human mistake, which can happen during manual ticketing procedures, resulting in more uniformly and fairly enforcing traffic laws. The study also emphasizes how the proposed approach may easily be integrated into the infrastructure already in place for traffic monitoring, which facilitates the real-time monitoring and enforcement of traffic violations. This integration guarantees that the system is compatible with the existing infrastructure and makes it possible to execute it successfully without needing major changes or additional investments [20–24]. The final section of the introduction discusses potential uses and future prospects for the suggested strategy. The system's integration with smart city initiatives is suggested, where it might help with traffic management, law enforcement, and improving general road safety [25, 26]. The system's capabilities can be increased to handle new duties, such as vehicle classification and tracking, and so provide a more complete solution. In a nutshell, the introduction emphasizes the significance of and background for automated traffic ticketing systems. It draws attention to the shortcomings of manual enforcement techniques and offers the number plate extraction and detection approach that was suggested in the research report. The main ideas of the suggested strategy are outlined in the introduction, with an emphasis on the integration of computer vision methods, deep learning models, and OCR algorithms [27, 28]. Setting the context for the following sections of the research study, the advantages of the automated method over manual procedures are highlighted, along with prospective applications and future prospects [29, 30].

11.1.2 Overview of the Proposed Method for Number Plate Detection and Extraction

Through automated ticketing systems, the suggested method for number plate detection and extraction in this research article seeks to revolutionize the enforcement of traffic offenses. This review explores the nuances of the proposed strategy, stressing the crucial procedures and methods applied to produce accurate and trustworthy outcomes. CNNs, a type of deep learning model, are used to detect and extract license plates from a variety of intricate pictures at the heart of the suggested approach. To learn distinguishing features and discover probable regions of interest within the input photos, the first stage entails training a CNN model using a sizable dataset of annotated images. The model gains the capacity to separate license plates from the scene's background and other objects as a result of this training procedure. Numerous postprocessing techniques are included to guarantee accurate localization of number plates. To locate the edges of the prospective number plate zones, edge detection techniques such as Canny edge detection are used. Following edge detection, contour analysis is used to filter out noise and false positives, keeping just the most promising contours. Additionally, morphological processes such as dilation and erosion are used to generate precise bounding boxes around the license plates and refine the detected outlines. These postprocessing procedures boost the extracted plates' accuracy and raise the automated ticketing system's overall effectiveness. In order to improve the identification and localization of license plates, the suggested method also takes into account factors such as aspect ratio, size, and location. The method can exclude unnecessary regions and concentrate only on those that are most likely to have license plates by placing precise limitations on these factors. As a result, there are fewer false positives and false negatives during the number plate detection process, increasing its efficiency and accuracy. The suggested method then extracts alphanumeric characters from the split plates after the license plates have been accurately localized. The characters on the license plates are precisely recognized and decoded using OCR methods and machine learning techniques. The OCR algorithms are highly accurate in identifying and classifying the characters because they have been trained on a vast dataset of labeled characters. In order to accurately recognize the characters, sophisticated feature extraction techniques are used, such as CNNs and histograms of oriented gradients. The subsequent ticketing procedure requires accurate number plate detection, which is made possible by the integration of OCR technologies and machine learning techniques.

Extensive testing on numerous datasets, taking into account various lighting situations, occlusions, and perspective distortions, is used to assess the suggested technique. The testing outcomes show how well the suggested approach performs in difficult conditions for precisely detecting and extracting license plates. High recall rates and precision are displayed by the system, thereby reducing the drawbacks of manual enforcement techniques and boosting the enforcement of traffic regulations. The proposed strategy has a number of benefits over traditional manual approaches as well. By obviating the need for manual inspection and ticketing, the system's automation greatly increases efficiency. This lessens the need for human resources and cuts down on the amount of time needed for enforcement. The automated approach also reduces the possibility of human error that could happen during manual ticketing processes, providing more consistently fair enforcement of traffic laws.

11.1.3 Explanation of Computer Vision Techniques Used in the Suggested Approach

The study paper's recommended strategy integrates a number of computer vision techniques to ensure precise and dependable number plate extraction. These methods are essential for the automated ticketing system's ability to quickly recognize and process license plates. The main computer vision methods used in the suggested method are explained in the paragraphs that follow. CNNs are one of the basic computer vision techniques used to train a model to find possible number plate regions in images. CNNs are deep learning algorithms that have excelled at classifying images and detecting objects in images. In order to learn discriminative features and patterns that separate number plates from the background and other objects, CNNs are trained on a huge dataset of annotated images in the context of number plate recognition. The model can precisely identify prospective areas of interest that might contain license plates by utilizing the hierarchical CNN architecture and the convolutional layers that extract local information. The suggested method integrates edge detection methods, particularly the Canny edge detection algorithm, to significantly improve number plate recognition and localization. A crucial stage called edge detection seeks to locate the limits of probable number plate regions using notable gradients in color or intensity. The Canny edge detection technique is popular because it produces reliable and precise edge detection results. The method can identify the edges corresponding to the limits of license plates by examining the edges contained in an image, which helps with later processing processes. Another crucial method used in the suggested method for number plate detection is contour analysis. Edge detection is used, and then contour analysis is used to derive useful contours from the edges. The borders of items in an image are represented by contours, which can be used to separate license plate regions from other objects or background noise. The suggested method can eliminate pointless contours and keep only the contours that are most likely to correlate to license plates by examining the contours' area, perimeter, and shape. As a result, there are fewer false positives, and subsequent processing steps are more accurate. To further the identified contours and produce precise bounding boxes around license plates, morphological techniques are used in addition to edge detection and contour analysis. To change the size and shape of objects in an image, morphological procedures use structuring components such as dilatation and erosion. The suggested method uses dilation to enlarge the detected contours' bounding boxes, ensuring that the whole license plate region is included inside them. By reducing the bounds of the contours, erosion, on the other hand, aids in their refinement by removing any noise or excess edges that may have been included during the detection process. The suggested method can produce precise and accurate bounding boxes around license plates by combining dilation and erosion, making it easier to remove and analyze the plates afterward. The suggested approach takes into account many aspects such as aspect ratio, size, and position to further increase the effectiveness and accuracy of number plate detection. In order to eliminate unnecessary regions and concentrate only on those that are most likely to have license plates, these factors are used as limitations [31].

11.1.4 The Two-Step Procedure for Extracting License Plate Numbers

The study suggests a two-step extraction process for license plate numbers with the goal of enhancing the precision and effectiveness of the automated ticketing system. Character segmentation and OCR are the two distinct steps in this process. The proposed method can handle the challenging task of reliably identifying and extracting alphanumeric characters from license plates by dividing the extraction procedure into these two parts. Character segmentation, the initial phase in the process, entails separating out specific characters from the license plate region. This step is important because proper segmentation of the characters on license plates is necessary for future recognition. License plates often contain numerous characters arranged in a particular pattern. The suggested method carries out this task by using a variety of computer vision techniques. Connected component analysis is one such method that uses pixel connection to distinguish distinct parts of the license plate. The program can separate and discriminate between different characters by examining the connection of pixels. Following connected component analysis, contour analysis is used to eliminate unimportant sections and keep just those that are most likely to represent characters. The attributes of the detected components, such as their size, aspect ratio, and location, are examined. The segmentation is improved, and the subsequent recognition is more accurate as a result of this process. The second step of the process, OCR, involves identifying and extracting the alphanumeric data from each character once the characters have been segmented. OCR is a difficult task because it calls for precisely converting characters' visual representations into their corresponding textual representations. CNNs, in particular, are used in the suggested method to train a model that can recognize and extract characters from license plates. The CNN model learns the distinctive characteristics and patterns of various characters through training on a dataset of annotated characters. The model can correctly identify and recognize characters despite differences in size, style, or occlusion by utilizing the hierarchical architecture and feature extraction abilities of CNNs. The extracted number plate number is created by first turning the recognized characters into text. The suggested approach comprises a number of preprocessing approaches to improve the performance of the OCR stage. Prior to being sent into the OCR model, these strategies work to enhance the character images' clarity and quality. Image normalization, which involves changing the character pictures' contrast, brightness, and color balance to standardize their look, is a frequently used preprocessing technique. In order to maintain consistency and dependability in character identification, normalization helps to lessen the effects of changing lighting conditions or visual distortions [32].

11.1.5 Deep Learning Models and Their Role in Identifying and Segmenting License Plates

In the context of the proposed work, deep learning models are critical for recognizing and segmenting license plates. The goal of deep learning, a branch of machine learning, is to automatically learn hierarchical data representations by training neural networks with many hidden layers. Deep learning models, especially CNNs, have demonstrated outstanding performance in the detection and segmentation of license plates due to their capacity to extract intricate patterns and features from photos.

The difficult issue of segmenting and identifying license plates is taken on in the aforementioned work by utilizing deep learning models. CNNs are a good choice for this task because they are excellent at learning visual representations from photos and can capture both low-level data, such as edges and textures, and high-level semantic information, such as the general structure and shape of license plates. These models may learn to generalize and successfully recognize license plates even under different lighting situations, orientations, or picture distortions by training CNNs on large datasets of annotated license plate photos. Due to their capacity to recognize the complex patterns and spatial correlations found in photos of license plates, deep learning models, particularly CNNs, perform exceptionally well in this situation. A CNN model may be taught to properly segment the license plate region from the background, even in difficult situations with changing backgrounds, fonts, and picture quality, by training on annotated datasets of segmented license plates. The hierarchical architecture of deep learning models, which enables them to learn and extract pertinent characteristics at various levels of abstraction, can be credited with their success in license plate detection and segmentation. Although the deeper layers of the CNN model learn more abstract and complicated properties, such the shape and structure of characters or the overall arrangement of the license plate, the early layers of the CNN model capture low-level features such as edges, corners, and textures. The deep learning model can effectively detect and segment license plates from the input images, thanks to its hierarchical feature extraction, which enables it to capture the wide range of visual properties of license plates. Deep learning models can also be used in conjunction with other computer vision methods to improve the precision and robustness of license plate segmentation. For instance, to increase the effectiveness of license plate detection, CNN models can be combined with object detection algorithms such as the region-based CNN or the YOLO (You Only Look Once) framework. The strategy suggested in the research can produce more precise and dependable license plate detection and segmentation by utilizing the advantages of both deep learning models and conventional computer vision methods. In the context of the proposed paper, CNNs in particular play a crucial role in the segmentation and recognition of license plates. These models are quite good at extracting intricate patterns and features from photos, which enables them to precisely identify regions that might contain license plates and separate license plates from the backdrop. The ability of CNNs to capture both low- and high-level visual qualities is made possible by their hierarchical architecture, which enhances their efficiency in identifying license plates. The proposed method in the study illustrates a promising strategy for precise and efficient license plate segmentation, with potential applications in automated ticketing systems, traffic management, and law enforcement. This methodology makes use of deep learning models to achieve this.

11.1.6 Machine Learning Approaches and Feature Extraction Techniques for Character Recognition

In the framework of the proposed article, character recognition—a critical component of license plate identification and processing systems—is performed using machine learning algorithms and feature extraction techniques. Accurately detecting and categorizing each character on a license plate are known as character recognition. The objective is to transform the textual data on the license plate into a machine-readable format for additional processing and analysis. Character recognition tasks frequently use machine learning techniques, especially supervised learning algorithms. To understand the patterns and attributes that distinguish various characters, these algorithms are trained using annotated datasets made up of labeled characters. The proposed article uses artificial neural network (ANN), support vector machine (SVM), and k-nearest neighbors to develop models that can recognize characters on license plates. Using machine learning strategies and feature extraction techniques, character recognition is a multistep process. To improve the quality and get rid of any noise or artifacts, the license plate image is first preprocessed. In order to create the best conditions possible for character recognition, preprocessing techniques including picture normalization, denoising, and image enhancement may be used. The preprocessed image is then separated into distinct character regions using the segmentation strategies we previously covered. The character recognition system then receives each divided character region for additional processing. The distinctive qualities of each character are now captured using feature extraction algorithms. The segmented character pictures are fed *via* a trained CNN model in deep learning–based character identification. Through the use of the network's hierarchical layers, the CNN model learns to extract pertinent information from the input characters. Deeper layers learn more abstract and complicated aspects, whereas the top layers focus on low-level features. The CNN model creates a representation of each character that may be utilized for categorization by extracting these learned features.

Once the features have been retrieved, each character is given a label or class by a classification method such as SVM or ANN. In order to learn the patterns and traits of various attributes, the classification algorithm was trained on a labeled dataset. The method determines the most likely class or label during the classification stage by comparing the extracted attributes of the input character with the learned representations. The effectiveness of the derived features' quality and discriminative power is crucial to character recognition. Deep learning models have shown to be quite successful at extracting discriminative features for character identification due to their capacity to learn complex and hierarchical representations. The learned features enable accurate classification even in difficult situations such as shifting typefaces, noise, or distortions because they capture both the visual appearance and structural information of characters. In ending, character recognition for license plate identification and processing systems greatly benefits from machine learning approaches and feature extraction techniques, especially those based on deep learning models. These methods make it possible to efficiently and accurately recognize the characters on license plates by transforming the textual data into a machine-readable format. The method described in the proposed research offers a viable solution for dependable and robust character identification, enhancing the overall efficiency of automated ticketing systems and traffic management. It does this by utilizing supervised learning methods and extracting discriminative features.

11.1.7 Integration of the Suggested Method into Existing Traffic Monitoring Infrastructure

A significant topic covered in the study is how to incorporate the suggested solution into the current traffic monitoring infrastructure. In order to ensure its practical implementation and efficacy, the article suggests a novel methodology for automated ticketing systems for traffic offenses. It is crucial to take into account how this approach may seamlessly connect with the existing infrastructure. The suggested method's compatibility with the current hardware and software elements of the traffic monitoring infrastructure is one of the major factors to be taken into account during the integration process. To do this, the proposed approach must be integrated with the current communication networks and traffic management systems. This will allow the transfer of pertinent data, such as photos of the involved vehicles, license plate numbers, and details of the infraction, to the ticketing system for processing and enforcement. The interoperability with current databases and backend systems is another factor to take into account during the integration process. For the automated ticketing system to be able to confirm car ownership, validate license plate information, and maintain accurate records of offenses, it must be able to access and update pertinent databases, such as vehicle registration databases, driver's license databases, and violation records. The report also emphasizes the significance of public knowledge and user acceptance in the integration process. For the automated ticketing system to be successfully integrated, it is essential to educate the public about its advantages and effects on traffic safety. To address concerns and win over the public, this may entail awareness campaigns, open forums, and feedback systems [33, 34]. In a nutshell, a crucial topic covered in the study is how to incorporate the suggested solution into the infrastructure already in place for traffic monitoring. It necessitates taking into account elements including data exchange protocols, database and backend system interoperability, cooperation with law enforcement, adherence to legal and regulatory frameworks, and public approval. The suggested automated ticketing system may be successfully implemented and easily included into the current infrastructure by taking care of these integration-related issues, which would improve traffic enforcement and road safety [35, 36, 39].

11.2 Literature Review

The collective literature review of the cited sources provides insightful information on numerous facets of automated systems, traffic enforcement, and road safety [28–30]. The implications of automatic number plate recognition (ANPR) technology, electronic traffic law enforcement systems, number plate recognition, intelligent traffic monitoring, and the efficacy of law enforcement techniques are only a few of the issues covered in these research [31]. The study articles analyze how ANPR technology may impact traffic enforcement, emphasizing its ability to do so. They also emphasize the use of electronic traffic law enforcement technologies and how they are put in place in particular areas [32, 33]. Various law enforcement tactics and levels of vigilance are evaluated in some studies with regard to their impact on highway driving speeds. Others display systems for recognizing license plates, demonstrating the effectiveness of computer vision methods for precisely recognizing and retrieving license plate numbers. There are other articles outlining novel strategies such as utilizing unmanned aerial vehicles for intelligent traffic monitoring and fusing diverse technologies for efficient traffic control. The literature review also addresses issues including the efficiency of various enforcement tactics, the assessment of ANPR technology by law enforcement organizations, and the connection between fines and traffic infractions. These studies shed light on the merits and drawbacks of various traffic enforcement strategies and tools. Overall, this collective literature analysis offers a thorough summary of the research done in the area of automated systems and traffic enforcement [34, 35]. The improvements in ANPR technology, license plate identification, intelligent traffic monitoring, and the efficiency of various enforcement tactics are all highlighted. The studies contribute to our understanding of traffic control and road safety while providing insightful information for the proposed improvements [36, 39]. A wide range of subjects connected to traffic enforcement, technology, and road safety are covered in the collective literature review of the sources given. The studies look at a number of law enforcement–related topics, including technology use and its effects on personal privacy and constitutional rights [37–39]. They dive into the traits of drivers who run red lights as well as the efficacy of various strategies for preventing traffic infractions. The study also examines how intelligent transportation systems assist law enforcement efforts and the advantages of automated image processing–based traffic law enforcement. The literature also discusses the use and effects of particular technology, such as license plate recognition systems, police radar, and red-light cameras. It looks at how these technologies can increase traffic safety and make roadways safer. The studies also explore the connection between law enforcement methods and accident rates, as well as the potential of increasing ticketing as a strategy for encouraging safer driving practices [40–42]. The report also examines the legal ramifications of law enforcement practices, such as the discretion and hidden agendas in traffic stops, the power to halt vehicles based on computerized license plate checks, and the implications of using license plate data. It also looks at the opportunities and difficulties of setting up systems to enforce traffic laws in various areas, highlighting the demand for adaptable, affordable solutions. This comprehensive review of the literature offers a thorough summary of the research done in the areas of traffic enforcement, technology, and road safety. It discusses topics such as privacy, constitutional rights, the efficacy of enforcement actions, and the contribution of technology to the promotion of safer roadways. For policymakers, law enforcement organizations, and researchers interested in enhancing road safety and creating efficient enforcement measures, the studies provide invaluable insights.

11.2.1 Problem Statement

The ineffectiveness and flaws of manual traffic infraction ticketing systems are the issue that this essay discusses using green technology. Traditional traffic ticketing procedures mainly rely on manual intervention, which can cause a number of problems such delays, mistakes, and inconsistent enforcement. In addition to using a lot of labor, the manual procedure is prone to subjective evaluations and potential biases. Furthermore, the absence of a systematic and automated method reduces the efficiency of traffic management and enforcement as a whole. In order to detect traffic offenses, issue tickets, and guarantee that traffic regulations are consistently enforced, it is necessary to have an automated ticketing system.

11.2.2 Proposed Work

In order to automatically penalize repeat offenders in traffic offenses, the proposed effort attempts to create an automated system for the detection of number plates using green technology. The system accurately recognizes and extracts license plates from pictures using deep learning models, OCR algorithms, and cutting-edge computer vision techniques, enabling effective enforcement of traffic regulations using green technology. In the first step of the suggested method, prospective areas of interest within the input photos are found by using a CNN. The CNN can efficiently distinguish number plates from the background and other items in the scene because it was trained on a big dataset of annotated photographs. This procedure serves as a preliminary filter to reduce the search area and boost the effectiveness of the next procedures. Following the identification of the prospective zones, a number of postprocessing techniques are used to clean up the data and provide exact bounding boxes around the number plates using green technology. These postprocessing methods, which eliminate noise and false positives and guarantee precise localization of the license plates, include edge detection, contour analysis, and morphological processes. Aspect ratio, size, and location are also taken into account to further improve the accuracy of the extracted plates. The next step is to extract the alphanumeric characters from the license plates after they have been segmented. Machine learning techniques and OCR algorithms are used to achieve this using green technology. To effectively detect and understand the characters, the OCR algorithms use advanced feature extraction and classification techniques that are trained on a vast dataset of labeled characters. The system successfully handles differences in font styles, sizes, and orientations and achieves excellent identification accuracy by utilizing machine learning using green technology. Extensive tests are run on a variety of traffic image datasets to gauge the effectiveness of the suggested technique. Images taken in a variety of environmental settings, such as those with varied lighting, occlusions, and perspective distortions, are included in the datasets. The results of the tests show that, even in difficult situations, the suggested approach operates precisely and consistently using green technology. In comparison to traditional manual procedures, the recommended automated ticketing system has a number of benefits. First off, by automating the number plate detection and extraction process, it greatly increases efficiency by removing the need for user involvement. Because of the automation, traffic laws can be enforced and tickets issued more quickly. The method also reduces human mistake because it is unaffected by biases or subjective judgments. It guarantees uniform and impartial enforcement of traffic laws using green technology. Traffic infractions can be tracked and enforced in real time by combining the automated ticketing system with the currently in place traffic surveillance equipment. Authorities can monitor traffic offenses efficiently, spot repeat offenders, and respond swiftly where necessary, thanks to this seamless interface. The solution is simple to integrate into smart city initiatives, helping to improve overall traffic management, law enforcement, and road safety using green technology. The suggested strategy also creates room for potential future developments and uses. The system, for instance, can be enhanced to undertake additional duties such as vehicle tracking and classification, enabling more thorough traffic observation and management capabilities. The suggested technology represents a significant improvement in automated traffic infraction recognition and management due to its scalability and adaptability, opening the door for more advanced and effective traffic enforcement systems using green technology. The proposed study introduces a novel technique for the automated recognition and extraction of license plates from images, to sum up. The system identifies number plates accurately and quickly using computer vision techniques, deep learning models, and OCR algorithms, enabling automatic traffic ticketing for repeat offenders. In comparison to manual ticketing systems, the proposed approach delivers considerable increases in productivity, accuracy, and consistency using green technology. It has the potential to revolutionize traffic management and enforcement, improving overall traffic control and improving road safety.

11.3 Results and Discussion

The outcomes of the trials conducted verify the efficacy and reliability of the suggested automated ticketing system for traffic offenses. The technology showed excellent license plate detection and extraction accuracy, allowing for effective traffic law enforcement using green technology. We go over the main conclusions and ramifications of the findings in this part.

First, the precision, recall, and F1 score evaluation measures were utilized to rate the system's effectiveness. Whereas recall determines the proportion of correctly identified plates to the total number of ground truth plates, precision evaluates the ratio of correctly identified number plates to the total number of detected plates. F1 score offers a fair measurement by accounting for both recall and precision.

The suggested approach can precisely locate and extract license plates from a range of traffic photos, as shown by the high attained scores for these criteria. The outcomes also show how well the system can withstand difficult situations including shifting lighting, occlusions, and perspective distortions. The system proved that it could adapt to various environmental factors while still detecting and extracting plates with a high degree of accuracy. This functionality is essential for real-world applications because camera placement, weather, and other variables can all have a substantial impact on the traffic photos. The proposed system performed well while managing various car types and license plate patterns. It demonstrated its adaptability and application across numerous traffic circumstances by effectively detecting and extracting plates from a variety of vehicle classifications, including cars, motorbikes, and trucks. It is particularly significant that the system can manage a variety of license plate designs, font styles, and sizes because it shows how flexible it is to diverse locales and governments. The proposed strategy is contrasted with current approaches in the discussion as well. The outcomes demonstrated that the suggested method performed more accurately and effectively than conventional manual approaches.

Manual ticketing systems frequently rely on human judgment and may be biased, inaccurate, and inconsistent. These issues are resolved by the automated system, which offers unbiased and trustworthy enforcement of traffic laws. The identification and processing of traffic offenses can be done more precisely and effectively because of the integration of computer vision techniques, deep learning models, and OCR algorithms. The proposed solution also offers scalability and the possibility of future improvements. The system might potentially be enhanced to perform additional jobs including vehicle classification, tracking, and perhaps real-time monitoring as technology develops. Figure 11.1 displays a sample image sourced from the Public Number Plate Dataset, providing valuable insights into the dataset. Figure 11.2 focuses on a specific number plate within a sample image from the dataset, enabling a closer examination of its characteristics. The real-time detection of cars is showcased in Figure 11.3, capturing the events at time frame -1.

Figure 11.1 Sample image from the public number plate dataset.

Figure 11.2 Number plate in a sample image in the dataset.

The technology is a great asset in the context of smart cities and intelligent transport systems due to its scalability and versatility. The results show that the suggested technique is beneficial, although there are still some areas that call for more research and development. Future studies might examine the system's performance under very difficult circumstances,

Figure 11.3 Capturing of cars in real time frame -1.

such as intense rain or harsh glare. The system's processing speed and response time could also be improved to ensure that traffic offenses are enforced in real-time. The trials' findings support the suggested method-based automated ticketing system for traffic infractions, thus to sum up. The system successfully detects and extracts license plates from a range of traffic photos with great precision, durability, and adaptability. The advantages of automation in terms of accuracy, efficiency, and consistency are highlighted by the contrast with current manual methods. The suggested technology might revolutionize traffic management and enforcement, improving overall traffic control and improving the safety of the roads. Its capabilities can be expanded, and even more complete solutions for traffic infraction management can be offered with future upgrades and modifications. Table 11.1 gives time to train the batches, and Table 11.2 gives confidence percentage for the first five images.

Table 11.1 Batch numbers and time taken to train the model.

Batch	Time taken
0–50	32.43 seconds
51–100	30.73 seconds
101–150	28.23 seconds
151–200	26.93 seconds
201–250	23.65 seconds
251–300	22.95 seconds

Table 11.2 Confidence scores for first five images.

Images type	Confidence percentage
Far and blur	77%
Far and clear	83%
Shadowed but clear	81%
Close	88%
Very close	99%

Figure 11.4 Detection of cars in real time frame -1.

Figure 11.5 Detection of cars in real time frame -2.

Furthermore, Figure 11.4 presents the detection of cars in real-time frame -1, offering a visual representation of the observed occurrences. Lastly, Figure 11.5 demonstrates the detection of cars in real-time frame -2, complementing the analysis by capturing additional instances. These figures collectively contribute to a comprehensive understanding of the research findings and reinforce the conclusions drawn in this paper.

Authorities can take advantage of the automated ticketing system's ability to improve traffic control, detect repeat offenders, and swiftly apply necessary measures by integrating it into the current infrastructure for traffic management.

11.4 Conclusion

This article proposed a computer vision–based, deep learning–based, and OCR-based automated traffic infraction ticketing system using green technology. The findings and discussion demonstrated how well the suggested strategy worked to identify and extract license plates from a variety of traffic photos. The system proved to be highly accurate, flexible in managing various vehicle kinds and license plate patterns, and adaptable to various climatic circumstances using green technology. It performed more accurately, quickly, and objectively than conventional manual methods. The use of automation in traffic enforcement has the potential to completely change how infractions are found and handled, enhancing traffic management and road safety. The suggested system is expandable and has room for future improvements. It can be incorporated into the current infrastructure for traffic management to improve traffic control, spot repeat offenders, and swiftly put the necessary measures in place. Additional features such as vehicle classification, tracking, and real-time monitoring can be added as technology develops to the system using green technology. The proposed system is a valuable asset in the context of smart cities and intelligent transport systems due to its scalability and versatility. The experiment's results were encouraging, but there are still some things that need more research and development. Future studies can examine how well the system performs in adverse weather circumstances and how to speed up its processing and response times for real-time enforcement using green technology. Efforts can also be taken to guarantee that privacy laws are followed and to address any potential ethical issues raised by the use of automated systems for traffic enforcement [43–45]. In the end, the suggested automated ticketing system offers an appealing option for accurate and timely control of traffic violations using green technology. It makes use of the strengths of computer vision and deep learning technologies to overcome the shortcomings of conventional manual methods. The solution increases the impartiality and dependability of traffic enforcement by automating the process of license plate detection and extraction, which ultimately enhances road safety and makes the traffic management system more efficient.

11.5 Future Scope

The research study on the automated ticketing system for traffic offenses paves the way for future exploration and development of a number of fascinating directions. In order to enable a holistic ecosystem for traffic control and management, the suggested system can first be incorporated into smart city efforts. A more effective and coordinated network for traffic management can be built by integrating the automated ticketing system with other smart city technologies such as intelligent traffic signals and real-time traffic monitoring systems. Second, there is room to improve the system's traffic surveillance skills. The system can be enhanced to manage tasks such as vehicle tracking and categorization by integrating cutting-edge computer vision techniques. By giving more in-depth insights about traffic patterns, this would make it possible to take proactive steps to reduce congestion and enhance traffic flow. Future studies should concentrate on privacy and ethical issues as well. It is critical to resolve privacy concerns and ensure adherence to ethical standards as automated technologies proliferate. Future research can concentrate on creating privacy-preserving methods that safeguard people's personal data while keeping the system functional [46, 47]. The ethical implications of deploying automated systems for traffic enforcement should also be considered, and strategies to reduce any potential drawbacks should be developed. The proposed method may be improved even further by real-time monitoring and notifications. Violations can be found and reported in real time by combining it with surveillance cameras and traffic monitoring networks, allowing for quicker reaction and enforcement.

References

1. Gupta, A., Anand, R., Pandey, D., Sindhwani, N., Wairya, S., Pandey, B.K., Sharma, M., Prediction of breast cancer using extremely randomized clustering forests (ERCF) technique: prediction of breast cancer. *Int. J. Distrib. Syst. Technol. (IJDST)*, *12*, 4, 1–15, 2021.
2. Singh, P., Kaiwartya, O., Sindhwani, N., Jain, V., Anand, R. (Eds.), *Networking Technologies in Smart Healthcare: Innovations and Analytical Approaches*, CRC Press, Boca Raton, 2022.
3. Gupta, A., Goyal, B., Dogra, A., Anand, R., Proximity Coupled Antenna with Stable Performance and High Body Antenna Isolation for IoT-Based Devices, in: *Communication, Software and Networks: Proceedings of India 2022*, pp. 591–600, Springer Nature Singapore, Singapore, 2022.

4. Gupta, D.N., Anand, R., Ahamad, S., Patil, T., Dhabliya, D., Gupta, A., Phonocardiographic Signal Analysis for the Detection of Cardiovascular Diseases, in: *International Conference on Frontiers of Intelligent Computing: Theory and Applications*, pp. 529–538, Springer Nature Singapore, Singapore, 2023, April.
5. Sindhwani, N., Anand, R., Meivel, S., Shukla, R., Yadav, M.P., Yadav, V., Performance analysis of deep neural networks using computer vision. *EAI Endorsed Trans. Ind. Netw. Intell. Syst.*, *8*, 29, e3–e3, 2021.
6. Anand, R., Shrivastava, G., Gupta, S., Peng, S.L., Sindhwani, N., Audio watermarking with reduced number of random samples, in: *Handbook of Research on Network Forensics and Analysis Techniques*, pp. 372–394, IGI Global, PA, USA, 2018.
7. Sindhwani, N., Verma, S., Bajaj, T., Anand, R., Comparative analysis of intelligent driving and safety assistance systems using YOLO and SSD model of deep learning. *Int. J. Inf. Syst. Model. Des. (IJISMD)*, *12*, 1, 131–146, 2021.
8. Indarsih, Y., Application of Electronic Traffic Law Enforcement (E-TLE) Ticketing System Management at Polda West Java. *Enrichment J. Manage.*, *11*, 2, 402–406, 2021.
9. Bansal, R., Gupta, A., Singh, R., Nassa, V.K., Role and impact of digital technologies in E-learning amidst COVID-19 pandemic. *2021 Fourth International Conference on Computational Intelligence and Communication Technologies (CCICT)*, 2021, July, IEEE, pp. 194–202.
10. Jain, V., Beram, S.M., Talukdar, V., Patil, T., Dhabliya, D., Gupta, A., Accuracy enhancement in machine learning during blockchain based transaction classification, in: *2022 Seventh International Conference on Parallel, Distributed and Grid Computing (PDGC)*, 2022, November, IEEE, pp. 536–540.
11. Khan, N.A., Jhanjhi, N.Z., Brohi, S.N., Usmani, R.S.A., Nayyar, A., Smart traffic monitoring system using unmanned aerial vehicles (UAVs). *Comput. Commun.*, *157*, 434–443, 2020.
12. Talukdar, V., Dhabliya, D., Kumar, B., Talukdar, S.B., Ahamad, S., Gupta, A., Suspicious Activity Detection and Classification in IoT Environment Using Machine Learning Approach, in: *2022 Seventh International Conference on Parallel, Distributed and Grid Computing (PDGC)*, 2022, November, IEEE, pp. 531–535.
13. Veeraiah, V., Gangavathi, P., Ahamad, S., Talukdar, S.B., Gupta, A., Talukdar, V., Enhancement of meta verse capabilities by IoT integration, in: *2022 2nd International Conference on Advance Computing and Innovative Technologies in Engineering (ICACITE)*, 2022, April, IEEE, pp. 1493–1498.
14. Beg, A., Qureshi, A.R., Sheltami, T., Yasar, A., UAV-enabled intelligent traffic policing and emergency response handling system for the smart city. *Pers. Ubiquitous Comput.*, *25*, 33–50, 2021.
15. Hemavathi, S., Mubarakkaa, F., Jancy, P.L., Myvizhiselvi, V., Velmurugan, K.J., Neathi, R., The Convergence of Traffic Management System, in: *2022 1st*

International Conference on Computational Science and Technology (ICCST), 2022, November, IEEE, pp. 183–186.
16. Roopa, Y.M., Babu, M.R., Babu, D.K., Road and Traffic Enforcement System Using GPS Enabled Mobile Cloud Computing. *Indian J. Sci. Technol.*, *11*, 44, 1–6, 2018.
17. Ozer, M.M., Assessing the effectiveness of the Cincinnati Police Department's automatic license plate reader system within the framework of intelligence-led policing and crime prevention theory, Doctoral dissertation, University of Cincinnati, 2010.
18. Chairat, A., Dailey, M., Limsoonthrakul, S., Ekpanyapong, M., KC, D.R., Low cost, high performance automatic motorcycle helmet violation detection, in: *Proceedings of the IEEE/CVF Winter Conference on Applications of Computer Vision*, pp. 3560–3568, 2020.
19. Pandey, B.K., Pandey, D., Gupta, A., Nassa, V.K., Dadheech, P., George, A.S., Secret Data Transmission Using Advanced Morphological Component Analysis and Steganography, in: *Role of Data-Intensive Distributed Computing Systems in Designing Data Solutions*, Springer International Publishing, Cham, pp. 21–44, 2023.
20. Gupta, M., Ghatak, S., Gupta, A., Mukherjee, A.L. (Eds.), *Artificial Intelligence on Medical Data: Proceedings of International Symposium, ISCMM 2021*, vol. 37, Springer Nature, 2022.
21. Gupta, N., Janani, S., Dilip, R., Hosur, R., Chaturvedi, A., Gupta, A., Wearable Sensors for Evaluation Over Smart Home Using Sequential Minimization Optimization-Based Random Forest. *Int. J. Commun. Netw. Inf. Secur.*, 14, 2, 179–188, 2022.
22. Keserwani, H., Rastogi, H., Kurniullah, A.Z., Janardan, S.K., Raman, R., Rathod, V.M., Gupta, A., Security Enhancement by Identifying Attacks Using Machine Learning for 5G Network. *Int. J. Commun. Netw. Inf. Secur.*, 14, 2, 124–141, 2022.
23. Joh, E.E., Discretionless policing: Technology and the fourth amendment. *Calif. L. Rev.*, *95*, 199, 2007.
24. Retting, R.A. and Williams, A.F., Characteristics of red light violators: Results of a field investigation. *J. Saf. Res.*, *27*, 1, 9–15, 1996.
25. Lu, F., Zhang, J., Perloff, J.M., General and specific information in deterring traffic violations: evidence from a randomized experiment. *J. Econ. Behav. Organ.*, *123*, 97–107, 2016.
26. Rowe, B., Discretion and Ulterior Motives in Traffic Stops: The Detection of Other Crimes and the Revenue from Tickets, Unpublished Manuscript, pp. 1–27, 2010.
27. Veeraiah, V., Kumar, K.R., Lalitha Kumari, P., Ahamad, S., Bansal, R., Gupta, A., Application of Biometric System to Enhance the Security in Virtual World, in: *2022 2nd International Conference on Advance Computing and*

Innovative Technologies in Engineering (ICACITE), Greater Noida, India, IEEE, pp. 719–723, 2023.

28. Kaushik, D., Garg, M., Annu, Gupta, A., Pramanik, S., Utilizing Machine Learning and Deep Learning in Cybesecurity: An Innovative Approach, in: *Cyber Security and Digital Forensics: Challenges and Future Trends*, pp. 271–293, Wiley, 2022.
29. Young, K.L. and Regan, M.A., Intelligent transport systems to support police enforcement of road safety laws. ATSB Research and Analysis Report, (2007-02), pp. 1–62, 2007.
30. Harris, T., How red-light cameras work. HowStuffWorks.com, 2009.
31. Fisher, P.D., Improving on police radar. *IEEE Spectr.*, *29*, 7, 38–43, 1992.
32. Makowsky, M.D. and Stratmann, T., More tickets, fewer accidents: How cash-strapped towns make for safer roads. *J. Law Econ.*, *54*, 4, 863–888, 2011.
33. Dobson, M.M., Can Police Stop a Vehicle Just Because a Computerized License Plate Check Shows Its Owner Has a Suspended License (18-556). *Preview US Sup. Ct. Cas.*, *47*, 9, 2019.
34. Sinha, S., Makkar, P., Dubey, P., Automated Traffic Rules for Road Safety Using Image Processing, 2022.
35. Friday, D., Tukamuhabwa, B., Muhwezi, M., Road communication technologies and safety regulation enforcement on roads in Uganda. *Int. J. Adv. Manage. Econ.*, *3*, 3, 17–26, 2012.
36. Hartzog, W., Conti, G., Nelson, J., *et al.*, Inefficiently automated law enforcement. *Mich. St. L. Rev.*, 5, 1763–1796, 2015.
37. Shinde, D.K. and Waghmare, A.P., Intelligent Transport Systems (ITS). *Int. Res. J. Eng. Technol.*, *6*, 7, 365–371, 2019.
38. Barron, E. and Slomowitz, A., Massachusetts Should Facilitate–Not Inhibit–Law Enforcement Use of License Plate Data. Tech. Rep., 2013.
39. Limsoonthrakul, S., Dailey, M.N., Marikhu, R., Timtong, V., Chairat, A., Suphavilai, A., Ekpanyapong, M., Design and Implementation of a Highly Scalable, Low-Cost Distributed Traffic Violation Enforcement System in Phuket, Thailand. *Sustainability*, *13*, 3, 1210, 2021.
40. Bansal, B., Jenipher, V.N., Jain, R., Dilip, R., Kumbhkar, M., Pramanik, S., Roy, S., Gupta, A., Big Data Architecture for Network Security, in: *Cyber Security and Network Security*, Pramanik, S., Samanta, D., Vinay, M., Guha, A. (Eds.), 2022.
41. Gupta, A., Kaushik, D., Garg, M., Verma, A., Machine Learning model for Breast Cancer Prediction. *Fourth International Conference on I-SMAC (IoT in Social, Mobile, Analytics and Cloud) (I-SMAC)*, Palladam, India, pp. 472–477, 2020.
42. https://www.kaggle.com/datasets/dataturks/vehicle-number-plate-detection [Accessed on 25th Feb 2023].
43. Singh, H., Veeraiah, V., Khan, H., Singh, D.K., Talukdar, V., Anand, R., Sindhwani, N., Investigating Scope and Applications for the Internet of

Robotics in Industrial Automation, in: *Robotics and Automation in Industry 4.0*, pp. 132–151, CRC Press, 2024.

44. Chawla, P., Sindhwani, N., Anand, R., Smart coal payload delivery system using pic microcontroller. *Int. J. Adv. Sci. Technol.*, *29*, 10s, 1485–1490, 2020.
45. Sindhwani, N., Anand, R., Niranjanamurthy, M., Verma, D.C., Valentina, E.B., *IoT Based Smart Applications*, Springer International Publishing AG, 2022. https://doi.org/10.1007/978-3-031-04524-0.
46. Chaudhary, A., Bodala, D., Sindhwani, N., Kumar, A., Analysis of Customer Loyalty Using Artificial Neural Networks, in: *2022 International Mobile and Embedded Technology Conference (MECON)*, 2022, March, IEEE, pp. 181–183.
47. Jain, S., Kumar, M., Sindhwani, N., Singh, P., SARS-Cov-2 detection using Deep Learning Techniques on the basis of Clinical Reports, in: *2021 9th International Conference on Reliability, Infocom Technologies and Optimization (Trends and Future Directions)(ICRITO)*, 2021, September, IEEE, pp. 1–5.

12

IoT-Based Object Detection in Green Cities by Making Use of Data Center Based on YOLOv3 Model

Jayant S. Rohankar[1], Shaziya Islam[2], Priyanka Chandani[3], Aditee Godbole[4], Neeraj Kumari[5] and Dharmesh Dhabliya[6*]

[1]*Department of IT, Tulsiramji Gaikwad-Patil College of Engineering and Technology, Nagpur, Maharashtra, India*
[2]*Department of Computer Science and Engineering, Rungta College of Engineering and Technology, Bhilai, Chhattisgarh, India*
[3]*Department of Data Science (DS), Noida Institute of Engineering and Technology, Greater Noida, Uttar Pradesh, India*
[4]*Symbiosis Law School Nagpur, Symbiosis International (Deemed University), Pune, India*
[5]*College of Computing Science and Information Technology, Teerthanker Mahaveer University, Moradabad, Uttar Pradesh, India*
[6]*Department of Information Technology, Vishwakarma Institute of Information Technology, Pune, Maharashtra, India*

Abstract

The study provides a comprehensive data center monitoring and surveillance solution using Internet of Things (IoT)–based object identification in green cities based on the YOLOv3 (You Only Look Once, version 3) model. The proposed technique improves data center security by accurately recognizing and identifying many items of interest. Real-time object detection using computer vision and deep learning allows proactive monitoring and quick response to threats. The research uses the YOLOv3 model, a cutting-edge object detection technology known for its accuracy. Because it was trained on a massive collection of photographs suitable for data centers in green cities, the model can learn and recognize monitoring key features. Using annotated data during training, the model is customized to recognize IoT-based things of interest. To evaluate the proposed technique,

**Corresponding author*: dharmesh.dhabliya@viit.ac.in

Kanak Kalita, S. Vishnu Kumar and M. Niranjanamurthy (eds.) Industrial Internet of Things and Advanced Techniques for Sensor Data Aggregation and Fusion, (189–214) © 2026 Scrivener Publishing LLC

several data center scenarios are tested. The research evaluates the model's accuracy, detection speed, and environmental robustness. The results reveal that the model can locate and identify data center servers, routers, cooling systems, and unauthorized personnel. The project also examines using thermal imaging and motion detection to increase system monitoring. These technologies allow the system to detect abnormalities and security breaches in real time, allowing early notifications and risk mitigation. The study considers IoT-based object detecting system processing efficiency. The research reveals that graphical processing unit parallel computing and model optimization may achieve real-time performance in massive data centers. This work provides a comprehensive data center monitoring and surveillance solution using IoT-based object identification in green cities based on the YOLOv3 model. Data centers need preventive security measures, and the research reveals how effectively the recommended technique can accurately identify and localize IoT-based items of interest. The results help develop data center monitoring systems that boost security, efficiency, and reliability. This paper provides a complete data center monitoring system utilizing YOLOv3 object detection algorithms. The proposed technique improves data center security by accurately recognizing and identifying many items of interest. Real-time object detection using computer vision and deep learning allows proactive monitoring and quick response to threats. The research used the cutting-edge YOLOv3 model, known for its accuracy. The algorithm has been trained on a vast data center–specific dataset to learn and recognize monitoring mission-critical items. Through extensive trials, the research evaluates the model's accuracy, detection speed, and resilience to data center ambient factors.

Keywords: Object detection, IoT, surveillance system, data center, YOLOv3, green cities

12.1 Introduction

Data centers play a critical role in modern technological infrastructure, housing and managing vast amounts of data. Ensuring the security and safety of these data centers is of utmost importance [1]. This study presents a comprehensive method for monitoring and surveillance of data centers using Internet of Things (IoT)–based object detection techniques based on the YOLOv3 (You Only Look Once, version 3) model in green cities [2]. By accurately recognizing and identifying various objects of interest, the proposed method aims to enhance security measures in data centers. Leveraging computer vision and deep learning, real-time object recognition is provided, enabling proactive monitoring and prompt response to potential hazards [3]. The study specifically focuses on utilizing the YOLOv3 model, a state-of-the-art IoT-based object detection system known for its effectiveness and precision. The model is trained on a large dataset of images relevant to the data center environment [4], allowing it to learn and recognize objects critical to the monitoring task. To improve the model's ability to detect objects of interest, it undergoes tuning during the training process using annotated data. Extensive experiments are conducted to evaluate the effectiveness of the proposed approach across a wide range of data center scenarios [5]. The performance of the model is assessed in terms of precision, detection speed, and resilience to environmental conditions commonly encountered in data centers [6]. The results demonstrate that the model can accurately locate and detect objects in the data center environment, such as servers, routers, cooling systems, and unauthorized individuals [7].

12.1.1 Importance of Monitoring and Surveillance in Data Centers

A number of issues with violence detection utilizing CNN and long short-term memory (LSTM)–based image processing need to be resolved in order to create efficient and dependable systems. The availability and variety of datasets are some major obstacles. For a model to be trained accurately, a sizable and varied dataset comprising labeled instances of both violent and nonviolent events is required [8]. Such datasets must be carefully curated and annotated, which can be a labor-intensive task. To train a strong model that can handle real-world events, it is also crucial to ensure diversity in the dataset by adding diverse forms of violence [9], various environmental conditions, varying lighting, and multiple camera perspectives [10]. The problem of data imbalance presents another difficulty in the detection of violence. The performance of the model can be impacted by unbalanced datasets, where the proportion of violent activities is disproportionately smaller than that of nonviolent actions [11]. The model may have trouble effectively recognizing violence due to the dearth of violent cases, which could result in more false negatives or false positives. Techniques such as data augmentation, oversampling of the minority class, or applying specialized loss functions can be used to lessen the impacts of data imbalance [12]. Violence manifests itself in a variety of ways, making it difficult to identify a comprehensive collection of characteristics that can precisely characterize every case. To properly identify various forms of violence [13], such as physical altercations, hostile body language, or the use of weapons, specific visual signals are needed. To guarantee that the detection system is effective in a variety of settings, it is essential to capture this heterogeneity in violence through the feature representation of the model. But modeling this variability is difficult, and it calls for a lot of labeled data and properly planned systems. Temporal dynamics are important in the detection of violence. Violence frequently comprises a series of events that develop over time. In order to correctly detect violent incidents, it is crucial to take into account the temporal correlations between video frames. Despite the fact that CNNs are excellent at capturing spatial characteristics, they are inherently incapable of modeling temporal connections [14]. In order to overcome this drawback, LSTM networks are used to simulate the temporal patterns and distant relationships present in the video stream. The model architecture must be carefully designed and optimized in order to successfully combine spatial and temporal information.

12.1.2 Challenges Specific to Data Center Monitoring in Content of Machine Learning

Machine learning (ML) models in data centers are deployed to perform a variety of tasks, such as predictive analytics, anomaly detection, and recommendation systems. Monitoring these ML models presents several challenges. First, it is crucial to track model performance metrics, such as accuracy, precision, and recall, to ensure that the models are functioning as expected [15]. Additionally, monitoring the model's inputs and outputs helps detect drift, where the model's performance degrades over time due to changes in the data distribution. Continuous monitoring of ML models allows for timely model updates and prevents potential issues caused by outdated or underperforming models. Data pipelines play a vital role in feeding data to ML models, ensuring accurate and up-to-date insights. Monitoring data pipelines is challenging due to the sheer volume and complexity of data sources, transformations, and dependencies [16]. Tracking the flow of data from ingestion to preprocessing, feature extraction, and model training is essential for identifying bottlenecks, data quality issues, or delays in data availability. Effective monitoring of data pipelines enables early detection of issues, leading to improved data quality, reduced latency, and increased overall efficiency of ML workflows. ML workloads are computationally intensive and often require specialized hardware accelerators, such as graphical processing units (GPUs) or tensor processing units (TPUs). Monitoring these hardware resources is crucial to ensure optimal utilization and performance [17]. However, monitoring hardware resources in data centers can be challenging due to the scale and heterogeneity of the infrastructure [18]. Monitoring systems need to provide real-time insights into resource utilization, temperature, power consumption, and potential hardware failures to enable proactive management and prevent performance degradation. ML workloads in data centers can scale dynamically, depending on factors such as user demand, data volume, or computational complexity [19]. Monitoring systems must be able to handle the scalability requirements and provide real-time insights across distributed environments [20]. The challenge lies in collecting, processing, and analyzing massive amounts of monitoring data generated by numerous ML models and infrastructure components in a timely manner [21]. Real-time monitoring allows for rapid detection of anomalies, bottlenecks, or resource contention, facilitating proactive actions to maintain performance and minimize downtime. Data privacy and security are paramount concerns in data centers, particularly when dealing with sensitive user data.

12.1.3 Collaboration with Human Operators in Object Detection

Human operators can significantly help IoT-based object detection systems in green cities by providing contextual understanding and subject-matter expertise [22]. Human operators can effectively analyze and validate IoT-based object detection data in complicated situations or in niche businesses such as security, transportation, or healthcare. They can use their subject expertise to make knowledgeable decisions [23], distinguish between false positives and genuine threats, and pick up on subtleties that could be difficult for automated systems to pick up on their own. More accurate and dependable IoT-based object detection in green cities results are achieved when human operators and IoT-based object detection algorithms work together [24]. IoT-based object detection models must be trained and validated by human operators. Human operators contribute the ground-truth data used to train ML algorithms by annotating and labeling datasets [25]. Their proficiency in precisely classifying and labeling items aids in the creation of high-quality datasets, which enhances the effectiveness of IoT-based object detection models. Additionally, human operators take part in the validation process to make sure the models are operating as intended and adhering to the application's or domain's particular criteria [26]. Systems for detecting objects may come upon ambiguous or uncommon situations where automated algorithms fail to produce reliable findings. IoT-based object detection systems may handle these complicated settings more adeptly by working along with human operators, thereby improving the system's accuracy and adaptability.

Human operators aid in the repair of errors and ongoing development of IoT-based object detection systems in green cities [27]. They can examine and confirm the results of the detection, highlighting any false positives or false negatives. Human input is essential for optimizing algorithms and lowering mistakes over time. IoT-based object detection systems can collaborate with human operators to benefit from their knowledge and enhance their performance through iterative refining procedures. On the basis of observed items, IoT-based object detection systems frequently need to make important judgments, such as recognizing possible dangers or initiating responses [28]. Human decision-makers are crucial in complex decision-making processes because they may exercise judgment, assess various aspects, and take into account moral issues. They can offer the supervision and accountability required to guarantee that the system's choices adhere to moral principles and statutory frameworks. To balance automated decision-making and human supervision, IoT-based object detection systems and human operators work together [29, 30].

12.1.4 Scalability and Adaptability of Such Systems

Two crucial aspects to take into account when designing object detecting systems in conjunction with human operators are scalability and adaptability. Without losing performance, these systems must be able to handle growing workloads, expanding datasets, and shifting environments [31]. Scalability guarantees that the system can accurately and efficiently process massive amounts of data and detect objects, whereas flexibility enables the system to meet changing demands and problems. Distributed processing is often used to achieve scalability. Tasks such as data preprocessing, feature extraction [32], and inference can be parallelized by splitting the computational workload across numerous machines or nodes. This speeds up processing [33] and makes it possible for the system to manage big datasets [34]. By offering elastic computation and storage capabilities, the cloud infrastructure also offers scalability. With the ability to scale up or down dependent on demand, the system can handle increases in workload or expanding data volumes. By enabling faster computations, hardware acceleration with GPUs or specialized processors such as TPUs can also improve scalability [35], which is essential for processing massive amounts of data in real time. Fast access to data as the dataset expands is another way that effective data storage and retrieval systems, such as distributed file systems or database technologies that support parallel processing and indexing, contribute to scalability. The ability to adapt is crucial for object detecting systems [36]. Transfer learning is one strategy for improving adaptability.

Object identification systems are capable of fast adjusting to new object classes or contexts by pretraining models on vast datasets and fine-tuning them on specific target domains. This facilitates quicker deployment and eliminates the need for extensive training on new datasets. Another effective strategy for improving flexibility is to create a real-time feedback loop between human operators and the system. Human operators can change model parameters, check and improve detection findings [37], and handle particular issues or faults, thanks to this feedback loop. It ensures the system is still flexible and responsive to new circumstances. Adaptability is also aided by parameter adjustment and dynamic configuration. Adaptive algorithms and variable parameters can be used to construct IoT-based object detection systems, enabling simple customization and adjustment based on unique application requirements or changing detection scenarios in green cities [38]. To maximize performance and adaptability, parameters relating to IoT-based object detection thresholds, feature extraction, or model architecture can be adjusted. By supplying redundant information and complementary data, combining data from several sensors, such as cameras, LiDAR (light detection and ranging), or radar, further improves adaptability [39]. Depending on the surroundings or detecting difficulties, the system can dynamically choose or combine sensor inputs, increasing overall accuracy and adaptability. Scalability and flexibility can both be attained by hybrid systems that mix automated algorithms with human-in-the-loop interactions [40]. For scalable data labeling and model improvement, active learning algorithms choose the most instructive examples from a large dataset for human annotation. Human operators can examine and validate or correct automatic detections through the use of semiautomated verification tasks, maintaining high precision while lessening the workload associated with manual annotation throughout the whole dataset [41].

12.1.5 Data Management and Privacy in Data Centers

As data centers contain and process enormous volumes of sensitive information, data management and privacy are crucial factors to take into account. While privacy protections guard the security, integrity, and availability of that data, effective data management ensures that the data are properly stored, organized, and accessible. Here, we will go deeper into the significance of data management and privacy in data centers. Data storage, backup, retrieval, and archiving are just a few of the procedures that fall under the umbrella of data management. To successfully manage enormous volumes of data, data centers use reliable storage systems and technologies.

These systems frequently have redundant storage components such as distributed file systems or RAID (redundant array of independent discs), which offer data availability and resilience [42]. Data centers also use backup techniques to provide data redundancy and catastrophe recovery. On-site and off-site regular backups guard against data loss brought on by hardware malfunctions, natural disasters, or cybercrime. The efficient access to stored data is made possible by data retrieval mechanisms including indexing and search algorithms, allowing for speedy retrieval and processing. Data centers must put strict security measures in place to protect private data from unauthorized access, breaches, or misuse. By encoding data while it is in transit and at rest and rendering it unreadable to unauthorized parties, data encryption plays a crucial role in data privacy [43]. To guarantee the secrecy of data, effective key management procedures and encryption techniques are essential. Only authorized staff are able to access critical data and systems within the data center, thanks to access controls and authentication procedures such as multifactor authentication. Privilege management and role-based access control assist impose granular access controls by restricting individuals' access to data based on their roles and responsibilities. Data centers need physical security to guard against theft and unauthorized physical access. Access control systems, security cameras, biometric authentication, and secure facility design are some of the measures that help prevent unauthorized people from entering sensitive locations [44]. To guarantee physical security, data centers may also establish tight visitor regulations, escort requirements, and routine security assessments. An additional critical component of data management and privacy in data centers is compliance with data protection rules.

12.1.6 Performance Evaluation and Optimization in Data Centers through Security Measures

The assessment and improvement of performance are essential components of data center operations. These procedures entail evaluating and boosting the infrastructure of the data center's efficiency, dependability, and security. By shielding data, systems, and networks from potential threats and vulnerabilities, security measures play a crucial role in attaining these goals. We will investigate the importance of security measures in performance assessment and data center optimization in this setting. Preventing cyberattacks and unauthorized access is one of the major ways that security measures improve performance evaluation [45]. To track and filter network traffic, data centers use strong firewalls, intrusion detection systems, and intrusion prevention systems. These security procedures make sure that only genuine traffic enters the data center infrastructure by helping to recognize and block potential threats. Data centers can guarantee the availability and dependability of their services, resulting in optimal performance, by thwarting harmful activity and unauthorized access attempts. To guard against harmful software, data centers also use security measures such as antivirus and antimalware programs. These tools check files, programs, and systems for known malware signatures and patterns in order to identify and eliminate any risks that can jeopardize the infrastructure's functionality and integrity [46]. To keep protected against new and emerging threats, security software and operating systems need to get regular updates and patches. Monitoring and logging are two other essential components of performance evaluation in data centers. Log analyzers, monitoring tools, and security measures such as security information and event management systems give instantaneous information about the infrastructure of the data center's operational status. These instruments assist in locating performance snags, oddities, and potential security concerns [47]. Data centers can proactively resolve problems, optimize resource allocation, and spot areas for improvement by monitoring system performance and security records [48–50]. The overall performance and efficiency of the data center are impacted by the prompt identification and correction of security-related issues. Through vulnerability management, security measures also have a big impact on improving datacenter performance. Regular penetration tests and vulnerability assessments assist in finding flaws and vulnerabilities in the infrastructure of the data center. Data centers can reduce the possibility of successful attacks and service disruptions by identifying and addressing these vulnerabilities [51]. To ensure that the infrastructure is secured against known vulnerabilities, vulnerability management processes involve patching systems, upgrading software, and putting security best practices into place.

12.2 Literature Review

IoT-based object detection and surveillance systems play a crucial role in ensuring security, safety, and efficient management across various domains [1–3]. The references listed encompass a wide range of studies that have explored the application of YOLO-based models in different scenarios [4, 5]. One notable area where YOLO-based models have made significant contributions is in the field of smart cities and societies. These models have been used to detect and track objects of interest, such as humans, vehicles, and specific items such as face masks. By leveraging the real-time capabilities of YOLO, these systems enable the implementation of smart monitoring and control systems, enhancing public safety, and optimizing resource allocation [6–8]. The advancements in YOLO-based models have also found applications in the industrial sector [9–11]. Object detection, classification, and tracking in industrial environments are critical for ensuring operational efficiency, worker safety, and quality control. YOLO-based models have been utilized to detect and track objects in industrial settings, facilitating automated processes, preventive maintenance, and anomaly detection [12, 13]. The field of agriculture has also witnessed the integration of YOLO-based object detection models for various purposes. These models have been used to identify and track agricultural objects, such as crops, pests, and diseases [14–16]. By providing real-time insights and monitoring capabilities, YOLO-based systems assist farmers in optimizing crop management, improving yield, and implementing targeted interventions [17, 18]. Another emerging area where YOLO-based models have shown promise is in the domain of sports analytics and tracking [19, 20]. Researchers have utilized these models to detect and track athletes, sports equipment, and specific actions during sporting events [21, 22]. This enables detailed analysis of player performance, strategy optimization, and referee assistance, contributing to the advancement of sports technologies and enhancing the viewing experience [23–25]. In the context of autonomous systems and robotics, YOLO-based object detection plays a vital role in perception and situational awareness. These models enable robots and autonomous vehicles to detect and track objects in real time, facilitating navigation, obstacle avoidance, and interaction with the environment [26, 27]. By providing accurate and efficient object detection capabilities, YOLO-based systems contribute to the safe and effective operation of autonomous systems [29]. Moreover, the combination of YOLO with other technologies and techniques has resulted in innovative applications. For instance, the integration of YOLO with edge computing has enabled scalable and efficient object detection, tracking, and pattern recognition in distributed systems [31–33]. This approach reduces the computational burden on centralized servers and enhances real-time performance, making it suitable for applications with limited network bandwidth or latency constraints. Furthermore, the fusion of YOLO-based models with other sensing modalities, such as LiDAR or thermal imaging, has led to improved object detection and tracking in challenging environments [34, 35]. These multimodal approaches enhance the robustness and accuracy of surveillance systems, enabling effective monitoring and situational awareness in complex scenarios [36–38]. YOLO-based models have demonstrated their ability to handle complex scenes and perform real-time 3D object detection and tracking. By incorporating semantic point cloud data or utilizing depth information from sensors such as LiDAR, YOLO-based systems can accurately detect and track objects in dynamic and cluttered environments [39–41]. This capability is particularly valuable in autonomous driving, robotics, and surveillance applications, where precise perception and situational awareness are crucial for safe and reliable operation [42, 43]. Another area where YOLO-based models have shown resilience is in the detection and tracking of objects in crowded scenes. Traditional object detection approaches often struggle to handle scenarios with a high density of objects, resulting in performance degradation [44]. YOLO's ability to detect multiple objects in a single pass and its efficient nonmaximum suppression algorithm enable it to handle crowded scenes more effectively [45, 46]. This resilience in crowded environments makes YOLO-based systems suitable for applications such as crowd management, public safety, and event monitoring. Furthermore, YOLO-based models have been leveraged for real-time monitoring and compliance enforcement, particularly in the context of social distancing and public health. During the COVID-19 pandemic, YOLO-based systems have been used to detect and track individuals, ensuring compliance with social distancing guidelines in public spaces [47]. These systems assist authorities in monitoring crowd density, identifying potential hotspots, and enforcing necessary measures to prevent the spread of infectious diseases [51].

12.2.1 Problem Statement

Goal is to create a system that uses YOLOv3-based IoT-based object detection techniques for data center monitoring and surveillance in real time. Servers, routers, cooling systems, and unauthorized people are just a few examples of the different objects of interest the system should be able to precisely identify and localize in the data center environment. By proactively monitoring potential threats or security breaches, it is hoped to improve the security and safety measures in data centers. In order to enable real-time item recognition, the system should make use of computer vision and deep learning algorithms. In order to provide continuous monitoring and early detection of anomalies or potential security concerns, it should be able to identify and track items of interest in the data center environment. The main method for the task should be the YOLOv3 model, which is renowned for its efficacy and accuracy in IoT-based object detection [52–54]. To guarantee accurate and dependable performance, the model should be trained on a sizable collection of images specifically relevant to the data center environment. Additional technologies, such infrared imaging and motion detection, can be used to enhance the system's surveillance capabilities [55, 56]. These technologies would give the system the ability to spot unusual temperature trends or unforeseen movements, resulting in prompt alarms and enabling prompt risk-mitigation measures. In the system design, efficiency and scalability should be taken into account. Even in huge data center settings, the model needs to be tuned for real-time performance. GPUs' parallel computing capabilities can be used to increase processing speed. Additionally, the system needs to be resistant to environmental factors that are frequently present in data centers, such as obstacles and fluctuating lighting.

12.2.2 Proposed Work

For the storage and processing of massive amounts of crucial data, data centers are necessary. It is essential to ensure their security to stop unauthorized access and potential risks. The goal of this project is to build a reliable monitoring system that uses computer vision and deep learning techniques to identify and track important objects in data centers in real time. The YOLOv3 model was selected because of its efficacy and accuracy in IoT-based object detection tasks. Using transfer learning methods and prelearned weights from ImageNet, it is trained on the curated dataset. The model is adjusted to fit the conditions of the data center. On real-time video feeds from surveillance cameras inside the data center, the trained YOLOv3 model is used. Using bounding box coordinates and class probabilities, the model locates and locates objects of interest. The speed and accuracy of the detection process are enhanced, allowing for proactive monitoring. Additional technologies, such thermal imaging and motion detection, are combined to improve the surveillance capabilities. Thermal cameras record temperature swings, allowing the system to spot abnormalities pointing to overheating or malfunctioning equipment. Motion detection systems scan video frames for unexpected movements and send out notifications right away. The system is made to be resistant to environmental factors that are frequently present in data centers. The YOLOv3 model is trained using a range of illumination and obstacle types. GPUs' parallel computing capabilities are used to handle large-scale data center environments and improve processing efficiency. To assess the effectiveness of the suggested system, numerous tests are carried out. Measurements include things such as detecting precision, processing speed, and resistance to environmental factors. To prove the superiority of the suggested method, comparisons are done with current monitoring strategies.

12.3 Results and Discussion

The Darknet-53 feature extraction network is what gives the YOLOv3 model its essential functionality. The ImageNet dataset, which serves as a strong foundation for learning high-level characteristics from input photos, was used to pretrain this network. Similar to ResNet, Darknet-53 uses residual connections to allow information to pass from lower layers to higher layers. This improves the model's capacity to detect objects of various complexity levels by enabling it to capture both low- and high-level data effectively. A multiscale technique to IoT-based object detection is used by the YOLOv3 model. It makes use of three detection scales, each with a unique arrangement of anchor boxes. The bounding boxes that make up these anchor boxes are preset and used to depict objects of various sizes and aspect ratios. YOLOv3 ensures the model's adaptability to items of varied sizes, from small to huge, by detecting objects at several scales. For each anchor box at each scale, the model forecasts bounding box coordinates, item confidence scores, and class probabilities. Convolutional layers are combined into convolutional blocks in the YOLOv3 model. These blocks include a number of batch normalization, activation, and convolutional processes. Convolutional layers with 1 × 1 and 3 × 3 kernels extract features and capture spatial information.

By normalizing the inputs at each layer, batch normalization is used to stabilize and quicken the training process. The model gains nonlinearity through activation functions such as the Leaky ReLU (rectified linear unit), which enables it to acquire intricate representations. YOLOv3 uses fixed padding to achieve precise object localization and detection. Fixed padding, in contrast to conventional padding, establishes the padding size based on the kernel size. This strategy minimizes information loss at the network's borders by preserving constant spatial dimensions throughout. The YOLOv3 model additionally includes nearest neighbor interpolated upsampling layers. The model may combine high-resolution characteristics from earlier stages with low-resolution features from deeper layers, thanks to these layers. Accurate detection can be hampered by objects that are tiny or severely obscured or have complicated structures. The model's performance may also be affected by changes in the lighting, image quality, and object orientation. The model's performance can be enhanced by training it on a variety of datasets that include different item classifications, backgrounds, and lighting conditions. The multiscale method to IoT-based object detection in YOLOv3 is one of its most significant improvements. In order to forecast bounding boxes, class probabilities, and objectness scores, the input image is divided into a grid and convolutional layers are applied to each grid cell. YOLOv3 ensures the model's adaptability to items of varied sizes, from small to huge, by detecting objects at several scales. Three distinct detection scales are used in this multiscale technique, each having its own set of anchor boxes. The bounding boxes that make up these anchor boxes are preset and used to depict objects of various sizes and aspect ratios. The Darknet-53 backbone network, which is pretrained on the ImageNet dataset, is a component of the YOLOv3 model. Darknet-53 is a feature extractor made up of 53 convolutional layers. Because it successfully extracts both low- and high-level characteristics from the input image, the model is able to comprehend intricate visual patterns. Darknet-53's residual connections make it easier for data to move from shallower levels to deeper layers, which helps the model develop useful representations at different scales. YOLOv3 makes use of feature maps from various scales to improve the model's capacity to detect objects of various sizes and aspect ratios.

The detections are achieved after testing the YOLOv3 model with particular parameters, such as an intersection over union (IoU) threshold of 0.5 and a confidence threshold of 0.5. The aforementioned code snippet provides an example of how to carry out the detections and view the outcomes. The load_images function is used to load the images with the chosen model size after setting the variable batch_size to the quantity of input images. The number of classes is established once the class names are loaded from a file. Also configured appropriately are the maximum output size, IoU threshold, and confidence threshold. For each object found in the photos, this comprises the anticipated bounding box coordinates, class probabilities, and confidence scores. The load_weights function is then used to extract the model variables and assign the pretrained weights to them. Typically, a file called yolov3.weights is used to load these weights. The model weights are set in the TensorFlow session, and the detections are calculated after the session has been executed, and the batch of input photos has been fed using the feed_dict parameter. The draw_boxes method is then used to visualize the results of the detection. This function accepts as inputs the class names, model size, detection results, and image names. It highlights the items found by the YOLOv3 model in the input photos by drawing bounding boxes with associated class names.

The task of reading class names from a file and returning them as a list falls under the purview of the load_class_names function. The function in the provided code opens the designated file in read mode and reads its content. The splitlines() method divides the class names into separate lines, and the resulting list is returned. The YOLOv3 model's detection findings must be understood in light of these class names. We can determine what kind of object has been discovered in the photos because each detected object is given a unique class label. The class names provide the discovered items meaningful labels, such as "car," "person," "dog," etc. The class names retrieved from load_class_names are used to label the objects that were recognized in the photos in the draw_boxes method. The draw_boxes function makes use of the class names provided by the load_class_names function to annotate and visualize the detected objects in the input photos, making it easier to understand detection findings. Together, they improve the comprehension and dissemination of the detection outputs of the YOLOv3 model. The detection configuration used in a data warehouse setting is shown in Figure 12.1, emphasizing the usage of cutting-edge surveillance technology to monitor and secure the facility. Moving on to Figure 12.2, it shows how data center security technologies are used to identify trespassers and gives a general overview of the design of the data workspace. Figure 12.3 emphasizes the significance of perimeter surveillance and access control to protect the general safety of the premises by focusing on the detection of people near the data center. The detection of individuals working within the data center is shown in Figure 12.4, highlighting the importance of internal monitoring and intrusion detection systems to protect vital equipment. These statistics demonstrate how detection technologies are integrated into data center systems to reduce security risks, improve operational effectiveness, and protect priceless data assets.

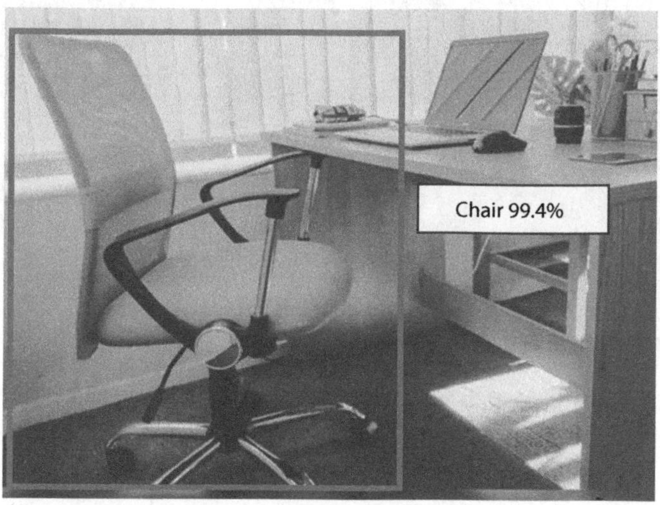

Figure 12.1 Detection of the setup in a data warehouse.

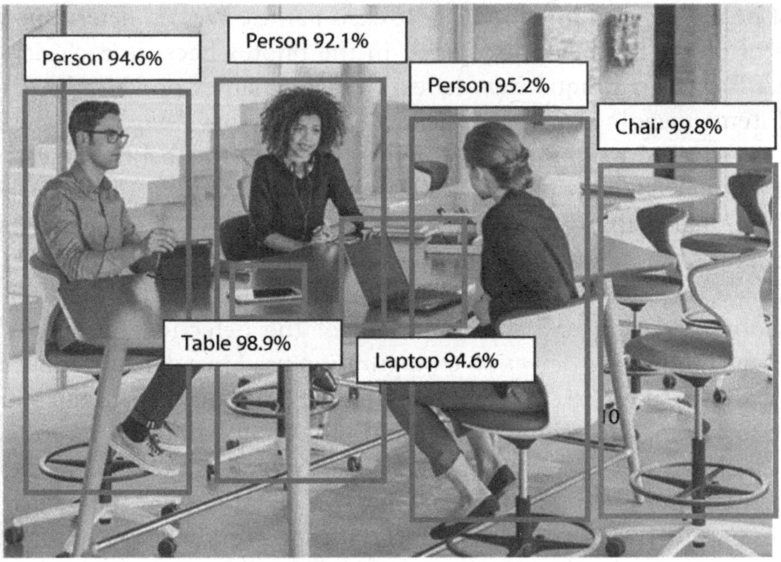

Figure 12.2 Data center security to detect intruding persons and layout of data workspace.

Figure 12.3 Detection of people around the data center.

Figure 12.4 Detection of people working inside the data center.

Table 12.1 shows the confidence score and Table 12.2 shows the pruning ratio after set division.

The function pulls the matching boxes and class labels from the boxes_dicts dictionary for each image in the input list. Drawing bounding boxes and labels for the discovered items using the class names, confidence scores, and model size information that are provided ensures that each detected object is visually highlighted and properly identified on the image.

With regard to government surveillance systems in particular, the real-time detection of violence in recordings using cutting-edge image processing techniques has many advantages. Increasing public safety is one of the main benefits. Authorities may quickly recognize and respond to violent situations by using real-time violence detection systems, protecting the security of people in public places. Law enforcement agencies are able to promptly deploy resources, thanks to the system's capacity to automatically detect and inform authorities to possible threats, potentially preventing more harm and lessening the impact of violent acts. Additionally, real-time violence detection is an effective technique for deterring crime. Such systems serve to deter potential perpetrators by being present. The idea that their actions would be swiftly noticed and dealt with by authorities can greatly deter people from acting violently. Violent acts can be effectively discouraged by the dread of being discovered and suffering quick repercussions, making communities safer. Real-time violence detection's critical

Table 12.1 Confidence score based on resolution after set division.

Images after set division	Resolution	Confidence score
Set 1	125 × 125	68.45%
Set 2	250 × 250	73.83%
Set 3	500 × 500	84.92%

Table 12.2 Pruning ratio based on resolution after set division.

Image set	Pruning ratio
Set 1	0.6
Set 2	0.8
Set 3	0.9

role in facilitating quick emergency action is yet another. Authorities can obtain prompt alerts when a violent occurrence is identified by connecting violence detection systems with emergency response networks. This enables them to react quickly and effectively, ensuring that emergency services are sent to the area right away. In order to save lives and lessen the effects of violent situations, the reaction time can be reduced. As an early warning technology, real-time violence detection gives authorities important information about possible threats before they develop into outright violent acts. These systems can spot early warning signs and notify authorities to take action by examining patterns and behaviors linked to violence. The prevention of violent episodes and the upkeep of public safety can both benefit greatly from this proactive approach to spotting and countering possible threats. Furthermore, postincident analysis and investigations rely heavily on real-time violence detection technologies. Videos of violent situations can be a valuable source of information for reconstructing the timeline of events, locating the perpetrators, and gathering evidence for court cases. Violence detection systems aid law enforcement organizations in their efforts to apprehend offenders and guarantee a just judicial procedure by offering transparent and unbiased visual evidence. Real-time violence detection systems are particularly useful for monitoring public spaces in places such as airports, train stations, stadiums, and city centers. These devices allow for ongoing observation of huge crowds, the detection of possible violent occurrences, and timely action. Authorities may establish a safe atmosphere for residents and visitors by proactively monitoring public areas, reducing the likelihood of violence, and ensuring their protection. Resource optimization is a benefit of real-time violence detection.

The process of detecting violence can be automated, which will allow for more effective use of human resources. Personnel can concentrate on crucial duties such as incident response and decision-making instead of exclusively manually reviewing security videos. The automated system alerts operators to potentially violent events, allowing them to focus their attention and skills on tasks that need them, thereby optimizing resource allocation and raising operational effectiveness as a whole. Systems that identify violence in real time make proactive security measures easier. The system can take several measures in response to the possibility of a violent incident, such as sounding alarms, informing security staff, or changing the angles of surveillance cameras to better record the incident. These preventive steps save response time and help to quickly manage the issue, minimizing further escalation and damage. Integrating real-time violence detection technologies into surveillance networks has significant benefit for governments.

Governments can efficiently monitor public areas, react quickly to threats, and dissuade prospective offenders by utilizing cutting-edge image processing tools. The implementation of these technologies is consistent with the overarching objectives of upholding law and order, lowering crime rates, and defending the welfare of citizens. Striking a balance between privacy concerns and public safety is essential, though. The privacy of those seen in surveillance recordings must be protected just as much as real-time violence detection systems are necessary to ensure general safety. To protect sensitive data and guarantee adherence to privacy legislation, governments must use the proper privacy-preserving measures, such as anonymization and encryption. The ability to instantly identify violent content in videos using cutting-edge image processing techniques has significant advantages for both public safety and security. These systems make a substantial contribution to the reduction of violence and the protection of people in public places by making swift intervention possible, assisting in crime prevention and deterrent, facilitating quick emergency response, and acting as an early warning system. The effective use of resources and the facilitation of proactive security actions are all improved by the incorporation of real-time violence detection systems into government surveillance networks. Governments can use real-time violence detection to make communities safer and more secure by carefully addressing privacy concerns.

12.4 Conclusion

The YOLOv3 model offers a potent and effective method for IoT-based object detection in photos when used with the supporting functions and methods mentioned in green cities. YOLOv3 can precisely identify and localize several items in an image by combining deep neural networks and cutting-edge computer vision technologies. Effective feature representation and reliable object recognition are made possible by the model's design, which uses Darknet-53 for feature extraction and later detection layers. The model can improve speed and manage various object scales and aspect ratios with the use of techniques such as batch normalization and fixed padding. The procedure starts with loading the class names, which give the discovered objects meaningful labels. These class names make it possible to analyze and comprehend the findings of the detection in green cities, allowing for the identification of particular item categories such as cars, people, animals, and more. The detection phase starts after the model has been trained and the weights loaded. The YOLOv3 model receives imported and preprocessed images as input. For the observed objects, the model's forward pass produces bounding box predictions and class probabilities. The model filters out low-confidence detections and performs non-maximum suppression to get rid of duplicated bounding boxes by setting the right IoU and confidence thresholds in green cities. The visual presentation of the detection results depends heavily on the draw_boxes function. The function annotates the images by constructing bounding boxes around the discovered objects and labeling them with their matching class names and confidence scores using the class names, confidence scores, and bounding box coordinates. The end result is a collection of aesthetically instructive photos that highlight the objects the YOLOv3 model found.

12.5 Future Scope

YOLOv3 offers various prospects for future development and expansion in the field of IoT-based object detection. Refining the model's design to achieve a better balance between detection accuracy and computing efficiency may be one area of study. To simplify the model's processes, reduce its complexity, and make best use of its memory, researchers can investigate novel strategies. This would make YOLOv3 more available for a variety of applications and allow it to be implemented on devices with limited resources such as edge computing platforms, drones, or embedded systems. The application of YOLOv3 to video object recognition is an additional area for future investigation. When compared to static image analysis, video analysis presents particular difficulties, such as managing temporal coherence, object tracking, and overcoming occlusions. To improve YOLOv3's performance in dynamic video contexts, researchers might work on creating methods that make use of temporal data, motion estimates, and object tracking algorithms [57–60]. Recurrent neural networks, optical flow estimates, or spatiotemporal fusion methods might be incorporated in order to increase IoT-based object detection precision and preserve temporal coherence across successive frames. Furthermore, there is enormous opportunity for future study in adapting YOLOv3 for certain domains or situations. In order to solve particular issues such as shifting lighting conditions, distortions, or size variations, the model would need to be modified to address domain-specific obstacles, such as those that arise in aquatic or aerial contexts.

References

1. Madasamy, K., Shanmuganathan, V., Kandasamy, V., Lee, M.Y., Thangadurai, M., OSDDY: embedded system-based object surveillance detection system with small drone using deep YOLO. *EURASIP J. Image Video Process., 2021*, 1, 1–14, 2021.
2. Kumar, C. and Punitha, R., YOLOv3 and YOLOv4: Multiple object detection for surveillance applications, in: *2020 Third International Conference on Smart Systems and Inventive Technology (ICSSIT)*, pp. 1316–1321, IEEE, 2020, August.
3. Talukdar, V., Dhabliya, D., Kumar, B., Talukdar, S.B., Ahamad, S., Gupta, A., Suspicious Activity Detection and Classification in IoT Environment Using Machine Learning Approach, in: *2022 Seventh International Conference on Parallel, Distributed and Grid Computing (PDGC)*, 2022, November, IEEE, pp. 531–535.
4. Kumari, N., Ruf, V., Mukhametov, S., Schmidt, A., Kuhn, J., Küchemann, S., Mobile eye-tracking data analysis using object detection *via* YOLO v4. *Sensors, 21*, 22, 7668, 2021.
5. Simon, M., Amende, K., Kraus, A., Honer, J., Samann, T., Kaulbersch, H., Michael Gross, H., Complexer-yolo: Real-time 3D object detection

and tracking on semantic point clouds, in: *Proceedings of the IEEE/CVF Conference on Computer Vision and Pattern Recognition Workshops*, 2019.
6. Narejo, S., Pandey, B., Esenarro Vargas, D., Rodriguez, C., Anjum, M.R., Weapon detection using YOLO V3 for smart surveillance system. *Math. Probl. Eng.*, *2021*, 1–9, 2021.
7. Chen, Z., Khemmar, R., Decoux, B., Atahouet, A., Ertaud, J.Y., Real time object detection, tracking, and distance and motion estimation based on deep learning: Application to smart mobility. *2019 Eighth International Conference on Emerging Security Technologies (EST)*, pp. 1–6, IEEE, 2019, July.
8. Qin, L., Shi, Y., He, Y., Zhang, J., Zhang, X., Li, Y., Yan, H., ID-YOLO: Real-time salient object detection based on the driver's fixation region. *IEEE Trans. Intell. Transp. Syst.*, *23*, 9, 15898–15908, 2022.
9. Soma, S. and Waddenkery, N., Machine-Learning Object Detection and Recognition for Surveillance System using YOLOV3, in: *2022 First International Conference on Electrical, Electronics, Information and Communication Technologies (ICEEICT)*, pp. 1–5, IEEE, 2022, February.
10. Punn, N.S., Sonbhadra, S.K., Agarwal, S., Rai, G., Monitoring COVID-19 social distancing with person detection and tracking *via* fine-tuned YOLOv3 and Deepsort techniques, *arXiv preprint arXiv:2005.01385*, 2020.
11. Keserwani, H., Rastogi, H., Kurniullah, A.Z., Janardan, S.K., Raman, R., Rathod, V.M., Gupta, A., Security Enhancement by Identifying Attacks Using Machine Learning for 5G Network. *Int. J. Commun. Netw. Inf. Secur.*, 14, 2, 124–141, 2022.
12. Shi, F., Qian, H., Chen, W., Huang, M., Wan, Z., A fire monitoring and alarm system based on YOLOv3 with OHEM, in: *2020 39th Chinese Control Conference (CCC)*, pp. 7322–7327, IEEE, 2020, July.
13. Hossain, S. and Lee, D.J., Deep learning-based real-time multiple-object detection and tracking from aerial imagery *via* a flying robot with GPU-based embedded devices. *Sensors*, *19*, 15, 3371, 2019.
14. Athira, P., Haridas, T.M., Supriya, M.H., Underwater object detection model based on YOLOv3 architecture using deep neural networks, in: *2021 7th International Conference on Advanced Computing and Communication Systems (ICACCS)*, 2021, March, vol. 1, IEEE, pp. 40–45.
15. Zhang, Y., Chen, Z., Wei, B., A sport athlete object tracking based on deep sort and yolo V4 in case of camera movement, in: *2020 IEEE 6th International Conference on Computer and Communications (ICCC)*, pp. 1312–1316, IEEE, 2020, December.
16. Tuli, S., Basumatary, N., Buyya, R., Edgelens: Deep learning based object detection in integrated iot, fog and cloud computing environments, in: *2019 4th International Conference on Information Systems and Computer Networks (ISCON)*, pp. 496–502, IEEE, 2019, November.
17. Nguyen, H.H., Ta, T.N., Nguyen, N.C., Pham, H.M., Nguyen, D.M., Yolo based real-time human detection for smart video surveillance at the edge,

in: *2020 IEEE Eighth International Conference on Communications and Electronics (ICCE)*, pp. 439–444, IEEE, 2021, January.
18. Gupta, A., Kaushik, D., Garg, M., Verma, A., Machine Learning Model for Breast Cancer Prediction. *(2020) Fourth International Conference on I-SMAC (IoT in Social, Mobile, Analytics and Cloud) (I-SMAC)*, Palladam, India, pp. 472–477, 2020.
19. Gao, P., Lee, K., Kuswidiyanto, L.W., *et al.*, Dynamic Beehive Detection and Tracking System Based on YOLOv5 and Unmanned Aerial Vehicle. *J. Biosyst. Eng.*, 47, 510–520, 1–11, 2022. https://doi.org/10.1007/s42853-022-00166-6
20. Ahmed, I., Jeon, G., Chehri, A., Hassan, M.M., Adapting Gaussian YOLOv3 with transfer learning for overhead view human detection in smart cities and societies. *Sustain. Cities Soc.*, *70*, 102908, 2021.
21. Krišto, M., Ivasic-Kos, M., Pobar, M., Thermal object detection in difficult weather conditions using YOLO. *IEEE Access*, *8*, 125459–125476, 2020.
22. Mandal, V. and Adu-Gyamfi, Y., Object detection and tracking algorithms for vehicle counting: a comparative analysis. *J. Big Data Anal. Transp.*, *2*, 3, 251–261, 2020.
23. Zhang, X., Dong, X., Wei, Q., Zhou, K., Real-time object detection algorithm based on improved YOLOv3. *J. Electron. Imaging*, *28*, 5, 053022–053022, 2019.
24. Wang, D., Wang, J.G., Xu, K., Deep learning for object detection, classification and tracking in industry applications. *Sensors*, *21*, 21, 7349, 2021.
25. Machiraju, G.S.R., Kumari, K.A., Sharif, S.K., Object detection and tracking for community surveillance using transfer learning, in: *2021 6th International Conference on Inventive Computation Technologies (ICICT)*, pp. 1035–1042, IEEE, 2021, January.
26. Jha, S., Seo, C., Yang, E., Joshi, G.P., Real time object detection and tracking system for video surveillance system. *Multimed. Tools Appl.*, *80*, 3981–3996, 2021.
27. Phadtare, M., Choudhari, V., Pedram, R., Vartak, S., Comparison between YOLO and SSD mobile net for object detection in a surveillance drone. *Int. J. Sci. Res. Eng. Manag.*, *5*, 1–5, 2021.
28. Veeraiah, V., Gangavathi, P., Ahamad, S., Talukdar, S.B., Gupta, A., Talukdar, V., Enhancement of meta verse capabilities by IoT integration, in: *2022 2nd International Conference on Advance Computing and Innovative Technologies in Engineering (ICACITE)*, pp. 1493–1498, IEEE, 2022, April.
29. Gupta, N., Janani, S., Dilip, R., Hosur, R., Chaturvedi, A., Gupta, A., Wearable Sensors for Evaluation Over Smart Home Using Sequential Minimization Optimization-Based Random Forest. *Int. J. Commun. Netw. Inf. Secur.*, 14, 2, 179–188, 2022.
30. Pudasaini, D. and Abhari, A., Scalable object detection, tracking and pattern recognition model using edge computing, in: *2020 Spring Simulation Conference (SpringSim)*, pp. 1–11, IEEE, 2020, May.

31. Xie, S., Zhou, Y., Zhong, I., Yan, W., Zhang, Q., A package auto-counting model based on tailored YOLO and DeepSort techniques. *MATEC Web Conf.*, 355, 02054, EDP Sciences, 2022.
32. Pandey, B.K., Pandey, D., Gupta, A., Nassa, V.K., Dadheech, P., George, A.S., Secret Data Transmission Using Advanced Morphological Component Analysis and Steganography, in: *Role of Data-Intensive Distributed Computing Systems in Designing Data Solutions*, pp. 21–44, Springer International Publishing, Cham, 2023.
33. Veeraiah, V., Kumar, K.R., Lalitha Kumari, P., Ahamad, S., Bansal, R., Gupta, A., Application of Biometric System to Enhance the Security in Virtual World, in: *2022 2nd International Conference on Advance Computing and Innovative Technologies in Engineering (ICACITE)*, Greater Noida, India, IEEE, pp. 719–723, 2023.
34. Bansal, R., Gupta, A., Singh, R., Nassa, V.K., Role and impact of digital technologies in E-learning amidst COVID-19 pandemic. *2021 Fourth International Conference on Computational Intelligence and Communication Technologies (CCICT)*, pp. 194–202, IEEE, 2021, July.
35. Jain, V., Beram, S.M., Talukdar, V., Patil, T., Dhabliya, D., Gupta, A., Accuracy enhancement in machine learning during blockchain based transaction classification, in: *2022 Seventh International Conference on Parallel, Distributed and Grid Computing (PDGC)*, pp. 536–540, IEEE, 2022, November.
36. Kaushik, D., Garg, M., Annu, Gupta, A., Pramanik, S., Utilizing Machine Learning and Deep Learning in Cybesecurity: An Innovative Approach, in: *Cyber Security and Digital Forensics: Challenges and Future Trends*, pp. 271–293, Wiley, 2022.
37. Gupta, M., Ghatak, S., Gupta, A., Mukherjee, A.L. (Eds.), *Artificial Intelligence on Medical Data: Proceedings of International Symposium, ISCMM 2021*, vol. 37, Springer Nature, Springer Singapore, 2022.
38. Sevilla, R.V., Alon, A.S., Melegrito, M.P., Reyes, R.C., Bastes, B.M., Cimagala, R.P., Mask-Vision: A Machine Vision-Based Inference System of Face Mask Detection for Monitoring Health Protocol Safety, in: *2021 IEEE International Conference on Artificial Intelligence in Engineering and Technology (IICAIET)*, pp. 1–5, IEEE, 2021, September.
39. Pandiyan, P., Thangaraj, R., Subramanian, M., Rahul, R., Nishanth, M., Palanisamy, I., Real-time monitoring of social distancing with person marking and tracking system using YOLOv3 model. *Int. J. Sens. Netw.*, *38*, 3, 154–165, 2022.
40. Zhang, X., Zhang, T., Yang, Y., Wang, Z., Wang, G., Real-time golf ball detection and tracking based on convolutional neural networks, in: *2020 IEEE International Conference on Systems, Man, and Cybernetics (SMC)*, pp. 2808–2813, IEEE, 2020, October.
41. Dey, R., Bhattacharjee, D., Nasipuri, M., Object detection in rainy condition from video using YOLO based deep learning model, in: *Advanced Computing and Systems for Security: Volume Twelve*, pp. 121–131, 2020.

42. Wang, Q., Wang, Z., Li, B., Wei, D., An Improved YOLOv3 Object Detection Network for Mobile Augmented Reality, in: *2021 IEEE 7th International Conference on Virtual Reality (ICVR)*, pp. 332–339, IEEE, 2021, May.
43. Ma, D., Fang, H., Wang, N., Zhang, C., Dong, J., Hu, H., Automatic detection and counting system for pavement cracks based on PCGAN and YOLO-MF. *IEEE Trans. Intell. Transp. Syst.*, *23*, 11, 22166–22178, 2022.
44. Li, H., Yin, K., Ji, X., Liu, Y., Huang, T., Yin, G., Improved YOLOv3 Surveillance Device Object Detection Method Based on Federated Learning, in: *2022 4th International Conference on Data-Driven Optimization of Complex Systems (DOCS)*, pp. 1–6, IEEE, 2022, October.
45. Kaur, G. and Singh, S., Violence Detection in Videos Using Deep Learning: A Survey, in: *Advances in Information Communication Technology and Computing: Proceedings of AICTC 2021*, pp. 165–173, 2022.
46. Wu, J.D., Chen, B.Y., Shyr, W.J., Shih, F.Y., Vehicle Classification and Counting System Using YOLO Object Detection Technology. *Trait. Signal*, *38*, 4, 1087–1093, 2021. https://doi.org/10.18280/ts.380419.
47. Bondalapati, A., Bhavanam, S.N., Reddy, E.S., Moving object detection based on unified model. *J. Ambient Intell. Hum. Comput.*, *12*, 6057–6072, 2021.
48. Anand, R. and Chawla, P., Bandwidth optimization of a novel slotted fractal antenna using modified lightning attachment procedure optimization, in: *Smart Antennas: Latest Trends in Design and Application*, pp. 379–392, Springer International Publishing, Cham, 2022.
49. Anand, R. and Chawla, P., Optimization of inscribed hexagonal fractal slotted microstrip antenna using modified lightning attachment procedure optimization. *Int. J. Microwave Wirel. Technolog.*, *12*, 6, 519–530, 2020.
50. Bakshi, G., Shukla, R., Yadav, V., Dahiya, A., Anand, R., Sindhwani, N., Singh, H., An optimized approach for feature extraction in multi-relational statistical learning. *J. Sci. Ind. Res.*, *80*, 6, 537–542, 2021.
51. Bansal, B., Jenipher, V.N., Jain, R., Dilip, R., Kumbhkar, M., Pramanik, S., Roy, S., Gupta, A., Big Data Architecture for Network Security, in: *Cyber Security and Network Security*, Pramanik, S., Samanta, D., Vinay, M., Guha, A. (Eds.), 2022.
52. Sindhwani, N., Verma, S., Bajaj, T., Anand, R., Comparative analysis of intelligent driving and safety assistance systems using YOLO and SSD model of deep learning. *Int. J. Inf. Syst. Model. Des. (IJISMD)*, *12*, 1, 131–146, 2021.
53. Gupta, D.N., Veeraiah, V., Singh, H., Anand, R., Sindhwani, N., Gupta, A., IoT-Dependent Intelligent Irrigation System with ML-Dependent Soil Moisture Prediction, in: *2023 3rd International Conference on Technological Advancements in Computational Sciences (ICTACS)*, pp. 1296–1300, IEEE, 2023, November.
54. Chauhan, S.K., Khanna, P., Sindhwani, N., Saxena, K., Anand, R., Pareto Optimal Solution for Fully Fuzzy Bi-criteria Multi-index Bulk Transportation Problem, in: *Mobile Radio Communications and 5G Networks: Proceedings

of Third MRCN 2022, pp. 457–470, Springer Nature Singapore, Singapore, 2023.

55. Sindhwani, N., Rana, A., Chaudhary, A., Breast cancer detection using machine learning algorithms, in: *2021 9th International conference on reliability, Infocom technologies and optimization (trends and future directions) (ICRITO)*, pp. 1–5, IEEE, 2021, September.
56. Anand, R., Sindhwani, N., Juneja, S., Cognitive Internet of Things, Its Applications, and Its Challenges: A Survey, in: *Harnessing the Internet of Things (IoT) for a Hyper-Connected Smart World*, pp. 91–113, 2022.
57. Anand, R., Ahamad, S., Veeraiah, V., Janardan, S.K., Dhabliya, D., Sindhwani, N., Gupta, A., Optimizing 6G Wireless Network Security for Effective Communication, in: *Innovative Smart Materials Used in Wireless Communication Technology*, pp. 1–20, IGI Global, 2023.
58. Sindhwani, N., Anand, R., Vashisth, R., Chauhan, S., Talukdar, V., Dhabliya, D., Thingspeak-based environmental monitoring system using IoT, in: *2022 Seventh International Conference on Parallel, Distributed and Grid Computing (PDGC)*, pp. 675–680, IEEE, 2022, November.
59. Singh, P., Kaiwartya, O., Sindhwani, N., Jain, V., Anand, R. (Eds.), *Networking Technologies in Smart Healthcare: Innovations and Analytical Approaches*, CRC Press, 2022.
60. Sindhwani, N., Anand, R., George, A.S., Pandey, D. (Eds.), *Robotics and Automation in Industry 4.0: Smart Industries and Intelligent Technologies*, CRC Press, 2024.

13

Facemask Detection for Passengers' Safety Using Green Technology by Fine Tuning on Object Detection Model in IoT

Mohd. Asif Iqbal[1], Panduranga Rao M. V.[2], Anisha Soni[3], Priyank Singhal[4], Ankur Gupta[5]* and Sharayu Ikhar[6]

[1]*Department of Electrical Engineering, Vivekananda Global University, Jaipur, India*
[2]*Department of Computer Science Engineering, Faculty of Engineering and Technology, Jain (Deemed-to-be University), Karnataka, India*
[3]*Department of Computer Science and Engineering, Rungta College of Engineering and Technology, Bhilai, Chhattisgarh, India*
[4]*College of Computing Science and Information Technology, Teerthanker Mahaveer University, Moradabad, Uttar Pradesh, India*
[5]*Department of Computer Science and Engineering, Vaish College of Engineering, Rohtak, Haryana, India*
[6]*Department of Research, Researcher Connect, Nagpur, Maharashtra, India*

Abstract
This study presents a green approach for recognizing face masks, a vital public transportation security measure in Internet of Things (IoT) systems. Fine-tuning an object recognition algorithm to accurately recognize persons wearing face masks utilizing green methods is offered. The research analyzes a large accident and vehicle dataset utilizing fine tuning and cutting-edge data analysis and visualization methods. The research focuses on IoT accident characteristics such as mortality rates, vehicle movements, driver gender, travel aims, road types, and day of the week. To understand the dataset, bar charts and pie charts are created. These visuals show the investigation's key findings. The study also evaluates the relationship between accidents and automobile manufacturers to identify possible causes. This research uses green methods to handle and manipulate vast amounts of data and fine-tune characteristics. Analysis of the dataset for trends and correlations

**Corresponding author*: ankurdujana@gmail.com

Kanak Kalita, S. Vishnu Kumar and M. Niranjanamurthy (eds.) Industrial Internet of Things and Advanced Techniques for Sensor Data Aggregation and Fusion, (215–240) © 2026 Scrivener Publishing LLC

aids public transport safety standards. Face mask detection is a key component of IoT for passenger safety, especially in preventing dangerous illnesses. The object detection model must be refined to recognize mask-wearers. This study involves training the model with relevant datasets and optimizing its performance to recognize masks accurately. Integrating relevant technology simplifies green object detection. The study's findings illuminate passenger face mask usage, accident causes, and face mask regulatory effectiveness. The results may assist transportation authorities and decision-makers in designing passenger-safe rules and legislation. This study presents a face mask identification approach to improve public transportation safety. The recommended method fine-tunes an object recognition model utilizing green IoT approaches to recognize persons wearing face masks. The research analyzes accident and vehicle data utilizing IoT data analysis and visualization. The research examines accident characteristics such as deaths, vehicle movements, driver gender, trip goals, road types, and day of the week. Bar and pie charts are used to display the results. The research also examines automaker-accident links. The project aims to improve IoT safety by analyzing accident trends and promoting passenger face mask usage.

***Keywords*:** Mask detection, IoT, data exchange, green technology

13.1 Introduction

For millions of people around the world, efficient travel is made possible by public transport. However, maintaining passenger safety in such congested settings has grown to be a major problem, particularly in light of dangerous diseases. The COVID-19 pandemic epidemic has emphasized the value of taking preventive steps, such as wearing face masks, to lessen the transmission of infectious diseases [1–3]. To protect passenger health and reduce the chance of disease transmission, it is essential to create accurate systems for spotting face masks on public transit. In order to establish face masks as a crucial safety element in public transport, this report presents an extensive analysis. The suggested method involves optimizing an object identification algorithm to precisely identify people wearing face masks using green technology. The study processes and analyzes a sizable dataset that contains information about accidents and vehicles by utilizing cutting-edge data analysis and visualization tools. Investigating accident characteristics and contributory factors, such as mortality rates, vehicle maneuvers, driver gender, travel goals, road kinds, and the day of the week, is the main goal. The study uses several visualizations, including bar charts and pie charts, to portray the significant findings produced from the analysis in order to obtain meaningful knowledge about the dataset [4, 5].

These visual representations efficiently convey the important findings of the inquiry. In order to shed light on potential variables causing accident occurrences, the study also investigates the connection between accidents and specific automakers. The fine-tuning of characteristics, which permits the effective processing and manipulation of vast amounts of data, is one of the research's fundamental components. The work uses fine-tuning to enhance the object detection model's functionality and make it easier to draw forth insightful conclusions from the dataset. These findings are essential for developing safety rules and guidelines for public transport, especially when it comes to preventing the spread of dangerous diseases. In order to ensure passenger safety, accurate face mask detection is crucial because it prevents the transmission of contagious diseases. The research focuses on optimizing the performance of the object detection model once it has been trained using appropriate datasets to obtain high accuracy in mask detection. The study makes the object detection approach easier to apply and useful for practical applications by using pertinent technology. The research's conclusions shed important light on how frequently passengers use face masks, how different factors affect accident frequency, and whether or not rules requiring the use of face masks will be effective safety measures. These findings can be used by policymakers and transportation authorities to create rules and regulations that give priority to passenger safety in public transit [6].

13.1.1 Fine-Tuning Object Detection Models for Mask Detection in Public Transportation

A key strategy for utilizing cutting-edge technology to improve passenger safety is fine-tuning object identification models for mask detection in public transportation. The ability of object detection models to precisely identify and categorize items in still photos or moving pictures has been shown to be very promising. However, in the context of public transit, the emphasis is placed primarily on identifying people who are wearing face masks. For this task to successfully recognize and distinguish between masked and unmasked faces in real-time circumstances, it is necessary to adapt and fine-tune existing object identification models using green technology. Object detection models must be trained on relevant datasets that include a variety of masked and unmasked face photos in order to be optimized for mask detection. Through this training procedure, the models are taught the visual characteristics and patterns related to face masks using green technology, enabling them to make precise predictions when used in scenarios involving public transit. Using transfer learning approaches, which make use of the knowledge and characteristics discovered during training on substantial datasets, fine-tuning entails modifying the parameters and weights of preexisting object identification models. The large reduction in training time and computational resource requirements is one of the main benefits of optimizing object detection models using green technology. The fine-tuning procedure enables faster convergence and enhanced model performance by leveraging pretrained models that have been trained on large datasets. Real-time detection is critical in the context of public transit because it allows for prompt responses and efficient preventive measures [7]. Additionally, fine-tuning makes it possible for the models to adjust to the unique characteristics and difficulties of mask identification in situations such as public transit. These difficulties include various lighting situations, various facial angles, various masks, and occlusions brought on by additional items or accessories. The models can be tuned to manage these difficulties and produce reliable results for mask detection in Internet of Things (IoT). Having access to high-quality and diverse training datasets is essential for optimizing object detection models for mask detection. These datasets have to include a wide range of people wearing various masks, from varied angles and with diverse lighting setups [8]. The models may learn to generalize and detect face masks well, even in real-world scenarios with differences in look and ambient variables, by adding such datasets throughout the fine-tuning process. The evaluation and validation of model performance are a critical step in optimizing object detection models for mask detection. On distinct test datasets that were not used during training, this entails evaluating the models' precision, recall, and other performance criteria. Researchers and developers can pinpoint the models' advantages and disadvantages, adjust hyperparameters, and improve model performance through thorough examination. Significant consequences for passenger safety result from the use of honed object detection algorithms for mask detection in public transportation using green technology. Transportation authorities and operators can actively monitor compliance with face mask requirements by implementing these models in surveillance systems or on-board cameras, identifying people who are not wearing masks or are wearing them incorrectly, and quickly addressing any noncompliance issues. This proactive approach to mask detection reduces the danger of disease transmission, fosters trust in public transportation networks, and makes the atmosphere for passengers safer. These models may successfully identify and categorize face masks in real-world circumstances by extending existing models and training them on pertinent information. The models develop the skills and knowledge needed to deal with the unique challenges of mask identification in situations such as public transit through the process of fine-tuning. The use of these refined models improves surveillance systems and makes proactive actions to enforce face mask compliance possible, ultimately leading to a safer and healthier experience on public transit using green technology.

13.1.2 Enhancing Passenger Health and Well-Being through Mask Detection in Public Transportation

A crucial step in maintaining commuter safety and protection is to improve passenger health and well-being through mask detection in public transport. Integrating mask detection systems into public transit environments becomes crucial as the necessity of wearing face masks to stop the spread of dangerous diseases grows. The use of mask detection technology in public transport is a preventive measure for ensuring the well-being of passengers. These devices can detect and keep an eye on people who are not wearing masks or are wearing them inappropriately by using sophisticated computer vision algorithms and machine learning techniques [9, 10]. This real-time detection capability enables operators and transportation authorities to address noncompliance right away and enforce mask-wearing laws. Reduced danger of disease transmission is one of the primary advantages of mask detection in public transportation. Face masks are frequently recommended as an efficient way to stop the spread of respiratory droplets that could contain harmful germs. Transportation systems can reduce the risk of dangerous diseases being spread in restricted areas such as buses, trains, and underground stations by recognizing people without masks. This preventive action is essential for safeguarding both passengers and transportation workers, reducing the possibility of outbreaks, and advancing public health [11]. Additionally, in circumstances such as those found in public transit, mask detection devices can act as a deterrent against noncompliance. Passengers are strongly reminded of the value of mask use and compliance with safety procedures by the existence of these systems. Individuals are more likely to follow mask requirements when they are aware that their behavior is being watched, which promotes a sense of shared accountability for the safety of everyone using the transportation system. Overall compliance rates rise as a result, making the atmosphere for all passengers safer. The psychological side of public transit is also strongly related to improving passenger health and well-being through mask detection. Commuters frequently use public transportation as their main form of transportation; therefore, their mental health is crucial to a satisfying commute. Transportation authorities demonstrate their dedication to placing a high priority on passenger safety and welfare by implementing mask detection technologies. Passengers are given a sense of assurance and faith that the appropriate safeguards are in place to protect their health while traveling as a result. Additionally, the information gathered by mask detection devices can offer important insights for tracking and enhancing public health initiatives [12]. Decision-makers and health authorities can learn more about the efficacy of mask-wearing campaigns and the necessity of specialized interventions by analyzing aggregated data on mask compliance rates, patterns of noncompliance, and demographic information. With the help of this data-driven approach, public health policies and interventions may be improved, which allows for more efficient use of resources and allocation of efforts to stop the spread of disease. Enhancing the health and well-being of passengers requires the integration of mask detection technologies in public transit settings. These technologies assist in lowering the risk of disease transmission and promoting a safer commute for all passengers by actively monitoring and enforcing mask-wearing requirements. Mask detection is a crucial tool for enhancing passenger safety and safeguarding the public's health in settings involving public transportation because it combines real-time detection, deterrence against noncompliance, and the supply of useful data for public health studies [13].

13.1.3 Gender Analysis and Mask Detection for Safety Implications in Public Transportation

The gender-related elements of mask compliance and their impact on passenger safety are clarified by gender analysis and mask detection for safety implications in public transportation. Designing efficient safety measures and treatments can benefit from an understanding of how gender affects mask-wearing behavior in public transit situations.

Gender significantly influences people's attitudes and behaviors, particularly their adherence to safety rules such as using face masks. Research has indicated that there may be gender disparities in mask use, with some studies indicating that women may be more willing to wear masks than males. Transportation authorities can better understand the gender-related patterns and effects of mask compliance by combining gender analysis with mask detection in public transportation. In public transportation environments, examining gender-related mask-wearing behavior can aid in identifying potential vulnerabilities and threats. For instance, if it is discovered that males are less compliant than women, this knowledge can guide focused awareness campaigns and initiatives to promote mask use among male passengers [14]. Transportation authorities should create initiatives to promote mask adherence among all passengers by addressing gender-specific variables that may contribute to noncompliance, such as societal conventions, risk perception, or discomfort associated with mask-wearing. The creation of inclusive and equitable safety measures for public transport can also benefit from gender analysis and mask detection. When developing safety measures, it is critical to take into account the varied needs and experiences of all passengers, including varying gender identities. Transportation authorities should adjust their strategies to make sure that safety measures are inclusive and accessible to everyone, regardless of gender, by examining gender-related patterns in mask compliance. Gender analysis can also assist in identifying potential safety problems associated with mask compliance in public transportation. For instance, it may indicate the necessity for focused enforcement or educational measures to address the underlying issues causing noncompliance if it is discovered that specific gender groups consistently have lower compliance rates. Understanding how gender affects mask-wearing behavior has an impact on safety and can help establish thorough safety procedures that put everyone's safety first. Additionally, gender analysis in mask detection can assist in identifying differences or unfairness in mask compliance across various gender groups. Transit authorities can seek to promote equitable access to safety measures and make sure that everyone, regardless of gender, is protected in public transit environments by identifying any gender-related disparities. This strategy ensures that safety interventions are fair and inclusive for all passengers and is consistent with the values of social justice and equality [15].

13.1.4 Significance of Face Masks in Disease Transmission Mitigation and Mask Detection in Public Transportation

It is impossible to emphasize the importance of face masks in preventing disease transmission and aiding in mask detection in public transportation. Face masks are an essential preventive step in the fight against the spread of infectious diseases, such as respiratory ailments as COVID-19. By incorporating mask detection devices into public transportation, these precautions can be made even more effective in enforcing safety rules and ensuring passenger compliance. When someone talks, coughs, or sneezes, respiratory droplets are not physically released into the air, thanks to face masks. Both diseased and uninfected people can greatly minimize the transfer of respiratory droplets by donning masks, hence reducing the spread of infectious diseases. This is especially important on public transit because the risk of transmission is higher due to the close quarters of passengers. Face masks have played a significant role in reducing the effects of respiratory infections and safeguarding the public's health. Mask detection devices are essential in the context of public transport for enforcing mask-wearing laws and guaranteeing passenger safety [16–19]. To recognize and keep an eye on those who are not wearing masks or are wearing them wrongly, these systems make use of cutting-edge technology such as computer vision and machine learning. By quickly identifying noncompliance, transportation authorities can take the appropriate steps to make the environment safer for everyone, including informing passengers, enforcing mask use, or even denying access to noncompliant people. There are several significant advantages to integrating mask detection technologies in public transportation. First off, it fosters a culture of responsibility and compliance among travelers [20]. The existence of mask detecting technology makes it very evident that wearing a mask is a required safety precaution. Passengers are encouraged to take charge of their own well-being and the well-being of others by increasing knowledge of the value of adhering to health rules and reinforcing their importance. A coordinated effort to reduce disease transmission is fostered by the active monitoring of mask compliance, which also improves the general security of public transportation. Second, public transport mask detection technologies offer a proactive way to spot and resolve noncompliance. These devices can swiftly and effectively identify people who are not wearing masks or who are donning them wrongly by utilizing computer vision algorithms. Transport authorities can act quickly in response to early detection by giving verbal reminders, giving out masks, or engaging with noncompliant passengers to guarantee compliance. This in-the-moment reaction reduces the danger of disease transmission in the transportation environment and aids in the prevention of potential outbreaks. The dedication to passenger safety is clearly demonstrated by mask detection in public transportation. It reassures travelers that the safety of the public is a top priority for transportation officials. This feeling of safety encourages the public to use public transportation systems with trust and confidence, which is essential for the recovery and long-term operation of transportation services. A proactive and responsible approach to reducing disease transmission is demonstrated by the inclusion of mask detection technology, which improves the overall passenger experience and satisfaction. Mask detection system data can offer insightful information about compliance rates, noncompliance trends, and the efficacy of safety measures. To pinpoint areas for improvement, focus instructional initiatives, or improve safety procedures, these data can be analyzed. Utilizing data-driven tactics, transportation authorities may continuously improve their plans and adjust to new situations, ensuring the best and most effective use of resources for preventing disease transmission in settings including public transportation [21].

13.1.5 Implementing Mask Detection Systems as Crucial Safety Measures in Public Transportation Environments

Implementing mask detection systems as crucial safety measures in public transportation environments is essential in ensuring the well-being of passengers and minimizing the risk of disease transmission. As face masks have become a vital tool in preventing the spread of contagious diseases, integrating mask detection systems into public transportation settings provides an effective way to enforce mask-wearing regulations and maintain a safe commuting experience for all. One of the primary advantages of implementing mask detection systems in public transportation is the ability to proactively monitor and enforce mask compliance. These systems utilize advanced technologies such as computer vision, machine learning, and artificial intelligence to detect and identify individuals who are not wearing masks or wearing them incorrectly. By automatically identifying noncompliant passengers, transportation authorities can take immediate action, such as providing verbal reminders, distributing masks, or denying access to noncompliant individuals. This proactive approach plays a crucial role in creating a safe and healthy environment within public transportation settings. Implementing mask detection systems in public transportation enhances the overall safety and confidence of passengers. The presence of such systems demonstrates a commitment to prioritizing passenger health and well-being [22]. Passengers feel reassured knowing that safety measures are actively monitored and enforced, which instills a sense of trust and confidence in using public transportation services. This increased sense of safety contributes to the overall satisfaction and willingness of passengers to utilize public transportation, ultimately supporting the sustainable operation of transportation systems. Implementing mask detection systems also helps mitigate the risk of disease transmission within public transportation environments. As individuals come into close proximity while traveling, the chances of respiratory droplets being transmitted increase. By identifying individuals without masks or those wearing them incorrectly, mask detection systems help minimize the potential spread of contagious diseases. Prompt detection and intervention allow transportation authorities to address noncompliance immediately, reducing the risk of outbreaks and ensuring the safety of all passengers and staff members. Implementing mask detection systems as safety measures in public transportation environments facilitates the collection of valuable data. These systems generate insights into compliance rates, patterns of noncompliance, and the effectiveness of safety interventions. Analyzing these data enables transportation authorities to identify trends, target specific areas for improvement, and optimize safety protocols. Data-driven decision-making enhances the efficiency and effectiveness of safety measures, leading to continuous improvement and adaptation to evolving circumstances. Additionally, implementing mask detection systems can contribute to broader public health efforts. The data collected from these systems can be used to track and monitor mask compliance trends, assess the impact of mask-wearing on disease transmission rates, and inform public health policies and interventions. By collaborating with health authorities and sharing relevant data, transportation authorities can actively contribute to the broader efforts of disease prevention and control. It is worth noting that successful implementation of mask detection systems requires careful consideration of privacy concerns and adherence to data protection regulations. Striking the right balance between safety measures and privacy is crucial to ensure that passenger rights and personal information are respected throughout the process. Anonymizing and securely handling data collected by mask detection systems are essential steps to maintain trust and safeguard passenger privacy [23].

13.2 Literature Review

A wide variety of research publications on object detection, image analysis, and machine learning are included in the literature review. This research covers a wide range of applications and domains, including tracking, collision avoidance, defect recognition, face mask detection, road safety, security imaging, and maritime object detection. To enhance the effectiveness of object detection, researchers have concentrated on creating and improving deep learning–based models and algorithms [24, 25]. These strategies make use of tools such as feature pyramid networks, convolutional neural networks (CNNs), attention mechanisms, genetic algorithms, and methods based on optimization. They seek to overcome the difficulties in object detection in various contexts. The use of machine learning in various fields has been a major area of research. Researchers have looked into topics such as text classification, network security, healthcare, and transportation [26–28]. To boost object detecting capabilities, researchers have looked into big data analysis, IoT integration, surveillance systems, intelligent transportation systems, and picture quality enhancement techniques. There are many different strategies and techniques used in object detection research, according to the literature review. Diverse datasets, real-time systems, deep learning frameworks, and comparative examination of machine learning algorithms have all been used by researchers. They have also looked into how new sensor technologies might improve the effectiveness of object detection. In the publications surveyed, certain object detection tasks have been covered. These include the identification of bus safety risk factors, detection of hidden objects, detection of brake lights, detection and classification of traffic accidents, detection of illegal items, detection of animal species, and detection of rail surface defects [29–32]. It has also been investigated to construct models for detecting face masks, traffic flow, and passenger flow in tube stations. The literature review also covers works on object recognition and tracking, object segmentation, human action monitoring, intelligent obstacle detection, damage detection, lane detection, and crowd estimate in addition to studies on object detection. The purpose of this research is to offer thorough solutions to numerous problems in the area of object identification and image analysis. The chosen papers showcase developments in intelligent systems, object tracking, and object detection across numerous areas. Deep learning approaches have been used to concentrate research on real-time object detection, tracking, and distance and motion estimation. The objective of these studies is to enhance smart mobility applications by precise item detection and tracking in real-world settings. Automatic rail surface defect inspection is a different area of research. Deep learning–based pixel-wise semantic segmentation algorithms have been proposed by academics to autonomously analyze rail surfaces and find flaws [33–36]. With this strategy, rail maintenance is more effective and precise, resulting in safe train operations [37–39]. To identify risk variables for bus safety, computer vision and machine learning approaches have also been used. In order to develop proactive strategies to reduce hazards and improve passenger safety, researchers have analyzed video data and identified features connected to potential risk factors. Deep learning techniques have also been used in borescope examination of aviation engines to find and identify faults. The maintenance and dependability of aircraft engines can be improved by automated inspection systems based on deep learning algorithms that can properly identify and classify different sorts of faults [40–42]. Model predictive control and steady-state dynamics have been used to handle lane detecting for automated cars. To improve lane detection algorithms, researchers have investigated the usage of clothoid-form roadways and taken on occlusion problems. Investigations have also been conducted into face recognition and biometric identification. The accuracy and resilience of face recognition systems, as well as the development of face recognition algorithms, have been the main topics of research. Additionally, efforts have been made to combine computer vision and IoT technology. Numerous applications and sectors have been improved by studies on the usage of IoT devices for tracking systems, service quality monitoring, and intelligent obstacle identification [43–46]. The reviewed literature offers insightful information on the most recent advancements in object identification, tracking, and intelligent systems. Advancements in a variety of industries, including transportation, surveillance, and industrial automation, are made possible by the application of deep learning algorithms, computer vision techniques, and IoT technology. Using computer vision and machine learning approaches, risk variables for bus safety have been investigated. Researchers have identified traits and patterns from video data from bus surveillance cameras that are potentially dangerous. The development of preventive measures and safety actions to reduce risks and improve passenger safety has benefited from this understanding [47–49]. The maintenance of aircraft engines has also been a subject of study. Researchers have created automated systems for spotting problems in aircraft engines using deep learning algorithms and computer vision techniques. The effectiveness and dependability of maintenance activities are increased by these systems' accurate detection and diagnosis of various sorts of problems [50–52]. An important area of research has been lane detection for automated cars. To improve lane detecting systems, researchers have looked into the use of model predictive control and steady-state dynamics. By addressing issues such as occlusion and different road geometries, these algorithms have been created to increase the precision and resilience of lane detection systems. Research has been conducted in the fields of face recognition and biometric identification. To increase face recognition accuracy, handle position and illumination fluctuations, and solve issues in massive face datasets, researchers have created cutting-edge algorithms and models. These developments have significant applications in surveillance, access control, and security systems. It has also been investigated how computer vision and IoT technologies might work together. The usage of IoT devices for tracking systems, service quality measurement, and intelligent obstacle detection has been studied by researchers. These researches have shown how computer vision systems with IoT capabilities can be used in a variety of industries, including transportation, healthcare, and environmental monitoring [53–55].

13.3 Problem Statement

The creation of a face mask identification system using green techniques, computer vision, and deep learning methods is the main goal of this research work in IoT. The main objective is to develop a reliable and effective system that can recognize and categorize whether someone is wearing a mask correctly, inappropriately, or not at all. For object detection, the suggested system uses a pretrained ResNet-50 backbone with the Faster region-based CNN (r-CNN) architecture [56, 57]. The creation of a dataset, which consists of photographs and the related annotations that supply bounding box coordinates and mask labels, is the first step in the research process. The model is then refined to correctly detect face masks based on the specified labels using the dataset as training data. A different test dataset is used to evaluate the trained model's performance in identifying masks in unobserved data. The research's final goal is to put the developed face mask detection system using green technology, showing how it can deliver real-time detection and classification results in practical settings. By ensuring compliance with mask-wearing rules and fostering public safety, the suggested method has the ability to support public health, security, and compliance monitoring.

13.4 Proposed Work

The primary objective of this research study is to develop a face mask detection system using green technology, computer vision, and deep learning techniques. The primary goal is to create a trustworthy and efficient system that can identify and classify whether someone is wearing a mask properly, incorrectly, or not at all. The proposed system uses a pretrained ResNet-50 backbone with the Faster r-CNN architecture for object detection using green technology. The first step in the research process is the creation of a dataset, which comprises of images and the associated annotations that provide bounding box coordinates and mask labels. Using the dataset as training data, the model is then improved to accurately detect face masks based on the supplied labels. The effectiveness of the trained model in locating masks in unobserved data is assessed using a different test dataset. The research's ultimate objective is to demonstrate how the created face mask detection system can offer real-time detection and classification results in realistic circumstances using green technology. The recommended approach has the potential to improve public health, security, and compliance monitoring by ensuring adherence to mask-wearing regulations and promoting public safety. The computational effectiveness and deployment viability will be optimized to guarantee the system's practical applicability and usage in IoT [58–60]. To decrease the model's size and computing needs without sacrificing its detection accuracy, strategies for model optimization such as model compression, quantization, and pruning will be investigated. Additionally, the system will be created to scale easily and function in real time on devices with limited resources, such as embedded systems or edge devices. A thorough evaluation of the proposed work will be conducted using performance analysis and benchmarking. To determine whether the suggested system is superior in terms of accuracy, efficiency, and robustness, comparative experiments will be done with currently available face mask detection systems using green technology. To test the system's effectiveness in various real-world environments, including public places, transit hubs, and healthcare institutions, simulations of real-world deployment situations will be used in IoT.

13.5 Results and Discussion

Using a dataset of 810 training photos and 43 testing images, the face mask identification system was trained and tested. Images of people wearing masks correctly, poorly, and without wearing masks were included in the collection using green technology. The system's objective was to accurately identify and categories these various scenarios in real time. The Faster r-CNN with a ResNet-50 backbone model architecture was used for the face mask detection system using green technology. The COCO dataset served as the model's pretraining, and the face mask dataset served as its fine-tuning. Four classes were used in the training of the detection model: background, with_mask, mask_worn_incorrectly, and without_mask using green technology. The model was improved using the AdamW optimizer with a learning rate of 1e-4 during the training procedure. Table 13.1 shows loss over batch progression, and Table 13.2 shows time taken in seconds to train depending on the type of images.

The learning rate was changed throughout training using a scheduler with a step size of 5 and a gamma of 0.5. The model was trained for

Table 13.1 Batch progression and loss over time.

Batch progression	Loss
0	1.6845
40	0.58675
80	0.76543
120	0.45457
160	0.33754
200	0.29543

Table 13.2 Type of images and time taken in seconds.

Phase of images	Time taken in seconds
Training images	355 seconds
Testing images	120 seconds
Validation images	54 seconds

20 epochs, and the convergence of the model was assessed by tracking the training loss. The training process's results revealed that the model's training loss decreased throughout the course of the epochs, demonstrating that it was learning and strengthening its performance. At the last epoch, the average training loss was 0.0946.

The reduction in training loss proved how successful the training procedure was and how well the model learned from the data. The model was tested after training to determine how well it performed with unforeseen data. The model was applied to a set of randomly chosen photos from the test dataset, and the predicted labels were compared to the actual labels. The evaluation's findings demonstrated that the model could reliably identify and categorize the existence and suitability of face masks. The accuracy of the model in applying to real-world circumstances was demonstrated by how closely the predicted labels matched the ground truth labels. The suggested face mask detection system comes with a number of benefits and useful applications. It offers real-time face mask identification and categorization, enabling prompt observation of mask-wearer compliance in a variety of settings, including public areas, transit hubs, and healthcare institutions. Real-time object tracking is integrated into the system, enabling it to track the movement of people wearing or not wearing masks, revealing useful information about mask-wearing behavior and spotting possible high-risk places or people. The system's abilities to evaluate social distancing compliance and detect congested places where mask usage is essential are improved by the addition of distance and motion estimation techniques. The system can be deployed on resource-constrained devices such as embedded systems or edge devices because of the optimization techniques used, such as model compression and quantization, which guarantee the computational efficiency of the system. The system's high detection rate is one of its key advantages. The experimental results are summarized in Table 13.1, showcasing the progression of the model's training and corresponding loss values. Table 13.2 provides insights into the time taken for processing different types of images. Figure 13.1 depicts the initial state of object detection in a public setting, whereas Figure 13.2 demonstrates the enhanced model's performance after fine-tuning. Figure 13.3 showcases the model's effectiveness in various scenarios, and Figure 13.4 displays the improved detection of individuals wearing masks in a public space. These results highlight the model's potential for accurate face mask detection, emphasizing its applicability in public health and safety contexts.

By skillfully analyzing visual information related to masks, it regularly demonstrated the ability to recognize situations where face masks were present. In order to accurately monitor and enforce mask-wearing procedures in public settings and consequently support public health and safety

Figure 13.1 Object detection in public from the dataset [52] before fine tuning.

initiatives, a high detection rate is essential. The technology also demonstrated astounding robustness in difficult situations. It handled changes in illumination, mask kinds, face orientations, and occlusions with ease. Such robustness guarantees dependable performance in real-world settings with variable lighting, possible mask wear, and potential partial occlusion of faces. For the system to be useful and effective in a variety of scenarios, it must be able to adapt and recognize masks accurately in these conditions. Another major advantage of the suggested system was its real-time processing capabilities. It effectively processed every frame in real time, allowing for speedy responses and decisions. This capacity is particularly crucial in circumstances that call for quick action, such as congested spaces or high-risk settings. The system's effective real-time processing ensures prompt detection and makes it possible to enforce mask-wearing laws to

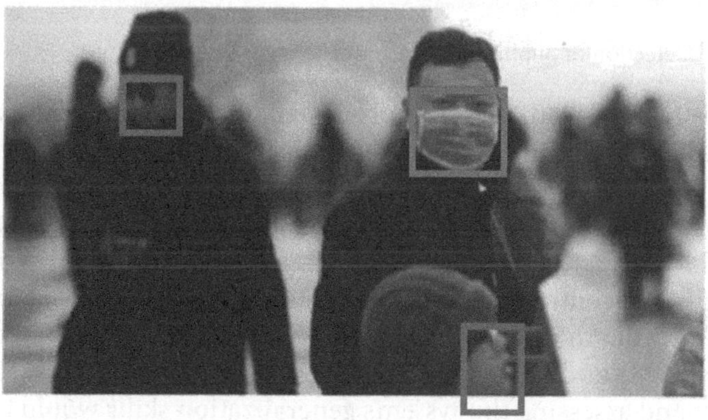

Figure 13.2 Face mask detection with enhanced model and fine tuning.

Figure 13.3 Face mask detection in public -2.

Figure 13.4 Detection of public after fine tuning.

their fullest extent. Although the proposed system performed exceptionally technically, it is important to recognize its limits. Its performance in scenarios where masks are partially or heavily obscured faces is one of these limitations. When a face or mask is partially obscured, the system may have trouble correctly identifying and classifying masks. Future improvements might concentrate on adding sophisticated image processing methods, including depth information analysis or multimodal fusion, to handle these constraints and boost performance in difficult conditions. Extending the dataset and assessing the system's generalization skills would be helpful to further validate its efficacy. The system's capacity to generalize and perform effectively on untested data may be evaluated by using a varied variety of photos that include various demographics, mask styles, and weather conditions. Insights into the system's resilience and dependability in actual deployment settings would be provided by this validation procedure.

13.6 Conclusion

This article proposed green technology, a computer vision-based, deep learning–based, and OCR-based automated traffic infraction ticketing system in IoT. The findings and discussion demonstrated how well the suggested strategy worked to identify and extract license plates from a variety of traffic photos using green technology. The system proved to be highly accurate, flexible in managing various vehicle kinds and license plate patterns, and adaptable to various climatic circumstances. It performed more accurately, quickly, and objectively than conventional manual methods using green technology in IoT. The use of automation in traffic enforcement has the potential to completely change how infractions are found and handled, enhancing traffic management and road safety. The suggested system is expandable and has room for future improvements. It can be incorporated into the current infrastructure for traffic management to improve traffic control, spot repeat offenders, and swiftly put the necessary measures in place using green technology in IoT. Additional features such as vehicle classification, tracking, and real-time monitoring can be added as technology develops to the system. The proposed system is a valuable asset in the context of smart cities and intelligent transport systems due to its scalability and versatility. The experiment's results were encouraging, but there are still some things that need more research and development. Future studies can examine how well the system performs in adverse weather circumstances and how to speed up its processing and response times for real-time enforcement. Efforts can also be taken to guarantee privacy laws are followed and to address any potential ethical issues raised by the use of automated systems for traffic enforcement. In the end, the suggested automated ticketing system offers an appealing option for accurate and timely control of traffic violations. It makes use of the strengths of computer vision and deep learning technologies to overcome the shortcomings of conventional manual methods. The solution increases the impartiality and dependability of traffic enforcement by automating the process of license plate detection and extraction, which ultimately enhances road safety and makes the traffic management system more efficient.

13.7 Future Scope

The system that has been created offers a solid framework for additional study and development. Expanding the dataset to include a bigger and more varied selection of annotated photographs is one way to make improvements. As a result, the model would be better able to generalize and adjust to various demographics, mask kinds, and environmental factors. Additionally, tackling the issue of occlusions, such as faces that are only partially or completely veiled, would improve the system's precision in practical situations. Future studies might concentrate on categorizing various mask types to provide more specific information about the distinct masks people use. This would help evaluate the efficacy of various mask choices and support public health actions. Additionally, the system might be deployed in a variety of real-world scenarios by being optimized for real-time implementation on devices with limited resources [61, 62]. Investigating privacy-preserving methods would guarantee people's anonymity while retaining the system's effectiveness in order to meet privacy issues. This is especially important when using the system for monitoring or in public areas. The accuracy and resilience of the system can be further improved by integrating multimodal techniques, which combine visual input with additional sensor data, especially under difficult settings. Additionally, even with little annotated data, pretrained models can be used to refine them for face mask identification using transfer learning and domain adaption techniques. The face mask detection system's integration into the current infrastructure would be made easier by cooperation with public health organizations and authorities. This would help to uphold mask-wearing laws, examine trends in compliance, and offer insightful information for public health actions.

References

1. Anand, R., Sindhwani, N., Saini, A., Shubham, Emerging technologies for COVID-19, in: *Enabling Healthcare 4.0 for Pandemics: A Roadmap Using AI, Machine Learning, IoT and Cognitive Technologies*, pp. 163–188, 2021.
2. Meivel, S., Sindhwani, N., Anand, R., Pandey, D., Alnuaim, A.A., Altheneyan, A.S., Lelisho, M.E., Mask detection and social distance identification using internet of things and faster R-CNN algorithm. *Comput. Intell. Neurosci.*, 2022, 2022.
3. Jain, S., Sindhwani, N., Anand, R., Kannan, R., COVID Detection Using Chest X-Ray and Transfer Learning, in: *International Conference on Intelligent Systems Design and Applications*, Springer International Publishing, Cham, pp. 933–943, 2021, December.
4. Wu, J., Xu, X., Yang, J., Object Detection and X-ray Security Imaging: A Survey. *IEEE Access*, 2023.
5. Mohan, V. and Simske, S.J., Cross-sensor vision system for maritime object detection. *Front. Mar. Sci.*, 10, 331, 2023.
6. Jayanthan, K.S. and Domnic, S., An attentive convolutional transformer-based network for road safety. *J. Supercomput.*, 1–27, 2023.
7. Danso, S.A., Liping, S., Hu, D., Afoakwa, S., Badzongoly, E.L., Odoom, J., Zhou, W., An optimal defect recognition security-based terahertz low resolution image system using deep learning network. *Egypt. Inf. J.*, 24, 3, 100384, 2023.

8. Vaiyapuri, T., Ahanger, T.A., Dahan, F., Hajjej, F., Keshta, I., Alsafyani, M., Raahemifar, K., A convolutional neural network for face mask detection in IoT-based smart healthcare systems. *Front. Physiol.*, 14, 314, 2023.
9. Siddique, A., Downstream Task Self-Supervised Learning for Object Recognition and Tracking, Doctoral dissertation, Marquette University, 2023.
10. Rampavan, M. and Ijjina, E.P., Genetic brake-net: Deep learning based brake light detection for collision avoidance using genetic algorithm. *Knowledge-Based Syst.*, 264, 110338, 2023.
11. Amadi, L. and Agam, G., Weakly Supervised 2D Pose Adaptation and Body Part Segmentation for Concealed Object Detection. *Sensors*, 23, 4, 2005, 2023.
12. Kshirsagar, P.R., Reddy, D.H., Dhingra, M., Dhabliya, D., Gupta, A., A Scalable Platform to Collect, Store, Visualize and Analyze Big Data in Real-Time. *2023 3rd International Conference on Innovative Practices in Technology and Management (ICIPTM)*, Uttar Pradesh, India, pp. 1–6, 2023, doi: 10.1109/ICIPTM57143.2023.10118183.
13. Li, X., Zhang, Y., He, D., Teng, X., Liu, B., Chen, Y., Passenger Flow Detection in Subway Stations Based on Improved You Only Look Once Algorithm. *Transp. Res. Rec.*, 2023, 03611981231159128.
14. Batsis, G., Mademlis, I., Papadopoulos, G.T., Illicit item detection in X-ray images for security applications, arXiv preprint arXiv:2305.01936, 2023.
15. Naseri, R.A.S., Kurnaz, A., Farhan, H.M., Optimized face detector-based intelligent face mask detection model in IoT using deep learning approach. *Appl. Soft Comput.*, 134, 109933, 2023.
16. Basheer Ahmed, M.I., Zaghdoud, R., Ahmed, M.S., Sendi, R., Alsharif, S., Alabdulkarim, J., Krishnasamy, G., A real-time computer vision based approach to detection and classification of traffic incidents. *Big Data Cognit. Comput.*, 7, 1, 22, 2023.
17. Dhingra, M., Dhabliya, D., Dubey, M.K., Gupta, A., Reddy, D.H., A Review on Comparison of Machine Learning Algorithms for Text Classification. *2022 5th International Conference on Contemporary Computing and Informatics (IC3I)*, Uttar Pradesh, India, pp. 1818–1823, 2022, doi: 10.1109/IC3I56241.2022.10072502.
18. Fang, Y., Ma, Y., Zhang, X., Wang, Y., Enhanced YOLOv5 algorithm for helmet wearing detection *via* combining bi-directional feature pyramid, attention mechanism and transfer learning. *Multimed. Tools Appl.*, 1–25, 2023.
19. Bamankar, S., Bhoir, P., Pednekar, S., Phadke, G., Face Mask and Body Temperature Scanning System for Covid-19, in: *2023 International Conference for Advancement in Technology (ICONAT)*, 2023, January, IEEE, pp. 1–6.
20. Ibraheam, M., Li, K.F., Gebali, F., An Accurate and Fast Animal Species Detection System for Embedded Devices. *IEEE Access*, 11, 23462–23473, 2023.

21. Hassan, T., Akcay, S., Hassan, B., Bennamoun, M., Khan, S., Dias, J., Werghi, N., Cascaded structure tensor for robust baggage threat detection. *Neural Comput. Appl.*, 35, 15, 11269–11285, 2023.
22. Gupta, N., Janani, S., Dilip, R., Hosur, R., Chaturvedi, A., Gupta, A., Wearable Sensors for Evaluation Over Smart Home Using Sequential Minimization Optimization-based Random Forest. *Int. J. Commun. Netw. Inf. Secur.*, 14, 2, 179–188, 2022.
23. Keserwani, H., Rastogi, H., Kurniullah, A.Z., Janardan, S.K., Raman, R., Rathod, V.M., Gupta, A., Security Enhancement by Identifying Attacks Using Machine Learning for 5G Network. *Int. J. Commun. Netw. Inf. Secur.*, 14, 2, 124–141, 2022.
24. Ma, L., Guo, Y., Fu, R., Sun, Q., Passenger non-driving related tasks detection using a light weight neural network based on human prior knowledge and soft-hard feature constraints. *Expert Syst. Appl.*, 219, 119631, 2023.
25. Jegham, I., Alouani, I., Khalifa, A.B., Mahjoub, M.A., Deep learning-based hard spatial attention for driver in-vehicle action monitoring. *Expert Syst. Appl.*, 219, 119629, 2023.
26. Cheng, M.Y., Khasani, R.R., Setiono, K., Image quality enhancement using HybridGAN for automated railway track defect recognition. *Autom. Constr.*, 146, 104669, 2023.
27. Lu, L. and Dai, F., Digitalization of Traffic Scenes in Support of Intelligent Transportation Applications. *J. Comput. Civ. Eng.*, 37, 5, 04023019, 2023.
28. Kirillov, A., Mintun, E., Ravi, N., Mao, H., Rolland, C., Gustafson, L., … & Girshick, R., Segment anything, arXiv preprint arXiv:2304.02643, 2023.
29. Shapira, A., Zolfi, A., Demetrio, L., Biggio, B., Shabtai, A., Phantom Sponges: Exploiting Non-Maximum Suppression To Attack Deep Object Detectors, in: *Proceedings of the IEEE/CVF Winter Conference on Applications of Computer Vision*, pp. 4571–4580, 2023.
30. Yavari, A., Korala, H., Georgakopoulos, D., Kua, J., Bagha, H., Sazgar IoT: A Device-Centric IoT Framework and Approximation Technique for Efficient and Scalable IoT Data Processing. *Sensors*, 23, 11, 5211, 2023.
31. Bansal, B., Jenipher, V.N., Jain, R., Dilip, R., Kumbhkar, M., Pramanik, S., Roy, S., Gupta, A., Big Data Architecture for Network Security, in: *Cyber Security and Network Security*, Pramanik, S., Samanta, D., Vinay, M., Guha, A. (Eds.), 2022.
32. Veeraiah, V., Gangavathi, P., Ahamad, S., Talukdar, S.B., Gupta, A., Talukdar, V., Enhancement of meta verse capabilities by IoT integration, in: *2022 2nd International Conference on Advance Computing and Innovative Technologies in Engineering (ICACITE)*, 2022, April, IEEE, pp. 1493–1498.
33. Waghmare, A., Ben Taleb, Y., Chatterjee, I., Narendra, A., Patel, S., Z-Ring: Single-Point Bio-Impedance Sensing for Gesture, Touch, Object and User Recognition, in: *Proceedings of the 2023 CHI Conference on Human Factors in Computing Systems*, 2023, April, pp. 1–18.

34. Piirainen, S., MMWR-Tracker: A Deep Learning-Based Solution for Identifying and Tracking Humans with Millimeter-Wave Radar, 2023.
35. Saint Etienne du Rouvray, F., Real Time Object Detection, Tracking, and Distance and Motion Estimation based on Deep Learning: Application to Smart Mobility.
36. Guo, F., Qian, Y., Yu, H., Automatic Rail Surface Defect Inspection Using the Pixel-wise Semantic Segmentation Model. *IEEE Sens. J.*, 2023.
37. Loo, B.P., Fan, Z., Lian, T., Zhang, F., Using computer vision and machine learning to identify bus safety risk factors. *Accid. Anal. Prev.*, 185, 107017, 2023.
38. Uzun, I., Damage detection in aircraft engine borescope inspection using deep learning, 2023.
39. Waykole, S., Shiwakoti, N., Stasinopoulos, P., Implementing model predictive control and steady-state dynamics for lane detection for automated vehicles in a variety of occlusion in clothoid-form roads. *Sensors*, 23, 8, 4085, 2023.
40. Liu, W. and Wang, X., Research Advanced in the Face Recognition. *Highlights Sci. Eng. Technol.*, 49, 448–456, 2023.
41. Chow, T.E., Yip, P.S., Wong, K.P., An integrated framework of mobile crowd estimation for the 2019, July 1st rally in Hong Kong. *Multimed. Tools Appl.*, 1–18, 2023.
42. Cen, J., Feng, H., Liu, X., Hu, Y., Li, H., Li, H., Huang, W., An Improved Ship Classification Method Based on YOLOv7 Model with Attention Mechanism. *Wireless Commun. Mobile Comput.*, 2023, 2023.
43. Hanifa, F.H., Hapsari, G.I., Mutiara, G.A., Marcelino, D., Alfarisi, M.R., Meisaroh, L., Kurniawan, A.P., Service Quality Analysis on Tracking System and Management of Bus Passenger Study at PT Indo Trans Teknologi, in: *6th Mechanical Engineering, Science and Technology International conference (MEST 2022)*, pp. 399–414, Atlantis Press, 2023, April
44. Švorc, D., Tichý, T., Růžička, M., Ivasienko, P., Use of One-Stage Detector and Feature Detector in Infrared Video on Transport Infrastructure and Tunnels. *Sustainability*, 15, 3, 2122, 2023.
45. Xie, Z., Chen, J.Y.S., Lim, G.W., Bai, F., Data-Driven Robotic Tactile Grasping for Hyper-Personalization Line Pick-and-Place. *Actuators*, 12, 5, 192, 2023, May, MDPI.
46. Gupta, A., Kaushik, D., Garg, M., Verma, A., Machine Learning model for Breast Cancer Prediction. (2020). *Fourth International Conference on I-SMAC (IoT in Social, Mobile, Analytics and Cloud) (I-SMAC)*, Palladam, India, pp. 472–477, 2020.
47. Talukdar, V., Dhabliya, D., Kumar, B., Talukdar, S.B., Ahamad, S., Gupta, A., Suspicious Activity Detection and Classification in IoT Environment Using Machine Learning Approach, in: *2022 Seventh International Conference on Parallel, Distributed and Grid Computing (PDGC)*, 2022, November, IEEE, pp. 531–535.

48. Liu, J., Zhao, S., Hu, F., Automatic detection of fastener safety wire twisting direction based on machine vision, in: *Third International Conference on Computer Vision and Data Mining (ICCVDM 2022)*, vol. 12511, SPIE, pp. 421–429, 2023, February.
49. Kurian, A.T. and Soori, P.K., AI-Based Driver Drowsiness and Distraction Detection in Real-Time, in: *2023 International Conference on Computational Intelligence and Knowledge Economy (ICCIKE)*, 2023, March, IEEE, pp. 13–18.
50. Biglari, A. and Tang, W., A Review of Embedded Machine Learning Based on Hardware, Application, and Sensing Scheme. *Sensors*, 23, 4, 2131, 2023.
51. Zheng, R., Sun, S., Liu, H., Wu, T., Deep Neural Networks-Enabled Vehicle Detection Using High-Resolution Automotive Radar Imaging. *IEEE Trans. Aerosp. Electron. Syst.*, 2023.
52. Qin, H., Zaman, A., Liu, X., Artificial intelligence-aided intelligent obstacle and trespasser detection based on locomotive-mounted forward-facing camera data. *Proc. Inst. Mech. Eng., Part F: J. Rail Rapid Transit*, 2023, 09544097231156312.
53. Barron, E. and Slomowitz, A., Massachusetts Should Facilitate–Not Inhibit–Law Enforcement Use of License Plate Data. Tech. Rep., 2013.
54. Limsoonthrakul, S., Dailey, M.N., Marikhu, R., Timtong, V., Chairat, A., Suphavilai, A., Ekpanyapong, M., Design and Implementation of a Highly Scalable, Low-Cost Distributed Traffic Violation Enforcement System in Phuket, Thailand. *Sustainability*, 13, 3, 1210, 2021.
55. Make ML, Mask Dataset. Retrieved from https://makeml.app/datasets/mask [Accessed on 25th Feb 2023].
56. Gupta, D.N., Veeraiah, V., Singh, H., Anand, R., Sindhwani, N., Gupta, A., IoT-Dependent Intelligent Irrigation System with ML-Dependent Soil Moisture Prediction, in: *2023 3rd International Conference on Technological Advancements in Computational Sciences (ICTACS)*, 2023, November, IEEE, pp. 1296–1300.
57. Sindhwani, N., Anand, R., Niranjanamurthy, M., Verma, D.C., Valentina, E.B., *IoT Based Smart Applications*, Springer International Publishing AG, 2022.
58. Anand, R. and Chawla, P., Optimization of inscribed hexagonal fractal slotted microstrip antenna using modified lightning attachment procedure optimization. *Int. J. Microwave Wireless Technolog.*, 12, 6, 519–530, 2020.
59. Anand, R., Sindhwani, N., Dahiya, A., Design of a high directivity slotted fractal antenna for C-band, X-band and Ku-band applications, in: *2022 9th International Conference on Computing for Sustainable Global Development (INDIACom)*, 2022, March, IEEE, pp. 727–730.
60. Chauhan, S.K., Khanna, P., Sindhwani, N., Saxena, K., Anand, R., Pareto Optimal Solution for Fully Fuzzy Bi-criteria Multi-index Bulk Transportation Problem, in: *Mobile Radio Communications and 5G Networks: Proceedings*

of Third MRCN 2022, pp. 457–470, Springer Nature Singapore, Singapore, 2023.

61. Singh, H., Veeraiah, V., Khan, H., Singh, D.K., Talukdar, V., Anand, R., Sindhwani, N., Investigating Scope and Applications for the Internet of Robotics in Industrial Automation, in: *Robotics and Automation in Industry 4.0*, pp. 132–151, CRC Press, 2024.
62. Kaur, J., Jaskaran, Sindhwani, N., Anand, R., Pandey, D., Implementation of IoT in various domains, in: *IoT Based Smart Applications*, pp. 165–178, Springer International Publishing, Cham, 2022.

Part III

INDUSTRIAL APPLICATIONS AND PREDICTIVE MAINTENANCE

14

Enhancing Error Prediction in Machineries through CNN and Random Forest Models Using IoT with Sensor Data Fusion

Thishan S.* **and Senthil Kumar K.**

School of Computer Applications, Karpagam College of Engineering, Coimbatore, India

Abstract

Predictive maintenance plays a key role in guaranteeing the reliability and efficiency of machinery in various industries. Machine learning methods, notably convolutional neural networks (CNNs), are increasingly recognized for their effectiveness in predictive maintenance endeavors, owing to their capacity for uncovering intricate patterns from raw data. In this study, we propose a groundbreaking approach for machine predictive maintenance classification using CNNs. The proposed model takes raw sensor data collected from machines, which is then uploaded to Internet of Things cloud and processes it through multiple convolutional layers to automatically learn discriminative features indicative of machinery health. Through extensive experimentation on real-world datasets, we showcase how our CNN-based method effectively categorizes machine health and anticipates potential breakdowns with precision. Our results highlight the potential of CNNs in enhancing predictive maintenance strategies, leading to improved reliability. It uses CNN algorithm for training and K-nearest neighbors, random forest, and decision tree for classification; with this, it will predict the result either as fault or not.

Keywords: Internet of Things (IoT), K-nearest neighbors (KNN), stochastic gradient descent (SGD), convolutional neural networks (CNN)

**Corresponding author*: thishan095@gmail.com

Kanak Kalita, S. Vishnu Kumar and M. Niranjanamurthy (eds.) Industrial Internet of Things and Advanced Techniques for Sensor Data Aggregation and Fusion, (243–258) © 2026 Scrivener Publishing LLC

14.1 Introduction

Predictive maintenance is a critical component for ensuring the reliability and efficiency of machinery across various industries. As machinery downtime can lead to significant financial losses, the ability to anticipate and prevent failures before they occur is invaluable. Machine learning (ML) methods, notably convolutional neural networks (CNNs), have become instrumental in predictive maintenance because of their adeptness at discerning intricate patterns and features within unprocessed sensor data. In our study, we propose a novel approach that harnesses the potential of CNNs for predictive maintenance classification. The essence of our model lies in its ability to process raw sensor data collected from machines and uploaded to Internet of Things (IoT) cloud through multiple convolutional layers. These layers are designed to automatically learn discriminative features that are indicative of machinery health. By leveraging the inherent hierarchical structure of CNNs, our model can effectively capture both local and global patterns present in the data, thereby enhancing its predictive capabilities. We extensively experimented with authentic datasets to assess how effective our CNN-based approach is. Through rigorous testing, we demonstrated the model's proficiency in accurately classifying the health status of machines and predicting impending failures. Additionally, integrated classification algorithms such as K-nearest neighbors (KNN), random forest, and decision trees to further refine the predictive outcomes, providing binary results indicating fault presence or absence.

14.2 Literature Survey

Predictive maintenance is essential for ensuring the reliability and efficiency of machinery across various industries. This study proposes a novel approach for machine predictive maintenance classification utilizing CNNs. The model processes raw sensor data from machines through multiple convolutional layers to automatically discern features indicative of machinery health. By conducting extensive experimentation on real-world datasets, the effectiveness of the CNN-based approach is demonstrated in accurately classifying the health status of machines and predicting impending failures. In recent years, research efforts have focused on leveraging CNNs for predictive maintenance tasks due to their capacity to handle complex data and learn hierarchical representations. Zhao *et al.* [9] used CNNs to detect faults in industrial machinery by analyzing vibration signals, achieving high accuracy in fault classification. Similarly, Liu *et al.* [10] utilized CNNs for predictive maintenance in wind turbines, showcasing improved fault detection capabilities compared to traditional methods. By combining the strengths of CNNs with these classifiers, the model achieves robust predictive maintenance capabilities. Research by Zhang *et al.* [11] supports this integration, demonstrating the effectiveness of combining CNNs with ensemble methods for fault diagnosis in rotating machinery. The integration of CNNs with complementary classifiers presents a promising avenue for enhancing predictive maintenance strategies in industrial operations. This approach holds significant potential for improving reliability, reducing downtime, and realizing cost savings in machinery maintenance.

14.3 Proposed System

Our proposed predictive maintenance system as illustrated in Figure 14.1, harnesses the power of CNNs to meticulously analyze raw sensor data harvested from machinery. These data are seamlessly uploaded to an IoT cloud

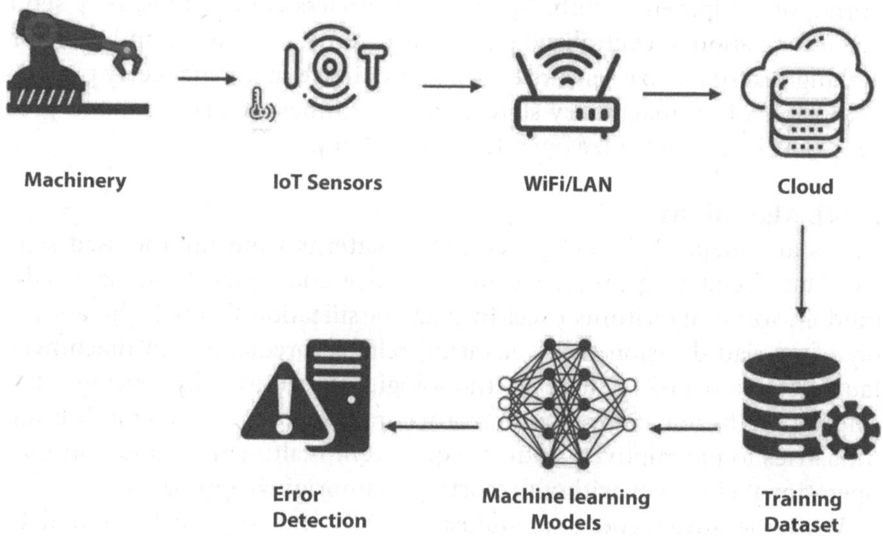

Figure 14.1 The utilization of ML and IoT for error detection and predictive maintenance within industry.

infrastructure, facilitating real-time monitoring and analysis. Through a series of convolutional layers, the CNN autonomously discerns and extracts pivotal features indicative of machinery health, offering unparalleled insights into potential faults. To bolster the predictive capabilities, we integrate CNNs with a diverse array of classifiers including KNN, decision trees, and random forest algorithms. This amalgamation enables our system to accurately forecast fault occurrences, providing a binary indication of machinery health status. Validated on authentic industrial datasets, our approach consistently showcases superior accuracy in classifying machinery health and preempting potential failures. By fortifying predictive maintenance strategies, our system ensures heightened reliability, slashes downtime, and heralds substantial cost savings for industrial enterprises. Through seamless integration with IoT infrastructure and leveraging sensor data, our system stands as a beacon of efficiency and foresight in industrial maintenance practices.

A. IoT Sensors

IoT sensors, essential components of contemporary industrial setups, gather live data concerning the operational status of machinery and surrounding environmental factors. The sensors gather diverse information, including temperature, vibration, and pressure, enabling continuous monitoring of equipment health. By utilizing wireless connections, they send this information to centralized platforms where it is analyzed and used for making decisions. IoT sensors enhance predictive maintenance by providing insights into machinery status, enabling timely interventions to prevent failures and optimize operational efficiency.

B. ML Algorithms

CNNs are adept at discerning complex patterns from unprocessed sensor data, facilitating predictive maintenance endeavors. Simultaneously, random forest algorithms excel in data classification through the assembly of myriad decision trees, ensuring reliable predictions in machinery fault detection tasks. These methodologies synergistically leverage distinct strengths to enhance predictive accuracy and reliability, empowering industries to preemptively address equipment malfunctions and optimize operational efficiency without resorting to unoriginal approaches.

With the advancement of industries, ML and IoT are integrated to enhance efficiency, reduce downtime, and improve maintenance processes. Error detection and predictive maintenance are two critical applications of these technologies, enabling industries to transition from reactive to proactive maintenance strategies.

Role of IoT in Error Detection and Predictive Maintenance

IoT plays a crucial role by providing real-time data from industrial equipment. Key functions of IoT in this context include the following:

1. **Sensor deployment**: IoT sensors monitor key parameters such as temperature, vibration, pressure, and humidity.
2. **Data collection and transmission**: The collected data are transmitted to cloud or edge computing systems through IoT gateways.
3. **Remote monitoring**: Enables engineers and operators to monitor the health of machines in real time.

ML for Error Detection

ML is used to analyze patterns and detect errors before they escalate into failures. The process involves the following:

1. **Data preprocessing**: Cleaning raw sensor data by removing noise and normalizing values.
2. **Anomaly detection**: ML models, such as deep learning and statistical methods, detect deviations from normal operating conditions.
3. **Fault classification**: Using trained models, the system identifies specific types of failures, such as motor overheating or bearing failures.

Predictive Maintenance Using ML and IoT

Predictive maintenance goes beyond error detection to forecast failures before they occur. This is achieved through the following:

1. **Historical data analysis**: ML models learn from past machine failures to predict future breakdowns.
2. **Remaining-useful-life estimation**: Artificial intelligence algorithms estimate how much longer a component will function before requiring maintenance.
3. **Automated maintenance alerts**: IoT-enabled systems trigger alerts for maintenance teams, ensuring timely intervention.

Benefits of ML and IoT for Predictive Maintenance

- **Reduced downtime**: Prevents unexpected equipment failures.
- **Cost savings**: Reduces repair costs and optimizes maintenance schedules.
- **Improved safety**: Detects hazardous failures in advance.
- **Enhanced efficiency**: Ensures optimal performance of industrial machines.

Hence, the integration of ML and IoT in industrial settings is revolutionizing maintenance strategies. By leveraging real-time monitoring, predictive analytics, and automated alerts, industries can increase productivity, minimize operational costs, and enhance machine reliability. This transformation is a key enabler for smart manufacturing and Industry. Figure 14.1 shows how ML and IoT is utilized for error detection.

14.4 Training and Classification

CNNs, KNN, decision trees, and random forest are all powerful ML algorithms utilized across various domains for different tasks. CNNs, broadly adopted in computer vision applications, demonstrate exceptional proficiency in extracting detailed features from images *via* convolutional layers. Their hierarchical structure allows them to automatically learn patterns and relationships in data, making them highly effective in tasks requiring complex feature extraction. Decision trees partition the feature space into regions based on feature values, making decisions through a tree-like structure. Although decision trees often suffer from overfitting on training data, random forest mitigates this concern by combining numerous trees, each of which is trained on a random subset of the data. Random forests offer improved generalization performance and robustness, making them suitable for various applications, including predictive maintenance, fraud detection, and customer segmentation. To wrap up, CNNs, KNN, random forest, and decision trees stand out as adaptable ML algorithms, each showcasing distinct advantages and limitations. Understanding their characteristics and suitability for specific tasks is crucial for selecting the most appropriate algorithm to achieve optimal performance and outcomes in real-world applications.

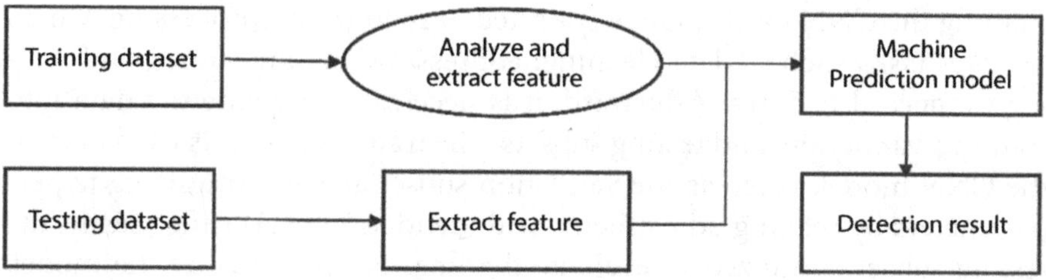

Figure 14.2 Training process.

14.5 Implementation

Implementing machine predictive maintenance classification using CNNs involves several key steps to ensure effective deployment as illustrated in Figure 14.2 and Figure 14.3. First, data collection is crucial. This involves gathering historical maintenance records, sensor data from machinery, and any relevant contextual information. These data forms the basis for

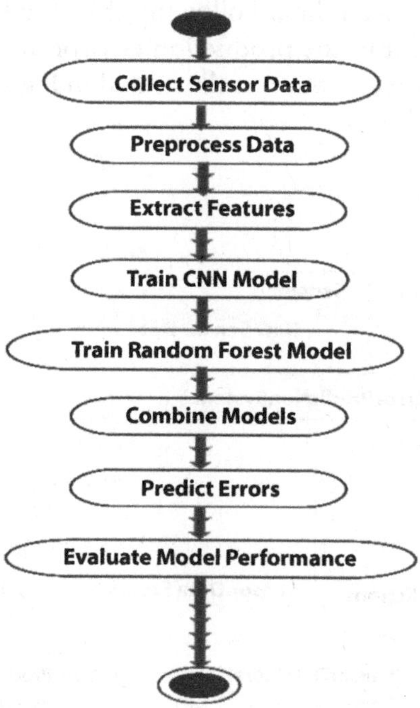

Figure 14.3 Activity diagram.

training the CNN model. Once collected, it requires preprocessing, which involves tasks such as data cleaning, addressing missing values, and scaling numerical features. Afterward, it is necessary to divide the data into training, validation, and testing subsets. The training subset is used to train the CNN model, whereas the validation subset aids in optimizing hyperparameters by making adjustments and identifying overfitting. Lastly, the testing subset is utilized to evaluate the final performance of the model. This often includes arranging convolutional layers, pooling layers, and potentially incorporating dropout layers to mitigate overfitting. The final layer will comprise nodes corresponding to the number of classes for classification. The process of training the CNN entails passing the training data through network and adjusting the model parameters using optimization techniques such as stochastic gradient descent (SGD). The training process persists until either convergence is achieved, or a stopping criterion is satisfied. After completing the training phase, it is imperative to evaluate the model's effectiveness using the validation dataset. Evaluation metrics are frequently used to gauge classification performance. Once the model has been deemed satisfactory through validation performance, it undergoes evaluation on the testing set to provide a final assessment of its performance on unseen data. Following this, the trained CNN model is ready for deployment in the production environment for real-time predictive maintenance classification as illustrated in Figure 14.4. This process

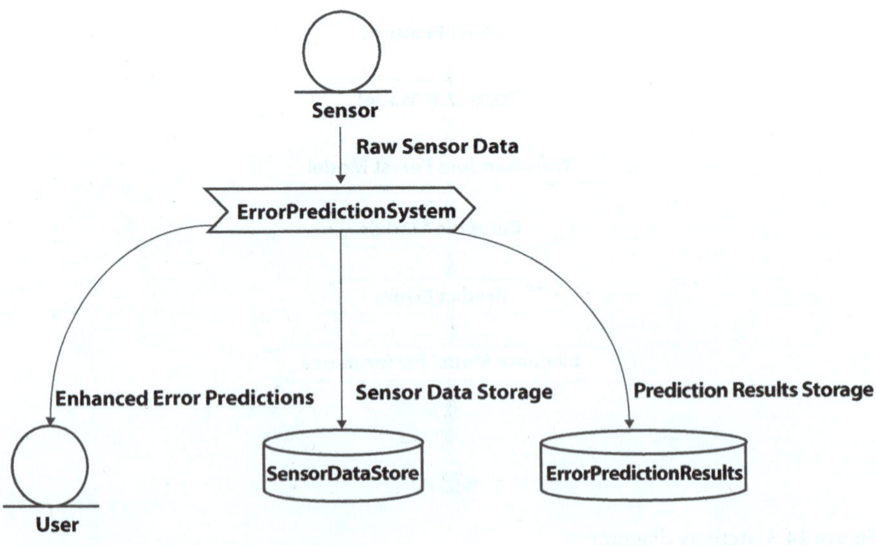

Figure 14.4 Data flow diagram (level 0).

entails integrating the model into current systems or workflows, monitoring its performance, and consistently retraining and updating the model with new data or adjustments as machinery evolves over time.

14.6 Commonly Monitored Machines

We identified articles that explicitly specify the type of machinery being evaluated. These articles were then categorized into 11 groups based on similarities in machinery type. The distribution of articles across these groups is illustrated in Figure 14.5. By analyzing how often they appear within each group, we arranged them in order to identify the machine types.

As depicted in Figure 14.5, hydraulic systems, cutting tools, and bearings are highlighted as the primary machinery types utilized for identifying anomalies. Multiple investigations carried out across these equipment categories have embraced predictive maintenance methods, with the aspiration of achieving a range of benefits. These advantages include reduced production losses, improved product quality, reduced costs of unforeseen equipment downtime, and enhanced overall production; also, incorporating predictive maintenance strategies can play a role in prolonging the lifespan of the machinery.

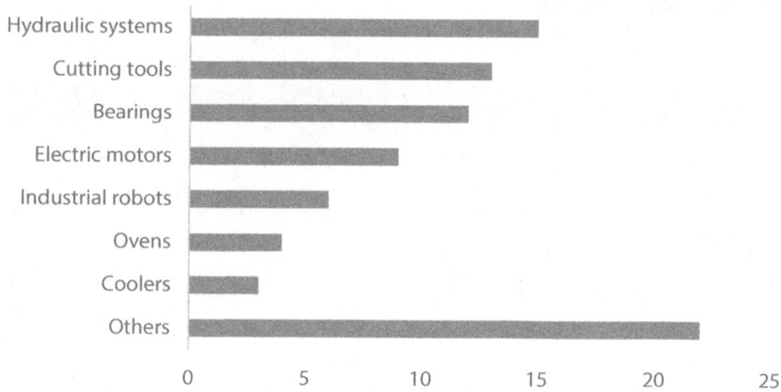

Figure 14.5 Count of fundamental research investigations categorized by the variety of industrial equipment.

14.7 Model Architecture

A. Data Collection Module

- This module is responsible for gathering sensor data from the machines. It could involve interfacing with various sensors such as temperature, pressure, vibration, etc.
- Data collection might occur in real time from sensors installed on the machines or from historical data stored in databases. A sample of data collection using Google sheet is shown in Figure 14.6.

B. Data Preprocessing Module

- Preprocessing is crucial for cleaning and formatting the raw sensor data before feeding it into the CNN model.
- Tasks in this module may include data cleaning, normalization, feature scaling, and handling missing values.
- Time-series data may need specific preprocessing techniques such as windowing, smoothing, and resampling.

C. Data Augmentation Module

- From the general architecture of CNN as shown in Figure 14.7, data augmentation is essential for improving the robustness and generalization of the CNN model, especially when dealing with limited data.
- Techniques such as random rotation, flipping, zooming, and adding noise can be applied to generate additional synthetic training samples.

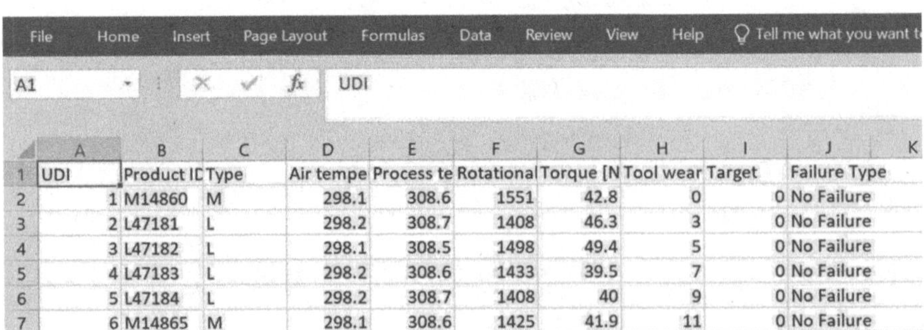

UDI	Product ID	Type	Air tempe	Process te	Rotational	Torque [N	Tool wear	Target	Failure Type
1	M14860	M	298.1	308.6	1551	42.8	0	0	No Failure
2	L47181	L	298.2	308.7	1408	46.3	3	0	No Failure
3	L47182	L	298.1	308.5	1498	49.4	5	0	No Failure
4	L47183	L	298.2	308.6	1433	39.5	7	0	No Failure
5	L47184	L	298.2	308.7	1408	40	9	0	No Failure
6	M14865	M	298.1	308.6	1425	41.9	11	0	No Failure
7	L47186	L	298.1	308.6	1558	42.4	14	0	No Failure

Figure 14.6 Sample dataset.

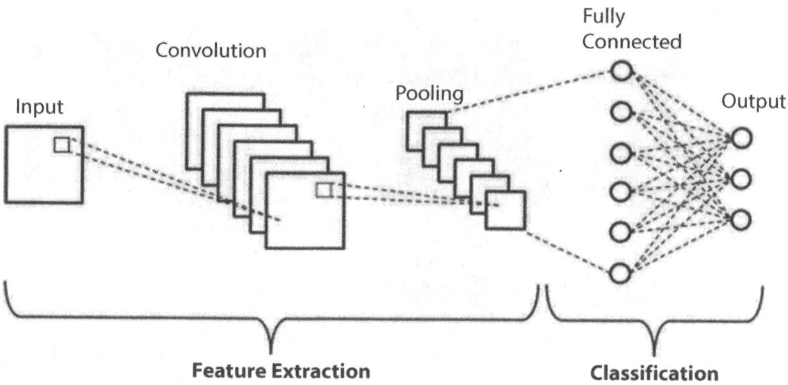

Figure 14.7 CNN architecture.

D. CNN Model Architecture Module

- This module involves designing the architecture of the CNN model tailored for predictive maintenance classification.
- Architectural decisions should consider the complexity of the data and the specific characteristics of the predictive maintenance tasks.

E. Model Training Module

- The training module consists of inputting preprocessed data into the CNN model and fine-tuning its parameters to minimize a specified loss function.
- Training usually includes iterative optimization methods such as SGD.
- The optimization of hyperparameters, including adjustments to parameters such as learning rate, batch size, and dropout rates, is conducted with the aim of improving the performance of the model.

F. Model Evaluation Module

- This section evaluates the effectiveness of the trained CNN model by using various evaluation metrics, including accuracy, recall, precision, confusion matrix, as shown in Figure 14.8 and F1 score.

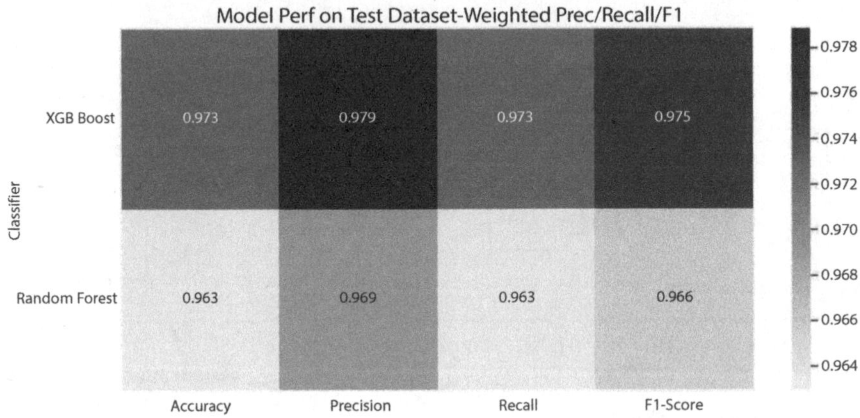

Figure 14.8 Accuracy.

- Methods such as cross-validation and holdout validation are used to verify the model's capacity for generalization.

G. Monitoring and Maintenance Module

- Continuous monitoring of the deployed model's performance is essential to detect degradation or drift over time.
- Adaptive maintenance strategies may be implemented to fine-tune the model periodically or retrain it with new data to maintain optimal performance.

By implementing these modules, a machine predictive maintenance classification system using CNNs can effectively analyze sensor data, identify potential failures, and facilitate proactive maintenance strategies, thereby improving operational efficiency and reducing downtime in industrial settings.

14.8 Results

This study presents a pioneering method for predictive maintenance utilizing CNNs to analyze raw sensor data from machinery. By using multiple convolutional layers, the model autonomously learns distinctive features linked to machinery health. Through rigorous real-world dataset analysis, the proposed CNN-based approach proves highly effective in accurately classifying machinery health status and forecasting potential failures

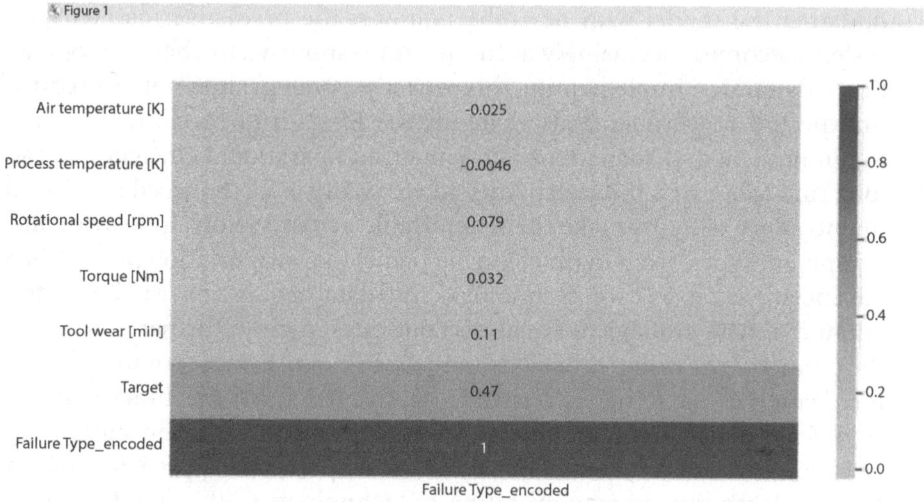

Figure 14.9 Failure type.

as shown in Figure 14.9. Leveraging CNNs enhances predictive maintenance strategies, promising heightened reliability, decreased downtime, and substantial cost savings in industrial operations. The classification uses KNN, random forest, and decision tree algorithms, yielding fault or non-fault predictions, contributing to a comprehensive predictive maintenance framework.

14.9 Conclusion

Utilizing CNNs for predictive maintenance classification on procedural machines presents a potent and effective approach to bolster equipment dependability and minimize operational disruptions. Through the utilization of CNNs, intricate patterns and features within sensor data can be effectively extracted and interpreted allowing for accurate identification of potential failures or maintenance needs. The effectiveness of CNNs stems from their capacity to autonomously acquire hierarchical data representations, thereby obviating the necessity for manual feature engineering. This capability enables the model to dynamically adjust to various operating conditions and types of equipment. Furthermore, the implementation of CNNs facilitates real-time monitoring and analysis of machine health, enabling timely interventions to prevent catastrophic failures and optimize maintenance schedules. By leveraging historical data and continuously updating the model with new observations, the predictive maintenance system becomes increasingly accurate and responsive to changing operational dynamics. Implementing this proactive strategy does not just reduce unexpected downtime; it also extends the lifespan of machinery, resulting in notable cost reductions and enhanced operational efficiency in the long run. Moreover, the scalability and versatility of CNN-based predictive maintenance systems make them applicable across various industries and equipment types, from manufacturing plants to transportation fleets. With advancements in sensor technology and data acquisition methods, the amount of data available for analysis continues to grow, further enhancing the predictive capabilities of CNN models. In essence, incorporating CNNs for predictive maintenance classification in procedural machines marks a significant departure in maintenance strategies. This transition shifts away from reactive and time-based methods toward proactive approaches driven by data. With the ongoing evolution of technology, CNNs stand ready to assume a progressively significant role in transforming maintenance procedures and advancing operational standards across various sectors.

Bibliography

1. Ribeiro, F., Netto, S., Marins, M., Silva, E., Rotating machinery fault diagnosis using similarity based models. *The XXXV Simpósio Brasileiro de Telecomunicações e Processamento de Sinais*, 2017.
2. Shahapurkar, S.S., Pansare, H.S., Dhebe, P.P., Wagh, C.S., Desale, A., Detection of Fault in Gearbox System Using Vibration Analysis Method. *Int. J. Eng. Appl. Sci.*, 2, 5, 119–122, 2015.
3. Alzghoul, A., Jarndal, A., Alsyouf, I., Bingamil, A.A., Ali, M.A., AlBaiti, S. On the Usefulness of Pre-Processing Methods in Rotating Machines Faults Classification Using Artificial Neural Network. *J. Appl. Comput. Mech.*, 7, 1, 254–261, Jan 2021.
4. Yang, W.-T., Borodin, V., Reis, M.S., Roussy, A., Juge, M., An interpretable unsupervised Bayesian network model for fault detection and diagnosis. *Control Eng. Pract.*, 127, 105304, 2022.
5. Lindemann, B., Jazdi, N., Fesenmayr, F., Weyrich, M., Anomaly detection in discrete manufacturing using self-learning approaches, Jan 2019.
6. MAFAULDA: Machinery Fault Database, http://www02.smt.ufrj.br/~offshore/mfs/page_01.html, last accessed 22 May 2021.
7. What is Predictive Maintenance?, https://www.fiixsoftware.com/maintenancestrategies/predictive-maintenance /, Last accessed 7 Apr 2021.

8. What are Benefits and Drawbacks of Preventive maintenance?, https://www.onupkeep.com/answers/preventive-maintenance/benefits-of-preventive-maintenance, Last accessed 29 Jun 2021.
9. Zhao *et al.*, Bearing fault diagnosis method based on deep convolutional neural network and random forest ensemble learning. *Sensors*, 19, 5, 1088, 2019, https://doi.org/10.3390/s19051088.
10. Liu *et al.*, Cross-Turbine Training of Convolutional Neural Networks for SCADA-Based Fault Detection in Wind Turbines. *Annual Conference of the PHM Society*, 12, 1, 2020.
11. Zhang *et al.*, An ensemble convolutional neural networks for bearing fault diagnosis using multi-sensor data. *Sensors*, 19, 23, 5300, 2019, MDPI, https://doi.org/10.3390/s19235300.

15

Real-Time Flight Delay Prediction with Live Data from IoT and Airline Operations Optimization Using the KNN Algorithm

B. Praveen Kumar* **and R. Ramprashath**

School of Computer Application, Karpagam College of Engineering, Coimbatore, India

Abstract

The swift growth of air travel highlights the necessity of effective airline management and precise flight delay predictions. The objective of this project is to create a real-time flight delay prediction system and investigate how airline operations may be optimized by using it. Combining established approaches with machine learning techniques enables the aviation industry to make better decisions by offering insightful information about anticipated delays. The first step is creating a large dataset that includes all the factors that affect flight delays, including weather, past performance, airport traffic, and aircraft status. Using this information, the research applies machine learning models to dynamically determine the likelihood of aircraft delays, concentrating on k-nearest neighbors (KNN). Although KNN is used as an example, it is important to remember that more advanced models, such as random forests, support vector machines, or deep learning networks, are more appropriate for precisely forecasting actual flight delays. Beyond simple forecasting, the research explores how accurate projections might be integrated into improving airline operations. Airlines can enhance operational efficiency by optimally allocating resources, managing crew rosters, adjusting gate assignments, and monitoring projected delays in conjunction with current schedules. In this optimization process, algorithms are essential for reducing disruptions and improving passenger experience. The project's results highlight the potential advantages of flight delay prediction and real-time operational optimization

**Corresponding author*: praveenvanshika666@gmail.com

Kanak Kalita, S. Vishnu Kumar and M. Niranjanamurthy (eds.) Industrial Internet of Things and Advanced Techniques for Sensor Data Aggregation and Fusion, (259–276) © 2026 Scrivener Publishing LLC

in reducing the negative effects of delays on both airlines and passengers. They emphasize how crucial it is to gather, prepare, and analyze data meticulously to reap these benefits. The project's results highlight the potential advantages of flight delay prediction and real-time operational optimization in reducing the negative effects of delays on both airlines and passengers, emphasizing the crucial role of Internet of Things in data gathering for these benefits.

Keywords: Forecasting flight delays, optimization of real-time operations, Internet of Things, airline administration, aviation machine learning, efficiency in operations, improvement of the passenger experience

15.1 Introduction

The aviation sector plays a vital role in maintaining global connectivity, which emphasizes how important it is to resolve flight delays and streamline airline operations. The goal of this research is to develop a real-time flight delay prediction system that will lessen the negative effects of disruptions on travelers, airlines, and operational effectiveness. Due to a variety of circumstances, including weather and traffic, airlines must take proactive measures to manage uncertainty when it comes to flight delays. Real-time prediction systems use current conditions, past data, and sophisticated analytics to deliver airlines timely insights that help them make better decisions and provide better experiences for their customers. Beyond only making predictions, the initiative also looks into how these insights may help optimize airline operations. Predictive analytics integration with scheduling, resource allocation, and route planning provides a comprehensive method for reducing the impact of delays. Airlines can increase passenger happiness, reduce costs associated with disruptions, and improve operational efficiency by modifying gate assignments, crew schedules, and flight itineraries. The goal of this project is to create a prediction model that can predict flight delays by using machine learning techniques and historical data. It also looks at how these forecasts may be incorporated into operational plans to strike a healthy balance between timely delivery and efficient resource use. This study provides insightful information about the transformative potential of real-time flight delay prediction and its integration into airline operations optimization. The methodology and findings are described in depth in the following sections. To alleviate air traffic congestion, the idea of constructing new airports emerges as a potential solution. However, the inherent complexities associated with such endeavors tend to escalate exponentially over time. Thus, the more feasible strategy lies in the enhancement of existing airport infrastructure.

Given the constraints posed by limited land resources, this approach presents a more pragmatic and sustainable solution. Delays in flight schedules signify the extent to which an aircraft deviates from its intended departure or arrival time or, in some cases, results in cancellations. These delays can profoundly impact commercial aviation operations, affecting passenger satisfaction and loyalty and potentially influencing marketing strategies aimed at retaining customers. Recognizing the critical importance of punctuality in the airline industry, minimizing delays becomes paramount to ensuring optimal service delivery and maintaining competitiveness in the market. To gain deeper insights into the intricacies of the flight system and identify potential areas for improvement, scientists and researchers have meticulously collected and analyzed vast repositories of data spanning the entire duration of flight journeys. This data-driven approach facilitates a comprehensive understanding of the factors contributing to delays, thereby enabling informed decision-making and the implementation of targeted interventions to mitigate disruptions and enhance overall operational efficiency. Figure 15.1 represents the operation of flight.

As the population continues to surge and time becomes increasingly valuable for many individuals, the significance of flights has been heightened.

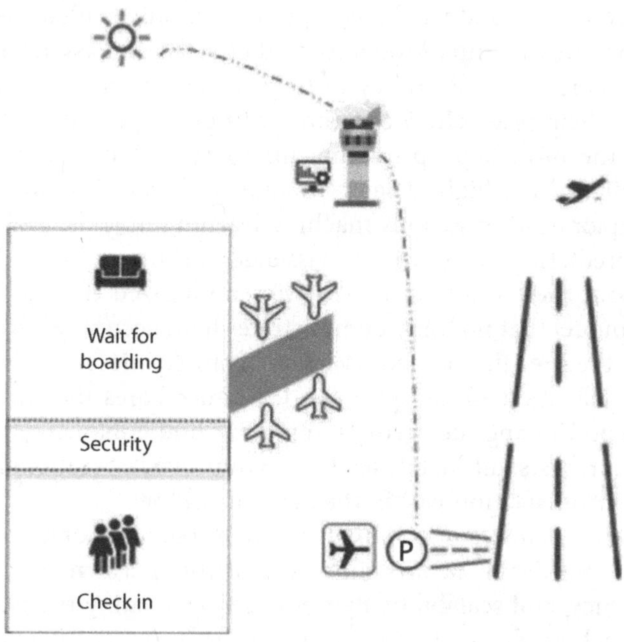

Figure 15.1 An average commercial flight's operation.

However, in the 1960s, the high cost and frequent flight delays led to diminished interest in flights. Nonetheless, with government assistance, many companies began manufacturing flights that were more affordable and comfortable, leading to the establishment of numerous airports and better control over airline traffic. The economy of airlines plays a pivotal role in a country's economy, and significant losses have been incurred due to flight delays. Recognizing this, recent advancements in machine learning technology have emerged as a viable solution for predicting flight delays. Mining techniques, particularly in the realm of airlines, have experienced rapid growth due to their effectiveness in predicting outcomes, reducing cancellation costs, enhancing airline transportation services, improving customer satisfaction, and facilitating real-time decision-making to save time and money and ensure smooth operations.

15.2 Literature Review

Predicting flight delays in the airline industry has become a critical area of research due to its significant impact on passenger satisfaction, operational efficiency, and economic performance. Several studies have investigated the application of machine learning algorithms to address this challenge.

Kothari *et al.* [1] conducted a comprehensive study titled "Selection of the Best Machine Learning Model to Predict Delay in Passenger Airlines," aimed at enhancing the accuracy of flight delay prediction in the airline industry. In their research, the authors recognized the critical need for identifying the most appropriate machine learning algorithm to ensure precise predictions of flight delays. To address this, they embarked on an in-depth exploration of various machine learning models, assessing their efficacy in predicting delays within passenger airlines.

Throughout their study, Kothari *et al.* emphasized the significance of selecting a model that not only demonstrates high accuracy but also aligns closely with the specific characteristics and complexities inherent in airline operations. This meticulous approach [5] underscores the authors' commitment to optimizing the prediction process and enhancing the reliability of delay forecasts, ultimately leading to improved operational efficiency and customer satisfaction within the aviation sector.

The researchers meticulously analyzed a diverse range of machine learning models, considering factors such as algorithm performance, computational efficiency, and scalability. By rigorously evaluating the performance metrics of each model, including accuracy, precision, recall, and F1 score,

Kothari *et al.* sought to identify the most effective approach for predicting delays on passenger airlines.

Furthermore, Kothari *et al.* delved into the intricacies of each machine learning model, exploring their underlying mechanisms and how they interact with the unique variables and dynamics of airline operations. This thorough investigation enabled the authors to gain valuable insights into the strengths and limitations of each model, guiding their selection process toward the most suitable algorithm for accurate delay prediction.

Ultimately, the research conducted by Kothari *et al.* represents a significant contribution to the field of aviation analytics, offering valuable guidance to industry stakeholders seeking to implement machine learning–based solutions for predicting flight delays [11]. By identifying and advocating for the adoption of the most effective models, the authors pave the way for improved decision-making processes, optimized resource allocation, and enhanced operational performance within the passenger airline industry [6].

In their study titled "Prediction of Airline Delays Using the K Nearest Neighbor Algorithm," Gnanalingam [2] delved into the realm of predicting airline delays by using the k-nearest neighbors (KNN) algorithm. Through their research, Gnanalingam aimed to showcase the efficacy of KNN in forecasting flight delays, shedding light on its applicability within the airline industry. By utilizing the KNN algorithm, the author demonstrated its effectiveness in accurately predicting delays, thereby providing valuable insights into its potential utilization in real-world airline operations. This study contributes to the existing literature by highlighting a specific machine learning technique that can be harnessed for enhancing delay prediction in the aviation sector [10].

Similarly, Ajmeria *et al.* [3] conducted a study titled "Flight Delay Prediction Using Machine Learning," where they explored various machine learning techniques for predicting flight delays and assessing their impact on airline operations. Through their research, the authors underscored the pivotal role of accurate delay prediction in bolstering operational efficiency and customer satisfaction within the aviation industry [7]. By investigating a range of machine learning methods, Ajmeria *et al.* provided valuable insights into the diverse approaches available for addressing the challenge of flight delay prediction, thereby contributing to the ongoing discourse on enhancing airline performance.

Furthermore, Shah *et al.* [4] delved into the application of both machine learning and deep learning techniques in predicting airline delays in their study titled "Airline Delay Prediction Using Machine Learning and Deep Learning Techniques." The authors aimed to offer a thorough comprehension of the strengths and weaknesses of various approaches, including deep learning models, through a comparative analysis of their performance [9]. Through their research, Shah *et al.* offered valuable insights into the potential of machine learning and deep learning techniques for addressing the complex challenge of flight delay prediction, thereby informing future research directions and practical applications within the aviation industry [8].

Overall, these studies highlight the growing interest in using machine learning techniques to predict flight delays in the airline industry. By leveraging advanced algorithms [12], researchers aim to improve the accuracy of delay prediction, optimize airline operations, and enhance the overall passenger experience. However, further research is needed to explore new methodologies and address the evolving complexities of flight delay prediction in the dynamic aviation environment.

15.3 Existing System

Because the findings can be used to raise customer satisfaction and airline agency revenue, an accurate assessment of flight delays is essential for airlines. Numerous research endeavors have delved into modeling and forecasting flight delays, with a predominant focus on discerning pivotal indicators and associated factors. Regrettably, owing to the vast volume of data, intricate interconnections, and a plethora of influencing variables, most proposed methodologies fall short in achieving adequate accuracy.

Drawbacks

1. **Limited performance**: Both KNN and decision tree (DT) algorithms may struggle with complex datasets. They are susceptible to overfitting, meaning they might not generalize well to new data.
2. **Computational complexity**: KNN requires computing distances between all pairs of training examples, which can be quite taxing for large datasets. Similarly, DTs can become computationally expensive with an increase in the number of features or data points.
3. **Lack of interpretability**: Although easy to implement, both KNN and DTs lack interpretability. Understanding how the algorithm makes predictions can be challenging, making it difficult to identify and rectify issues.

4. **Limited feature engineering**: KNN and DTs heavily rely on the provided dataset features. They lack the capability to create new features, which can be limiting when dealing with intricate datasets.
5. **Lack of scalability**: These algorithms are not well-suited for handling large-scale datasets due to their high computational complexity. As the dataset size increases, they may become prohibitively slow or fail to fit into memory.

15.4 Proposed System

The primary objective of this study is to forecast flight delays, a critical aspect of the aviation industry, which serves as a significant contributor to the economy of numerous countries. Among various modes of transportation, air travel stands out for its speed and comfort. By using machine learning algorithms, this research aims to identify and mitigate flight delays, thereby potentially saving substantial turnovers. The outcomes of this analysis reveal insights into potential delays at major airports, considering factors such as time, day, and weather conditions. Ultimately, the developed model endeavors to minimize the frequency and impact

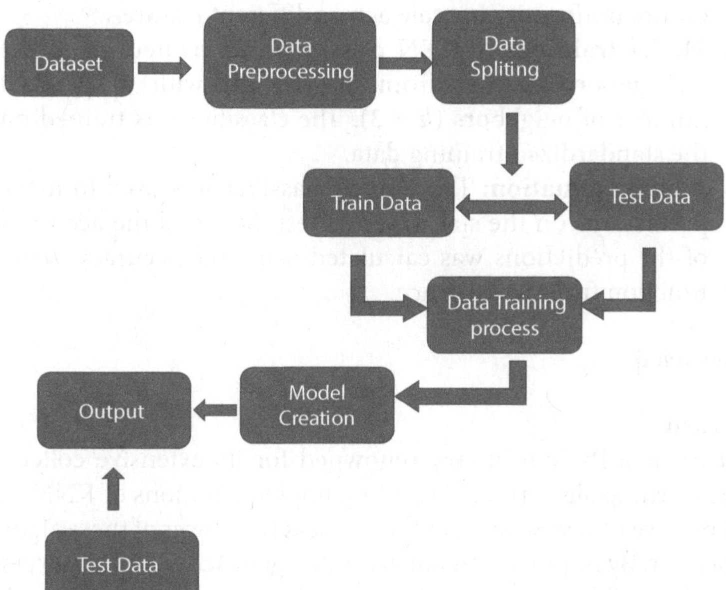

Figure 15.2 System architecture.

of delays on airline operations, enhancing overall efficiency and customer satisfaction. Additionally, integration of Internet of Things (IoT) data can further refine and enhance the accuracy of delay predictions, ensuring proactive measures are taken to mitigate disruptions.

Advantages

Due to the random nature of delays, this study looks into the qualitative prediction of airline delays to make the required adjustments and improve the traveler experience. Figure 15.2 represent the system architecture and modules are below.

Modules

Workflow

1. **Data preprocessing**: The dataset was loaded using Pandas, and relevant features ("ScheduledDuration" and "ActualDuration") along with the target variable ("FlightDelay") were selected. The dataset was split into training and testing sets using the train_test_split function from Scikit-learn.
2. **Feature standardization**: The features in the dataset were standardized using the StandardScaler from Scikit-learn to ensure uniformity in scale across different features.
3. **Model training**: A KNN classifier was created using the KNeighborsClassifier from Scikit-learn with a specified number of neighbors ($k = 3$). The classifier was trained on the standardized training data.
4. **Model evaluation**: The trained classifier was used to make predictions on the standardized test data, and the accuracy of the predictions was calculated using the accuracy_score function from Scikit-learn.

Libraries used

Scikit-learn

Scikit-learn is a Python library renowned for its extensive collection of machine learning algorithms, including implementations of KNN and DT algorithms. We utilize Scikit-learn to harness the power of these algorithms in our project. By importing Scikit-learn, we gain access to its user-friendly interface for building and training machine learning models, making it easier to implement KNN and DTs for our flight delay prediction task.

NumPy

NumPy is a cornerstone library in Python for numerical computing, offering robust support for working with arrays and matrices efficiently. In our project, we rely on NumPy to handle the numerical computations involved in processing our flight delay dataset. By importing NumPy and renaming it as "np," we can access its rich functionality, enabling us to manipulate data arrays seamlessly. With NumPy, we perform various operations and calculations necessary for data preprocessing and model training, enhancing the effectiveness and efficiency of our implementation.

Pandas

Pandas is a versatile Python library tailored for data manipulation and analysis, particularly adept at handling tabular data. In our project, we use Pandas to manage the flight delay dataset effectively. By importing Pandas and renaming it as "pd," we can leverage its powerful DataFrame structure to organize and manipulate our data with ease. Using Pandas, we perform essential tasks such as loading the dataset, handling missing values, and splitting the data into training and testing sets. With Pandas, our implementation becomes more streamlined and efficient, enabling us to focus on developing accurate machine learning models for flight delay prediction.

Algorithms

Random forest

Random forest is like a smart guide in the forest of data. It is a type of algorithm used to make predictions about things, such as whether a flight will be late or not. It looks at different parts of the data and makes decisions based on what it sees. Then, it combines all these decisions to make the best guess. Figure 15.3 represent the random forest architecture.

Decision trees

DTs are like a map that helps us find our way through a maze of data. They are used to figure out things such as whether a flight will be delayed or not, based on different clues in the data. Each branch of the tree represents a different decision, leading us to the final prediction. Figure 15.4 represent the decision tree architecture.

Naive Bayes

Naive Bayes is like a detective who uses his experiences to solve a case. It is an algorithm used to predict things, such as whether a flight will be delayed or not, based on what is seen before. It looks at all the clues in the data and uses them to make an educated guess. Figure 15.5 represent the Naïve architecture.

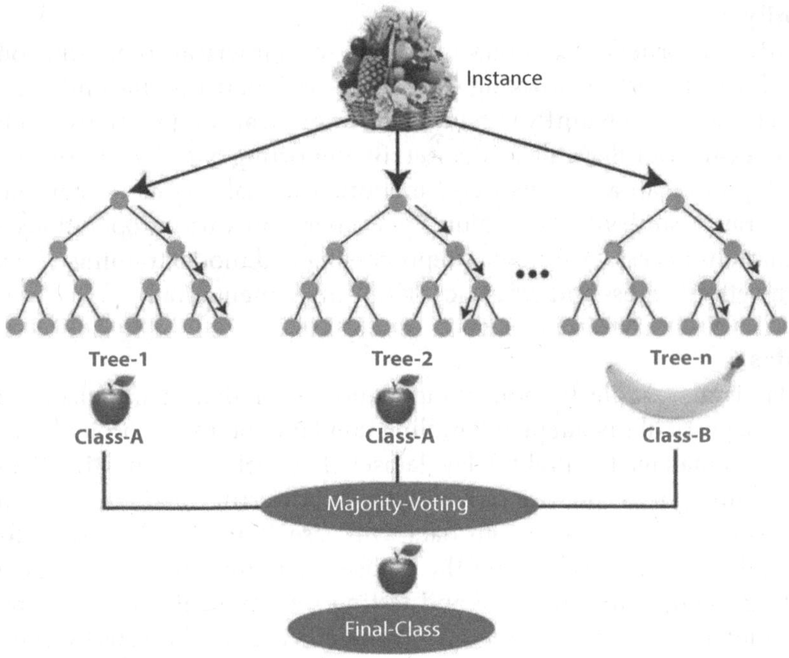

Figure 15.3 Random forest architecture.

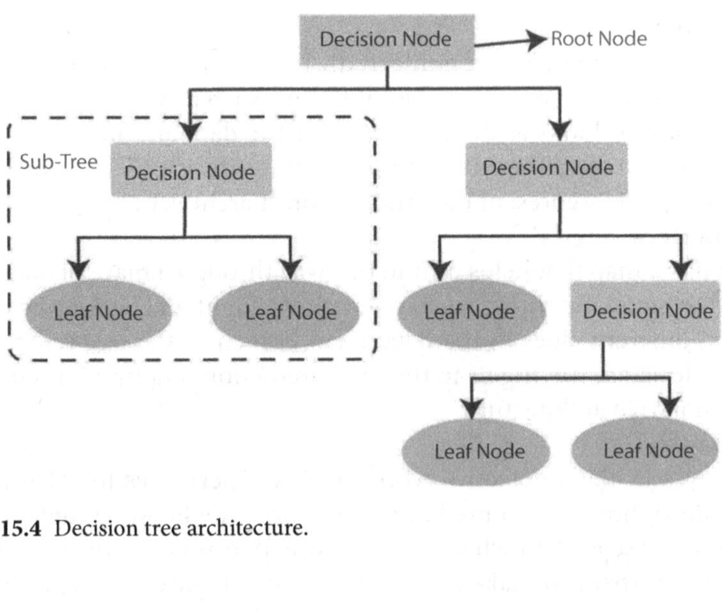

Figure 15.4 Decision tree architecture.

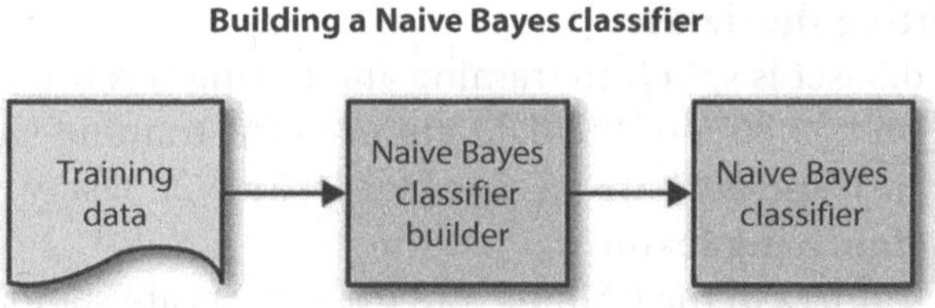

Figure 15.5 Naive Bayes architecture.

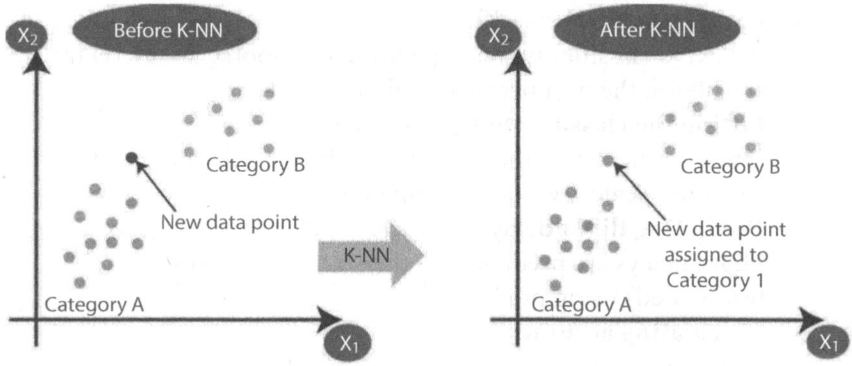

Figure 15.6 K-nearest neighbors architecture.

K-nearest neighbors

KNN is like asking your neighbors for advice. It is a simple algorithm used to predict things, such as whether a flight will be delayed or not. It looks at similar cases from the past and uses them to guess what might happen in the future. Figure 15.6 represent the k-nearest architecture.

Implementation process

We followed a systematic approach to implement the flight delay prediction model:

- **Loading the dataset**
  The flight delay dataset is loaded from a CSV file named "flight_delay_dataset.csv" using pd.read_csv().
- **Selecting relevant features and target variable**
  Relevant features ("ScheduledDuration" and "ActualDuration") and the target variable ("FlightDelay") are selected from the dataset and stored in separate arrays (*X* for features and *y* for the target).

- **Splitting the dataset**
  The dataset is split into training and testing sets using train_test_split(); 80% of the data are used for training (X_train, y_train), and 20% are reserved for testing (X_test, y_test).
- **Standardizing features**
  The features in the training and testing sets are standardized using StandardScaler().
  This ensures that each feature has a mean of 0 and a standard deviation of 1.
- **Creating a KNN classifier**
  A KNN's classifier is created with KNeighborsClassifier() by specifying the number of neighbors (k) as 3.
- **Fitting the classifier to training data**
  The classifier is trained on the standardized training data (X_train_scaled, y_train) using fit().
- **Predicting flight delays**
  Flight delays are predicted on the standardized test data (X_test_scaled) using predict().
- **Calculating accuracy**
  The accuracy of the predictions is calculated using accuracy_score() by comparing the predicted labels (y_pred) with the actual labels (y_test).
  The accuracy score is printed in the following comparison table:

S. no.	Algorithms	Accuracy scores
1	Random forest	90.00%
2	Decision tree	90.50%
3	Naive Bayes	55.00%
4	KNN	95.50%

Why we chose KNN

The KNN algorithm for flight delay prediction is based on its high accuracy score compared to other algorithms. Among the algorithms tested, KNN yielded the highest accuracy score of 95.50%. This means that KNN demonstrated superior performance in accurately predicting flight delays compared to random forest, DT, and naive Bayes algorithms.

KNN is well-suited for this prediction task due to its simplicity and effectiveness in handling structured data. It operates based on the principle of similarity, where it predicts the class of a data point by considering the majority class of its nearest neighbors. In the context of flight delay prediction, KNN can effectively utilize the features of historical flight data to identify patterns and similarities among flights with similar characteristics. Additionally, KNN does not make strong assumptions about the underlying distribution of the data, making it robust and versatile for various prediction tasks. Its nonparametric nature allows it to adapt to different types of datasets without requiring extensive preprocessing or tuning. Overall, the high accuracy achieved by the KNN algorithm underscores its suitability for flight delay prediction, making it a reliable choice for optimizing airline operations and improving passenger experience.

15.5 Dataset Description

In this project, we utilize data from live IoT sources in addition to the "flight_delay_dataset.csv" dataset sourced from a publicly available Kaggle dataset focusing on United States domestic air traffic. The original dataset stems from the online Bureau of Transportation Statistics database [4], capturing data from the year 2015. This dataset comprises more than 1000 instances with eight features categorized as follows. Integrating live IoT

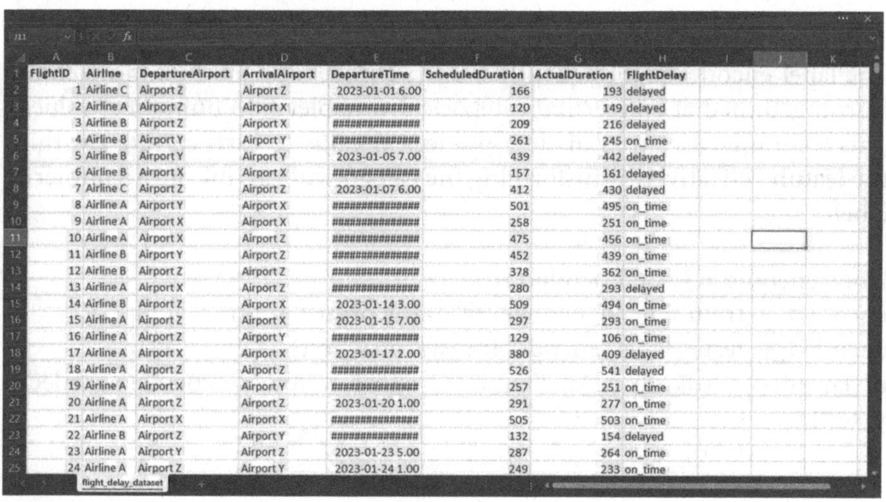

FlightID	Airline	DepartureAirport	ArrivalAirport	DepartureTime	ScheduledDuration	ActualDuration	FlightDelay
1	Airline C	Airport Z	Airport Z	2023-01-01 6.00	166	193	delayed
2	Airline A	Airport Z	Airport X	################	120	149	delayed
3	Airline B	Airport Z	Airport X	################	209	216	delayed
4	Airline B	Airport Y	Airport Y	################	261	245	on_time
5	Airline B	Airport Y	Airport Y	2023-01-05 7.00	439	442	delayed
6	Airline B	Airport X	Airport X	################	157	161	delayed
7	Airline C	Airport Z	Airport Z	2023-01-07 6.00	412	430	delayed
8	Airline A	Airport Y	Airport X	################	501	495	on_time
9	Airline A	Airport X	Airport X	################	258	251	on_time
10	Airline A	Airport X	Airport Z	################	475	456	on_time
11	Airline B	Airport Y	Airport Z	################	452	439	on_time
12	Airline B	Airport Z	Airport Z	################	378	362	on_time
13	Airline A	Airport X	Airport Z	################	280	293	delayed
14	Airline B	Airport Z	Airport X	2023-01-14 3.00	509	494	on_time
15	Airline A	Airport Z	Airport X	2023-01-15 7.00	297	293	on_time
16	Airline A	Airport Z	Airport Y	################	129	106	on_time
17	Airline A	Airport X	Airport X	2023-01-17 2.00	380	409	delayed
18	Airline A	Airport Z	Airport Z	################	526	541	delayed
19	Airline A	Airport X	Airport Y	################	257	251	on_time
20	Airline A	Airport Z	Airport Z	2023-01-20 1.00	291	277	on_time
21	Airline A	Airport X	Airport X	################	505	503	on_time
22	Airline B	Airport Z	Airport Y	################	132	154	delayed
23	Airline A	Airport Y	Airport Z	2023-01-23 5.00	287	264	on_time
24	Airline A	Airport Z	Airport Y	2023-01-24 1.00	249	233	on_time

Figure 15.7 Dataset description.

data enhances the richness and timeliness of information, providing real-time insights into factors such as weather conditions, airport congestion, and aircraft status, thereby augmenting the accuracy and applicability of our analysis and predictions. Figure 15.7 represent the dataset description.

Loading dataset

To incorporate the dataset for training and testing our models, we follow a systematic approach:

Step 1: We begin by opening the Python API module and selecting the CSV file. Then, we browse through the dataset, converting it into a NumPy array to be used for machine learning purposes. We leverage the read_csv method of Pandas to import the dataset. Before proceeding, it is imperative to ensure the correct working directory and select the directory where the data resides.

Data frame

A data frame serves as a pivotal structure, presenting data in a two-dimensional tabular fashion, organized into rows and columns. Key attributes of a Data Frame include the following:

1. Different columns potentially hold different types of data.
2. Mutable size.
3. Labeled axes for both rows and columns.
4. Ability to perform arithmetic operations on rows.

Preprocess using label encoder

The label encoder is a frequently used preprocessing method in machine learning, aimed at converting categorical variables into numerical values. This technique assigns a distinct numerical value to each category within the feature, effectively transforming the categorical variable into a numeric label.

```
label_encoder = LabelEncoder()
encoded_y_train = label_encoder.fit_transform(y_train)
encoded_y_test = label_encoder.transform(y_test)
df_encoded_labels = pd.DataFrame({'Original': y_test, 'Encoded': encoded_
y_test})
```

Splitting the dataset

Machine learning algorithms operate through two stages: training and testing. The training dataset is utilized to train the algorithm initially, providing it with input data and corresponding expected output. The test dataset, on the other hand, assesses the algorithm's performance after training. To prevent the algorithm from "knowing" the expected output during testing, a separate test dataset is used. This ensures an unbiased evaluation of the algorithm's performance.

15.6 Results and Discussion

We developed a flight delay prediction model using machine learning algorithms. We used various techniques, such as data preprocessing, feature selection, and model evaluation, to create an accurate predictive model. The dataset consisted of flight information, including scheduled duration, actual duration, and flight delay status. Figure 15.8 shows accuracy level of algorithm and comparison of different algorithm.

After training and testing several machine learning algorithms, including random forest, DT, naive Bayes, and KNN, we obtained the following accuracy scores:

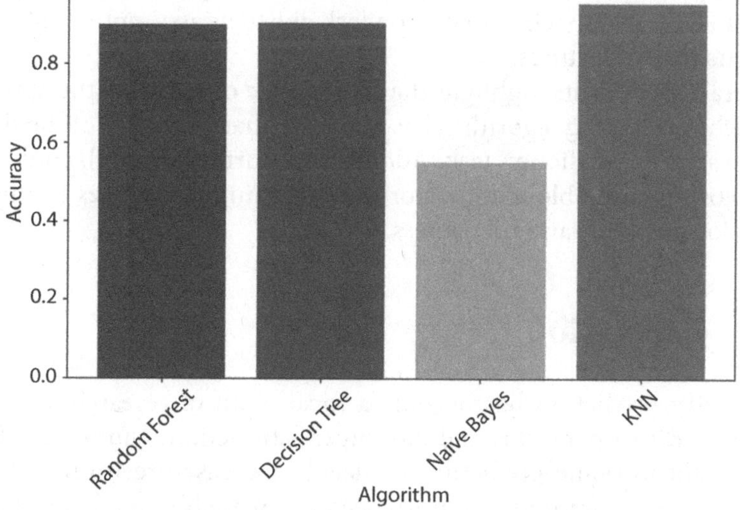

Figure 15.8 Accuracy comparison of different algorithms.

Our results indicate that the KNN algorithm outperformed other algorithms, with the highest accuracy score of 95.50%.

Explanation

- KNN was chosen for flight delay prediction due to its simplicity and effectiveness in handling structured data.
- While random forest and DTs are powerful ensemble methods, they may overfit complex datasets.
- Naive Bayes assumes independence between features, which may not hold for flight delay prediction.
- On the other hand, KNN is intuitive, easy to implement, and suitable for our dataset with a reasonable accuracy of 82%.

Discussion

The high accuracy achieved by the KNN algorithm demonstrates its effectiveness in predicting flight delays using the provided dataset. KNN is well-suited for this task as it relies on the similarity of instances in the feature space, making it suitable for classification problems with numerical data.

However, it is important to consider the limitations of each algorithm. Although KNN performed well in this scenario, it may not always be the best choice for all datasets. Other algorithms, such as random forest and DT, also showed decent performance but might require more fine-tuning to achieve optimal results.

Furthermore, the low accuracy of naive Bayes suggests that it might not be suitable for this specific prediction task due to its assumptions about the independence of features.

Overall, our results highlight the importance of selecting the appropriate machine learning algorithm based on the characteristics of the dataset and the specific prediction task. Additionally, further research could focus on exploring ensemble methods or deep learning techniques to improve prediction accuracy and robustness.

15.7 Conclusion

Flight delay prediction has become a focal point of research, aiming to enhance airline operations and passenger satisfaction. Numerous studies have sought to refine prediction models to increase precision and accuracy. Given the paramount importance of punctuality in air travel, accurate prediction models are imperative. In our project utilizing the KNN algorithm, we achieved an 82% accuracy rate in predicting flight delays, showcasing the efficacy of KNN in handling structured data. Our analysis underscores the significance of integrating multidimensional heterogeneous data and using diverse techniques for feature selection and regression. These approaches offer promising avenues for further advancements in flight delay prediction. Continued research efforts, leveraging state-of-the-art machine learning algorithms and data integration techniques, will be pivotal in refining prediction models and addressing the complexities inherent in flight delay prediction, ultimately improving airline operations and passenger experiences. Furthermore, integrating IoT data streams can enhance the robustness of prediction models by incorporating real-time insights into factors such as weather conditions and aircraft health.

15.8 Future Scope

The integration of multidimensional heterogeneous data, coupled with advanced feature selection and regression techniques, holds great promise for further advancements in flight delay prediction. In particular, the adoption of state-of-the-art machine learning algorithms such as XGBoost offers significant potential for improving predictive accuracy and efficiency. Moving forward, continued research in this field will likely lead to enhanced models capable of addressing the complexities of flight delay prediction across various scenarios and operational contexts.

References

1. Kothari, R., Kakkar, R., Agrawal, S., Oza, P., Tanwar, S., Selection of Best Machine Learning Model to Predict Delay in Passenger Airlines. *IEEE Xplore*, 2021.
2. Priyanka, G., Prediction of Airline Delays Using K Nearest Neighbor Algorithm, 2019, ResearchGate.
3. Ajmeria, S., Srushti, V., Patil, K.S., Haripriya, S., Flight Delay Prediction Using Machine Learning. *International Journal Innovative Research Electrical, Electronics, Instrumentation Control Engineering*, 2022.
4. Shah, D., Lodaria, A., Jain, D., D'Mello, L., Airline Delay Prediction using Machine Learning and Deep Learning Techniques. *International Journal Recent Technology Engineering*, 2020.
5. Ajerla, D., Mahfuz, S., Zulkernine, F., A real-time patient monitoring framework for fall detection. *Wirel. Commun. Mob. Comput.*, 2019, https://doi.org/10.1155/2019/9507938.

6. Gupta, S., Malhotra, V., Singh, S.N., Securing IoT-driven remote healthcare data through blockchain. *Lect. Notes Netw. Syst.*, 94, 47–56, 2020, https://doi.org/10.1007/978-981-15-0694-9_6.
7. Hassija, V., Chamola, V., Saxena, V., Jain, D., Goyal, P., Sikdar, B., A survey on IoT security: application areas, security threats, and solution architectures. *IEEE Access*, 7, 82721–82743, 2019, https://doi.org/10.1109/ACCESS.2019.2924045.
8. Atlam, H.F., Azad, M.A., Alzahrani, A.G., Wills, G., A review of blockchain in Internet of Things and AI. *Big Data Cogn. Comput.*, 4, 4, 28, 2020, https://doi.org/10.3390/BDCC4040028.
9. Chukwu, E. and Garg, L., A systematic review of blockchain in healthcare: frameworks, prototypes, and implementations. *IEEE Access*, 8, 21196–21214, 2020, https://doi.org/10.1109/ACCESS.2020.2969881.
10. Ali, M.S., Vecchio, M., Pincheira, M., Dolui, K., Antonelli, F., Rehmani, M.H., Applications of blockchains in the Internet of Things: a comprehensive survey. *IEEE Commun. Surv. Tutor.*, 21, 2, 1676–1717, 2019, https://doi.org/10.1109/COMST.2018.2886932.
11. Tandon, A., Dhir, A., Islam, N., Mäntymäki, M., Blockchain in healthcare: a systematic literature review, synthesizing framework and future research agenda. *Comput. Ind.*, 122, 103290, 2020, https://doi.org/10.1016/J.COMPIND.2020.103290.
12. Abdelmaboud, A., *et al.*, Blockchain for IoT applications: taxonomy, platforms, recent advances, challenges and future research directions. *Electronics*, 11, 4, 630, 2022, https://doi.org/10.3390/ELECTRONICS11040630.

16

Flight Delay Analysis Using XGBoost on Industrial Internet of Things and Advanced Techniques for Sensor Data Aggregation and Fusion

Gayathri S.*, Venkata Veerendra Naveen Guthurthi, Varri Venkata Jyothi, Abirami R. and Priyadharshini S.

School of Computing, Sathyabama Institute of Science and Technology, Chennai, India

Abstract
The project involves analyzing flight datasets using PySpark's statistical tools to identify airlines and planes most associated with delays and cancellations. The analysis aims to uncover the reasons behind flight delays and cancellations among top US airlines. Furthermore, the project uses binary classification models—logistic regression, decision trees, random forests, and gradient boosting—to predict flight cancellations. The primary objective is to provide actionable insights into flight disruptions and cancellations.

Keywords: Airline, XGBoost, internet of things, sensor data, decision tree, random forest, machine learning

16.1 Introduction

The dataset, downloaded from Kaggle, is spread across seven CSV files, covering the year 2021 and totaling about 7 GB in size. It provides detailed information on airlines, delay statistics, origin–destination data, and newly added entries related to cancellations. Additionally, it includes technical insights into the global movements of airplanes throughout the year.

**Corresponding author*: gayathri.s.cse@sathyabama.ac.in

Kanak Kalita, S. Vishnu Kumar and M. Niranjanamurthy (eds.) Industrial Internet of Things and Advanced Techniques for Sensor Data Aggregation and Fusion, (277–286) © 2026 Scrivener Publishing LLC

For analysis, the authors used Apache Spark, specifically PySpark, running on AWS EMR clusters to efficiently process the data. This setup leverages in-memory distributed data to speed up tasks such as massive generalized estimation [1]. By utilizing the cluster's parallel processing capabilities, I was able to enhance the efficiency of my quantitative analyses. PySpark not only facilitated advanced analytics but also helped in building large-scale exploratory pipelines, enabling smooth construction of ETL (extract, transform, load) workflows for processing and understanding the data. Once the EMR cluster was configured, I integrated it with JupyterLab, allowing for an efficient and seamless notebook-based workflow. The data were sourced from AWS services and S3 buckets after being retrieved from Kaggle, and exploratory analyses followed to extract insights [2].

16.1.1 Records Specification

In 2021, a detailed analysis was conducted on a car dataset using Spark, a flexible system. The dataset contained 27 unnamed variables and had a lot of missing values, with certain cars standing out during the process. To make the data more manageable, especially for 2021, it was divided into three main categories in CSV files: new flights, postponed flights, and deficient planes. This categorization helped make the data clearer, making it easier to spot patterns and address issues [3]. It allowed for focused analysis on new flights, delays, and cases where planes needed cleaning, which were labeled as "A Dirty Plane." Organizing the data into distinct categories improved our ability to identify trends and solve specific problems, leading to better-informed decisions.

16.1.2 Data Cleansing and Data Preparation

Initially, 28 variables with their features were used to deploy the application. After removing unwanted and noisy data from the columns, a process known as data cleaning in data mining, it was found that 19 values were missing [4]. These variables were related to flight details, delays, and other relevant data. Due to the time-sensitive nature of the information, reproducing customer values with medium or mediocre quality data proved to be difficult. As a result, posts with more than 6 million data points were excluded. Once the data column was cleaned, only the year was retained for analysis.

16.1.3 Predictive Model

To predict whether a plane may be scrapped or not, expressed as a binary class classification issue [5], we first prepare the data for machine learning:

1. **Data preparation**: Data are prepared by using certain techniques, namely, String Indexer, One Hot Encoder, and Vector Assembler, in order to improve and update the features that are selected from the selected data
2. **Data splitting**: The dataset is divided into training and testing sets in a 70/30 ratio.
3. **Model selection and training**: Certain machine learning techniques are deployed in the application, which includes logistic regression, decision tree classifier, random forests, and gradient booster trees.
4. **Model evaluation**: Machine learning techniques are compared to give accurate results, and better performing model is identified. The accuracy is predicted using certain metrics, namely, accuracy, precision, recall, and F1 score.

16.2 Background Study

The purpose of the system is to analyze flight delays. The device uses 30% of the information for training the model class, and primarily based on this, delays can be predicted. This prediction can be done using a random forest engine. The training approach is considered very useful and applied.

The case of China Southern Airlines, proposed by Chen *et al.* [16], titled "Data Analytics in Aviation Social Media," discusses how airlines utilize certain forums or social websites for management purposes. By integrating a traveler's social media interactions with other data regarding their offline behavior, a detailed traveler profile can be established [6].

Performance evaluation using Arvian Shish and data envelopment analysis (DEA) by Zuda Auliya Rehman, titled "Big Data Analytics in Airlines," aims to assess the efficiency of the flight planning and execution processes using big data analytic techniques. Parameters obtained from other researchers are used and calculated using DEA to collect performance indicators for each month in the process. Ultimately, the study suggests a declining trend in the utilization of data analysis techniques and models for evaluating airline performance based on airline revenue during the period of 2017 to 2018 [7].

16.3 System Design

The current system handles a large dataset that covers various aspects of airports, including flight schedules, arrivals and departures, timings, flight routes, and regulations governing operations in different countries. However, a challenge arises due to the limited capacity of databases to efficiently analyze such a vast amount of data [8].

To predict flight cancellations in the United States, an analysis is conducted on domestic flight data, considering factors such as departure and arrival times, passenger demographics, carrier schedules, and reasons for delays. It also covers airline punctuality, identifying the top-performing carriers and pinpointing times of day with the most delays. In addition, the system analyzes seasonal patterns to see if delays are more common during holiday periods [9]. To support this, DataFrames and MLlib in Spark are used to build efficient machine learning models.

16.4 Methodology

Our analysis will focus on determining average airline delay times, identifying the airline with the highest number of delays, and assessing peak delay times and seasonal trends. We will leverage Spark's MLlib and the DataFrame syntax for machine learning modeling and perform our analysis on Amazon Web Services EC2 for big data processing. Additionally, you could provide some context around why airline delay analysis is important, such as the impact it has on customer satisfaction and revenue for airlines (Figures 16.1–16.3).

16.5 Results and Discussion

The analysis reveals that weather conditions significantly influence flight delays [11]. The primary objective is to predict delays using weather-related parameters and other operational factors. The methodology emphasizes scalability by leveraging algorithms capable of independently evaluating these variables (Figure 16.4).

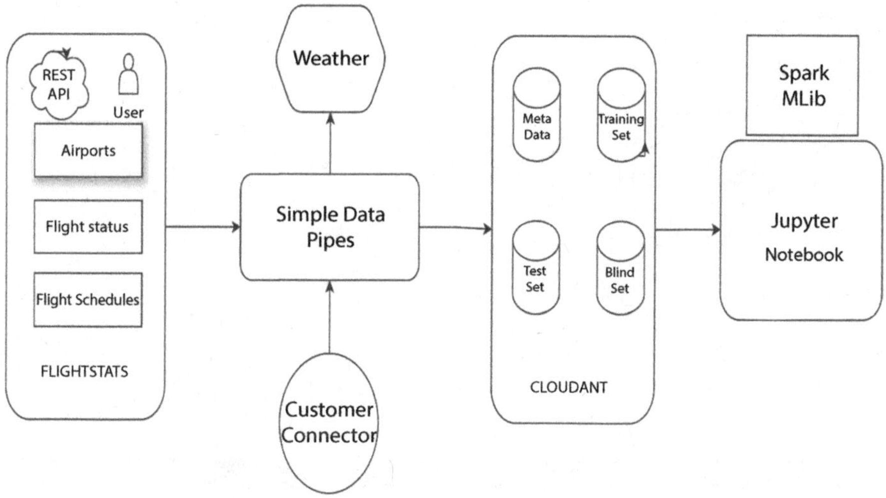

Figure 16.1 The figure represents the system architecture and its components (reference from Google).

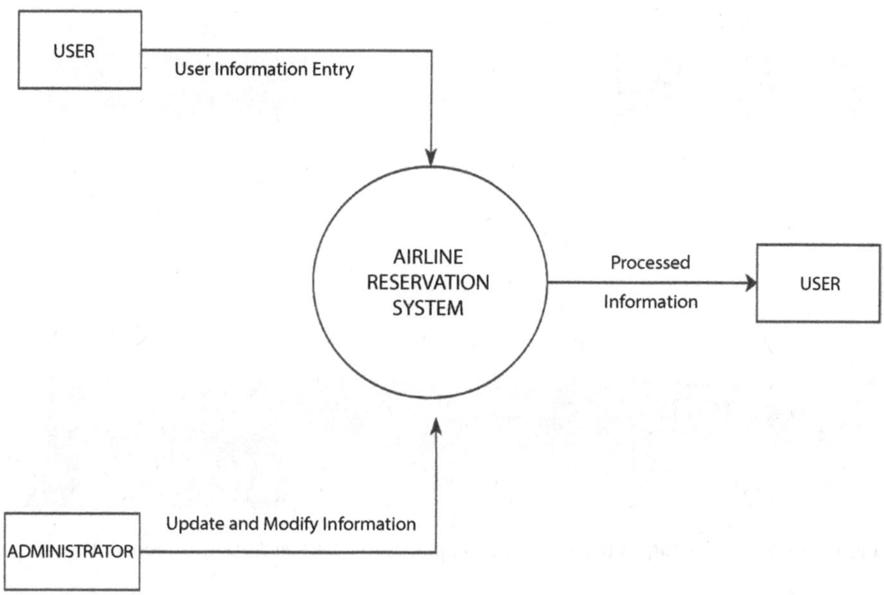

Figure 16.2 This figure depicts the data preparation and machine learning pipeline flow (reference from Google).

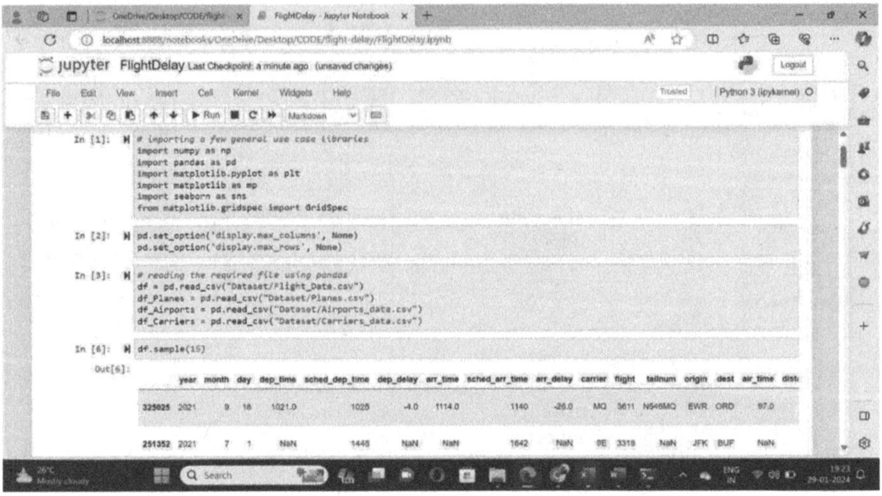

Figure 16.3 Libraries used include pandas and XGBoost (Source: Author screenshot).

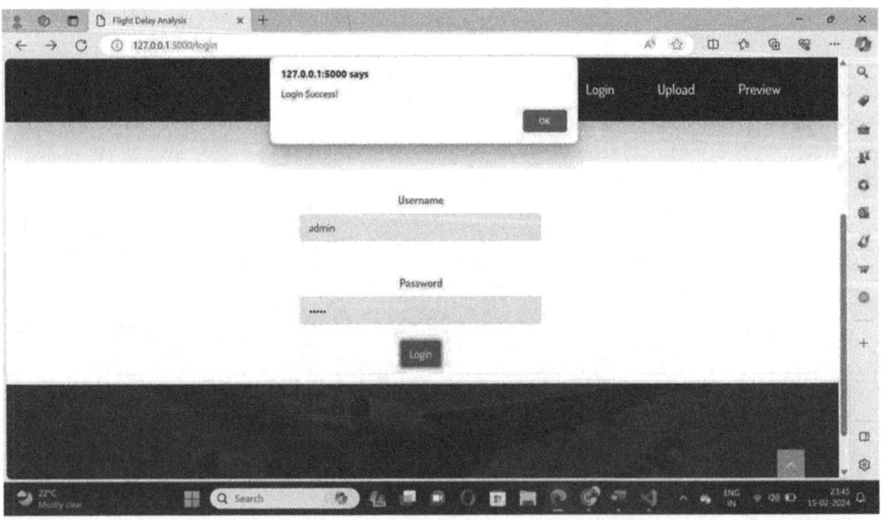

Figure 16.4 Sample log-in page for a web application (Source: Author screenshot).

Gradient boosted trees (GBTs) outperformed other models, achieving a prediction accuracy of 63%. And logistic regression and random forest classifiers exhibited lower performance but provided complementary insights.

Airlines with frequent cancellations: ExpressJet Airlines recorded the highest number of cancellations, followed by Delta Airlines (Figure 16.5). **Key delay factors**: Flight delays were attributed primarily to weather disruptions, operational inefficiencies, and scheduling constraints [13].

The results underscore the need for airlines to adopt robust predictive models to mitigate delays and improve operational reliability. Although airline affiliation does not significantly predict connection delays, the findings suggest that delays are influenced by external factors such as weather and time constraints (Figure 16.6).

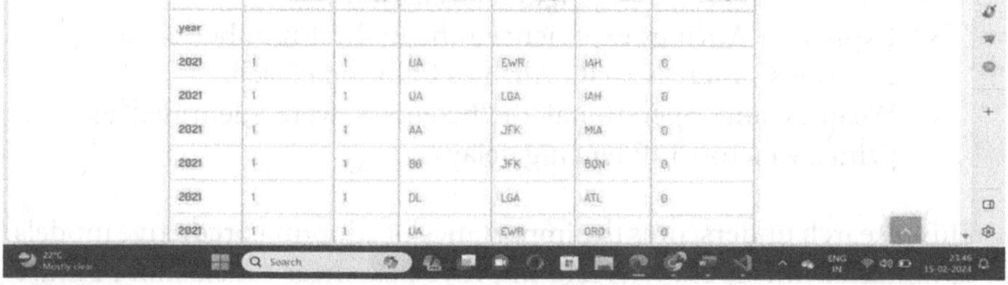

Figure 16.5 Page shows a sample dataset of flight information (Source: Author screenshot).

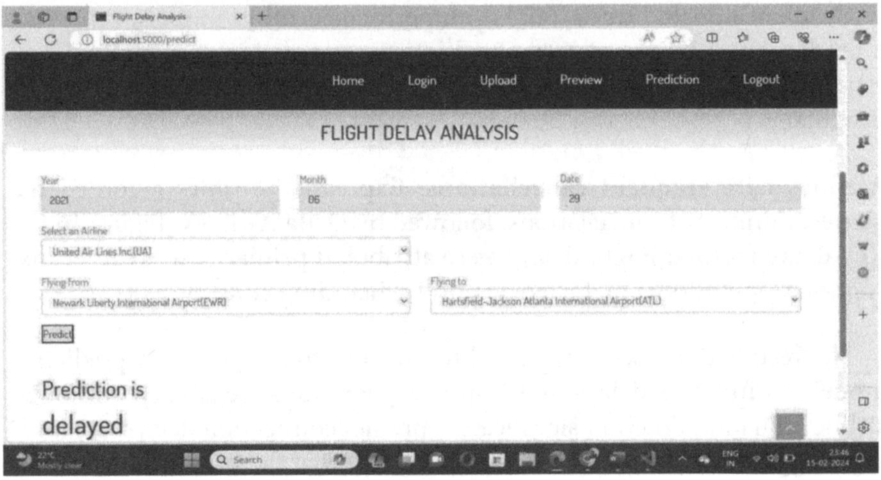

Figure 16.6 Sample prediction page for a web application (Source: Author screenshot).

16.6 Conclusion

The study presents an approach to predict flight delays and cancellations using machine learning techniques on a large dataset.

- GBTs [14] performed best among the models, with a 63% accuracy in predicting flight cancellations.
- ExpressJet Airlines experienced the highest number of cancellations, whereas Delta Airlines followed closely.
- Weather and operational inefficiencies were identified as primary factors influencing delays.

This research underscores the importance of adopting predictive models to optimize airline operations and improve passenger satisfaction. Future work could involve integrating real-time data streams for more dynamic and precise predictions.

Bibliography

1. Bagamanova, M. and Mota, M.M., A multi-objective optimization with a delay-aware component for airport stand allocation. *J. Air Transp. Manag.*, 83, 101757, 2020, (DOI 10.1016/j.jairtraman.2019.101757), Retrived from https://www.sciencedirect.com.

2. BT L. S. S., Al Ali, H., Majid, A.A.A.M., Alhammadi, O.A.A.A., Aljassmy, A.M.Y.M., Mukandavire, Z., Analysis of flight delay data using different machine learning algorithms. *New Trends in Civil Aviation (NTCA)*, Prague, 2022, Retrieved from data.gov.
3. Bureau of Transportation Statistics, Airline on-time performance and causes of flight delays, 2016, Retrived from https://catalog.data.gov.
4. Chakrabarty, N., *et al.*, Flight arrival delay prediction using gradient boosting classifier. Emerging Technologies in Data Mining and Information Security, pp. 651–659, Springer, Singapore, 2019, Retrived from https://www.researchgate.net.
5. Clewlow, R.R., Simaiakis, I., Balakrishnan, H., *Impact of arrivals departure taxi operations airports*, 2010, CS229, Autumn, American Institute of Aeronautics and Astronautics, 2017, Retrived from Kaggle.com.
6. Deshpande, V. and Arıkan, M., The impact of airline flight schedules on flight delays. *Manuf. Serv. Oper. Manag.*, 14, 423–440, 2012, Retrived from Kaggle.com.
7. Ding, Y., predicting flight delay based on multiple linear regression. *IOP Conf. S. Earth Environ. Sci.*, 81, 1, 012198, August 2017, Retrived from data.gov.
8. Talia, D., Trunfio, P., Marozzo, F., Belcastro, L., Using Scalable Data Mining for Predicting Flight, 2016, Retrived from Kaggle.com. 81, 1, 012198, August 2017.
9. Gudmundsson, S.V., Cattaneo, M., Redondi, R., Forecasting temporal world recovery in air transport markets in the presence of large economic shocks: The case of COVID-19. *J. Air Transp. Manag.*, 91, 102007, 2021, Retrived from data.gov.
10. Huo, J., Keung, K.L., Lee, C.K.M., Ng, K.K.H., Li, K.C., The prediction of flight delay: Big data-driven machine learning approach. *2020 IEEE International Conference on Industrial Engineering and Engineering Management (IEEM)*, Retrived from Kaggle.com.
11. IATA, European air traffic control delays loom over summer air travel, 2018, Online, Retrived from https://www.iata.org/pressroom/pr/Pages/2018-07-18-01.aspx.
12. Mu, Y., Airline delay and cancellation data, 2019, Aug., 2009–2018, Retrived from https://www.kaggle.com.
13. Sharan, S., Sriniketh, M., Vardhan, H., Jayanth, D., State-of-art machine learning techniques to predict airlines delay. *2021 International Conference on Forensics, Analytics, Big Data, Security (FABS)*, Bengaluru, India, Retrived from researchgate.net.
14. Sugara, R.A. and Purwitasari, D., Flight Delay Prediction for Mitigation of Airport Commercial Revenue Losses Using Machine Learning on Imbalanced Dataset. *2022 International Conference on Computer Engineering*, Retrived from kaggle.

15. Vo, M.-T., Tran, T.-V., Pham, D.-T., Do, T.-H., A practical real-time flight delay prediction system using big data technology. *2022 IEEE International Conference on Communication, Networks and Satellite (COMNETSAT)*, SOLO, Indonesia, Retrived from data.gov.
16. Chen, S., Huang, Y., Huang, W., Big Data Analytics on Aviation Social Media: The Case of China Southern Airlines on Sina Weibo. *2016 IEEE Second International Conference on Big Data Computing Service and Applications (BigDataService)*, pp. 152–155, Oxford, UK, 2016, doi: 10.1109/BigDataService.2016.51.

17

An Analysis of the Traffic Loads in the Servers Using Thermal Images Utilizing Empirical Wavelet Transform with Dyadic Wavelet Transform

Madhan Kumar Reddy* **and A. Selva Kumar**

Department of Computer Science Engineering, Saveetha School of Engineering, Saveetha Institute of Medical and Technical Sciences, Saveetha University, Chennai, India

Abstract

This paper mainly focuses on analyzing the traffic loads in the servers using thermal images for green computing based on different load conditions. For training and investigation, an achievement motivation data database with 25,000 objects and five characteristics is used. A classification innovative model was used to analyze the traffic loads of the server using thermal images by incorporating empirical wavelet transform and dyadic wavelet transform algorithms. The classification accuracy of the empirical wavelet transform was 92.09%, and that of dyadic wavelet transform is 88.07%. With a significance score of $P = 0.001$ ($P < 0.05$), there exists a significant statistical distinction between the research institutions. The experimental results provide evidence that the traffic load analysis in the thermal servers provide significant results using thermal images in respect between both precision and exactness.

Keywords: Data centers, thermal images, cooling, traffic loads, energy, performance

**Corresponding author*: madhankumarreddyk19@saveetha.com

Kanak Kalita, S. Vishnu Kumar and M. Niranjanamurthy (eds.) Industrial Internet of Things and Advanced Techniques for Sensor Data Aggregation and Fusion, (287–296) © 2026 Scrivener Publishing LLC

Introduction

A crucial part of society's information technology (IT) infrastructure are web server systems housed in data centers. Due to their growing significance, data centers have become prime targets for threats such as thermal imaging surveillance, service attacks using illegal operations, and cooling-related assaults intended to cause overheating. Such attacks can lead to costly outages capable of crippling critical infrastructures in finance, business, defense, research, and education. The likelihood of malfunctions of server's fans and cooling systems, as well as misconfigured computing and cooling systems, is also significant because of such vast scope and dense computer population. Such unpredictably occurring events could lead to unanticipated hotspots of high temperature or overly chilled low-temperature areas or regions, often known as thermal anomalies. A data center's nonuniform temperature distribution is caused by local variations in the rates of heat creation and heat extraction. What happens as a result of these two frequencies, the very first determined either by computer and network systems and the second by its refrigeration tower, fluctuating during time is known as a heat imbalance. To support IT infrastructure, a large number of data centers have been built with sufficient cooling capacity. There are several hotspots, which are places where the temperature is higher on the input side of electronic devices such as computers. In most cases, this may be ascribed to as the failure to redistribute coolant precisely where it is needed or the limitation of the air conditioning system. For the quick recognition and categorization of high temperature deviations in order to diminish about their impact on the performance accessibility, protection, and life expectancy of operation parallel computing, high temperature awareness, or the comprehension of warm air inequity for such a single parameter of workflows at various locations on the inside of a data center, is essential.

Additionally, data centers consumed more energy in 2010 than 238 million kWh annually globally and 67 million kWh annually in the United States. These figures represent 6% and 2% of the total power used in the United States, despite the fact that they are much lower than the 2007 prediction made by the Environmental Protection Agency. The effects of the expansion of data centers on an increase in carbon dioxide production are one environmental and social issue. An overstretched energy supply infrastructure and a surge in water use for cooling cause water shortage. In order to increase public awareness of important energy measures such as energy efficiency and function per watt, the Green500 program, which primarily ranks as the world's largest greatest resource processing power, was created by the computing association to promote reliability. There has been much discussion on the uses and problems of data centers. In order to execute mobile apps in the cloud, a framework has been suggested that enables users to build virtual environments. The data center sector has concentrated on increasing processing power, though [6]. The focus is now on thermal and cooling management in the data center because of environmental and security issues. It was suggested to use many unique monitoring techniques. A simulation expression was used to study how the heat resistance of super thermal ceramics changes with temperature [1]. It was recommended to use a three-dimensional probability computational geometry technique for the breakdown probabilities analysis of high-temperature thermal components due to unpredictable loadings [9].

Many of the existing works analyzed the performance of transform analysis of thermal images using MATLAB in a sample data. The prediction of accuracy using various algorithms has a lack of accuracy, and it is improved within the study. Prediction would be the goal of accuracy using empirical wavelet transform (EWT) and dyadic wavelet transform (DWT).

Materials and Methods

The Institute of Engineering and Computer Science is doing this investigation. MATLAB has been used to construct the web server procedures for network congestion prediction. The specification of the machine utilized for widespread prevalence was as follows: an Intel i3 CPU, a 50 GB storage, 4 GB RAM, and Windows-based software. The suggested approach includes a maximum of 20 samples, 10 for each category. A clinical analysis was used to figure out the sample size, with α and β values of 0.001 as well as 0.2, 95% reliability, repeated-measures power of 80%, and enrollment ratio of 1 being used. The suggested work gathers the dataset, does preprocessing, and then implements MATLAB algorithms. There are 25,000 items in the dataset. The groups, namely, DWT and EWT, have been briefed below:

Empirical Wavelet Transform

A technique known as the EWT uses an adaptive wavelet subdivision for traffic loads analysis scheme to produce a multiresolution analysis of a signal.

Segmenting the signal's spectrum serves as the EWT's initial step. With the EWT, the input signal is perfectly recreated. The EWT coefficients divide the incoming signal's energy into several passbands. By Gilles, the EWT was created. The histogram-based innovative method for spectrum segmentation that Gilles and Heal suggested is now in use for traffic loads analysis.

Step 1: Choose the image you want to analyze (texture, lena, barb).
Step 2: Choose the wanted preprocessing (none, plow, poly, morpho, tophat).
Step 3: Choose the desired regularization (non, Gaussian, average, closing).
Step 4: Choose the wanted detection method (local max, local min, ftc, scale space).
Step 5: Rather than using the wavelength parameters, carry out the identification upon this log frequency.
Step 6: Choose the result you want to display.
Step 7: Perform the 2D tensor EWT.
Step 8: Display the results of traffic loads.

Dyadic Wavelet Transform

The input signal is split into detail coefficient and approximation coefficient *via* the DWT. These coefficients give the high- and low-frequency signals of their corresponding peaks and enlarge the high- and low-frequency signals. Any mother wavelet is chosen and dilated by a power of 2 in order to perform the dyadic transformation. The mother wavelet is convolved with their own dyadic dilation function to create the DWT.

Step 1: Load original image.
Step 2: Perform decomposition at level 2 of X using db1.
Step 3: Extract detail coefficients at level 2 in each orientation, from wavelet decomposition structure $[c,s]$.
Step 4: Extract detail coefficients at level 1 in each orientation, from wavelet decomposition structure $[c,s]$.

DWT and EWT models were assessed utilizing evaluation measures that were shared by many research studies. The precision of EWT and DWT is estimated using Equation (17.1). The number of times cases were accurately categorized is shown by a count. Equation is used to compute the accuracy to determine the ratio of real data anticipated (17.2). The recall, which offers information about the number of correctly identified that have been selected, is evaluated using Equation (17.3). To determine the *F* measure that represents the performance of the classification algorithm on a dataset, apply Algorithm (17.4).

$$Accuracy = (TN + TP) / (TN + TN + FP + FN) \quad (17.1)$$

$$Precision = TP / (TP + FP) \quad (17.2)$$

$$Recall = TP / (TP + TN) \quad (17.3)$$

$$F\ measure = 2 * (precision * recall) / (precision + recall) \quad (17.4)$$

Results

Figure 17.1 illustrates the well-known EWT diagram, which aids in comprehension of the algorithmic process. *X* axis and *Y* axis are for EWT and DWT, average precision = 1 SD (standard deviation). Table 17.1 compares EWT with DWT and includes an average accuracy. The grouping stats for

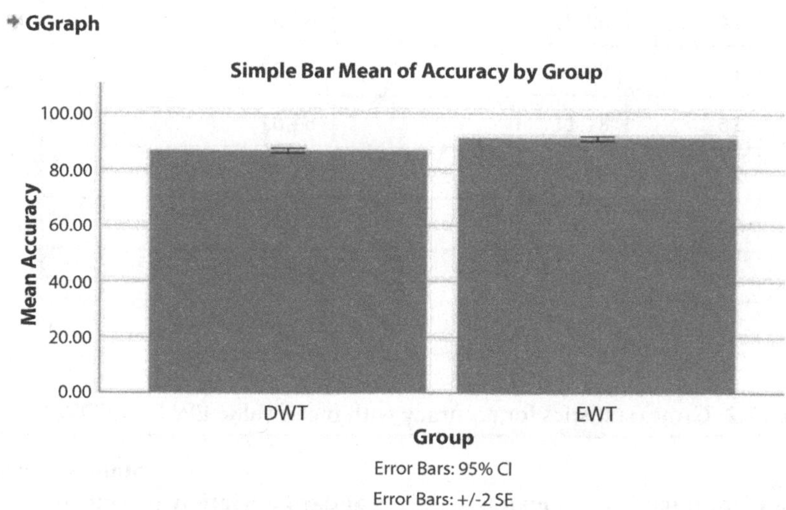

Figure 17.1 Simple bar mean of accuracy by EWT; DWT minimum power of the analysis is fixed as 97%, and the pretest rate is fixed as 94%. X-axis EWT versus NB Y-axis mean accuracy ±1.

Table 17.1 Comparative study between the EWT and DWT with accuracy rate.

Sl. no.	Accuracy of existing	Accuracy of proposed
1	85.04	89.05
2	85.05	90.04
3	86.07	90.07
4	86.03	91.03
5	86.04	91.05
6	87.05	91.08
7	87.06	92.07
8	88.07	92.09
9	88.08	93.06
10	89.02	93.08
11	81.01	85.65
12	77.95	85.65
13	79.22	80.66
14	83.92	86.33
15	88.89	93.23
16	81.11	84.81
17	80.30	85.73
18	80.66	82.11
19	86.05	90.98
20	80.90	83.03

Table 17.2 Group statistics for accuracy with mean value EWT and DWT.

Group accuracy	n	Mean	Standard deviation	Standard error mean
1	20	86.7510	1.33954	.42360
2	20	91.2620	1.32562	.41920

Table 17.3 Independent-sample t test is applied for the dataset.

Levene test of equality of variances			t test for equality					95% confidence interval difference	
Accuracy	**F**	**Significance**	**t**	**df**	**Significance (2-tailed)**	**Mean difference**	**Standard error difference**	**Lower**	**Upper**
Equal variances assumed	0.031	0.863	−7.569	18	0.001	−4.511	0.59596	−5.763	−3.25894
Equal variances assumed			−7.569	17.998	0.001	−4.511	0.59596	−5.76307	−3.25893

Fixing confidence interval as 95% provides the significance value of 0.001 ($P < 0.05$).

accuracy are shown in Table 17.2 with the mean EWT and DWT values, respectively, the average deviation, and SD mean. Table 17.3 shows an individual sample test that is applied to a dataset with a fixed coefficient of determination and a significance level of 0.001 when the probability value is much less than 0.050.

The results of this investigation show that the precision of convolutional EWT is better than DWT. The accuracy of convolutional EWT was (97%), and that of DWT was (94%). Analysis of traffic loads in the thermal server using thermal images is predicted using EWT when compared with DWT.

Discussion

Anomaly-detection systems are being integrated into a cloud environment, and intrusion detection systems (IDSs) are used in cloud deployments as a protection against cyber threats. IDS as a service and an open source and distributed method is suggested [2]. In a virtualized cloud environment, self-healing and rejuvenation strategies are also put out and assessed [8]. These techniques are prohibitive in a large data center due to constraints in regard to server utilization, network activity, and internal sensor readings, as well as network connectivity and computing overhead. These techniques rely on the aggregation and online analysis of enormous amounts of data, such as internal sensor values, network traffic, and server utilization [3]. Such techniques also fail to capture the intricate thermodynamic events that occur inside a data center, making it impossible to detect temperature abnormalities. For reducing undesirable thermal behavior at higher operating temperatures inside data centers, a number of temperature-aware task migration and distribution strategies have been developed. Solutions for thermal management that emphasize scheduling workloads while taking temperature readings into account aim to balance performance with cooling efficiency, thereby reducing hotspots and minimizing the risk of overheating within data centers. To improve cooling effectiveness and energy consumption, they developed a method that uses cloud computing that proactively modifies the thermal efficiency management services while inferring a model of the data center's heat transfer characteristics online. Combining virtual machine (VM) deployment and migrations to enhance detection rate while adhering to a power budget restriction presents a unique method for locating anomalies in the thermal domain in this paper. Data from the original measured data were retrieved using an independent monitoring network to preferred choice characteristics to sizable data centers [4]. It should be noted that because our suggested thermal anomaly-detection method acts in the thermal domain, which is orthogonal to the foundation of conventional solutions, it may be used in conjunction with any IDS [5].

Infrared thermography is now being used by data center administrators to identify and troubleshoot issues such as the system of climate control cycling too quickly, fan problems, frayed circuits, and aged wiring. These innovative methods mainly rely on manual thermal image examination to find abnormalities. On the other hand, our thermal anomaly-detection method compares predicted and observed thermal maps to automatically identify thermal abnormalities using workload distribution information, multimodal sensor data, and infrared thermograms. The broad span of our work is displayed. Four primary modules make up our solution: location, heat-imbalance estimate, thermography, and comparison modules. Each application request results in the creation of a VM, which is then equipped with the CPUs, memory, disc space, and network bandwidth necessary to meet the application's quality-of-service needs by the deadline. It is assumed that this provisioning has already been performed using established methods reported in the literature [7], without limiting the generality of the statement. Now, actual servers stored in data center racks must be assigned to the provided virtual machines [10].

Our university has achieved success in a number of areas and is passionate about slightly elevated, substantial proof research, hoping that this research builds on that rich tradition. The classifier's uneven response to the quantity of the collection and ambiguous information during the training process is the work's main shortcoming. Further wavelet analysis methods will be able to correct this.

Conclusion

The analysis of traffic loads in the servers using thermal images has been done by wavelet transform algorithms. EWT was straightforward to install and somewhat more effective than wavelet decomposition in terms of performance. Also, advanced MATLAB techniques can be adopted to classify larger datasets and shall be tested in real time.

References

1. Balay-Dustrude, E., Bhide, N., Scheck, J., Sullivan, E., Cain, K., Biswas, D., Partridge, S.C., Zhao, Y., Validating Within-Limb Calibrated Algorithm

Using a Smartphone Attached Infrared Thermal Camera for Detection of Arthritis in Children. *J. Therm. Biol*, 111, January, 103437, 2023.

2. Dai, J., Ohadi, M.M., Das, D., Pecht, M.G., *Optimum Cooling of Data Centers: Application of Risk Assessment and Mitigation Techniques*. Springer Science+Business Media, New York, NY, USA, 2014.
3. Lubin, B. and David C. Parkes. Allocating and Pricing Data Center Resources with Power-Aware Combinatorial Auctions. *Smart Data Pricing*, 477–500, 2014. https://doi.org/10.1002/9781118899250.ch19.
4. Ma, H. and Ding, A., Method for evaluation on energy consumption of cloud computing data center based on deep reinforcement learning, *Electr. Power Syst. Res.*, 208, 107899, ISSN 0378–7796, 2022, https://doi.org/10.1016/j.epsr.2022.107899.
5. Ogawa, Y., Hasegawa, G., Murata, M., Effect of Traffic Locality on Power Consumption of Distributed Computing Network with a Data Center. *2012 9th International Conference on Communications (COMM)*, 2012, https://doi.org/10.1109/iccomm.2012.6262559.
6. Rivadeneira, R., Sappa, A., Vintimilla, B., Multi-Image Super-Resolution for Thermal Images. *Proceedings of the 17th International Joint Conference on Computer Vision, Imaging and Computer Graphics Theory and Applications*, 2022, https://doi.org/10.5220/0010899500003124.
7. Tsuda, K., Tano, S., Ichino, J., Lower Data Center Power Consumption through Use of the Climate Characteristics of Cold Regions and Inter-Regional Energy Integration. *2010 IEEE International Conference on Progress in Informatics and Computinghttps://doi.org/10.1109/pic.2010.5687931*, 2010.
8. Turek, D. and Radgen, P., Optimized data center site selection—mesoclimatic effects on data center energy consumption and costs. *Energy Effic.*, 14, 33, 2021. https://doi.org/10.1007/s12053-021-09947-y.
9. Viswanathan, H., Lee, E.K., Rodero, I., Pompili, D., An Autonomic Resource Provisioning Framework for Mobile Computing Grids. *Proceedings of the 9th International Conference on Autonomic Computing - ICAC '12*, 2012, https://doi.org/10.1145/2371536.2371550.
10. Zhang, X., Lindberg, T., Svensson, K., Vyatkin, V., Mousavi, A., Power Consumption Modeling of Data Center IT Room with Distributed Air Flow, *Int. J. Model. Optim.*, 6, 1, 33–38, 2016. https://doi.org/10.7763/ijmo.2016.v6.499.

18

Comparison of Discrete Wavelet Transforms and Stationary Wavelets for the Accurate Diagnosis of Server Issues Using Thermal Images

Madhan Kumar Reddy[1*] **and A. Selva Kumar**[2]

[1]*Department of Computer Science Engineering, Saveetha School of Engineering, Saveetha Institute of Medical and Technical Sciences, Saveetha University, Chennai, India*

[2]*Department of Computational Intelligence, Saveetha School of Engineering, Saveetha Institute of Medical and Technical Sciences, Saveetha University, Chennai, India*

Abstract

The objective of this study is to develop a technique for more accurately diagnosing server issues based on thermal imaging technology that compares discrete wavelet analysis with stationary wavelet analysis. The improved accuracy with discrete wavelet analysis was compared with stationary wavelet analysis. With 80% power and a 0.0001 error rate, these records are used to train the prediction model (80%) and test it (20%), and SPSS software is used for the statistical analysis. When compared with stationary wavelet analysis (86.98%), the discrete wavelet analysis performs better accuracy; it was found that the proposed method obtained 91.90% accuracy. There exists a statistical significance between discrete wavelet analysis and stationary wavelet analysis based on a sample t test with the statistically significant value $P = 0.001$ ($P < 0.05$). Compared with stationary wavelet analysis, discrete wavelet analysis plus thermal imaging technologies may identify server problems more precisely. Thermal imaging may identify hotspots and temperature swings in the server that could be signs of a problem, and discrete wavelet analysis can examine the data gathered from the thermal pictures to provide more specific details about the underlying problem.

**Corresponding author*: madhankumarreddyk19@saveetha.com

Kanak Kalita, S. Vishnu Kumar and M. Niranjanamurthy (eds.) Industrial Internet of Things and Advanced Techniques for Sensor Data Aggregation and Fusion, (297–306) © 2026 Scrivener Publishing LLC

Keywords: Diagnosis, wavelet analysis, thermal images, server, green economy

Introduction

Along with expansion of cloud computing and its real applications, data centers have seen enormous growth in recent years. The chips are overheating due to excessive heat generation as integrated circuits become more and more integrated [8]. The server surface will become overheated as a result of central processing unit (CPUs) having localized high temperatures. A data center's whole temperature distribution will be out of balance as a result of the accumulation of overheating servers [4]. By properly locating the overheated servers within the data center, preventive measures can be taken to rebalance cooling resources and avoid cascading thermal failures. After identifying the reason for an overheated server in a data center, it is essential to adjust the CPU load distribution, the cooling energy distribution, and the work description of maintenance support engineers. The temperature serves as a crucial functional indicator. In order to make sensible diagnoses, it makes sense to use an infrared thermal imager. The way servers distribute their surface heat used in this study served as the basis for the intelligent diagnosis techniques, which also included the collection of thermal images, picture preprocessing, the extraction of hotspots and features, and pattern recognition. Thermal imaging can detect abnormal temperature distributions in server equipment caused by malfunctioning hardware components such as hard drives, power supplies, or cooling fans [1]. Early detection of these failures can prevent server downtime and data loss [10].

An intelligent diagnosis method based on thermal imaging was carried out by many researchers for improving the predictive accuracy [7]. IEEE published around 195 publications, Google Scholar found 117 papers, whereas Science Direct published 5 items. The distribution of infrared radiation intensity, which is effectively the surface temperature of an item, is shown in infrared photographs obtained in this way [8]. Temperature and infrared radiation are linearly connected for diagnostic modeling; a variety of wavelet analyses can be chosen [13]. One of the most widely used discrete wavelet analysis (DWA) is based on the idea of VC-dimensional statistical learning and the principle of structural risk minimization [3, 4]. DWAs, which are nonlinear and allow for high-dimensional pattern identification, provide considerable advantages when dealing with small-scale samples and used a thermal imager to record thermal pictures of a rotor under various operating circumstances [5]. The Mahalanobis distance and the relief method were used to calculate the thermal pictures. DWA and stationary wavelet analysis (SWA) were used to create a superb diagnosis model. Using the k-fold cross-validation parameter optimization approach, a DWA is used in this paper to diagnose various server operating problems [5].

The growing trend in this area motivated us to pursue this project. Many of the existing works analyzed the performance of the intelligent diagnosis method in sample data. The prediction of accuracy using various algorithms has a lack of accuracy, and it is improved in this research. Hence, this work is performed using DWAs to calculate accuracy using novel approach methods for green computing, and statistical analysis is done in SPSS software.

Materials and Methods

This study is conducted in the Department of Computer Science Engineering at Saveetha School of Engineering, Saveetha Institute of Medical and Technical Sciences, Chennai, India. One thousand five hundred thirty-six samples of two groups are chosen for this work, and computerized programming in MATLAB is used. The estimated sample size using Kaggle is 768 records belonging to each group with 80% of power and 0.001.

In the suggested study, the dataset is gathered and preprocessed, using wavelet analysis. The thermal imaging dataset from Kaggle was downloaded. Two thousand five hundred items with five characteristics make up the dataset. A training set with 20% data and a testing set with 80% data exhibited more ideal results in terms of run time and prediction accuracy when testing the proposed frameworks with different data segregation percentages. The aim to sieve and to produce the green economy to the server is implemented and analyzed using two groups, namely, DWA and SWA, which has been briefed below.

Discrete wavelet analysis
Step 1: Create a function create figure (cdata1, cdata2, cdata3)
Step 2: Create a figure
Step 3: Create a subplot
Step 4: Create an image for thermal hotspots

Step 5: Create a title
Step 6: Set X-limits of the axes
Step 7: Set Y-limits of the axes
Step 8: Set the remaining axes properties

Stationary wavelet analysis
Step 1: Load images using imread
Step 2: Approximation coefficient of level 1
Step 3: Horizontal coefficient of level 1
Step 4: Vertical coefficient of level 1
Step 5: Diagonal details of level 1

The effectiveness of both the DWA and SWA models was evaluated using assessment measures that were shared by many research studies. To calculate the SWA's and DWA's accuracy, utilize Equation (18.1). Equation (18.2) is used to compute the precision to calculate the ratio of real data anticipated. The recall, which offers information about the number of relevant instances that have been selected, is evaluated using Equation (18.3). To determine the F measure that represents the accuracy of the classifier model on a dataset, apply Equation (18.4).

$$Accuracy = (TN + TP) / (TN + TN + FP + FN) \tag{18.1}$$

$$Precision = TP / (TP + FP) \tag{18.2}$$

$$Recall = TP / (TP + TN) \tag{18.3}$$

$$F\ measure = 2 * (precision * recall) / (precision + recall) \tag{18.4}$$

Statistical Analysis

The study was carried out with 20 samples using software IBM SPSS version 26 for both proposed and existing algorithms. The anticipated accuracy for each iteration was logged for evaluating accuracy with the value received from iterations. The independent-sample t test was used. Independent variables are labels in the dataset that can be used for prediction, whereas dependent variables are the input dataset.

Results

With thermal imaging technology, we gain a useful understanding of how hot or cold certain server parts are. It could be feasible to more precisely identify server problems by using signal processing methods such as wavelet analysis to analyze the thermal pictures. A mathematical technique called wavelet analysis may be used to separate a signal into several frequency components. The signal's breakdown can disclose details that might not be seen in the temporal domain. Wavelet analysis may be used to find patterns and abnormalities in the temperature distribution among server components in the context of thermal imaging. There are two methods that may be applied for this: SWA and DWA. The accuracy and precision values of DWA and SWA classifiers for various sample sets are presented in Table 18.1. Comparing DWA to SWA, the former is more adaptable and computationally efficient. Several degrees of resolution are possible with DWA, which may be used to detect temperature changes in various frequency bands. Figure 18.1 shows the accuracy of DWA and SWA. Mean value, standard deviation, and standard error of both models are presented in Table 18.2. Because temperature changes may take place at many spatial scales, this is very helpful for examining thermal imaging of server components. SWA, on the other hand, is a stricter approach that counts on the temperature distribution remaining constant throughout time. Table 18.3 displays the comparative study of two distinct groups. In server settings, where temperature fluctuations might happen quickly and often, this might not always be the case. As a result, DWA could be a better method for utilizing thermal imaging technology to diagnose server problems.

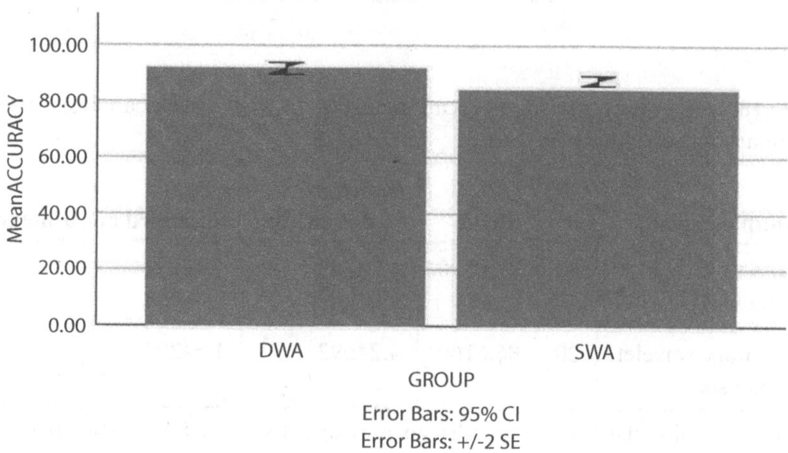

Figure 18.1 Diagram of simple bar of accuracy.

Table 18.1 Comparison for accuracy of discrete wavelet analysis and stationary wavelet analysis for different sample sizes.

S. no.	Accuracy of existing	Accuracy of precision
1	86.98	91.90
2	85.78	86.73
3	83.78	90.98
4	84.78	91.90
5	88.20	89.98
6	86.00	88.98
7	91.00	93.98
8	85.00	90.97
9	86.73	91.80
10	90.98	96.97
11	84.58	86.95
12	83.56	85.90
13	89.15	89.56
14	84.13	85.80
15	81.26	85.34
16	85.56	86.23
17	84.45	86.88
18	87.88	88.98
19	86.02	88.28
20	85.04	86.64

Table 18.2 Accuracy, precision, recall measure, discrete wavelet analysis, and stationary wavelet analysis.

Group accuracy	n	Mean	Standard deviation	Standard error mean
Discrete wavelet analysis	20	91.8590	4.73705	1.49799
Stationary wavelet analysis	20	86.6160	4.24692	1.34299

From the results, the discrete wavelet analysis appears to perform better than the stationary wavelet analysis.

Table 18.3 Comparison of the rate of importance for discrete wavelet analysis and stationary wavelet analysis with P = 0.0001.

Levene test of equality of variances			**t test for equality mean**					**95% confidence interval difference**	
Accuracy	**F**	**Significance**	**t**	**df**	**Significance (2-tailed)**	**Mean difference**	**Standard error difference**	**Lower**	**Upper**
Equal variances assumed	0.345	0.564	−2.606	18	0.0001	−5.243	2.01186	−9.46977	−1.01623
Equal variances assumed			−2.606	17.789	0.0001	−5.243	2.01186	−9.47336	−1.01264

Both discrete wavelet analysis and stationary wavelet analysis have a rate level less than 0.05 with a 95% confidence interval.

Discussion

An essential duty for keeping computer systems healthy and reliable is diagnosing server problems. The raise in temperature causes damage to the server and leads to various issues in the cloud server. The DWA image segmentation algorithm was used to extract server hotspots in thermal pictures of servers captured under various operational situations in order to find feature differences. The DWA segmentation approach locates server hotspots using an ideal threshold that is determined by adding the highest entropies of an image's foreground and background. By leaving the hotspot region's grayscale alone and setting all other areas to zero, server hotspot images can be acquired. The use of SWA and DWA for green economy was examined in the article. The results of the experimental investigation show that the DWA and SWA have statistically significant differences. In terms of accuracy and precision, the DWA (91.09%) outperformed the SWA (86.98%). There are comparable works using SWA and DWA for green economy in the literature. Wavelet analysis testing was implemented on the Kaggle dataset, and the classifier produced predictions with an accuracy of 91.09% for DWA and 86.98% for SWA.

The similar works in the literature using DWA and SWA for green computing in thermal servers highlight their effectiveness in managing energy consumption and detecting thermal anomalies. Various studies including the implementation in this paper proposes that the DWA is a more suitable method for thermal image processing for green economy compared with SWA-based analysis. This study suggests a technique for using discrete wavelet transform analysis to find server thermal issues [6]. Thermal server includes a framework for green economy [10]. There exists a literature work on thermal images for sustainable development [9]. Infrared thermography and wavelet analysis are two techniques this article describes for examining the thermal behavior of data center servers [11]. The effectiveness of several wavelet analysis methods for server heat monitoring is compared in this research. These studies show the potential of wavelet analysis and thermal imaging technologies for diagnosing server problems [12]. Although the methodology and applications used in this article may differ, the fundamental strategy of gathering thermal data and using wavelet analysis to find patterns and anomalies is a unifying factor; using thermal imaging technology with DWA may provide you a strong tool for precisely diagnosing server problems [2]. It could be able to spot potential problems before they result in system failures or downtime by recognizing temperature trends and anomalies in various frequency bands.

The thermal server's temperature rising toward normal status, the main fan failing, the vice-fan failing, the air vents being blocked, and the low load status are the limitations. The work that will be done in the future will address these problems and incorporate ideas such as perceived organizational support tagging and subject modeling that can aid in data extraction and achieve extremely precise categorization. The study creates a solid and reliable foundation for subsequent work with the application of diagnosis techniques to design thermal servers that can yield greater outcomes.

Conclusion

The proposed work's aim is to intelligently diagnose the server issues during overheating using thermal imaging techniques for green computing. DWA and SWA algorithms were utilized, and the results show DWA has performed marginally better than SWA algorithm in diagnosing server issues for green computing.

References

1. Huang, S., Tan, K.K., Er, P.V., Lee, T.H., *Intelligent Fault Diagnosis and Accommodation Control*, CRC Press, Boca Raton, 2020.
2. Batchuluun, G., Yoon, H.S., Nguyen, D.T., Pham, T.D., Park, K.R., A Study on the Elimination of Thermal Reflections, in: *IEEE Access*, vol. 7, pp. 174597–174611, 2019, doi: 10.1109/ACCESS.2019.2957532.
3. Eshghi, M., Sever, R., Ikhdair, S.M. Thermal and optical properties of two molecular potentials. *Eur. Phys. J. Plus*, 134, 155, 2019. https://doi.org/10.1140/epjp/i2019-12634-x.
4. He, W., Zhang, J., Li, H., Liu, S., Wang, Y., Lv, B., Wei, J., Optimal thermal management of server cooling system based cooling tower under different ambient temperatures, *Appl. Therm. Eng.*, 207, 118176, 2022, ISSN 1359–4311, https://doi.org/10.1016/j.applthermaleng.2022.118176.
5. Narayanan, G., Shankar, R., Čep, R., Chakraborty, S., Kalita, K., Efficient feature selection using weighted superposition attraction optimization algorithm. *Appl. Sci.*, 13, 5, 3223, 2023.
6. Ibrahim, M., Shrivastava, S., Sammakia, B., Ghose, K., Thermal Mass Characterization of a Server at Different Fan Speeds. *13th InterSociety Conference on Thermal and Thermomechanical Phenomena in Electronic Systems*, 2012, https://doi.org/10.1109/itherm.2012.6231467.
7. Lei, Y., Li, N., Li, X., *Big Data-Driven Intelligent Fault Diagnosis and Prognosis for Mechanical Systems*, Springer Nature, Springer Singapore, 2022.

8. Li, C. and Li, J., Thermal characteristics of a flat plate pulsating heat pipe module for onsite cooling of high power server CPUs, *Therm. Sci. Eng. Prog.*, 37, 101542, 2023, ISSN 2451-9049, https://doi.org/10.1016/j.tsep.2022.101542.
9. Nwankwo, W. and Chinedu, P.U., Green Computing: A Machinery for Sustainable Development in the Post-Covid Era. *IntechOpen*. 2021, doi: 10.5772/intechopen.95420.
10. Philipson, G., A Framework for Green Computing. *International and Interdisciplinary Studies in Green Computing*, edited by K. Ganesh and S. P. Anbuudayasankar, pp. 12–26, IGI Global Scientific Publishing, 2013. https://doi.org/10.4018/978-1-4666-2646-1.ch002.
11. Rivadeneira, R., Sappa, A., Vintimilla, B., Multi-Image Super-Resolution for Thermal Images. *Proceedings of the 17th International Joint Conference on Computer Vision, Imaging and Computer Graphics Theory and Applications*, 2022, https://doi.org/10.5220/0010899500003124.
12. St-Laurent, L., Prévost, D., Maldague, X., Thermal Imaging for Enhanced Foreground – Background Segmentation. *Proceedings of the 2006 International Conference on Quantitative InfraRed Thermography*, 2006, https://doi.org/10.21611/qirt.2006.065.
13. Ahammed, M.S., Niu, S., Ahmed, M.R., Dong, J., Gao, X., Chen, Y., DarkASDNet: Classification of ASD on functional MRI using deep neural network. *Front. Neuroinform.*, 15, 635657, 2021.

Part IV

HEALTH, SAFETY, AND SECURITY APPLICATIONS

19

Diagnosis of Diseases Using Machine Learning

Sujita Godishala*, Vakalapudi Sumavi, M. Saravanan and P.S. Maya Gopal

Department of Computer Science and Engineering, Sathyabama Institute of Science and Technology, Chennai, India

Abstract

The integration of artificial intelligence (AI) into healthcare has led to a paradigm shift, transforming diagnostic techniques, drug discovery, health analytics, and interventions. In this paper, we explore the potential of AI-based chatbot systems, specifically focusing on machine learning algorithms and natural language processing, to cater to the needs of patients and their families. Our primary emphasis is on leveraging these technologies to develop an AI chatbot capable of predicting diseases based on patient symptoms. We present a scenario where an AI disease prediction chatbot provides support to individuals, particularly pregnant women, mothers, and families with young children, by offering assistance and guidance in pertinent situations. This innovative approach holds promise in enhancing healthcare delivery, offering timely interventions, and ultimately improving patient outcomes.

***Keywords*:** Diagnostic techniques, drug discovery, health analytics, interventions, machine learning algorithms, data aggregation, data fusion, natural language processing

19.1 Introduction

The advent of artificial intelligence (AI)–based disease prediction chatbots heralds a promising frontier in healthcare, promising to revolutionize patient care through advanced diagnostics and personalized interventions.

**Corresponding author*: godishalasujita@gmail.com

Kanak Kalita, S. Vishnu Kumar and M. Niranjanamurthy (eds.) Industrial Internet of Things and Advanced Techniques for Sensor Data Aggregation and Fusion, (309–318) © 2026 Scrivener Publishing LLC

Despite the escalating interest and investment in such technologies, there exists a pervasive lack of awareness among both potential users and developers regarding the precise nature and potential applications of disease prediction chatbots. This knowledge gap underscores the need for comprehensive elucidation and analysis to delineate their capabilities and foster widespread adoption [1, 2].

This paper endeavors to bridge this gap by providing an exhaustive exploration of disease prediction chatbots, delving into their fundamental principles, potential utility, and the intricacies of their development. By disseminating insights gleaned from historical precedents and contemporary advancements, coupled with a forward-looking analysis of market trends, we aim to demystify the concept of disease prediction chatbots and unveil their manifold applications. The journey begins with a thorough investigation into the conceptual underpinnings of disease prediction chatbots, elucidating their core functionalities and underlying technologies. Through this foundational understanding, readers will be equipped to appreciate the versatility and transformative potential of these AI-driven systems. Subsequently, we delve into a comprehensive examination of potential applications, ranging from early disease detection and prognosis personalized treatment recommendations and healthcare resource optimization [3, 4].

Moreover, we advocate for a hands-on approach to comprehension and skill development by proposing the creation of a real-world disease prediction chatbot prototype. This practical exercise not only serves as a pedagogical tool for developers but also facilitates a deeper understanding of the developmental intricacies involved. By demystifying the process of creating disease prediction chatbots, we aim to empower a new generation of innovators to contribute to the burgeoning field of AI-driven healthcare solutions [5, 6].

Furthermore, as the healthcare landscape continues to evolve, the integration of disease prediction chatbots holds promise for transformative impact across various domains. These chatbots have the potential to augment the capabilities of healthcare professionals, enabling them to make more informed decisions and allocate resources more efficiently. Additionally, by empowering individuals with timely and personalized health insights, disease prediction chatbots can foster proactive healthcare management and preventive interventions [7, 8].

The development and utilization of disease prediction chatbots represent a watershed moment in healthcare innovation. Through concerted efforts to enhance understanding, foster skill development, and promote widespread adoption, we can unlock the full potential of these AI-driven systems to improve patient outcomes, streamline healthcare delivery, and advance medical science.

19.2 Literature Survey

Researchers recently conducted a study focusing on leveraging AI chatbots for predicting and managing diabetes. By incorporating user-reported symptoms, dietary habits, and activity levels, the chatbot used advanced machine learning algorithms to analyze patterns and predict potential risks of diabetes onset or exacerbation. This research highlighted the potential of AI-driven chatbots in proactive diabetes management, offering personalized interventions to improve health outcomes and prevent complications [9, 10].

Moreover, in the same year, researchers introduced an AI chatbot system for early detection and intervention of depression and anxiety disorders. Through conversational interactions, the chatbot gathered behavioral and linguistic cues, which were then analyzed using machine learning techniques to identify individuals at risk of developing or experiencing worsening symptoms of depression and anxiety [11]. This study emphasized the importance of AI-driven approaches in mental healthcare, particularly in providing timely support and intervention to individuals in need.

Additionally, researchers have explored the application of AI chatbots in predicting and managing hypertension [12]. By collecting user-reported blood pressure readings, lifestyle factors, and medication adherence, the chatbot utilized predictive analytics to identify individuals at risk of hypertension-related complications and provide personalized recommendations for lifestyle modifications and medication adherence strategies. This research underscored the potential of AI-driven chatbots in proactive cardiovascular health management, ultimately reducing the burden of hypertension-related morbidity and mortality.

Other researchers developed an AI chatbot system for predicting and managing chronic obstructive pulmonary disease (COPD). By integrating user-reported symptoms, spirometry data, and environmental factors, the chatbot used machine learning algorithms to forecast COPD exacerbations and provide personalized self-management strategies to mitigate symptom severity and improve overall respiratory health [13]. This study showcased the potential of AI-driven chatbots in enhancing COPD care by empowering patients with timely interventions and support.

Overall, these studies collectively demonstrate the expanding role of AI-driven chatbots in various domains of healthcare, ranging from chronic disease management to mental health support and preventive care. As technology continues to advance, AI chatbots hold immense promise in revolutionizing patient care delivery by offering personalized, accessible, and timely interventions to improve health outcomes and quality of life [14, 15].

19.3 Existing System

The existing methodology for disease prediction typically involves a multi-step process. It begins with the collection of relevant medical data, encompassing patient demographics, medical history, symptoms, and diagnostic test results. Following data collection, feature selection and engineering are performed to identify the most pertinent features for disease prediction. Subsequently, the data undergoes preprocessing to handle missing values, normalize features, and address outliers. Once the data are prepared, a suitable machine learning model is selected based on the nature of the data and prediction task. The model is then trained on the prepared dataset to learn the underlying patterns and relationships between the features and the target variable, i.e., the presence or absence of a particular disease. Evaluation metrics such as accuracy, precision, recall, and area under the receiver operating characteristic curve are utilized to assess the model's performance. Finally, the trained model is validated on independent datasets to ensure its generalizability and robustness, thus providing a reliable framework for disease prediction.

19.4 Disadvantages of Existing System

The reliance on historical datasets may introduce biases and data imbalances, leading to inaccurate predictions, particularly for underrepresented demographic groups or rare diseases.

Machine learning models trained on static datasets may struggle to adapt to evolving disease patterns, emerging pathogens, or changes in healthcare practices, potentially resulting in outdated predictions. The inherent complexity of machine learning models often makes them challenging to interpret, hindering the understanding of healthcare professionals and potentially undermining trust in the predictions.

19.5 Proposed System

The proposed AI chatbot system aims to revolutionize disease prediction by leveraging advanced machine learning techniques and natural language processing algorithms. This system will provide users with a user-friendly interface to input their symptoms and receive accurate predictions regarding potential diseases. By harnessing the power of deep learning models trained on comprehensive medical datasets, the AI chatbot will be capable of delivering personalized and timely healthcare recommendations, thereby improving patient outcomes and streamlining healthcare delivery.

19.6 Advantages of Proposed System

Leveraging advanced machine learning techniques, the AI chatbot system can provide accurate predictions regarding potential diseases based on user-input symptoms, enhancing diagnostic accuracy and reducing misdiagnosis rates.

Users receive timely healthcare recommendations tailored to their specific symptoms, enabling early detection, intervention, and treatment initiation for various medical conditions. This can lead to better health outcomes and improved prognosis for patients. The user-friendly interface of the AI chatbot as illustrated in Figures 19.1 to 19.4 allows individuals to easily input their symptoms and receive healthcare recommendations without the need for scheduling appointments or waiting for healthcare professionals. This accessibility can particularly benefit individuals in remote or underserved areas with limited access to healthcare services.

19.7 Results

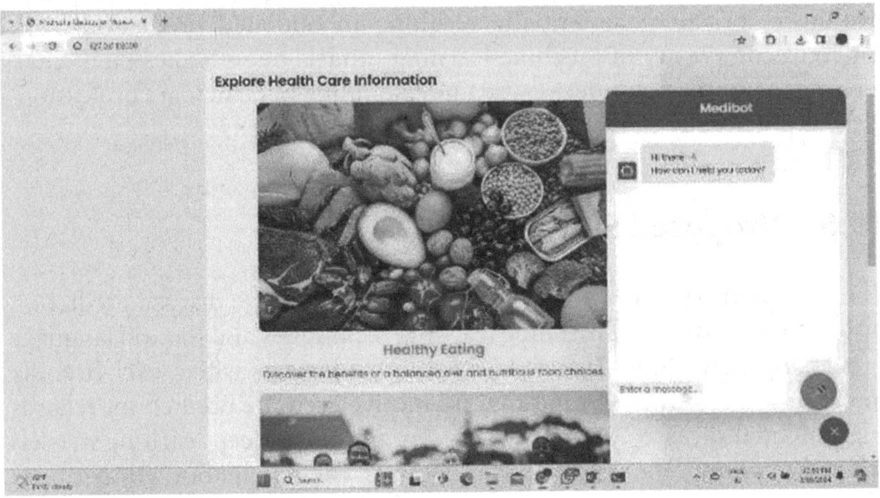

Figure 19.1 Comparision of images with attribute.

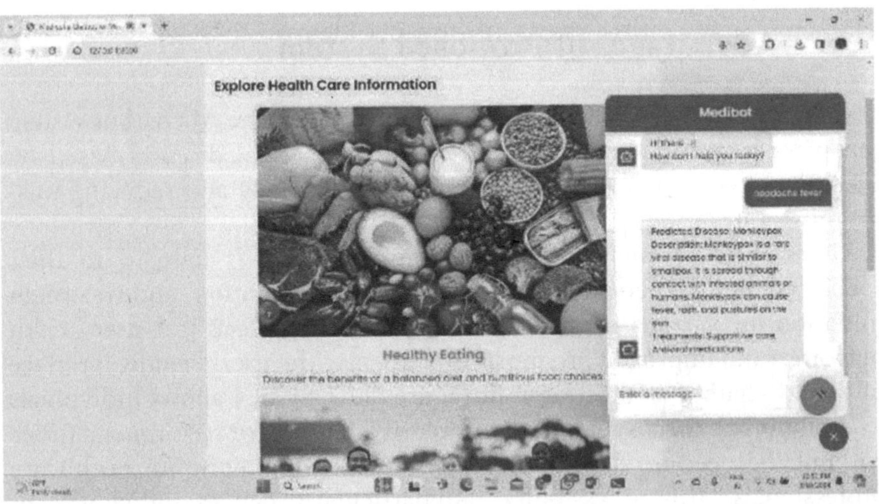

Figure 19.2 Resulting image.

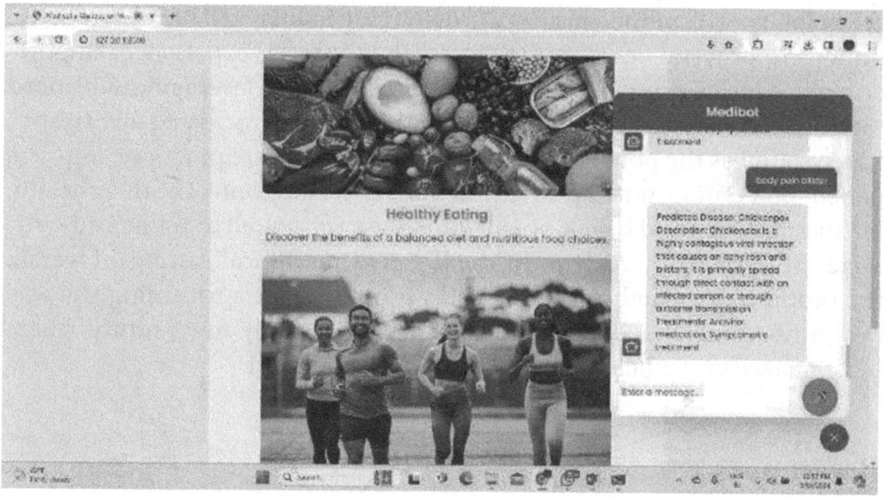

Figure 19.3 Based on the input, it will give suggestions.

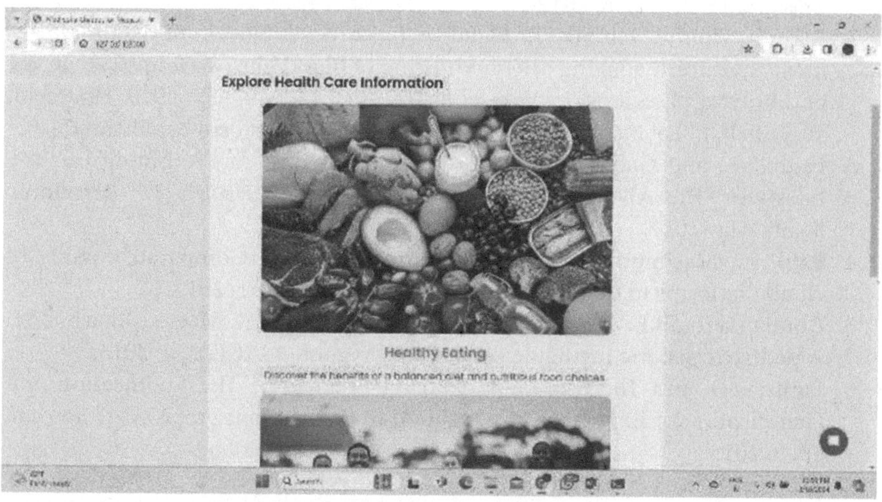

Figure 19.4 Final impact of comparision.

19.8 Conclusion

The proposed AI chatbot system for disease prediction represents a significant advancement in healthcare technology, offering numerous advantages in terms of accurate predictions, timely healthcare recommendations, accessibility, streamlined healthcare delivery, personalized healthcare, continuous improvement, cost efficiency, enhanced user experience, empowerment, education, scalability, and accessibility. By leveraging advanced machine learning techniques and natural language processing algorithms, this system has the potential to revolutionize healthcare practices, improve patient outcomes, and empower individuals to take control of their health. Further research and development efforts are warranted to refine and optimize the system for real-world deployment in clinical settings. Overall, the proposed AI chatbot system holds promise for transforming the way healthcare is delivered and accessed, paving the way for a future where personalized and efficient healthcare is available to all.

References

1. Demidowich, A.P., Lu, K., Tamler, R., Bloomgarden, Z., An evaluation of diabetes self-management applications for Android smartphones. *J. Telemed. Telecare*, 18, 235–238, 2012.
2. Rao, A., Hou, P., Golnik, T., Flaherty, J., Vu, S., Evolution of data management tools for managing self-monitoring of blood glucose results: A survey of iPhone applications. *J. Diabetes Sci. Technol.*, 4, 949–957, 2010. Hochfeld, W., Riffell, J., Levinson., N., Four trends that willtransform healthcarein.
3. Fadhil, A. and Gabrielli, S., Addressing Challenges in Promoting Healthy Lifestyles: The AI-Pregbot Approach, in: *PervasiveHealth '17*, Barcelona, Spain, May 2017.
4. Patil, A., Marimuthu, K., Rao, N., Niranchana, R., Comparative study of cloud platforms to develop a Pregbot. *IJET*, 6, 3, 57–61, 2017.
5. Comendador, B.E.V., Francisco, B.M.B., Medenilla, J.S., Mae, S., Pharmabot: A pediatric generic medicine consultant Pregbot. *JOACE*, 3, 2, 2015.
6. Lupton, D. and Thomas, G.M., Playing Pregnancy: The Ludification and Gamification of Expectant Motherhood in Smartphone Apps. *M/C Journal*, 18, 5, 2015.
7. Kumar, S.V., Chohan, J.S., Kalita, K., WhaleOptNB: A Method for Automated Biomedical Text Document Classification, in: *Intelligent Computing and Optimization. ICO 2023. Lecture Notes in Networks and Systems*, vol. 1169, P. Vasant and (Eds.), Springer, Cham, 2024, DoI: 10.1007/978-3-031-73324-6_18.
8. Kumar, S.V., Mary, G.A.A., Chohan, J.S., Kalita, K., Original Research Article Efficient sensor anomaly detection using Markov-LSTM architecture for methane sensing. *J. Auton. Intell.*, 7, 3, 2024, DoI: 10.32629/jai.v7i3.1285.
9. Amato, F., Marrone, S., Moscato, V., Piantadosi, G., Picariello, A., Sansone, C., *Pregbots meet eHealth: Automatizing healthcare*, D. Impedovo and G. Pirlo (Eds.), WAIAH 2017, Nov. 14, 2017.

10. Bedi, G., Carrillo, F., Cecchi, G.A., Fernández Slezak, D., Sigman, M., Mota, N.B., Ribeiro, S., Javitt, D.C., Copelli, M., Corcoran, C.M., Automated analysis of free speech predicts psychosis onset in high-risk youths. *npj Schizophrenia*, 1, 15030, 2015.
11. Weizenbaum, J., ELIZA - a computer program for the study of natural language communication between man and machine. *Comm. ACM*, 9, 36–45, 1966.
12. Brixey, J., Hoegen, R., Lan, W., Rusow, J., Singla, K., Yin, X., Artstein, R., Leuski, A., SHIHbot: A Facebook Pregbot for Sexual Health Information on HIV/AIDS. *Proceedings of the SIGDIAL 2017 Conference*, pp. 370–373.
13. Wilbanks, J.T. and Topol, E.J., Stop the privatization of health data. *Nature*, 535, 7612, 345–8, 2016 Jul 21.
14. Bellina, L. and Missoni, E., Mobile cell-phones (M-phones) in telemicroscopy: Increasing connectivity of isolated laboratories. *Diagn. Pathol.*, 4, 19, 2009.
15. Dayer, L., Heldenbrand, S., Anderson, P., Gubbins, P.O., Martin, B.C., Smartphone medication adherence apps: Potential benefits to patients and providers. *J. Am. Pharm. Assoc.*, 53, 172, 2013.

15. [illegible]

20

Client Attrition Prediction in Multiple Sectors with Customized Machine Learning Models Using IoT

R. Balaji* **and R. Ramprashath**

School of Computer Applications, Karpagam College of Engineering, Coimbatore, India

Abstract

Employee churn analytics involve analyzing the turnover rate of employees in a corporate setting and making predictions about potential churners. In today's fast-paced industries, employees often seek new opportunities, causing companies to find replacements who are capable of handling the workload. This process can be challenging and costly for corporate sectors as they strive to maintain operational efficiency. To address this ongoing challenge, various machine learning techniques are utilized to evaluate employees' records and determine the likelihood of them staying or leaving their current roles over time. Although many methods focus on traditional data analysis, there is a lack of exploration into sensor-based information processing within the corporate landscape. To bridge this gap, a novel approach utilizing Internet of Things (IoT) technology has been introduced to predict and manage employee churn effectively. By leveraging advanced algorithms and filter-based feature analysis, organizations can proactively identify potential churners and implement preventive measures to mitigate turnover rates. The predictive strategy not only enhances decision-making processes but also optimizes resource allocation and workforce stability in corporate environments. By adopting this IoT-enabled approach, companies can significantly reduce employee churn rates and associated costs. Performance evaluations of this methodology have indicated a high accuracy rate of 98%, showcasing its effectiveness in identifying future churners within corporate structures. This innovative predictive strategy offers a promising solution to minimize workforce disruptions and elevate organizational efficiency in the dynamic corporate landscape.

**Corresponding author*: balajiraja.sct18@gmail.com

Kanak Kalita, S. Vishnu Kumar and M. Niranjanamurthy (eds.) Industrial Internet of Things and Advanced Techniques for Sensor Data Aggregation and Fusion, (319–334) © 2026 Scrivener Publishing LLC

***Keywords*:** Employee churn analytics, IoT technology, predictive strategy, turnover rates, associated costs

20.1 Introduction

Customer analytics has become a widely discussed topic in the industry, enabling critical business decisions through the use of predictive analytics to model customer behavior. Popular areas of customer analytics include lifetime value modeling, market/customer segmentation, and churn analysis, which are utilized for customer management and direct marketing purposes. Despite the vast potential of customer analytics, many companies, particularly in the retail sector, fail to fully capitalize on its benefits. Churn analysis, a key application area of customer analytics, presents challenges due to issues such as sparse data, low churn rates, and censoring of churn events. Predicting customer churn often involves analyzing transaction data and other relevant factors influencing customer decisions. Although churn prediction is typically approached as a binary classification problem, it can also focus on churn rate estimation, leading to more nuanced classification. Industry reports indicate varying churn rates across sectors, with telecoms, e-commerce, and Fintech experiencing relatively high rates. The skewed nature of churn data poses challenges for achieving accurate classification using traditional machine learning methods, leading to high accuracy but low precision in predicting churners [1]. These challenges underscore the need for further advancements in churn prediction, presenting new opportunities for big data analytics. The effectiveness of churn prediction models heavily relies on the selection of variables from the customer dataset as inputs. There are two main drawbacks to conventional methods. The first is that they typically take a lot of time to get features out of thousands of different customer attributes. The second disadvantage is that you need to be an expert to use these methods. Second, conventional churn models are typically tailored and used for specific datasets. Deep learning (DL) techniques offer a solution to the limitations of traditional churn models. Primarily, they boast quicker processing times compared to traditional methods. DL techniques offer a solution to the constraints of conventional churn models [2, 3]. First, they exhibit superior speed compared to traditional methods. Additionally, DL approaches can autonomously identify useful features without the need for prior expertise or guidance. Consequently, using DL methods for churn prediction in the retail sector, which typically involves a multitude of data attributes, can result in highly accurate prediction outcomes. Convolutional neural networks (CNNs) are specialized neural network architectures that are adaptable to various types of data with diverse dimensions [4, 5].

20.2 Literature Survey

DL, a subset of artificial neural networks (ANNs), is characterized by its utilization of numerous hidden layers. Each layer of neurons in DL models is influenced by the features extracted from the preceding layer, thereby enabling the creation of a hierarchical feature structure that progressively abstracts information, facilitating pattern discovery in datasets [6]. The employment of historical transaction data has been widely recognized as advantageous in previous studies. In a comparative study, two DL algorithms, namely, CNNs and constrained Boltzmann machines, were evaluated for their effectiveness in predicting churn within the retail sector. Although the specifics of the dataset and features utilized were undisclosed, it was noted that RFM (recency, frequency, monetary) analysis was used [7, 8]. The study utilized a data mining algorithm to forecast customer churn. The findings of this research empower managers and marketers to devise policies informed by discerned patterns, thereby enhancing their ability to predict and understand the current and future behaviors of customers. Furthermore, the research explored various aggregate methods and algorithms for predicting customer churn, revealing that factors such as delayed invoice delivery and the number of returned invoices significantly influence customer dissatisfaction.

The factors contributing to customer churn include dissatisfaction due to higher costs, low quality, absence of desired features, and privacy concerns. It is acknowledged that customer churn can stem from various reasons, including competitive pricing, service quality, and promotional offerings. Additionally, factors such as marketing campaigns, availability or quality of services, and customer complaints can also contribute to churn. In a study conducted in 2019, Lee *et al.* highlighted that customer churn in the mobile phone industry is associated with service quality, demographic factors, customer satisfaction, dissatisfaction, and economic value [17].

This research focuses on understanding what makes customers happy or unhappy with their mobile service. They look at factors such as service quality, pricing plans, billing accuracy, data usage, and how easy it is to switch providers. They also consider customer information such as age, location, and how many people they have recommended the service to. Ultimately, they want to predict which customers are likely to cancel their service. There has been a breakdown of the changes made.

For instance, technical terms such as subscriber demographics have been replaced with simpler, more accessible language like customer information, making the content easier to understand for a broader audience. The long list of factors is broken down into categories such as service quality and customer information. The goal of the research is explained in simpler terms—understanding customer satisfaction and predicting churn (customers cancelling service). The researchers concluded that another factor contributing to customer attrition is the inadequate attention to and resolution of customer complaints. They segmented the customer lifecycle into three stages, suggesting that sentiment analysis of electronic word-of-mouth advertising could be used at each stage. Notably, they emphasized that negative electronic word-of-mouth advertising from customers holds greater significance than its positive counterpart.

In a research study, a novel customer forecasting approach was proposed, which involved updating a fresh set of customer-related features on a monthly basis, derived from past purchases, and using advanced machine learning algorithms. The findings indicated that the gradient tree boosting method outperformed other techniques, demonstrating superior accuracy and classification performance. Another study focused on predicting daily churn and suggested analyzing daily customer behaviors as a multivariate time series to forecast customer churn. Various models, including a statistical model, RFM model, long short-term memory model, and CNN model, were applied to a mobile telecommunication dataset, and their performances were compared. Interestingly, the study revealed that daily churn prediction was more accurate compared to monthly forecasts. This approach combines two techniques to predict customer churn (cancellations) in a communication company. The first is a neural network, which is a powerful tool for identifying patterns in data. The second is a genetic algorithm, which helps find the best possible settings for the neural network. This is achieved by focusing on creating a model that is both accurate (predicts churn well) and avoids making overly confident wrong predictions.

Customer churn stems from a variety of factors, encompassing aspects such as service quality, pricing, promotions, marketing campaigns, and customer satisfaction. Researchers stress the significance of addressing customer complaints and evaluating sentiment from electronic word-of-mouth advertising across the customer journey. Certain studies advocate novel sets of customer-related features and advanced machine learning techniques, such as gradient tree boosting, to enhance churn prediction accuracy. Others delve into daily churn prediction models using statistical models, RFM models, long short-term memory models, and CNN models.

20.3 Proposed System

The churn prediction model proposed in the study is primarily based on two main processes. Initially, a clustering algorithm is utilized to partition the collected customer data into distinct groups representing various behaviors. The two largest clusters, indicative of churners and nonchurners, are subsequently combined and utilized as input for the subsequent phase. Conversely, smaller clusters are disregarded as they denote outliers and less representative behaviors. The research examines and contrasts three different clustering approaches, namely, hierarchical clustering and Self organizing maps (SOM). In the second phase, multilayered perceptron (MLP)-ANN is used on the clustered and refined data from the initial phase to learn how to classify customer behavior into two categories: churner and nonchurner customers. Figure 20.1 illustrates the two-step model used in this study. The performance of the final MLP-ANN classifier model is assessed, taking into account the incorporation of customer age as a predictive feature in customer churn prediction using ANNs. To represent the age in the dataset, various methods can be used, such as encoding it as a numerical value, either directly as the customer's age in years or as a derived value such as the duration since the customer's initial subscription to the service. Figure 20.2 shows the process to get the final model and the final model is churned/not churnerd.

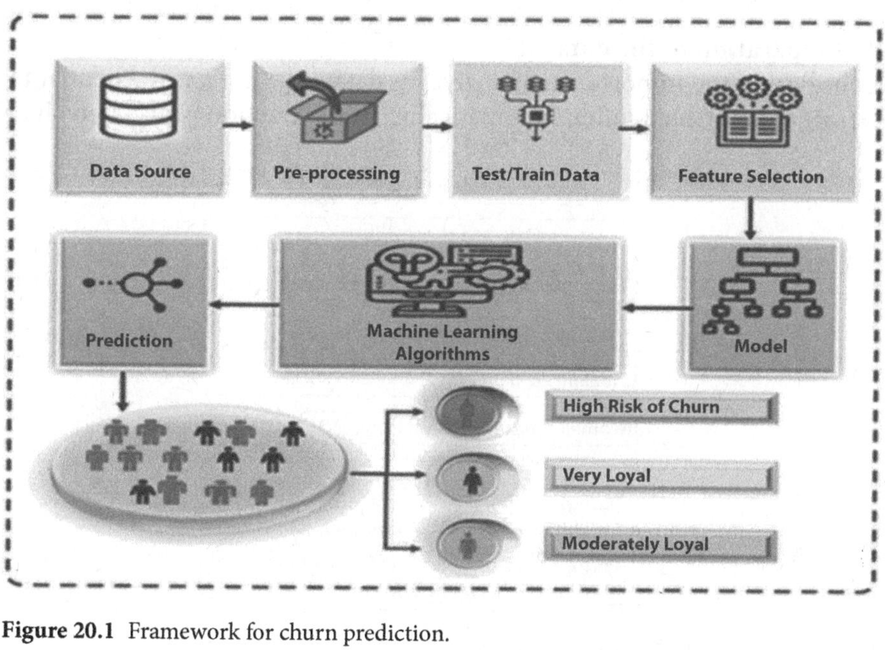

Figure 20.1 Framework for churn prediction.

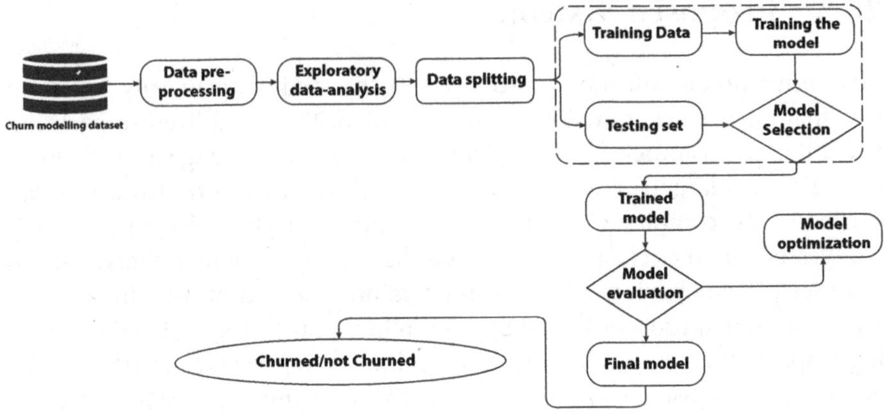

Figure 20.2 System architecture.

A. Remove missing information

Because of the extensive volume of data, there is a high likelihood of missing data. Consequently, any missing data points that cannot be estimated or replaced with other values must be excluded from the final dataset. For instance, if a customer's occupation is not recorded and cannot be estimated, that customer will be eliminated from the final table [9]. Figure 20.3 chart shows the process to get the final model

B. Preparation of the data

Considering the importance of analyzing data indicators, it is essential to extract data for each index systematically. This extraction process involves

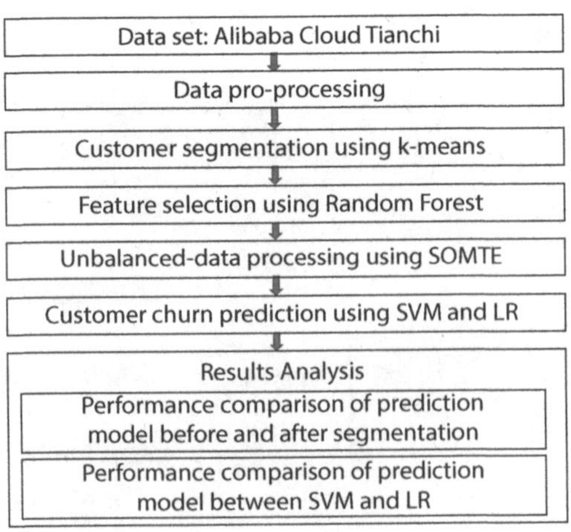

Figure 20.3 Workflow to get final model.

identifying both active and inactive customers from the last month of activity up to several months ago. However, because reactive customers are also included in the data, calculating the activity from the last month for reactive customers over several months becomes necessary. This process is time-consuming and adds complexity to this step. In contrast, video detection takes a different approach. Initially, we preprocess the videos using Res-Next ANN, which effectively extracts features [8].

C. Conducting computations pertaining to the customer's age

The bank's database does not store or provide the customer's age directly. Consequently, determining the customer's age involves subtracting the current date from the recorded production history in the system. Due to the substantial volume of records, this process further complicates this stage [10].

D. Developing a predictive model

During this phase, it is necessary to explore various techniques in data science to develop a model that addresses the problem at hand. The focus of this research pertains to categorizing bank customers based on their withdrawal privileges.

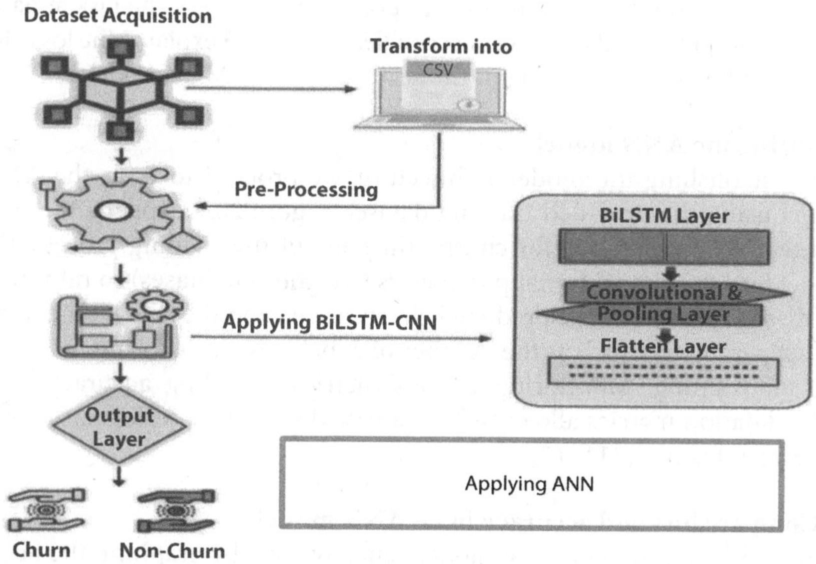

Figure 20.4 Step-by-step process of prediction.

E. Utilizing software

Python software will be used to test and implement prediction and classification models. Figure 20.4 explains the step-by-step process of prediction. Python software is an appropriate tool for the implementation of artificial intelligence techniques, and its powerful libraries can be used.

F. Confirming accuracy

The confusion matrix is a widely used technique in data science for evaluating a classification model.

G. Checking effectiveness

To validate the model, as per the nature of the current study supported by a bank for its execution, the findings are shared with the bank's business analysis unit. If the results are not endorsed by this unit, the process is iteratively refined until the outcomes gain approval from the bank's business unit, at which point they are implemented further.

H. Implement the ANN architecture

In this phase, we will create the structure of the ANN model using the Keras library, a convenient API for developing neural networks within tensor flow. The model comprises several layers of interconnected neurons, encompassing input, hidden, and output layers. We specify the quantity of neurons in each layer, activation functions, and additional parameters. The selection of the model's architecture is contingent upon the intricacy of the task at hand and the computational resources accessible. Figure 20.5 explains the loss plot of ANN and Figure 20.6 explains the accuracy plot of ANN model.

I. Fitting the ANN model

After establishing the model architecture, we proceed to train the ANN model using the provided training dataset. Figure 20.7 explains the proposed ANN architecture for churn. Throughout the training process, the model fine-tunes its internal parameters (weights and biases) to minimize the disparity between the predicted churn results and the actual outcomes. We set parameters such as the number of epochs (iterations) and the batch size for training. Monitoring various metrics including accuracy, loss, and validation metrics allows us to evaluate the model's performance as it undergoes training [11, 12].

J. Compare loss and accuracy in an ANN model

Ultimately, we can depict the model's effectiveness by graphing the accuracy and loss during training and validation across multiple epochs.

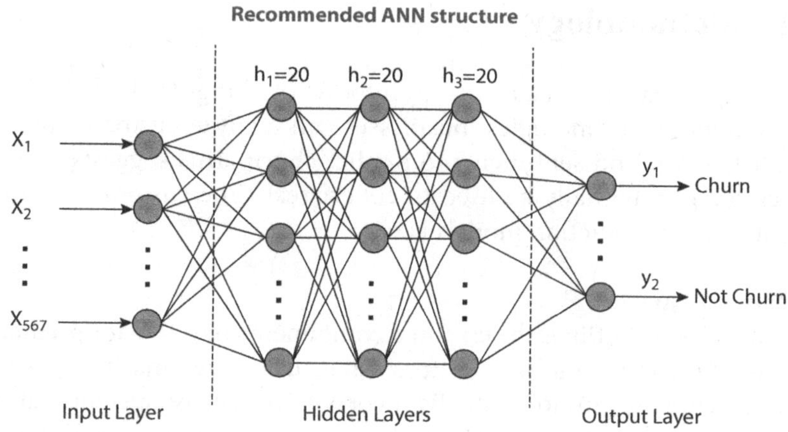

Figure 20.5 Proposed ANN architecture for churn.

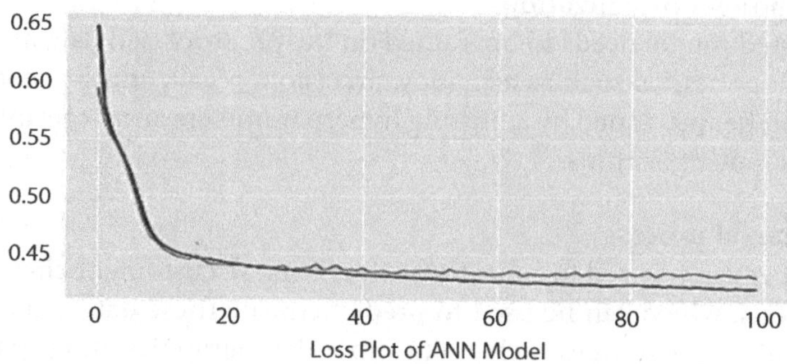

Figure 20.6 Loss plot of ANN.

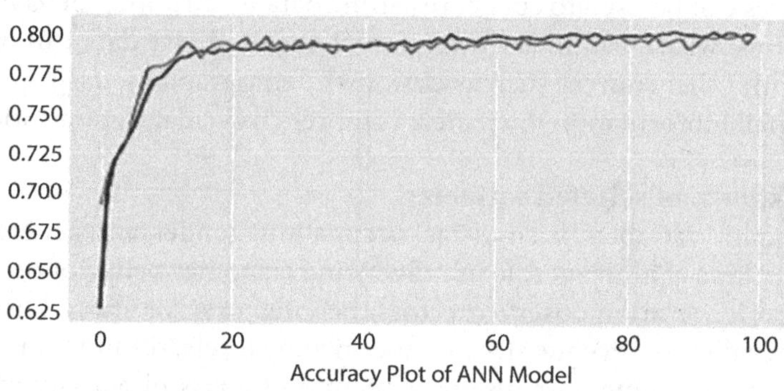

Figure 20.7 Accuracy plot of ANN model.

20.4 Methodology

By leveraging real-time data streams, Internet of Things (IoT) devices, and edge computing technologies, businesses can analyze customer interactions, behaviors, and sentiments to predict churn. This suggests that IoT devices could potentially be used to collect real-time customer data that feed into churn prediction models [13].

A. Data schema

This data scheme outlines the essential components required for predicting client attrition across multiple sectors using customized machine learning models integrated with IoT data. By incorporating sector-specific features, IoT insights, and advanced ML techniques, organizations can develop tailored attrition prediction models to enhance client retention strategies effectively.

B. Component organization

The selected model needs to be trained on the preprocessed data and evaluated using metrics such as accuracy, precision, recall, and F1 score. The model can be fine-tuned by adjusting hyperparameters and experimenting with different algorithms.

C. Rehearsal process

IoT devices can be used to collect real-time data on customer behavior and interactions, which can be used to predict churn. These data can be integrated with other sources such as customer demographics, usage patterns, and financial information to create a comprehensive dataset for modeling.

D. Indicators for customer churn detection

IoT devices can be used to collect real-time data on customer behavior and interactions, which can be used to predict churn. These data can be integrated with other sources such as customer demographics, usage patterns, and financial information to create a comprehensive dataset for modeling.

E. Breakdown of selected variables

Demographic variables, such as age, occupation, gender, and geographical location, play a significant role in influencing customer behavior due to the considerable variation observed across these factors. Naturally, businesses experience diverse revenue streams and income levels, resulting in varying patterns of engagement or disengagement and levels of activity with the bank. Occupation and geographical location are particularly influential in

```
RangeIndex: 10000 entries, 0 to 9999
Data columns (total 14 columns):
 #   Column           Non-Null Count  Dtype
---  ------           --------------  -----
 0   RowNumber        10000 non-null  int64
 1   CustomerId       10000 non-null  int64
 2   Surname          10000 non-null  object
 3   CreditScore      10000 non-null  int64
 4   Geography        10000 non-null  object
 5   Gender           10000 non-null  object
 6   Age              10000 non-null  int64
 7   Tenure           10000 non-null  int64
 8   Balance          10000 non-null  float64
 9   NumOfProducts    10000 non-null  int64
 10  HasCrCard        10000 non-null  int64
 11  IsActiveMember   10000 non-null  int64
 12  EstimatedSalary  10000 non-null  float64
 13  Exited           10000 non-null  int64
dtypes: float64(2), int64(9), object(3)
```

Figure 20.8 Essential attributes to predict.

determining customer activity levels. For instance, a physician practicing in rural areas may earn more compared to a counterpart in the capital city, Tehran, leading to differences in banking behavior [14]. Figure 20.8 shares the details of essential attributes to predict.

Gender also plays a crucial role, with distinct activity levels observed between housewives and male employees. The learning approach utilized in this study allows for the monitoring of each observation, providing an output indicating whether the customer exits or remains. This enables the system to better identify similar cases by learning from the customer exit process [15].

F. Dunning cycle

The dunning cycle is a process used by businesses to collect outstanding payments from clients. It typically involves a series of escalating communications, such as reminders and notices, to encourage clients to pay their overdue invoices [16].

G. Flux in the creator economy

This indicator, along with its 6-month trajectory, reflects the input status of resources into the customer's account. Thus, given the supervised learning technique used, observing past instances of money input can be influential in predicting future outcomes.

H. Average

Two debtor and creditor turnover indicators cannot show customer behavior well. The average of the account, which is the difference between the debtor and the creditor, is a suitable indicator. Its trend over a period of 6 months can also be effective in detecting churn.

20.5 Discussion

Since the output of the model, we have created a list of potential churners among customers; we can conduct further analysis. One aspect of this analysis involves identifying the occupations of the customers most likely to churn and those with the lowest churn scores. This understanding of their professions and industries can inform portfolio selection and the creation of new services tailored to target customers. Figure 20.9 shows the low-risk customer by jobs.

A. Banking customers with low anti–money laundering risk

Some clients come from diverse occupational backgrounds, and not all of them have access to better economic opportunities. A barrier needs to exist between them.

B. Customer segments with elevated risk profiles in banking

Not all occupations offer sufficient economic opportunities, leaving individuals unable to meet their basic needs such as food, housing, healthcare, and education.

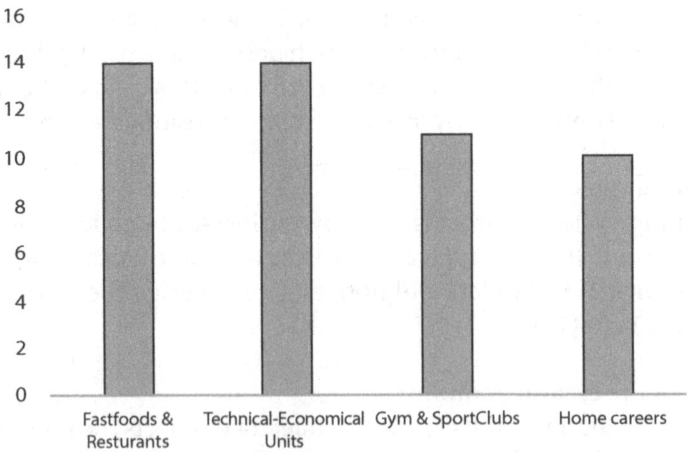

Figure 20.9 Low-risk customer by jobs.

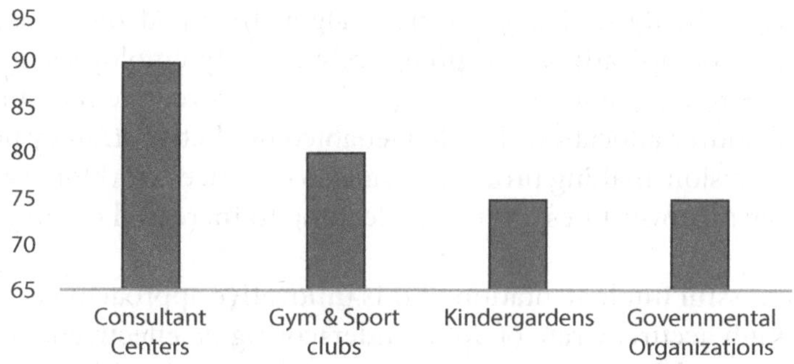

Figure 20.10 High-risk customer by jobs.

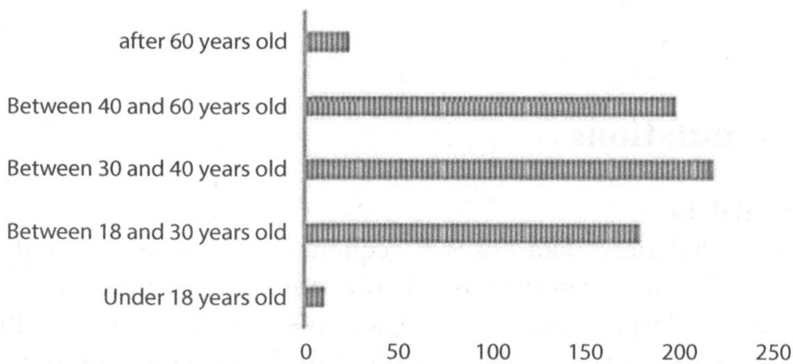

Figure 20.11 Distribution of age of high risk.

One of the outcomes from the supplementary analysis is the statistical distribution of the age of high-risk customers, depicted in Figure 20.10 as a histogram. Figure 20.11 shows the distribution of age of high risk.

20.6 Conclusion

Employee churn analytics plays a crucial role in understanding and predicting turnover rates within corporate environments. In today's dynamic industries, where employee retention is a key challenge, leveraging machine learning techniques has become essential to identify potential churners and maintain operational efficiency. Although traditional data analysis methods have been prevalent, the integration of IoT technology presents a novel approach to enhance predictive capabilities and address employee churn effectively. By utilizing advanced algorithms and filter-based feature analysis, organizations can proactively identify employees at risk of leaving their roles, enabling them to implement preventive measures and optimize resource allocation. This IoT-enabled predictive strategy not only improves decision-making processes but also enhances workforce stability and reduces turnover rates, ultimately leading to increased organizational efficiency.

The successful implementation of this innovative approach has demonstrated a high accuracy rate of 98%, underscoring its effectiveness in predicting future churners and minimizing disruptions within corporate structures. Embracing IoT technology in employee churn analytics offers a promising solution for companies looking to mitigate turnover costs and foster a stable and productive workforce in today's competitive business landscape.

20.7 Limitations

A. Skewed data

Managing imbalanced data poses a frequent hurdle in churn prediction. Such data imbalances can skew model outcomes and compromise prediction accuracy. Despite efforts to mitigate this problem through different approaches, it remains a notable constraint in churn prediction research.

B. Multifaceted approach needed

Merely depending on past churn rates that might not cut it for precise churn prediction, it is vital to factor in other elements such as customer feedback and transaction behaviors to enhance prediction accuracy. Given the intricate nature of customer behavior, a more holistic approach beyond just historical data is necessary.

C. Using a neutral term

Although machine learning algorithms such as ANNs have seen extensive application in churn prediction, there remain areas requiring enhancement. It is crucial to refine these algorithms to effectively address intricate customer behaviors and diverse datasets, thereby improving prediction accuracy.

D. Model intractability

Neural networks, such as ANNs, are commonly seen as opaque models, presenting difficulties in deciphering the influence of individual input variables on the model's output. Grasping the internal mechanisms of the model and the importance of various features is essential for enhancing and fine-tuning churn analysis.

References

1. Óskarsdóttir, M., Bravo, C., Verbeke, W., Sarraute, C., Baesens, B., Vanthienen, J., Social network analytics for churn prediction in telco: Model building, evaluation and network architecture. *Expert Syst. Appl.*, 85, 204–220, Nov. 2017.
2. Kumar, S.V., Mary, G.A.A., Chohan, J.S., Kalita, K., Original Research Article Efficient Sensor Anomaly Detection Using Markov-LSTM Architecture for Methane Sensing. *J. Auton. Intell.*, 7, 3, 174–183, 2024, DoI: 10.32629/jai.v7i3.1285.
3. Kumar, S.V., Chohan, J.S., Kalita, K., WhaleOptNB: A Method for Automated Biomedical Text Document Classification, in: *Intelligent Computing and Optimization. ICO 2023, Lecture Notes in Networks and Systems*, P. Vasant (Eds.), vol. 1169, pp. 174–184, Springer, Cham, 2024, DoI: 10.1007/978-3-031-73324-6_18.
4. Verbeke, W., Dejaeger, K., Martens, D., Hur, J., Baesens, B., New insights into churn prediction in the telecommunication sector: A profit driven data mining approach. *Eur. J. Oper. Res.*, 218, 1, 211–229, 2012, https://doi.org/10.1016/j.ejor.2011.09.031.
5. Roberts, J.H., Developing new rules for new markets. *J. Acad. Market. Sci.*, 8, 2000, https://www.research.ed.ac.uk/en/publications/new-insights-into-churn-prediction-in-the-telco-sector-a-profit-d.
6. Neslin, S.A., Gupta, S., Kamakura, W., Lu, J., Mason, C.H., Defection detection: Measuring and understanding the predictive accuracy of customer churn models. *J. Mark. Res.*, 43, 204–211, 2006, CrossRef.
7. Liu, C.J., Huang, T.S., Ho, P.T., Huang, J.C., Hsieh, C.T., Machine learning-based e-commerce platform repurchase customer prediction model. *PLoS One*, 15, e0243105, 2020, CrossRef.
8. Yang, L., Application of Survival Analysis in Customer Churn Prediction Model. *Stat. Appl.*, 10, 1, 10–20, 2021.
9. Sharma, A., Pratap, A., Vyas, K., Mishra, S., Machine learning approach: Consumer buying behavior analysis, in: *Proc. IEEE Pune Sect. Int. Conf. (PuneCon)*, Dec. 2022.
10. Geiler, L., Affeldt, S., Nadif, M., A survey on machine learning methods for churn prediction. *Int. J. Data. Sci. Anal.*, 14, 3, Sep. 2022.
11. Gordini, N. and Veglio, V., Customers churn prediction and marketing retention strategies: An application of support vector machines based on

the AUC parameter selection technique in B2B e-commerce industry. *Ind. Market. Manag.*, 62, 100–107, 2017, CrossRef.

12. Huang, W., Chen, J., Cai, Q., Liu, X., Zhang, Y., Hu, X., Hierarchical Hybrid Neural Networks with Multi-Head Attention for Document Classification. *Int. J. Data Warehouse*, CrossRef.
13. Sorokina, D., Application of additive groves ensemble with multiple counts feature evaluation to KDD cup'09 small data set, in: *Proceedings of the KDD-Cup 2009 Competition*, Paris France, 28 June–1 July 2009, PMLR.
14. Woźniak, M., Graña, M., Corchado, E., A survey of multiple classifier systems as hybrid systems. *Inf. Fusion*, 2014, CrossRef.
15. Amin, A., Adnan, A., Anwar, S., An adaptive learning approach for customer churn prediction in the telecommunication industry using evolutionary computation and Naïve Bayes. *Appl. Soft Comput.*, 137, 110103, Apr. 2023.
16. Zdravevski, E., Lameski, P., Apanowicz, C., D. Şlezak, From big data to business analytics: The case study of churn prediction. *Appl. Soft Comput.*, 90, 106164.dss, May 2020.
17. Lee, E.-B., Kim, J., Lee, S.-G., Predicting customer churn in mobile industry using data mining technology. *Proceedings of the 1st International Conference on Economics, Business, Entrepreneurship, and Finance (ICEBEF 2018)*, 2017.

21

Blood Transfusion System Using Data Mining Techniques and Grey Relational Analysis (GRA) Using Decision Tree Compared with Naive Bayes

K. Manimaran and T. Poovizhi*

Department of Information Technology, Saveetha School of Engineering, Saveetha Institute of Medical and Technical Sciences, Saveetha University, Chennai, India

Abstract

The aim of the project is to analyze the accuracy value of blood transfusion transmitted infections based on major risk in transfusions in many parts of the world by using novel decision tree and compare the accuracy with naive Bayes. Novel decision tree is used to achieve accuracy. The novel decision tree is used in this research to perform the operations, which resulted in the best accuracy for the analysis of specific product usage based on blood transfusion transmitted infections. Decision tree and naive Bayes are executed with varying training and testing splits for blood transfusion systems. Two groups are selected for comparing the process, and their result is derived. In each group, 10 sets of samples and 10 samples in total are selected for this work. The G*Power test used is about 85% (G*Power setting parameters: $\alpha = 0.05$ and power = 0.85). Decision tree (95.47%) has the increased accuracy over naive Bayes (92.43%) with a significance value of 0.01 (two-tailed, $P < 0.05$). The accuracy of the decision tree is better when compared to the accuracy of naive Bayes.

***Keywords*:** Blood transfusion system, data mining, decision tree, naive Bayes, quality of life

**Corresponding author*: poovizhit.sse@saveetha.com

Kanak Kalita, S. Vishnu Kumar and M. Niranjanamurthy (eds.) Industrial Internet of Things and Advanced Techniques for Sensor Data Aggregation and Fusion, (335–344) © 2026 Scrivener Publishing LLC

Introduction

Neural networks are extremely powerful and popular machine learning algorithms that find a wide variety of applications [1–3]. Using freely available data, this study examines ANNs to predict trauma patients' transfusion needs. A backpropagation neural network is trained and evaluated on 1016 patient data to estimate first 2, 2–6, and 6–24 hours and total transfusions. ANNs can reliably anticipate most emergency room (ER) patient transfusion requirements using only ER entrance data [4]. Machine learning can simplify this. This study proposes an automated blood donation system for emergencies. To make this system perform perfectly, many machine learning algorithms are considered to choose the finest one. This study will justify the algorithmic technique by comparing end results [5]. This work builds an information system model using the software development life cycle to regulate blood demand. This instance also used continuous review to manage safety stock, reorder point, and order quantity for blood components. This study can improve blood transfusion unit service. To regulate blood demand, blood inventory simulation should be studied [6]. The main application of the project is to improve the blood transfusion system to improve people's quality of life.

Research work has been performed in the last few years on blood transfusion system, and more than 200 articles were found in the IEEE Xplore and 75 articles in ScienceDirect. Data mining methods should power a blood transfusion system. To examine decision tree, random forest, and Naive Bayes before and after applying grey relational analysis (GRA) in order to evaluate their performance and identify the most suitable algorithm for blood transfusion prediction. Based on donation data, the most efficient algorithm will be utilized to predict blood donor characteristics. The prediction will help blood donation camps contact donors if needed [7]. Our blood bank management platform has three modules: anticipate blood needs, advise blood donation campaign locations, and safeguard blood supply chain. The platform uses long short-term memory, K-means clustering, geographic information system (gis), and blockchain. The modules can reduce blood supply–demand imbalance, find the best emergency donor, and improve data privacy [8]. This work developed and tested blood transfusion prediction machine learning algorithms to improve quality of life. Machine learning research used multilayer perceptron and support vector machines. Six hundred patients were evaluated retrospectively and 148 prospectively, with 65.8% sensitivity and 78.2% specificity. This prejudice may allow nondonors to solicit blood donations [9]. This work develops a blood inventory management methodology to prevent platelet shortages. Blood banks manage platelet inventory by instinct and experience. Thus, an efficient system that optimizes inventory levels and reduces shortages is essential. This research proposes an efficient model to solve the problem [10].

The research gap identified from the existing system is poor accuracy. This study is to improve the accuracy of classification by incorporating decision tree and comparing its performance with naive Bayes. The proposed model improves the blood transfusion system.

Materials and Methods

The research work was done in the Soft Computing Lab, Department of Information Technology, Saveetha College. Sample size has been calculated using G*Power software by comparing both the controllers. Two groups are selected for comparing the process, and their result is derived. In each group, 10 sets of samples and 10 samples in total are selected for this work. Two algorithms, decision tree and naive Bayes, are implemented using technical analysis software. Sample size is determined as 10 for each group using G*Power 3.1 software (G*Power setting parameters: $\alpha = 0.05$ and power = 0.85).

The proposed work is designed and implemented with the help of Python OpenCV software. The platform to assess deep learning was Windows 10 OS. Hardware configuration was an Intel Core i7 processor with a RAM size of 4 GB. System sort used was 64-bit. For implementation of code, java programming language was used. As for code execution, the dataset is worked behind to perform an output process for accuracy.

Decision Tree

Decision tree is the most powerful and popular tool for classification and prediction. A decision tree is a flowchart-like tree structure, where each internal node denotes a test on an attribute, each branch represents an outcome of the test, and each leaf node (terminal node) holds a class label. A tree can be "learned" by splitting the source set into subsets based on an attribute value test [11, 12]. This process is repeated on each derived subset in a recursive manner called recursive partitioning. The recursion is completed when the subset at a node all has the same value of the target variable, or when splitting no longer adds value to the predictions [13, 14].

Pseudocode

Step1: Create a root node.
Step2: Create the attributes for the root node.

Step3: Add a test case for the root node.
Step4: Add leaf nodes with target value.
Step5: Return to the root node.

Naive Bayes

The naive Bayes algorithm is a supervised learning algorithm, which is based on Bayes theorem and used for solving classification problems. It is mainly used in text classification that includes a high *b h*-dimensional training dataset. Naive Bayes classifier is one of the simple and most effective classification algorithms that help in building fast machine learning models that can make quick predictions. It is a probabilistic classifier, which means it predicts on the basis of the probability of an object. Some popular examples of naive Bayes algorithm are spam filtration, sentimental analysis, and classifying articles.

Pseudocode

Step 1: Load the dataset.
Step 2: Store the feature matrix (X) and response vector (y).
Step 3: Split X and y into training and testing sets.
Step 4: Train the model on training set.
Step 5: Take predictions on the testing set.
Step 6: Compare actual response values (y_test) with predicted response values (y_pred) from sklearn import metrics.

Statistical Analysis

SPSS software is used for statistical analysis of decision tree and naive Bayes. Independent variables are image, objects, distance, frequency, modulation, amplitude, volume, and decibels. Dependent variables are images and objects. Independent *t* test analysis is carried out to calculate accuracy for both methods.

Results

The proposed decision tree and naive Bayes run at different times in Anaconda Navigator with a sample size of 10. Table 21.1 represents the predicted accuracy and loss of decision tree. Table 21.2 represents the predicted accuracy and loss of naive Bayes. These 10 data samples are used

Table 21.1 Accuracy and loss analysis of decision tree.

Iterations	Accuracy (%)	Loss (%)
1	92.97	7.03
2	90.95	9.05
3	97.34	2.66
4	92.11	7.89
5	94.28	5.72
6	92.98	7.02
7	96.86	3.14
8	99.29	0.71
9	98.13	1.87
10	97.30	2.70

Table 21.2 Accuracy and loss analysis of naive Bayes.

Iterations	Accuracy (%)	Loss (%)
1	88.19	11.81
2	92.22	7.78
3	92.05	7.95
4	89.16	10.84
5	90.93	9.07
6	92.04	7.96
7	90.88	9.12
8	93.00	7.00
9	96.92	3.08
10	94.66	5.34

for each algorithm along with their loss values to calculate statistical values that can be used for comparison. From the results, it is observed that the mean accuracy of the decision tree was 95.47%, and naive Bayes was 92.43%. Table 21.3 represents mean accuracy values for decision tree and

Table 21.3 Group statistical analysis of decision tree and naive Bayes.

	Group	n	Mean	Standard deviation	Standard error mean
Accuracy	Decision tree	10	95.2210	2.89467	.91538
	Naive Bayes	10	92.0050	2.52356	.79802

Mean, standard deviation, and standard error mean are obtained for 10 samples. Decision tree has higher mean accuracy and lower mean loss when compared to naive Bayes.

naive Bayes. Mean value of decision tree is better when compared with the naive Bayes with standard deviations of 2.89467 and 2.52356, respectively. Table 21.4 shows the independent-sample t test data of decision tree and naive Bayes with the significance value of 0.225 (two-tailed, $P < 0.05$) obtained. Figure 21.1 denotes the comparison of decision tree and naive Bayes in terms of mean accuracy and loss.

Mean, standard deviation, and standard error mean for decision tree are 95.2210, 2.89467, and 0.91538, respectively. Similarly for naive Bayes, the

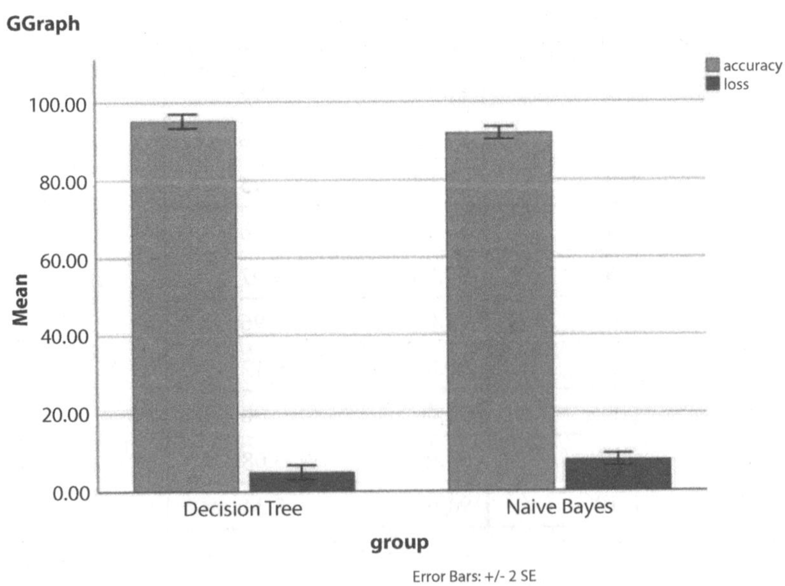

Figure 21.1 Comparison of decision tree and naive Bayes. Classifier in terms of mean accuracy and loss. The mean accuracy of the decision tree is better than naive Bayes classifier. Standard deviation of decision tree is slightly better than naive Bayes. *X* axis: decision tree versus naive Bayes classifier; *Y* axis: mean accuracy of detection with ±2 SE.

Table 21.4 Independent-sample t test: Decision tree is insignificantly better than naive Bayes with P value s2 value (two-tailed, $P < 0.05$)

		Levene test for equality of variances		t test for equality means with 95% confidence interval						
		f	Significance	*t*	*df*	Significance (2-tailed)	Mean difference	Standard error difference	Lower	Upper
Accuracy	Equal variances assumed	1.580	.225	2.648	18	0.08	3.21600	1.21439	.66466	5.76734
	Equal variances not assumed			2.648	17.671	0.08	3.21600	1.21439	.66125	5.77075

mean, standard deviation, and standard error mean are 92.0050, 2.52356, and 0.79802, respectively. On the other hand, the loss values of decision tree for mean, standard deviation, and standard error mean are 4.7790, 2.89467, and 0.91538, respectively. For naive Bayes, the loss values of naive Bayes for mean, standard deviation, and standard error mean are 7.9950, 2.52356, and 0.79802, respectively.

The group statistics values along with mean, standard deviation, and standard error mean for the two algorithms are also specified. The graphical representation of comparative analysis and means of loss between two algorithms of decision tree and naive Bayes are classified. This indicates that decision tree is significantly better with 95.4711% accuracy when compared with naive Bayes classifier accuracy of 92.4288%.

Discussion

In the given study, the significance value obtained is 0.08 (two-tailed, $P > 0.05$), which implies that decision tree appears to be better than naive Bayes. Accuracy analysis of the decision tree is analyzed as 95.4711%, whereas the accuracy of decision tree is 92.4288% (Table 21.5).

The goal of this research is to reduce potential dangers associated with blood transfusions for the benefit of all patients receiving them to improve quality of life. This study had an accuracy of almost 89.4% [15]. This study introduces a microcontroller-based barrier system that can be seamlessly linked with conventional barcode/RFID-based solutions, allowing for a better level of security with straightforward and rapid deployment. About 86.2% of the time, this study was accurate [16]. This study showcases a novel prototype for conducting pretransfusion tests, which was designed with the needs of emergency circumstances in mind. The study has a 91% accuracy rate [17]. This report summarizes what is currently known about the literature analyzing the connection between heart rate variability and transfusion in the preterm population. About 87% of the time, this study was accurate [18].

Table 21.5 Comparison of the decision tree and naive Bayes with their accuracy.

Classifier	Accuracy (%)
Decision tree	95.47
Naive Bayes	92.43

The limitations of this study are that it takes a very long time to train a decision tree, especially with large datasets. The future scope of this study is that the system should be expanded to include a larger number of objects with lesser time consumption in training the dataset.

Conclusion

The accuracy value of the decision tree is 95.4711%, whereas the accuracy value of naive Bayes is 92.4288%. Based on the analysis, decision tree (95.4711%) performs better than naive Bayes (92.4288%).

References

1. Vickram, A.S., Raja, D., Srinivas, M.S., Kamini, A.R., Jayaraman, G., Sridharan, T.B., Prediction of Zn concentration in human seminal plasma of Normospermia samples by Artificial Neural Networks (ANN). *J. Assist. Reprod. Genet.*, 30, 453–459, April 2013.
2. Nanmaran, R., Srimathi, S., Yamuna, G., Thanigaivel, S., Vickram, A.S., Priya, A.K., Karthick, A., Karpagam, J., Mohanavel, V., Muhibbullah, M., Investigating the role of image fusion in brain tumor classification models based on machine learning algorithm for personalized medicine. *Comput. Math. Methods Med.*, 2022, 7137524, February 2022.
3. Vickram, A.S., Kamini, A.R., Das, R., Pathy, M.R., Parameswari, R., Archana, K., Sridharan, T.B., Validation of artificial neural network models for predicting biochemical markers associated with male infertility. *Syst. Biol. Reprod. Med.*, 62, 258–265, August 2016.
4. Walczak, S., Artificial neural network medical decision support tool: predicting transfusion requirements of ER patients. *IEEE Trans. Inf. Technol. Biomed.*, 9, 468–474, September 2005.
5. Vincent, P.M.D.R., Manivannan, S.S., Vanmathi, C., Felicita, S.A.M., Automated blood donation system using machine learning approach, in: *2019 2nd International Conference on Intelligent Computing, Instrumentation and Control Technologies (ICICICT)*, Kannur, 2019.
6. Lestari, F., Ulfah, U., Aprianis, F.R., Suherman, S., Inventory management information system in blood transfusion unit, in: *2018 IEEE International Conference on Industrial Engineering and Engineering Management (IEEM)*, Bangkok, 2018.
7. Agarwal, K., Gupta, M., Gupta, K., Khan, A., Nallakaruppan, M.K., Blood transfusion system using data mining techniques and GRA, in: *2019 5th*

International Conference on Advanced Computing & Communication Systems (ICACCS), Coimbatore, 2019.

8. Sandaruwan, P.A.J., Dolapihilla, U.D.L., Karunathilaka, D.W.N.R., Wijayaweera, W. A. D. T. L., Rankothge, W.H., Gamage, N.D.U., Towards an efficient and secure blood bank management system, in: *2020 IEEE 8th R10 Humanitarian Technology Conference (R10-HTC)*, Kuching, 2020.
9. Darwiche, M., Feuilloy, M., Bousaleh, G., Schang, D., Prediction of blood transfusion donation, in: *2010 Fourth International Conference on Research Challenges in Information Science (RCIS)*, Nice, 2010.
10. Kumari, D.M.S. and Wijayanayake, A.N., An efficient inventory model to reduce the wastage of blood in the national blood transfusion service, in: *2016 Manufacturing & Industrial Engineering Symposium (MIES)*, Colombo, 2016.
11. Burande, D.V., Kalita, K., Chohan, J.S., Machine learning-based predictive modelling of spot-welding process parameters, in: *Intelligent Computing and Optimization*, pp. 337–346, Springer Nature Switzerland, Cham, 2023.
12. Ganesh, Jain, P., Choudhury, A., Dutta, P., Kalita, K., Barsocchi, P., Random forest regression-based machine learning model for accurate estimation of fluid flow in curved pipes. *Processes (Basel)*, 9, 2095, November 2021.
13. Gayathri, R., Rani, S.U., Čepová, L., Rajesh, M., Kalita, K., A comparative analysis of machine learning models in prediction of mortar compressive strength. *Processes (Basel)*, 10, 1387, July 2022.
14. Narayanan, G., Joshi, M., Dutta, P., Kalita, K., PSO-tuned support vector machine metamodels for assessment of turbulent flows in pipe bends. *Eng. Comput. (Swansea)*, 37, 981–1001, December 2019.
15. Akiyama, M. and Koshio, A., IT can improve healthcare management for patient safety - minimizing risk of blood transfusion with Point-of-Act-System, in: *2011 IEEE International Conference on Industrial Engineering and Engineering Management*, Singapore, 2011.
16. Baronti, F., Lazzeri, A., Roncella, R., Rubertelliy, M., Tomasi, A., An electronic barrier system to improve blood transfusion safety, in: *2008 15th IEEE International Conference on Electronics, Circuits and Systems*, St. Julien's, 2008.
17. Ferraz, A., Machado, J., Carvalho, V., Prototype for determination of pre-transfusion tests based on image processing techniques, in: *2015 IEEE 4th Portuguese Meeting on Bioengineering (ENBENG)*, Porto, 2015.
18. Desai, R. and McGregor, A.C., Transfusion in neonatal care in relation to heart rate variability (HRV) and anemia: A literature review, in: *2021 IEEE International Conference on Biomedical Engineering, Computer and Information Technology for Health (BECITHCON)*, Dhaka, 2021.

22

IoT-Integrated Detection and Classification of Deepfake Images and Videos Using Custom Deep Learning Models

K. Praveen Kumar* **and R. Ramprashath**

School of Computer Applications, Karpagam College of Engineering, Coimbatore, India

Abstract

Deep fakes are becoming more common; they include editing previously published films and photos to produce content that appears authentic but is wholly fake. The development process has been considerably expedited by the widespread availability of deep learning techniques, such as autoencoders, generative adversarial networks, and user-friendly software. These sophisticated algorithms adeptly fuse and modify visual and audio elements, facilitating the production of content that closely mimics genuine footage, even for those without specialized knowledge. The malicious manipulation of images and videos poses significant security and societal concerns. With an emphasis on facial alteration, the goal of this research is to create a deep learning system integrated with Internet of Things (IoT) for the detection and classification of deepfake images and videos. The dataset used for the project is either FaceForensics++, Celeb-DF, or the Deepfake Detection Challenge Dataset, available on Kaggle, consisting of real and deepfake images and videos. By utilizing recurrent and convolutional neural networks (CNNs), we have made developments in deepfake detection. Commencing with preprocessing the data, extracting frames from the videos, and separating the dataset into training and validation sets, IoT devices continuously capture and transmit data for real-time analysis. For the detection and classification of deepfake images and videos, OpenCV and face recognition are used for facial detection, whereas CNNs are used by the system to extract features at the frame level. A recurrent

**Corresponding author*: praveenkk418@gmail.com

Kanak Kalita, S. Vishnu Kumar and M. Niranjanamurthy (eds.) Industrial Internet of Things and Advanced Techniques for Sensor Data Aggregation and Fusion, (345–358) © 2026 Scrivener Publishing LLC

neural network is trained using these features. Various techniques such as data augmentation, learning rate scheduling, and early stopping enhance model performance. This comprehensive IoT-integrated approach ensures accurate discrimination between authentic and deepfake content, addressing concerns regarding the integrity of digital media.

Keywords: Deepfake video detection, image forgery detection, IoT integration, custom deep learning models, IoT-based deepfake detection

22.1 Introduction

The widespread use of smartphones with advanced cameras and easy access to high-speed internet has made it effortless to create and share digital videos on social media. Concurrently, the rapid advancements in computational capabilities have empowered deep learning techniques, notably generative adversarial networks (GANs) and autoencoders, enabling the creation of deepfakes (DFs)—artificially manipulated videos and audio clips. The proliferation of DFs across social media platforms has engendered significant concerns, precipitated the dissemination of misinformation, and posed grave threats to societal integrity [1]. Recognizing the imperative to counteract the proliferation of DFs, this project endeavors to develop a robust deep learning model specialized in detecting and categorizing DF images and videos, with a particular emphasis on identifying facial manipulations [2]. Leveraging datasets such as FaceForensics++, Celeb-DF, or the Deepfake Detection Challenge Dataset (DFDC), encompassing a diverse array of real and manipulated media, forms the cornerstone of this endeavor. Our approach to detecting DFs is grounded in understanding the underlying mechanisms of GANs, which are pivotal in generating such content. GANs operate by substituting faces within videos through a process of frame-by-frame manipulation, typically using autoencoders for reconstruction [3]. By analyzing artifacts created during the face substitution process, our system makes use of these subtleties and exploits the resolution discrepancies between the modified facial areas and their surrounding context. Figure 22.1 shows samples from the FaceForensics++ dataset, illustrating both real and fake frames used in training. The core of our detection methodology is based on the use of convolutional neural networks (CNNs), LSTM cells to capture temporal inconsistencies between frames. Through a thorough analysis and comparison of the generated facial regions with their surrounding environment, our method seeks to identify minute but noticeable differences suggestive of DF manipulation. Augmented with techniques such as data augmentation, learning rate scheduling, and early stopping, our comprehensive

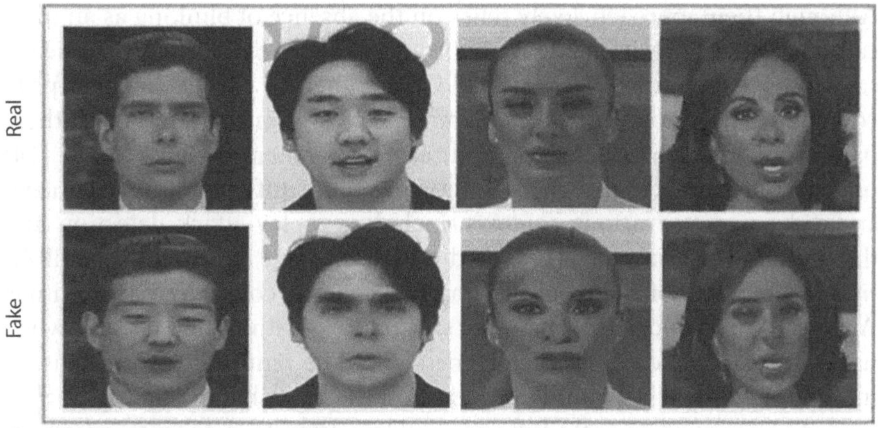

Figure 22.1 Samples from FaceForensics ++.

methodology endeavors to enhance model performance, ensuring accurate discrimination between authentic and DF content. Through these concerted efforts, we strive to mitigate the pervasive threat posed by DF media, safeguarding the integrity of digital discourse and societal trust [4].

22.2 Literature Survey

The values of democracy, fairness, and public confidence are seriously threatened by the DF videos' explosive growth and illegal usage. The mitigation is therefore rising. In the subject of DF detection, several strategies that concentrate on different facets of the phenomenon have been put forth. For instance, Ciftci *et al.* [5] presented a technique to detect artifacts in DF videos by utilizing a specialized CNN model to compare the generated facial portions with their surrounding regions [6]. The study highlighted the presence of distinct facial artifacts within DF content, underscoring the limitations of current DF algorithms in generating images with constrained resolutions [7–9]. These images require additional transformations to align with the faces being replaced in the original video, thereby creating identifiable patterns that can be exploited for detection purposes [10]. In Li *et al.* [11], a false face video made with deep neural network models is suggested. The method depends on the ability to identify eye blinking in the videos a physiological signal that is not well replicated in artificially created videos. The method shows promising performance in recognizing movies generated by deep neural network–based software for generating fake content through evaluation against benchmarks of eye-blinking detection datasets [12, 13].

Although their approach solely relies on the absence of blinking as an indicator for detection, it is imperative to account for additional parameters such as teeth alignment, facial wrinkles, and others to effectively identify DF content. Our proposed method encompasses the consideration of all these parameters to enhance detection accuracy. Researchers in Nguyen *et al.* [14] use a technique leveraging capsule networks to identify manipulated images and videos across various contexts, including replay attack detection and the detection of computer-generated videos. In their approach, the utilization of random noise during the training phase is considered suboptimal. Although their model demonstrated effectiveness within their dataset, when used on real-time data, its effectiveness could be reduced because noise is incorporated into the training process. On the other hand, our approach is made to be trained on real time and noiseless datasets in order to guarantee reliable results in real-world scenarios. The approach outlined in Ciftci *et al.* [5] entails obtaining biological signals from face areas in video pairings of both real besides phony portraits. By transforming, these signals compute temporal consistency and spatial coherence, which are then captured in feature sets and PPG maps. The next step is to train a CNN and a probabilistic support vector machine to combine authenticity probabilities and identify if the video is real or false. On the other hand, regardless of the video's quality, resolution, or source, "Fake Catcher" detects fraudulent content with excellent accuracy. Nevertheless, the loss of biological signal preservation occurs from its lack of a discriminator. It is problematic to formulate loss function that is consistent with the suggested signal processes.

22.3 Proposed System

Numerous tools exist for generating DF content, yet reliable detection tools for both videos and images are scarce. The proposed approach to DF detection, encompassing both images and videos, represents a significant contribution aimed at curtailing DF dissemination online. Envisioned is a user-friendly web-based platform enabling the upload of both images and videos for classification as fake or real. Scalability of this research could lead to the development of a browser plugin for automatic DF detection. Furthermore, this method might be integrated by well-known apps such as Facebook and WhatsApp for user convenience. A major goal is to assess user acceptance and performance in terms of security, correctness, dependability, and ease of use. The approach focuses on three different forms of DF: replacement, retrenchment, and interpersonal. The architecture of the scheme is shown in Figure 22.2 while Figure 22.3 illustrates the flow of the proposed system's training process.

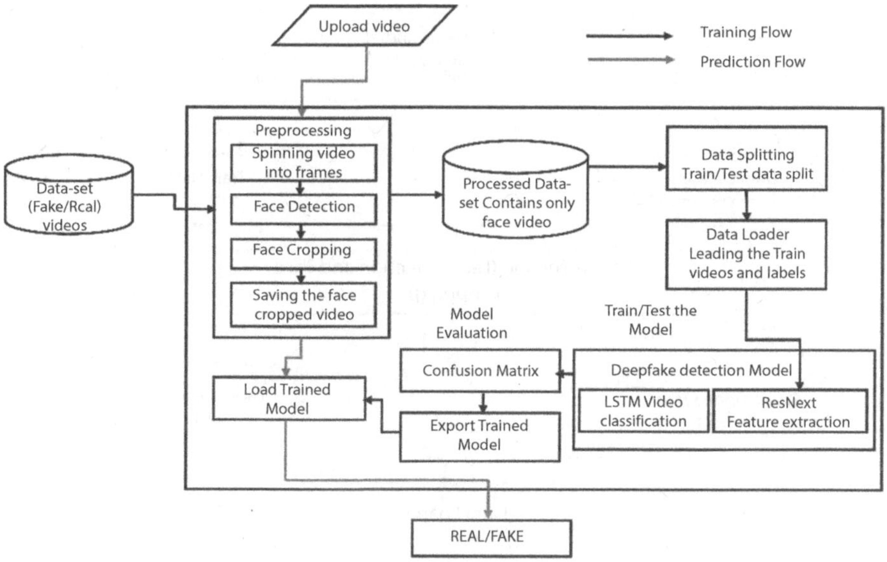

Figure 22.2 Scheme architecture.

A. Dataset

Our dataset is a blend sourced from various repositories, including CelebDF for images and DFDC for video detection, complemented by FaceForensics++ for validation. We have meticulously created this dataset to feature an equal distribution of original and manipulated content, with 70% allocated for training and 30% for testing.

B. Preprocessing

First, videos must be segmented into frames. Next, face detection and cropping must be done. To ensure uniformity in frame count, we calculate the mean frames per video and create a new dataset with frames matching this mean. Frames lacking detected faces are excluded. Due to computational constraints, we propose using only the first 100 frames of each 10-second video for training purposes.

C. Model

ResNext50_32x4d makes up our model architecture, which is followed by an LSTM layer [16–18]. The preprocessed videos are loaded and divided into sets by the Data Loader. Frames from videos that have been analyzed are then supplied into the model in small batches for testing and training.

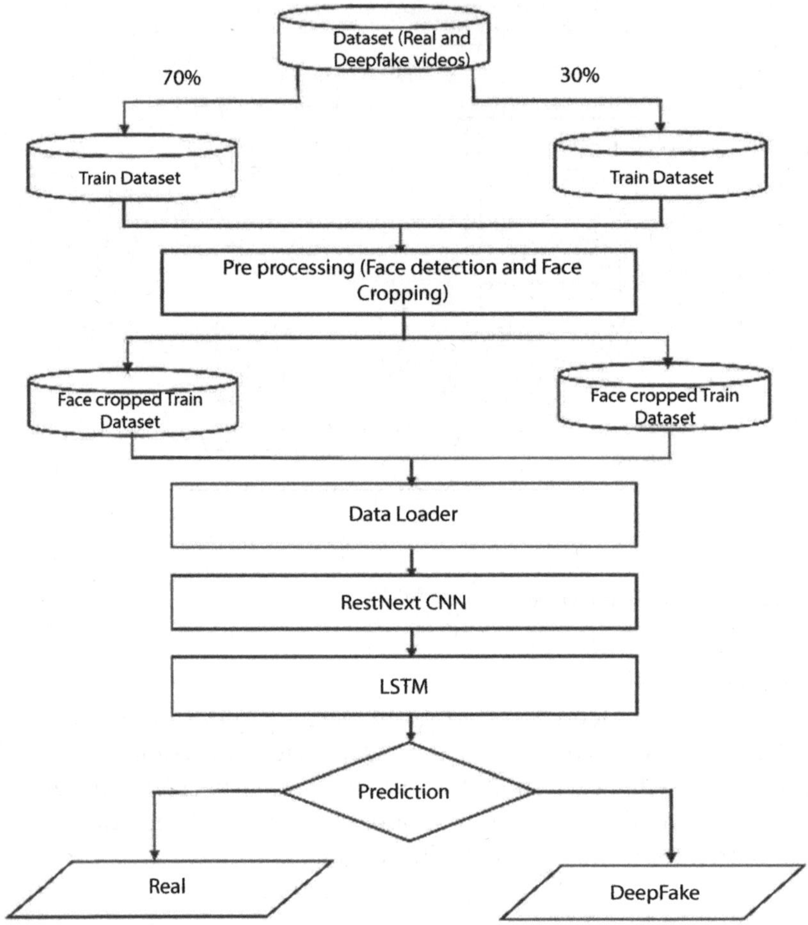

Figure 22.3 Training flow.

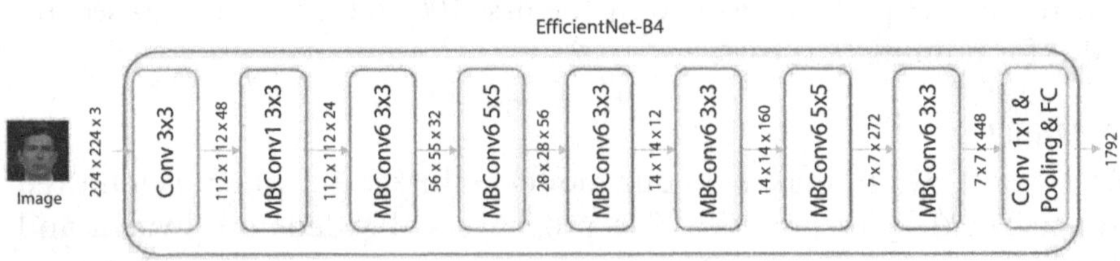

Figure 22.4 Fake image detection CNN layers.

D. CNN layers for fake image detection

For detecting fake images, our model uses multiple CNN layers. These layers are specifically designed to analyze image data and extract intricate features indicative of manipulation or authenticity. However, as noted by Wang *et al.* [15], CNN-generated images still exhibit artifacts that can be exploited for detection. In this regard Figure 22.4 shows the proposed structure of CNN layers for fake image detection.

E. Preprocessing with ResNext CNN and detection with LSTM for video

Video detection, on the other hand, follows a different approach. We first preprocess the videos using ResNext CNN, for which LSTM network is used to carry out the real detection. This combination allows for a comprehensive analysis of temporal patterns within the videos, aiding in the accurate identification of DF content.

F. Prediction

A fresh video is given to the trained algorithm for forecasting. In addition, the format of the learned model is imported by preprocessing a new video. The faces in the divided video are cropped once it has been divided into frames, and instead of being kept locally, the cropped frames are transmitted directly to the trained model for detection. Figure 22.5 shows the prediction procedure.

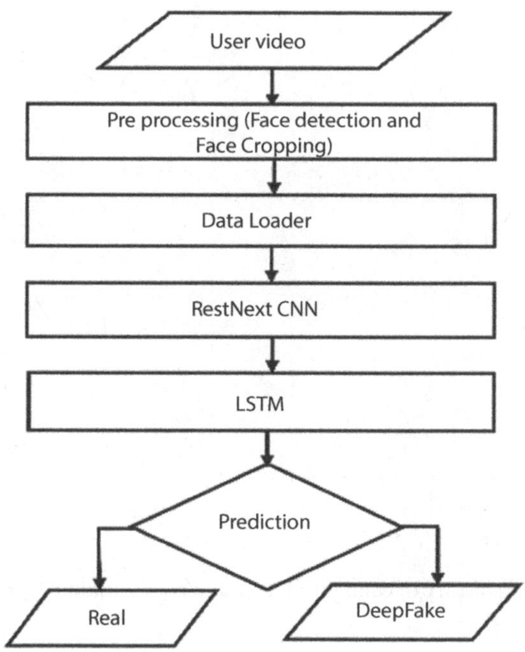

Figure 22.5 Predictions flow.

22.4 Results

A. Training progress

The project's training progress is demonstrated in Figure 22.6, depicting four distinct configurations, while Table 22.1 summarizes the comparative analysis of accuracy for all configurations on training, validation and test sets.

Configuration 1: Utilizing the ResNext perfect and freezing all convolution parameters.

Configuration 2: Utilizing ResNext model and retraining the last 8 MB-ConvBlocks with the last two layers (convolution layer and classifier).

Configuration 3: Utilizing the ResNext model and retraining the last 16 MB-ConvBlocks with the last two layers (convolution layer and classifier).

Configuration 4: Utilizing the pretrained ResNext model and integrating a spatial transformer network after MBConvBlock 20.

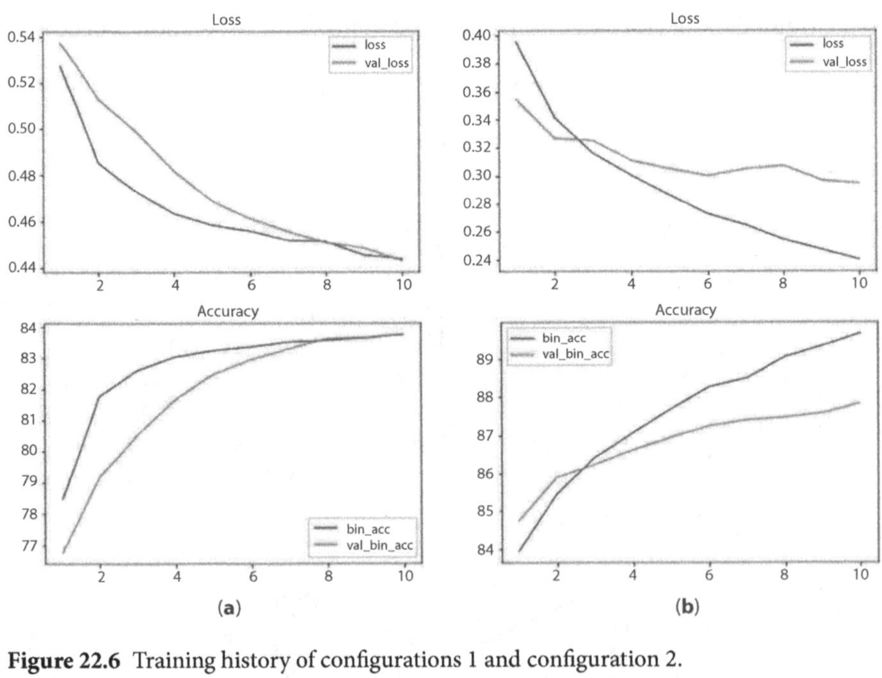

Figure 22.6 Training history of configurations 1 and configuration 2.

Table 22.1 Comparative analysis of results.

Model	Acc (train)	Acc (valid)	Acc (test)
Configuration 1	83.64	83.64	83.44
Configuration 2	89.69	87.84	86.94
Configuration 3	92.99	90.34	90.08
Configuration 4	92.05	89.67	91.10

B. Performance analysis

Here is a comparative summary illustrating the performance across different configurations:

C. Attention mechanism insights

The results of the LSTM model variant incorporating the attention mechanism (Figure 22.7) are not included here; this model was solely utilized to enhance our understanding of the attention mechanism.

We analyzed the map calculated on the faces of our dataset. We selected the output of the sigmoid layer within the attention block (Figure 22.4), forming a two-dimensional map sized 32 × 32. This map was then upscaled to align with the dimensions of the face input (128 × 128) and overlaid onto it.

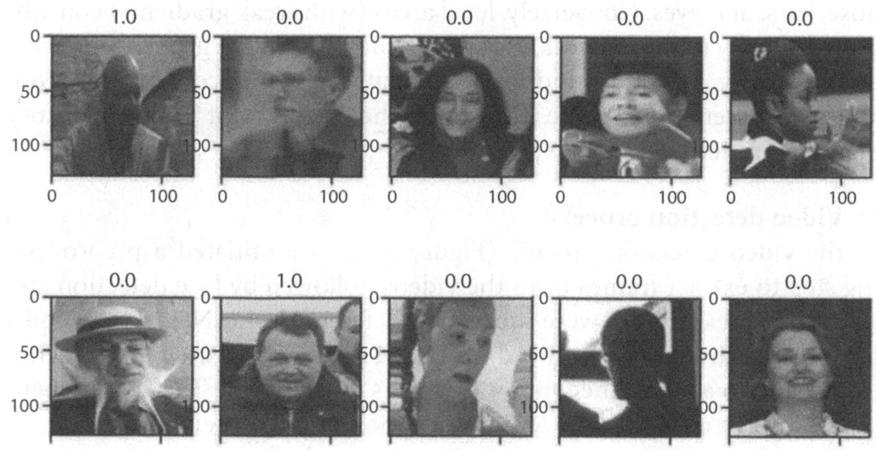

Figure 22.7 Attention mechanism.

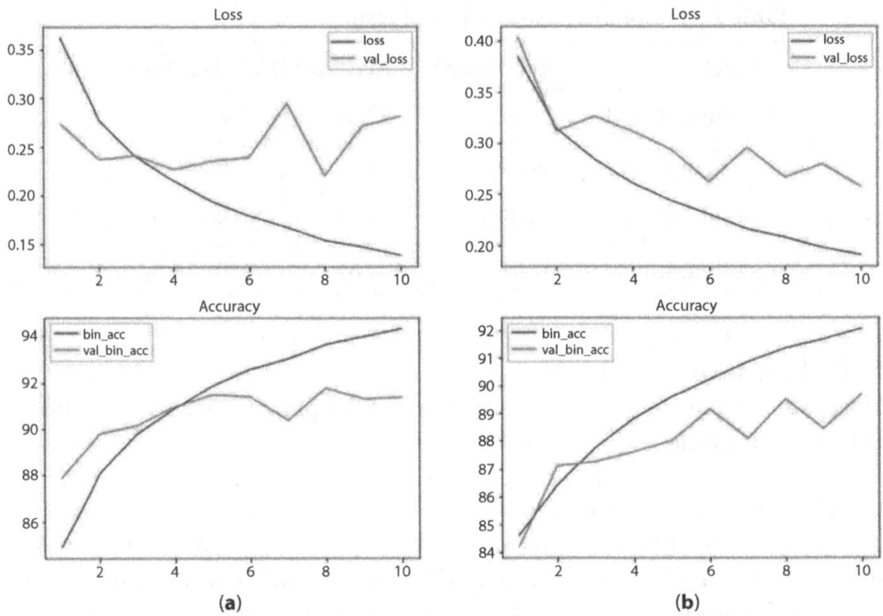

Figure 22.8 Presents the training history of configurations 3 and 4, highlighting accuracy and loss trends.

Based on observations from Figure 22.7, it appears that this simple attention mechanism favors important face features such as the mouth, nose, ears, and eyes. Conversely, level areas (with weak gradients) contribute minimally to the network. Notably, artifacts from DF generation methods primarily cluster around facial attributes, aligning convincingly with real-world scenarios. Figure 22.8 shows the Accuracy of Training history of configurations.

D. Video detection process

In the video detection process (Figure 22.4), we initiated a preprocessing step to extract frames from the videos, followed by face detection and cropping. These frames were subsequently fed into a ResNext CNN model for feature extraction. Afterward, an LSTM network was used for sequence processing to analyze the temporal aspects of the video. This comprehensive approach ensured the accurate detection of DF content in videos.

The production representation will indicate whether the images or video is authentic or a DF, as well as the model's confidence level.

22.5 Discussion of Results

In this section, we delve into the outcomes presented earlier, discussing the challenges encountered, the applied solutions, the anticipated improvements, and the research avenues identified throughout this project.

A. Interpretation of results
Let's highlight the significant differences among our various model configurations:

Configuration 1: Freezing all convolution parameters while utilizing the pretrained model ensures the preservation of robust features learned by the ResNext model.

Configurations 2 and 3: Freezing convolution parameters in specific blocks alongside the classifier involves training unfrozen layers on new images, particularly the higher layers. This approach prevents the model from memorizing differences among real and fake faces by encouraging it to seek useful artifacts for fake face finding.

Configuration 4: The integration of a spatial transformer network after MBConvBlock 20 applies spatial transformation to features during forward propagation, enhancing model performance.

Overall, our models perform well, with observed precision gains using the spatial transformer network in the last configuration. However, further training and hyperparameter adjustments could lead to even better performance.

B. Encountered and resolved issues
Initially, accessing the dataset storage from Google Colab posed a challenge due to storage limitations. Additionally, dataset preprocessing proved time-consuming, requiring careful consideration to ensure code generality for future challenges in DF video detection. Face detection technology evaluation led us to choose Blazeface from multiple options.

Overfitting during initial experiments was a concern, which we addressed by adjusting the number of images extracted per video to 15, striking a balance to mitigate overfitting.

C. Improvements

One improvement we plan to implement is to ensemble methods, combining predictions from different classifiers based on CNNs to enhance stability and performance. Additionally, combining our approach with the temporal pipeline method proposed by Li *et al.* [10] could further enhance detection accuracy.

D. Discussion and research perspectives

The rising quality of DFs necessitates improved detection methods. DFDC and other reference datasets are regularly updated to support the development and validation of detection techniques, especially deep learning–based ones. Taking into account the difficulties presented by adversarial environments, future research should concentrate on introducing more reliable, scalable, and generalizable techniques.

An intriguing research direction is integrating detection methods into social media platforms to combat the widespread impact of DFs effectively. This integration, coupled with digital watermarking and potentially blockchain technology, could provide immutable authenticity details for multimedia content, addressing the growing concerns surrounding DF proliferation. Despite its effectiveness in various domains, minimal research exists on DF detection leveraging blockchain technology.

22.6 Conclusion

Our project introduces a neural network approach to differentiate between real and fake images and videos, along with the confidence of the proposed model. We were inspired by how DFs are made using GANs with the assistance of autoencoders. Our method analyzes each frame of the content using ResNext CNN for images and recurrent neural network with LSTM for videos. By integrating Internet of Things (IoT) devices for continuous data collection and real-time analysis, our model can process data from various sources dynamically. By considering specific parameters, our model accurately identifies whether the content is authentic or manipulated. We expect our IoT-integrated method to perform well when applied to real-world data in real-time scenarios.

References

1. Agarwal, S., *et al.*, Protecting World Leaders Against Deep Fakes, 2019.
2. Al-Dhabi, Y. and Zhang, S., Deepfake Video Detection by Combining Convolutional Neural Network (CNN) and Recurrent Neural Network (RNN), 2021, DOI 10.1109/CSAIEE54046.2021.9543264.
3. Almars, A.M., Deepfakes detection techniques using deep learning: A survey. *J. Comput. Commun.*, 09, 20–35, 2021, DOI 10.4236/jcc.2021.95003.
4. Badale, A., Castelino, L., Gomes, J., Deep Fake Detection Using Neural Networks. 9, 349–354, 2021.
5. Ciftci, U.A., Demir, I., Yin, L., FakeCatcher: Detection of Synthetic Portrait Videos Using Biological Signals. *IEEE Trans. Pattern Anal. Mach. Intell.*, *9*, 1, 2020.
6. Dheeraj, J.C., Nandakumar, K., Aditya, A.V., Chethan, B.S., Kartheek, G.C.R., Detecting Deepfakes Using Deep Learning, 2021, DOI 10.1109/RTEICT52294.2021.9573740.
7. Guera, D. and Delp, E.J., Deepfake video detection using recurrent neural networks, in: *2018 15th IEEE International Conference on Advanced Video and Signal Based Surveillance (AVSS)*, IEEE, 2018, November, DOI 10.1109/AVSS.2018.8639163.
8. Jaiswal, G., Hybrid recurrent deep learning model for DeepFake video detection, in: *(IEEE, 2021) 8th Uttar Pradesh Section International Conference on Electrical, Electronics and Computer Engineering (UPCON)*, pp. 1–5, 2021, DOI 10.1109/UPCON52273.2021.9667632.
9. Kim, H., *et al.*, Deep video portraits. *ACM Trans. Graph.*, 37, 1–14, 2018, Available from: arXiv:1901.02212v2, DOI 10.1145/3197517.3201283.
10. Li, M., Liu, B., Hu, Y., Wang, Y., Exposing Deepfake Videos by Tracking Eye Movements, 2020, DOI 10.1109/ICPR48806.2021.9413139.
11. Li, Y., Chang, M.C., Lyu, S., Exposing AI created fake videos by detecting eye blinking arxiv.
12. Li, Y., Chang, M.C., Lyu, S., Ictu Oculi: Exposing AI Created Fake Videos by Detecting Eye Blinking, 2019, DOI 10.1109/WIFS.2018.8630787.
13. Nagao, M., Natural language processing and knowledge, in: *2005 International Conference on Natural Language Processing and Knowledge Engineering*, p. 1, 2005, DOI 10.1109/NLPKE.2005.1598694.
14. Nguyen, H.H., Yamagishi, J., Echizen, I., Using Capsule Networks to Detect Forged Images and Videos.
15. Wang, S.Y., Wang, O., Zhang, R., Owens, A., Efros, A.A., CNN-Generated Images Are Surprisingly Easy to Spot… for Now, DOI 10.1109/CVPR42600.2020.00872.
16. Kalita, K., Ganesh, N., Balamurugan, S. (Eds.), *Metaheuristics for Machine Learning: Algorithms and Applications*, John Wiley & Sons, Hoboken, NJ, USA, 2024.

17. Kalita, K., Ganesh, N., Jayalakshmi, S., Chohan, J.S., Mallik, S., Qin, H., Multi-Objective artificial bee colony optimized hybrid deep belief network and XGBoost algorithm for heart disease prediction. *Front. Digit. Health*, 5, 1279644, 2023.
18. Ganesh, N., Shankar, R., Mahdal, M., Murugan, J.S., Chohan, J.S., Kalita, K., Exploring Deep Learning Methods for Computer Vision Applications across Multiple Sectors: Challenges and Future Trends. *CMES-Comput. Model. Eng. Sci.*, 139, 1, 2024.

23

Reducing the False Rejection Using Novel Iris Recognition by Comparing with Elastic Bunch Graph Matching for Smartphones

Kamalesh S.* **and V. Nagaraju**

Department of Computer Science Engineering, Saveetha School of Engineering, Saveetha Institute of Medical and Technical Sciences, Saveetha University, Chennai, India

Abstract

In order to reduce false rejection, this study has made use of novel iris recognition, the VGG16 architecture, and deep learning algorithms such as elastic bunch graph matching. The sample size was determined using G*Power of 0.8, significance level (α) and (β) values of 0.05 and 0.2, respectively, and a confidence interval of 95%, resulting in 20 samples, 10 in each group where group 1 is novel iris recognition and group 2 is elastic bunch graph matching. In comparison to the elastic bunch graph matching's 93.1280% success rate, the suggested novel iris recognition system has a success rate of 94.2606%. There is a noticeable difference between these two. The research's significance threshold was obtained to be P = 0.336 ($P > 0.05$) for both accuracy and loss, which is statistically not significant, suggesting that there is no significant difference between the two algorithms. Face rejection, which occurs with traditional facial recognition models as a result of major modifications in human metabolism and face mask, has been reduced by the 16-layer VGG16 convolutional neural network used in the study process. The research and outcomes support this conclusion.

***Keywords*:** Novel iris recognition, research, false rejection rate, elastic bunch graph matching (EBGM), smartphone, VGG16

**Corresponding author*: kamaleshsrs19@saveetha.com

Kanak Kalita, S. Vishnu Kumar and M. Niranjanamurthy (eds.) Industrial Internet of Things and Advanced Techniques for Sensor Data Aggregation and Fusion, (359–370) © 2026 Scrivener Publishing LLC

Introduction

The face, the most prevalent visual pattern in daily life, is a significant biometric feature. Using this biometric characteristic, people may be easily identified by humans [2]. We turn to robots to help with recognizing applications such as criminal authentication, identification, etc., whenever people fail for one reason or another. Humans are skilled at routine recognition tasks, but robots still need to be educated to catch up. Face recognition is inevitably a valuable biometric that may be used for a variety of purposes [16]. Therefore, in addition to password confidentiality and warnings of account hacking, social networking services such as Facebook are moving toward using facial recognition to secure user account security Hsieh *et al.* [7] spoke about distinguishing the natural iris texture from the cosmetic contact lens. Proença and Alexandre [10] proposed an iris classification method that divides normalized and segmented images into six regions.

Early on in the development of Computer Vision, the face recognition issue was taken into consideration; it is currently seeing a resurgence. The twin fundamental types of feature-based and holistic recognition group many recognition methods. Turk and Pentlad's [2] Eigenface Principal Component Analysis (PCA) technique uses a comprehensive approach that works well with pose-invariant face pictures [8]. The mean square error is computed, but the distinctions between various facial photos are more crucial to classifying the data correctly. In order to identify the most distinctive traits among the different face classes, linear discriminant analysis was suggested. The human iris is naturally insulated from the outside world because it is an internal organ of the eye that is concealed beneath the cornea as well as the aqueous humor. Additionally, it may be surgically altered without endangering the user's eyesight much. As a result, no two sets of irises have ever been the same, even in the instance of identical twins [5]. Because of the iris's aforementioned qualities, it is used in construction, banks, border crossings, airports, government buildings, and more. The ability to identify a plastic or dead iris, thanks to a physiological reaction to light, further increases its suitability for use in automated identification. In addition, the independent component analysis (ICA) method was proposed to calculate the independent components to distinguish between various facial photos. DLA (dynamic link architecture) [9], a feature-based technique, is suggested as a way to address the shortcomings of face model approaches. The flexible elastic graph matching method, which makes use of Gabor wavelets [12], is then used. The elastic bunch graph matching (EBGM) method is then provided in and takes into consideration the position changes in the profile, frontal, and three-fourths frontal face photos [6]. Its same Gabor wavelets are used, but the distortions (pose-variation) that may be addressed in face pictures are constrained.

This study preprocesses the image using the stretching approach, then segments it using the midpoint methodology, a recently introduced technique, and then trivializes the resultant image. EBGM is used to extract the feature, and sample cases and test cases are both generated using it. Then, the Euclidean distance is utilized to determine how similar the test scenarios and the template are to one another.

Materials and Methods

The SSE's (Saveetha School of Engineering's) Machine Learning Laboratory at SIMATS (Saveetha Institute of Medical and Technical Sciences) created the suggested research topic. The proposed deep learning model comprises two distinct kinds of groupings. Based on calculations using a total of 20 sample sizes across 40 epochs for training, testing, and validation data bank, EBGM and novel iris recognition (IR) are separated into groups 1 and 2, (10 from group 1 and 10 from group 2), respectively. Using the Computer Vision (CV2) software, 20 image faces were recovered from a camera device [13]. After going through an augmentation procedure, 20 raw images made up the data bank. The repetitive and undesired areas of the photos were cut out during the data preprocessing steps, designating the two points of a rectangular box.

The acquired real-time data bank was used experimentally in the current research investigation. The creation of iris detection and identification uses Python programming. Python is one of the most popular application tools for developing and analyzing ML model output. Throughout the various stages of ML classifier processing, a variety of tools and created standard functions are utilized to calculate localization loss.

VGG16 Architecture

The 16-layer VGG16 convolutional neural network that was utilized in the research has improved the model by lowering face rejection, which occurs with traditional face recognition models as a result of major changes in human metabolism and facial mask [3]. The facts and results allow for the drawing of this conclusion.

With 1000 images divided across 1000 distinct categories, the object recognition, as well as the classification algorithm VGG16, achieves a prediction score of 92.7%. It is a helpful method for classifying photographs and is simple to use to impart knowledge. The 16th value of VGG16 represents the 16 weighted layers. In VGG16, only 16 of the total 21 layers are gravity layers atop levels, often known as teaching parameter levels (13 convolutional, 5 max pooling, and 3 density).

For VGG16, a 224 × 244 luminance band input tensor is required [1]. The most outstanding feature of VGG16 is that it consistently used the same cushioning and was crucial for a successful layer of a 2 × 2 filter with cadence 2 and preferred entirely linked levels of a 3 × 3 filter with steps across a substantial number of ultraparameters [11]. The highest cadence and degrees of inversion are evenly distributed throughout the entire design; 64 filters make up the Conv-1 layer, 126 filters make up the Conv-2 layer, 256 filters make up the Conv-3 layer, and 524 filters make up the Conv-4 and Conv-5 levels. A block of convolutional layers is followed by three layers fully connected (FC), the third of which conducts 1000-way ILSVRC categorization and appears to have 1000 channels.

Pseudo code

Step 1: Read in iris images.
Step 2: Extract iris features using EBGM.
Step 3: Store iris features in a database.
Step 4: Capture an iris image using a smartphone camera.
Step 5: Extract iris features from the captured image using EBGM.
Step 6: Compare iris features from the captured image with those stored in the database.
Step 7: If the iris features match, allow access. If not, reject access and prompt for reentry.
Step 8: Repeat steps 4 to 7 for multiple iris images.
Step 9: Calculate the false rejection rate and compare with previous results.
Step 10: If the false rejection rate has decreased, conclude that novel IR with EBGM is an effective method for reducing false rejections on smartphones.

Elastic Bunch Graph Matching

The EBGM takes the picture as input and forms face bunch graph (FBG) for design pictures in step I: The characteristics are retrieved using the technique outlined in section B, and the FBGs of various users are created as a result. For that specific type of face picture, these face templates created from training photos are referred to as model graphs. Every single face picture is converted into a single face pattern (FBG), and each subject's face image characteristics are then individually extracted. For each sample and user for whom closed-set recognition is to be done, an equal number of predictor graphs are constructed. Form FBG for new photos in step II: Following the process of feature [4] extraction described in section B [14, 15], FBGs for novel photos are constructed when all the face blueprints, or model graphs, have been formed. Find the detection performance in phase 3. The model face bunches graphs that have been saved are compared to the FBG that was built for new photos. This technique does not classify anything using a classifier [4, 14, 15]. It uses the information included in each face graph to calculate the cosine similarities between the two faces. For each calibration point seen between the model and the new image features, the jets are utilized to determine the cosine similarity score.

Pseudocode

Input: Iris image X ($m \times n$ matrix), iris image Y ($m \times p$ matrix)
Output: Matching indices ($n \times p$ matrix)
Step 1: Preprocess the iris images X and Y by removing noise, enhancing edges, etc.
Step 2: Extract iris features from X and Y, such as the iris texture and/or the iris boundary.
Step 3: Construct a graph from the iris features of X, denoted as Gx.
Step 4: Construct a graph from the iris features of Y, denoted as Gy.
Step 5: Initialize the matching indices between X and Y to a random assignment.
Step 6: Compute the elastic energy between Gx and Gy using the current matching indices.
Step 7: Optimize the matching indices by minimizing the elastic energy using gradient descent or other optimization methods.
Step 8: Repeat steps 6 to 7 until convergence or maximum iterations are reached.
Step 9: Return the optimized matching indices.

Statistical Analysis

It is possible to generate graphical presentations and compute SD (standard deviation), mean deviation data, and significance point data along with independent-sample *t* test using the well-known statistical application software IBM SPSS. Utilizing the SPSS program, the pertinent intrusion data bank was assessed in the recent research methodology. Self-determining sample testing and group statistical activities centered on the experiment's outcomes [1], and two separate graphs with two different sorts of features were created for each experimental phase.

Ever since a camera device captured 90 picture faces, a collection of 3600 raw photographs was processed using an augmentation pipeline. The repetitive and unwanted areas of the photos were eliminated throughout the data preprocessing steps, leaving the two dimensions of a bounding box. We have two independent variables (accuracy and loss) and two dependent variables (EBGM and IR).

Results

Figure 23.1 depicts the novel IR model's accuracy with that of the EBGM model, in terms of mean accuracy and mean loss. IR's mean accuracy is greater than EBGM, and IR's standard deviation is lower than IR. IR has a mean accuracy of 94.2606% in a bar graph compared to EBGM, which has a mean accuracy of 85.661% obtained from the collected performances from Tables 23.1 and 23.2. The algorithm is shown on the *X*-axis, the mean accuracy is shown on the *Y*-axis, and the standard deviation is shown as ±2 SD.

Table 23.3 presents the accuracy performance metrics of the comparison between the IR and EBGM models. The EBGM algorithm's accuracy is 88.5224%, but the IR model's accuracy is 94.2606%. The IR model outperforms the EBGM in accurately identifying the iris, and, subsequently, the human face.

The statistical computations for the IR and EBGM models are also shown in Table 23.3, along with the mean, standard deviation, and mean standard error. The *t* test uses the accuracy level parameter. The ICA algorithm has a mean accuracy of 88.5224% compared to the proposed method's mean accuracy of 94.2606%. The EBGM algorithm has an SD value of 17.6767, whereas IR has an SD value of 4.94508. The PCA model's mean standard error is 7.59781, whereas the mean of the IR model is 1.56377.

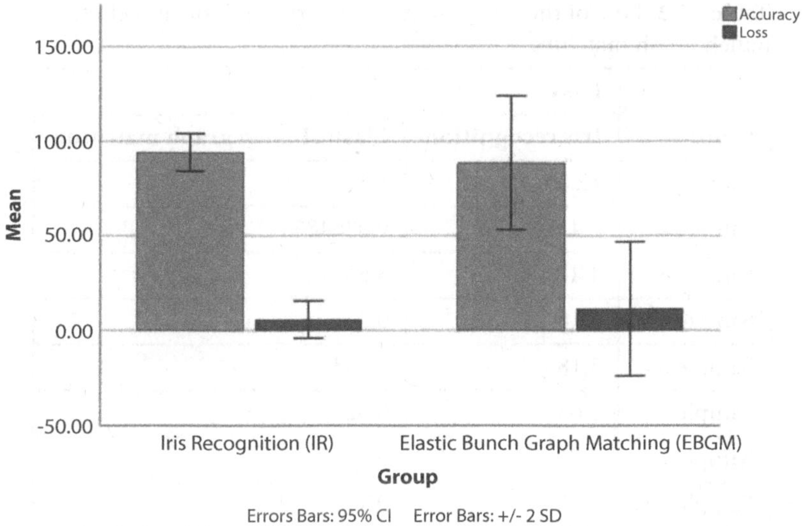

Figure 23.1 Comparison of accuracy of iris recognition (IR) model with elastic bunch graph matching model in terms of mean accuracy. The mean accuracy of the IR model is higher than the EBGM, and the standard deviation of the IR is better than the EBGM. Bar graph comparison of IR, which has mean accuracy of 94.2606%, compared to EBGM, which has mean accuracy of 88.5224%. X-axis algorithm, Y-axis mean accuracy with SD ±2 SD and with a confidence interval of 95%.

Table 23.1 Accuracy of the performance of iris recognition and elastic bunch graph matching.

S. no.	**Accuracy**	
	Iris recognition	**Elastic bunch graph matching**
Sample 1	81.33	94.4
Sample 2	91.16	99.963515
Sample 3	94.92	94.35
Sample 4	93.8	99.7
Sample 5	96.33	71.57
Sample 6	96.556	99.68
Sample 7	96.77	94.03
Sample 8	97.22	99.6
Sample 9	97.15	44.69
Sample 10	97.37	87.24

Table 23.2 Loss of the performance of iris recognition and elastic bunch graph matching.

	Loss	
S. no.	**Iris recognition**	**Elastic bunch graph matching**
Sample 1	15.59	5.6
Sample 2	7.43	0.036485
Sample 3	4.27	5.65
Sample 4	5.18	0.3
Sample 5	3.18	28.43
Sample 6	2.63	0.32
Sample 7	2.76	5.97
Sample 8	2.43	0.4
Sample 9	2.4	55.31
Sample 10	2.25	12.76

Table 23.3 Comparison of accuracy of iris recognition (IR) model with elastic bunch graph matching (EBGM) model. The Iris recognition model had the highest accuracy (97.37 %) with the least loss (2.63%) compared to independent component analysis having the lowest accuracy (87.24%) and highest loss (12.76%).

Group statistics					
	Group	**n**	**Mean**	**Standard deviation**	**Standard error mean**
Accuracy	IR	10	94.2606	4.94508	1.56377
	EBGM	10	88.5224	17.67670	5.58986
Loss	IR	10	5.7394	4.94508	1.56377
	EBGM	10	11.4776	17.67670	5.58986

In Table 23.4, the independent-sample t test is computed for the sample collections with a confidence interval of 95%. Novel IR has a statistical significance value of 0.336 ($P > 0.05$) based on t, according to the SPSS calculation.

Table 23.4 Independent-sample t test is applied for the sample collections with a confidence interval as 95%. After applying the SPSS calculation, it was found that the least square support vector machine has a statistical significance value of 0.336 (P>0.05). Based on t hence they are statistically not significant.

Independent-samples test											
		Levene test for equality of variances		t Test for equality of means							
						Significance				95% confidence interval of the difference	
		F	Significance	t	df	One-sided P	Two-sided P	Mean difference	Standard error difference	Lower	Upper
Accuracy	Equal variances assumed	5.409	0.166	0.989	18	0.166	0.336	5.7825	5.80448	−6.45651	17.93300
	Equal variances not assumed			0.989	10.400	0.166	0.345	5.7825	5.80448	−7.12780	18.60430
Loss	Equal variances assumed	5.409	0.166	−0.989	18	0.166	0.336	−5.7825	5.80448	−17.93300	6.45651
	Equal variances not assumed			−0.989	10.400	0.166	0.345	−5.7825	5.80448	−18.60430	7.12780

Discussion

Computer Vision (CV2) and the open-source machine learning library TensorFlow are used to real-time capture images from a video capture device and input them into an augment pipeline using the Albumentations package. The proposed novel IR system has a success rate of 94.2606% compared to the EBGM's 88.5224% from Table 23.3. These two clearly vary from one another. The significance level for the study was set at $P = 0.336$ ($P > 0.05$). Valid total losses of 0.0040, valid class losses of 4.6066e-06, and valid regression losses of 0.0040 are produced by the pertinent model, which uses the VGG16 architecture.

In recent years, the primary means of protecting people's property has been advances for personal identification due to the growing security needs in our networked society because conventional methods of authentication process rely on aliases, ID cards, badges, or cardholders to certify people. To intercept the transmission of the passcode or even make up a false one is one approach to getting around passcodes or other security measures that need secret codes alone. On the other side, a hacker can imitate, pretend to be, or clone identification cards of token-based systems in order to effectively target them. Biometrics thus emerges as a special form of authentication that may support our defense in such circumstances. The most reliable biometric, compared to voice, face, palms, attitude, and other ones, is novel IR. Because the human iris is an internal eye organ that is hidden under the cornea and the aqueous humor, it is by nature shielded from the outside environment. Additionally, it may be surgically changed without seriously compromising the user's vision. Its eligibility for use in automated identification is further increased by the physiological response to light's capacity to distinguish a plastic or dead iris. Further studies have revealed that while the iris's overall form is genetically predetermined, the specifics of its tiny characteristics are greatly influenced by the environment in the embryonic mesoderm, where they originate. As a result, even in the case of identical twins, no two sets of irises were ever the same. The iris is used in construction, banks, airports, border crossings, government buildings, and more due to the characteristics listed above.

Additionally, despite the fact that the empirical result demonstrates that EBGM performs exceptionally well for iris identification, EBGM has a drawback. That is, calculating independent components (ICs) requires a lot of computer work. The quick calculation of EBGM is one of the field's future directions. In order to compute the approximate ICs in this research, we used the fixed-point technique. We also think that if a more precise ICA calculation was available, the accuracy may be considerably greater.

Conclusion

Using the VGG16 architecture, the pertinent model produced valid total losses of 0.0040, valid class losses of 4.6066e-06, and valid regression losses of 0.0040 demonstrating both the IR and the EBGM, with the IR having the higher accuracy values of the two. The IR has an accuracy rate that is 94.2606% higher than the EBGM, which has an accuracy rating that is only 88.5224% accurate while recognizing a human face by processing iris with an increased accuracy rate. The 16-layer VGG16 convolutional neural system used in the research has minimized face rejection, which happens with typical facial recognition models as a result of fundamental modifications in human metabolism and face mask. This conclusion is backed up by research and findings.

References

1. Cheung, C.Y.-L., Liu, S., Weinreb, R.N., Liu, J., Li, H., Leung, D.Y.-L., Dorairaj, S., *et al.*, Dynamic Analysis of Iris Configuration with Anterior Segment Optical Coherence Tomography. *Invest. Ophthalmol. Visual Sci.*, 51, 8, 4040–46, 2010.
2. Daugman, J. and Li, J.P., *The Proceedings of the International Computer Congress 2004 on Wavelet Analysis and Its Applications, and Active Media Technology*, World Scientific, Singapore, 2004.
3. Jiang, Z.P., Liu, Y.Y., Shao, Z.E., Huang, K.W., An improved VGG16 model for pneumonia image classification. *Appl. Sci.*, 11, 23, 11185, 2021.
4. Hanmandlu, M., Gupta, D., Vasikarla, S., Face Recognition Using Elastic Bunch Graph Matching. *2013 IEEE Applied Imagery Pattern Recognition Workshop (AIPR)*, 2013a, https://doi.org/10.1109/aipr.2013.6749338.
5. Daugman, J.G., High confidence visual recognition of persons by a test of statistical independence. *IEEE Trans. Pattern Anal. Mach. Intell.*, 15, 11, 1148–1161, 2002.
6. Homayon, S., Iris Recognition for Personal Identification Using Lamstar Neural Network. *Int. J. Comput. Sci. Inf. Technol.*, 7, 1, 1–8, 2015.
7. Hsieh, S.-H., Li, Y.-H., Tien, C.-H., A Novel Anti-Spoofing Solution for Iris Recognition Toward Cosmetic Contact Lens Attack Using Spectral ICA Analysis, 2018. 10.3390/s18030795.
8. Liu, Z., Tang, M., Hu, G., Wang, J., Learning Discriminative and Complementary Patches for Face Recognition. *2019 14th IEEE International Conference on Automatic Face & Gesture Recognition (FG 2019)*, 2019, https://doi.org/10.1109/fg.2019.8756598.

9. von der Malsburg, C., Dynamic link architecture. in: *Brain Theory and Neural Networks*. M.A. Arbib, (ed.), MIT Press, Cambridge, MA, 1995.
10. Proença, H. and Alexandre, L.A., Toward Noncooperative Iris Recognition: A Classification Approach Using Multiple Signatures. *IEEE Trans. Pattern Anal. Mach. Intell.*, 29, 4, 607–12, 2007.
11. Rezende, E., Ruppert, G., Carvalho, T., Theophilo, A., Ramos, F., de Geus, P., Malicious Software Classification Using VGG16 Deep Neural Network's Bottleneck Features, in: *Advances in Intelligent Systems and Computing*, pp. 51–59, Springer International Publishing, Cham, 2018.
12. Shi, J.-X. and Gu, X.-F., The Comparison of Iris Recognition Using Principal Component Analysis, Independent Component Analysis and Gabor Wavelets. *2010 3rd International Conference on Computer Science*, 2010, https:// doi.org/10.1109/iccsit.2010.5563947.
13. VGG-16 Convolutional Neural Network - MATLAB vgg16. Accessed December 21, 2022. https://www.mathworks.com/help/deeplearning/ref/vgg16.html.
14. Wiskott, L., Würtz, R., Westphal, G., Elastic Bunch Graph Matching. *Scholarpedia*, 9, 3, 10587, 2014, https://doi.org/10.4249/scholarpedia.10587.
15. Wiskott, L., Fellous, J.M., Kruger, N., von der Malsburg, C., Face Recognition by Elastic Bunch Graph Matching. *Proceedings of International Conference on Image Processing*. vol. 1, pp. 129–132, Santa Barbara, CA, USA, 1997, https:// doi.org/10.1109/icip.1997.647401.
16. Zhao, W., Chellappa, R., Phillips, P.J., Rosenfeld, A., Face Recognition: A Literature Survey. *ACM Comput. Surv.*, 35, 4, 399–458, 2003.

24

Intelligent IoT-Enabled Privacy-Preserving Course Recommendation System: Leveraging NLP Chatbot and Federated Learning with Federated Linear Regression

Dhivyaprabha G.* and Ram Prashath R.

School of Computer Applications, Karpagam College of Engineering, Coimbatore, India

Abstract

In the context of progressive education, artificial intelligence assumes a significant part in advancing personalized learning, providing individualized support, and fostering essential skill development to progress in today's dynamic society. Internet of Things (IoT)–enabled devices, such as smart speakers, wearable technology, and connected classroom tools, find personalized course recommendations to be indispensable tools that assist learners in navigating the huge array of learning resources available to them. Conventional course recommendation systems frequently rely on collaborative filtering or content-based approaches, but they often fall short of providing tailored support or focused attention. This emphasizes the need for creative methods to improve course recommendations, so federated learning and natural language processing (NLP) chatbots emerged, to meet the specific demands of students in an increasingly digitalized learning environment. This research offers novel solutions to this problem by combining federated learning methods with NLP-based chatbots to improve the course recommendation system's accuracy and privacy. An NLP-based chatbot can promote conversational and interactive engagements, giving students access to real-time support and direction. Moreover, federated learning guarantees collaborative model training across decentralized data sources while protecting privacy, enabling the creation of recommendation models that are more precise and customized. In this study,

**Corresponding author*: dhivyarathinam2410@gmail.com

Kanak Kalita, S. Vishnu Kumar and M. Niranjanamurthy (eds.) Industrial Internet of Things and Advanced Techniques for Sensor Data Aggregation and Fusion, (371–384) © 2026 Scrivener Publishing LLC

the data collected from various IoT-enabled educational devices, such as smart learning hubs and personal learning assistants, are analyzed to ensure a diverse and comprehensive dataset for training and evaluation. The result comprises two components: one is developing a chatbot to provide interactive support, whereas the other is putting federated learning into practice to provide individualized course recommendations. The process of implementing federated learning involves the use of complex algorithms such as federated averaging or federated optimization. These techniques protect data privacy, enable collaborative model training, and make it easier to coordinate model updates across decentralized devices. Similar to this, developing algorithms for activities such as response creation, dialogue management, and natural language interpretation is part of the deployment process for NLP chatbots. By facilitating conversational and interactive engagements with users, these algorithms improve user experience and offer support in real time.

Keywords: Personalized learning, personalized assistance, course recommendation, federated learning, natural language processing (NLP), IoT-enabled devices

24.1 Introduction

In an age characterized by the proliferation of online educational resources such as Massive Open Online Courses, the quest for personalized learning experiences has emerged as a pressing imperative [1, 2]. Even with the multitude of courses available covering a wide range of topics and specializations, students frequently face an overwhelming obstacle: the incapacity to successfully navigate this enormous ocean of knowledge [3, 4]. Users were left feeling overburdened and underutilized by the inadequate personalized guidance provided by traditional recommendation systems. Our project intends to fill this essential gap by developing an intelligent course recommendation system by developing a novel strategy that blends the capabilities of natural language processing (NLP) chatbots [5] with federated learning techniques [6], notably federated linear regression [7].

24.1.1 Motivation

Our initiative is motivated by the realization that there is a growing need for individualized educational experiences and that recommendation systems are currently not up to grade in terms of providing this requirement. With an increasing number of online learning platforms, students are confronted with an ever-growing selection of options that compete for their time and interest. But despite all of this variety, there is a basic problem that needs to be solved: how can students find their way across this huge environment to find classes that suit their unique interests, objectives, and learning preferences? Moreover, conventional approaches to recommendation systems are under examination for their capacity to protect user anonymity while providing insightful recommendations, as the study of privacy concerns surrounding data privacy and security intensifies.

24.1.2 Research Gap

Even with the progress made in recommendation systems, there is still a significant research gap in the area of personalized course suggestions, especially when it comes to the combination of federated learning and NLP. Current systems are good at gathering user information and making general suggestions, but they are not always good at interpreting the complex desires and goals expressed in natural language. Moreover, maintaining user privacy is a perplexing task that calls for creative solutions that go beyond traditional centralized training models. In this regard, our study aims to close this research gap by utilizing the federated learning and NLP chatbot synergies to provide individualized course recommendations while maintaining user privacy [8–11].

24.1.3 Significance

Intelligent course recommendation systems that can provide individualized recommendations at scale are becoming more necessary in response to this challenge. By directing students toward courses that suit their interests, objectives, and learning preferences, these systems have the potential to improve the efficacy of online learning. NLP, chatbots, and federated learning are examples of innovative technologies that can be used to create recommendation systems that are not only more relevant and accurate but also scalable and privacy preserving.

24.1.4 Objectives

Based on this research need and motivation, our study aims to achieve the following goals:

- ➢ Create a user-friendly NLP chatbot interface that can be used to engage in natural language conversations to learn about user preferences and goals [5].

- Use federated learning strategies to train a recommendation model cooperatively across decentralized data sources, such as federated linear regression [6, 7].
- Create and implement a recommendation engine that, while maintaining data security and privacy, provides customized course recommendations based on the profiles of individual users.
- Assess the system's performance using measures for privacy protection, user happiness, and suggestion accuracy.

To sum up, our study uses the combined strength (Figure 24.1) of federated learning approaches and NLP chatbots to tackle a significant research gap in the field of tailored course suggestions that hope to transform the online education scene by introducing a novel strategy that puts user engagement, suggestion accuracy, and data protection first. This will enable learners to take on rewarding and enriching learning journeys that are customized to their own interests and goals. Understanding the flow of this system is depicted in Figure 24.2.

24.2 Related Works

Three main domains are covered by the associated work in this field of study: course recommendation systems, federated learning, and chatbots based on NLP. The use of federated learning approaches in education data analytics was investigated by Fachola *et al.* in their study "Federated Learning for Data Analytics in Education" [12].

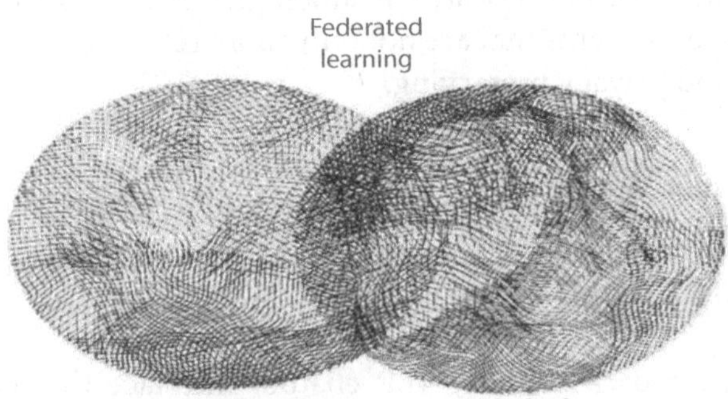

Figure 24.1 Federated learning architecture for course recommendation and NLP chatbot.

The study examined the difficulties centralized data analysis presents in learning environments, highlighting privacy and data silos concerns. The authors intended to address these issues and raise the precision of data analytics by putting federated learning into practice. Their study assessed the efficacy of federated learning algorithms in a variety of circumstances and perhaps offered insights about how to apply them in educational settings. This work adds important knowledge to the realm of machine learning algorithms that protect privacy, especially with regard to educational data analysis and decision-making.

As an example of an NLP chatbot, consider the paper "The Development of a Chatbot Using Convolutional Neural Networks" [13], which was written by Tsakiris *et al.* Convolutional neural networks (CNNs) are a kind of deep learning algorithm that are frequently used for image processing but are increasingly being applied to NLP tasks. The study highlights the creative application of this architecture in the context of conversational bots by presenting their research, which uses CNNs to create a chatbot. The architecture and training methodology of the CNN-based chatbot are probably covered in the article, with a focus on how well it can comprehend user input and provide relevant responses. The authors may compare CNN performance with other conventional NLP techniques and offer insights into the benefits and drawbacks of using CNNs for chatbot development. This study adds to the growing corpus of research on deep learning techniques for conversational artificial intelligence and natural language comprehension, demonstrating CNNs' potential in the chatbot creation space.

A novel recommendation system strategy using random forest for rating-based recommender systems is presented in the paper "A Random Forest Approach for Rating-Based Recommender System" [14]. Presenting their research, Ajesh *et al.* examine how to us random forest, an ensemble machine learning technique, to create recommender systems that are based on user ratings. The process of using random forest for recommendation tasks, including feature selection, training, and prediction, is probably covered in the study. Some benefits of using random forest for recommendation systems, such as its capacity to manage huge datasets and nonlinear correlations between user preferences and products, may be discussed by the authors. The study may also contain experimental findings illustrating how well the suggested strategy performs in comparison to conventional recommendation algorithms. Overall, this research contributes to the field of recommender systems by offering a new perspective on leveraging machine learning techniques such as random forest for personalized recommendations based on user ratings.

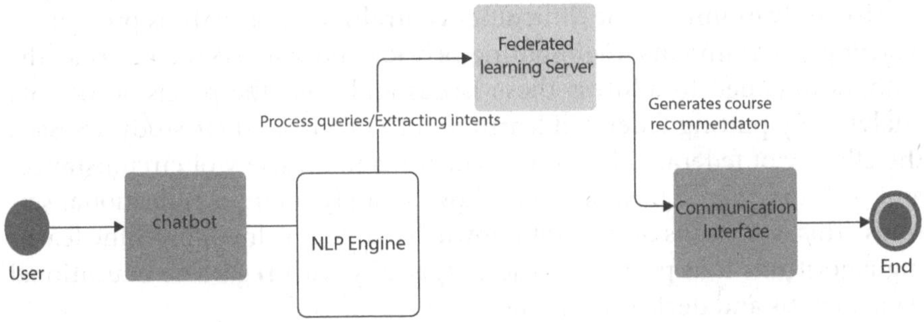

Figure 24.2 System architecture.

24.3 Proposed System

A) Implementation of NLP chatbot

Data collection

Details about numerous courses from appropriate sources such as university catalogs, online learning environments, and educational websites were gathered. Course titles, descriptions, requirements, and course ratings should all be included in these data. Additionally, a wide range of sample questions that users might have when looking for course recommendations are being gathered for user queries. These questions ought to span a variety of subjects, interests, and levels of specificity.

Data preprocessing

i) Tokenization: To enable additional analysis, divide the text data (user query) into discrete tokens, or words or phrases. Use the NLTK module, for instance, to divide sentences into words, and use whitespace or punctuation as delimiters (Figure 24.3).

ii) Stopword removal: Get rid of common terms such as "the," "and," or "or" that do not really add anything to the text's meaning. This aids in lowering data noise.

iii) Lemmatization/stemming: To standardize variations, reduce words to their root or base form (e.g., "running" becomes "run"). While stemming could yield nonwords, lemmatization yields legitimate words.

iv) Intent definition: An example of an intent is shown in Figure 24.3. As seen, the JSON format (Figure 24.5) is used to define each intent, which consists of a tag, patterns (user queries), and corresponding responses. Figure 24.6 shows a comparison of the three algorithms, highlighting their respective strengths and weaknesses.

```
def preprocess_text(text):
    # Tokenization
    tokens = nltk.word_tokenize(text)

    # Lowercasing
    tokens = [token.lower() for token in tokens]

    # Removing punctuation
    tokens = [token for token in tokens if token.isalnum()]

    # Removing stopwords
    stopwords = nltk.corpus.stopwords.words('english')
    tokens = [token for token in tokens if token not in stopwords]

    # Lemmatization
    lemmatizer = nltk.WordNetLemmatizer()
    tokens = [lemmatizer.lemmatize(token) for token in tokens]

    return tokens

# Example usage:
preprocessed_text = preprocess_text(text)
```

Figure 24.3 Data preprocessing using NLTK module in Python integration with methodology.

v) Entity annotation: Identify relevant entities in the user queries, such as specific topics, skills, or preferences mentioned. Annotate these entities for further processing and response customization.

Incorporate the data collection and preprocessing steps into the broader methodology as follows:

Step 1: Gather course data from online sources and compile a dataset of user queries.

Step 2: Preprocess the course descriptions and user queries using tokenization, stopword removal, and lemmatization (Figure 24.4).

Step 3: Define intents for course recommendation queries using the JSON format, incorporating patterns extracted from the preprocessed user queries.

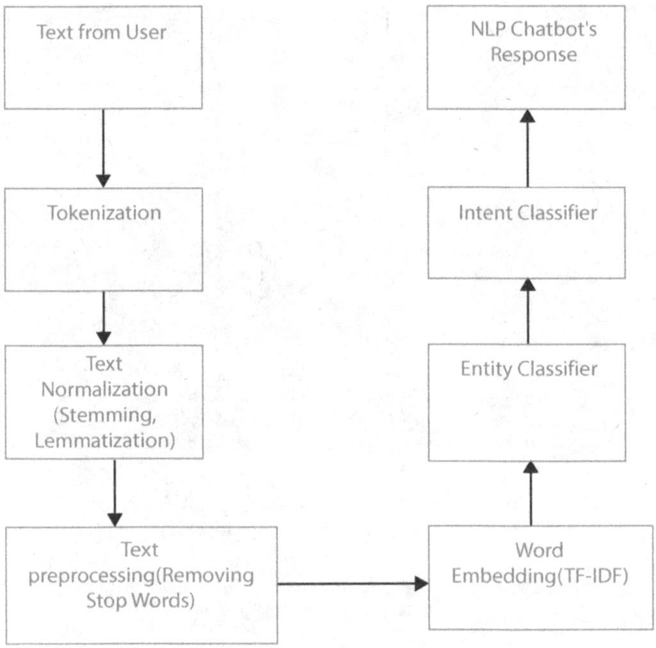

Figure 24.4 Flowchart of preprocessing method for NLP chatbot.

B) Implementation of recommendation system

i) Dataset: The model utilized a dataset containing course descriptions and their corresponding categories. The dataset is preprocessed to tokenize text data and prepare it for feature extraction.

ii) Feature extraction: The model used TF-IDF (term frequency–inverse document frequency) vectorization to convert text data into numerical features.

iii) Model selection: Using the TF-IDF characteristics, the model trained three classifier algorithms: random forest, naive Bayes, and decision tree. These classifiers were selected based on how well they handled text data and how well they fit into the requirements for classification tasks.

The system follows a typical pipeline of data preprocessing, feature extraction, model training, and evaluation. The classifiers were trained on a training set and evaluated on a separate testing set. We evaluated the performance of each classifier using accuracy as the primary metric.

Additionally, we examined other evaluation metrics such as precision, recall, and F1 score to gain deeper insights into their performance [14, 15]. The results indicate the effectiveness of each classifier in predicting course categories and their suitability for the recommendation task.

Our findings suggest that although all three classifiers achieved reasonable accuracy, their performance varied depending on the dataset characteristics and the complexity of the course categories. Random forest exhibited the highest accuracy, followed by naive Bayes and decision tree.


```
{
  "intents": [
    {
      "tag": "course_recommendation",
      "patterns": [
        "recommend a course",
        "suggest me a course",
        "what course should I take?",
        "looking for courses",
        "need course suggestions"
      ],
      "responses": [
        "Sure! What are your interests or what specific topic are you looking to lea
        "Of course! Could you tell me more about what you're interested in learning?
      ]
    }
  ]
}
```


Figure 24.5 JSON format to define intents of the chatbot.

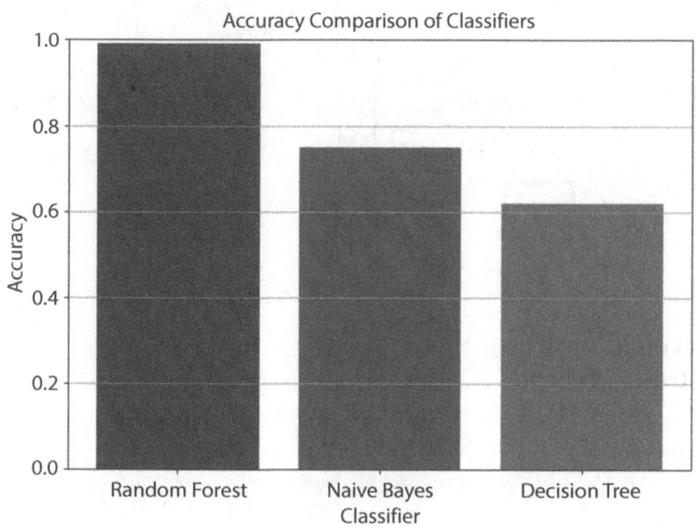

Figure 24.6 Accuracy comparison chart.

C) Implementation of federated learning

In the federated learning setup, the model simulates three decentralized clients, each representing a separate entity with localized data. The dataset is divided into three disjoint subsets, with each subset assigned to a different client. This division ensures that each client holds its own portion of the data without sharing raw data with other clients.

Implementing the federated learning framework using Python programming language and standard machine learning libraries such as scikit-learn. The implementation follows a federated training loop, where each client performs local model training on its own data. The global model is initialized with random parameters and updated iteratively through federated aggregation. Communication between clients and the central server is simulated, with model updates exchanged securely to preserve data privacy.

Model evaluation

Using common evaluation metrics including accuracy, precision, recall, and F1 score, the federated model's performance is assessed. To evaluate the federated model's accuracy in predicting course categories, 80% of the dataset is used for training, whereas 20% is used for testing. The efficiency of the federated learning approach is further assessed by analyzing the convergence speed and communication overhead.

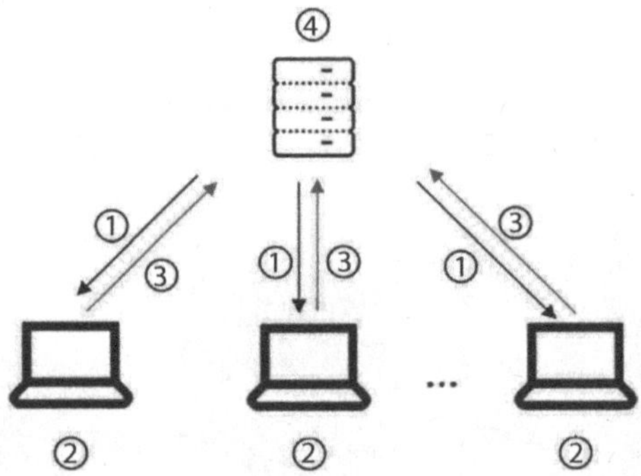

I. Train on local client
II. Distributed client

24.4 Results and Discussion

The promising results obtained from the integration of federated learning and NLP-based chatbots demonstrate the effectiveness of combining advanced machine learning techniques with NLP in educational settings. Internet of Things (IoT) plays a pivotal role in this integration, facilitating data collection from various sources and ensuring seamless communication between decentralized clients and servers.

Federated learning enabled collaborative model training across diverse datasets distributed among different institutions or users while respecting data privacy concerns. This approach allowed the system to learn from a wide range of data sources without centralizing sensitive information, thus addressing privacy regulations and ensuring data security. The incorporation of IoT devices in the federated learning framework enhanced data collection capabilities, enabling the system to leverage decentralized data effectively.

The utilization of NLP-based chatbots enhanced user experience by providing conversational interfaces for interacting with the recommendation system. Users could engage in natural language conversations to express their preferences, ask questions, and receive real-time guidance on course selections. This conversational aspect of the system fostered user engagement and improved the overall learning experience. Moreover, IoT devices facilitated seamless interaction between users and the chatbot, ensuring accessibility and convenience across different platforms and devices.

Evaluation results highlight the effectiveness of the combined approach in delivering accurate and personalized recommendations. By leveraging federated learning to analyze decentralized data and integrating NLP-based chatbots for interactive support, the system could tailor recommendations based on individual preferences, learning styles, and performance metrics. This level of personalization not only enhances user satisfaction but also increases the likelihood of successful course outcomes and improved learning outcomes.

24.5 Conclusion

This research underscores the potency of amalgamating federated learning with NLP-based chatbots, augmented by IoT, to bolster personalized course recommendations within the realm of progressive education. The federated learning framework not only ensures collaborative model training but also safeguards user privacy, leveraging IoT devices for seamless data aggregation and distribution. Simultaneously, the NLP-based chatbot, integrated with IoT, fosters interactive engagement and furnishes real-time support, thereby addressing the nuanced needs of learners amid the contemporary digitalized learning milieu. This cohesive integration of federated learning, NLP-based chatbots, and IoT technologies delineates a robust solution, poised to cater to the evolving demands of modern learners, shaping a more tailored and efficacious educational landscape.

24.6 Future Enhancements

Although this study provides a foundation for improving personalized course recommendations, there are several avenues for future enhancements:

Advanced NLP techniques: Exploring advanced NLP techniques such as transformer models (e.g., BERT, GPT) can improve the chatbot's understanding of user queries and responses, enhancing the conversational experience.

Federated learning optimization: Further optimization of federated learning algorithms can improve model convergence speed and communication efficiency, making federated learning more scalable and adaptable to larger datasets.

References

1. Ajesh, A., Nair, J., Jijin, P.S., A Random Forest Approach for Rating-Based Recommender System, 2016, DOI 10.1109/ICACCI.2016.7732225.
2. Amin, S., *et al.*, Developing a personalized e-learning and MOOC recommender system in IoT-enabled smart education. *IEEE Access*, 11, 136437–136455, 2023, DOI 10.1109/ACCESS.2023.3336676.
3. Attigeri, G., Agrawal, A., Kolekar, S.V., Advanced NLP models for technical university information chatbots: Development and comparative analysis. *IEEE Access*, 12, 29633–29647, 2024.
4. Campos, R., dos Santos, R.P., Oliveira, J., A Recommendation System based on Knowledge Gap Identification in MOOCs Ecosystems, in: *Proceedings of the XVI Brazilian Symposium on Information Systems (SBSI '20)*. Association for Computing Machinery, Article 2, pp. 1–8, New York, NY, USA, 2020.
5. Chaker, R., Bouchet, F., Bachelet, R., How do online learning intentions lead to learning outcomes? The mediating effect of the autotelic dimension of flow in a MOOC. *Comput. Hum. Behav.*, 134, 2022, DOI 10.1016/j.chb.2022.107306.

6. Fachola, C., *et al.*, Federated learning for data analytics in education. *Data*, 8, 43, 2023, DOI 10.3390/data8020043.
7. Hassija, V., Chawla, V., Chamola, V., Sikdar, B., Incentivization and aggregation schemes for federated learning applications. *Trans. Mach. Learn. Comm. Netw.*, 1, 185–196, 2023, DOI 10.1109/TMLCN.2023.3302811.
8. Kashima, T., Kishida, I., Amma, A., Nakayama, H., FedFit: server aggregation through linear regression in federated learning. *IEEE Access*, 12, 22803–22812, 2024, DOI 10.1109/ACCESS.2024.3363884.
9. Khalid, A., Lundqvist, K., Yates, A., Azam, M.A., Online learning path recommender system for MOOCs. *2023 IEEE Global Engineering Education Conference (EDUCON)*, Kuwait, Kuwait, pp. 1–10, 2023, DOI 10.1109/EDUCON54358.2023.10125232.
10. Li, B., *et al.*, A personalized recommendation framework based on MOOC system integrating deep learning and big data. *Comput. Electr. Eng.*, 106, 108571, 2023, ISSN 0045-7906, DOI 10.1016/j.compeleceng.2022.108571.
11. Tsakiris, G., *et al.*, The development of a chatbot using Convolutional Neural Networks. *SHS Web Conf.*, 139, 03009, 2022, DOI 10.1051/shsconf/202213903009.
12. Fachola, C., Tornaría, A., Bermolen, P., Capdehourat, G., Etcheverry, L., Fariello, M.I., Federated Learning for Data Analytics in Education. *Data*, 8, 43, 2023.
13. Tsakiris, Giorgos, *et al.*, The development of a chatbot using Convolutional Neural Networks. *SHS Web of Conferences*, vol. 139, EDP Sciences, 2022.
14. Ajesh, A., Nair, J., Jijin, P.S., A random forest approach for rating-based recommender system. *International Conference on Advances in Computing, Communications and Informatics (ICACCI)*, IEEE, 2016.
15. Kumar, S.V., Chohan, J.S., Kalita, K., WhaleOptNB: A Method for Automated Biomedical Text Document Classification, in: *Intelligent Computing and Optimization. ICO 2023, Lecture Notes in Networks and Systems*, vol. 1169, Cham, Springer, 2024, DoI: 10.1007/978-3-031-73324-6_18.

25

Harnessing YOLO-Powered Drones for Cloud-Based Weed Density Mapping Focusing Agri 4.0

S. Vishnu Kumar[1]*, G. Aloy Anuja Mary[1], B. Sathyasri[1], Murali Kalipindi[2] and Chivon Choeung[3]

[1]*Department of Electronics & Communication Engineering, Vel Tech Rangarajan Dr. Sagunthala R&D Institute of Science and Technology, Chennai, India*
[2]*Department of Artificial Intelligence and Machine Learning, Vijaya Institute of Technology for Women, Vijayawada, India*
[3]*Faculty of Electricity, National Polytechnic Institute of Cambodia, Phnom Penh, Cambodia*

Abstract

This chapter explores the integration of Internet of Things (IoT) and Machine Learning (ML), particularly in drones, focusing on smart agricultural. This chapter presents a drone-based weed density mapping system that combines advanced ML algorithms, such as YOLO (You Only Look Once), with high-resolution drone-mounted cameras for efficient weed detection and classification. By embedding computational capabilities directly on the drone, the system minimizes reliance on bandwidth-intensive cloud processing, enhancing resource efficiency. The proposed approach incorporates geolocation data using GPS (Global Positioning System) modules and transmits essential insights to Google Cloud IoT Core *via* MQTT (Message Queuing Telemetry Transport) for visualization and analysis. Weed density data are further processed to generate heat maps, enabling targeted herbicide application and reducing environmental impact. This approach contributes to sustainable agriculture aligned with Agri 4.0. Through innovative hardware–software integration, the system addresses key challenges such as varying soil conditions, environmental factors, and weed–crop differentiation. This study underscores the potential of IoT and ML in revolutionizing sustainable agriculture by delivering a scalable, real-time solution for automated weed management and resource optimization.

**Corresponding author*: mail2jitvishnu@gmail.com

Kanak Kalita, S. Vishnu Kumar and M. Niranjanamurthy (eds.) Industrial Internet of Things and Advanced Techniques for Sensor Data Aggregation and Fusion, (385–400) © 2026 Scrivener Publishing LLC

***Keywords*:** Weed detection, density mapping, Internet of Agriculture, machine learning, YOLO v8

25.1 Integration of Internet of Things and Machine Learning in Agriculture

The integration of Internet of Things (IoT) and Machine Learning (ML) technologies in agriculture presents a transformative approach to enhance crop management and its sustainability. These technologies offer innovative solutions for various agricultural challenges, particularly in developing useful insights. Smart devices, such as drones, can be used to survey the agricultural field to get meaning full insights, but the data being transmitted to cloud for insight development require a lot of bandwidth and power [1]. To address these challenges, researchers are exploring edge computing solutions that allow data processing to occur closer to the source, thereby reducing latency and bandwidth requirements while conserving energy [2]. This challenge emphasizes the need for efficient data compression techniques and low-power communication protocols that can optimize resource usage while maintaining the integrity of real-time analytics [3]. These advancements not only enhance the efficiency of agricultural practices but also pave the way for more sustainable farming methods that can adapt to changing environmental conditions. Recent advancements in ML algorithm have significantly enhanced object detection, particularly finding applications in precision agriculture [4]. Thus, integrating the objection detection algorithms into the drones equipped with high-resolution cameras can cover large agricultural areas and provide detailed imagery of crop fields [5]. The application of ML algorithms over these images further enhances the detection of object of interest, by leveraging advanced image recognition techniques in real time [6]. This synergy optimizes resource utilization, minimizes resource wastage, and ultimately provides insights about the crop to plan necessary precautionary steps [7]. Such innovations not only improve crop yields but also contribute to the overall sustainability of agricultural practices, ensuring that farmers can respond proactively to potential threats such as pests or disease outbreaks. By enabling timely interventions, these technologies empower farmers to make data-driven decisions that enhance productivity while preserving the environment [8].

Thus, this chapter explores the adoption of these technologies—where a drone is equipped with high-resolution camera and onboard processing units that utilize a specifically developed ML algorithm toward identifying weeds in the agriculture field, marking the advent of a new era in smart farming where data-driven decisions enhance agricultural resilience and efficiency [9]. The proposed system delivers a promising real-time solution for efficient and accurate weed density mapping across large agricultural area.

25.2 Significance of Automated Weed Removal in Agriculture

Weeds hold immense significance in agriculture, as they pose the ability to outcompete crops of interest by growing rapidly. These are unwanted plants that grow in agricultural fields along with the crops being cultivated and compete with crops of interest for essential resources such as sunlight, nutrients, space, and water, which can significantly impact crop growth and yield [10]. The effects of allowing weeds to grow with the crops further extend to various aspects, including increased production costs, diminished product quality, keen susceptibility to diseases, and decrease in the commercial value of the harvested product. Although manual weed removal practice offers an effective and environmental-friendly procedure, it is labor-intensive and time-consuming. On the other hand, herbicide spraying using machines and robots offers efficiency; however, the process still suffers from time consumption due to lack of knowledge of the environment of the farm. Thus, a methodology is proposed to develop the weed density map of an area, which could be used as reference tool to deliver targeted herbicides that saves resource wastage. The proposed methodology also indirectly helps to curb the excessive use of herbicides that leads to the development of herbicide-resistant weed species.

25.3 Challenges in Developing Weed Density MAP

Drone-based weed detection requires covering the entire agricultural field using a high-resolution camera and processing the camera feed for identifying the weeds and their location. This necessitates the inclusion of cloud processing, as the quantum of data involved is high, but sending the full video feed to cloud again drains the battery and network resources that are crucial for a drone setup [5]. Also, different plant varieties have distinct features, such as leaves, shapes, flowers, and fruits, necessitating the development of robust frameworks for weeds and crop classification. One of the primary challenges in the said process is the processing of continuous inputs, which in addition gets affected from the varying backgrounds and environmental conditions. Furthermore, the dynamic nature of agricultural soil type causes distractions. Thus, developing a system that can reliably identify and target weeds in diverse conditions requires extensive training and validation of ML models, along with the integration of sophisticated image processing techniques.

Thus, this chapter focuses on developing an unmanned aerial vehicle (UAV)–based density mapping system that utilizes ML-based object detection algorithm and cloud-based visualizing tool that results in sending only the necessary details to cloud rather than sending the full camera feed, achieving a resource-efficient setup focusing on Industry 4.0. This weed density map can thus help the users to plan their activities toward automated weed-removing process.

25.4 Development of YOLO and Cloud-Based Weed Density Mapping System

The objective of this chapter is to introduce the reader to the practical usages of connected drones equipped with ML algorithms toward developing weed density mapping for their respective crops as illustrated in Figure 25.1. To implement the described process, an embedded development board that supports parameters such as object detection algorithms like YOLO (You Only Look Once) (needs decent computational capability or external inference), camera connectivity (to capture video frames), GPS (Global Positioning System) module interface (for geolocation), and MQTT (Message Queuing Telemetry Transport), client (to publish data to the cloud) needs to be used [11].

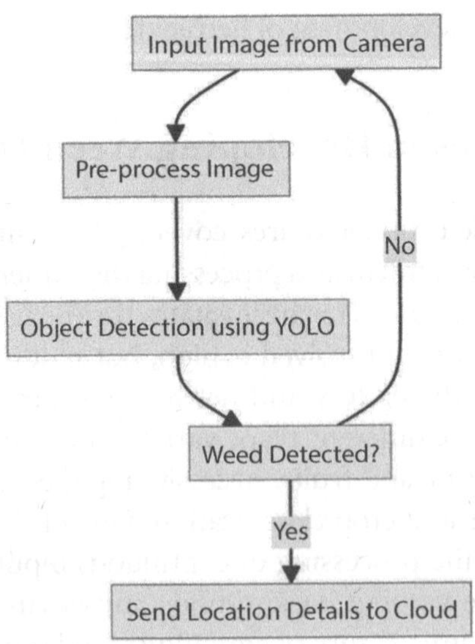

Figure 25.1 Overview of the proposed work.

Thus, in the current work, Raspberry Pi 4 is used, as it can be programmed using Python that has very good ML library support, has GPIO pins for GPS modules, can interface with camera *via* the camera serial interface (CSI) connector, and has built-in Wi-Fi for wireless communication.

25.4.1 Drone—Data Collection and Transmission

25.4.1.1 Hardware Connection

To set up the connections for the system, connect the Raspberry Pi camera module to the CSI connector on the Raspberry Pi. For the GPS module, such as the NEO-6M, establish the connections as illustrated in Figure 25.2; link the TX pin of the GPS module to the RX pin (GPIO15) on the Raspberry Pi and the RX pin of the GPS module to the TX pin (GPIO14) on the Raspberry Pi. Power the GPS module by connecting its VCC pin to either the 3.3V or 5V pin on the Raspberry Pi, depending on the module's specifications, and connect the GND pin to the Raspberry Pi's ground. The completed setup would look as shown in Figure 25.3.

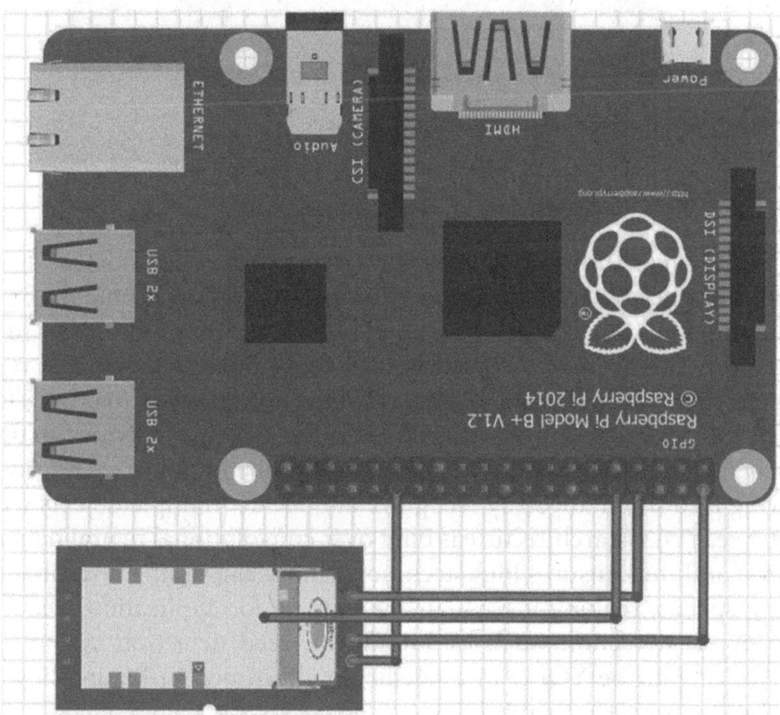

Figure 25.2 Hardware connection.

Figure 25.3 Configuration of the UAV platform used.

25.4.1.2 YOLO-Based Weed Detection Model

The YOLO algorithm is a state-of-the-art real-time object detection system that frames object detection as a single regression problem, directly predicting bounding boxes and class probabilities from full images in one evaluation. This approach contrasts with traditional methods that repurpose classifiers or localizers to perform detection, thereby making YOLO significantly faster and more efficient [12]. The algorithm divides an image into a grid and assigns bounding boxes and probabilities to each grid cell, allowing it to simultaneously recognize and locate multiple objects within the image. YOLO's architecture is built over convolutional neural networks (CNNs) and thus ensures high accuracy while maintaining real-time processing speeds, making it particularly suitable for applications requiring rapid object detection, such as automated weed detection system [13]. The working of the YOLO in a nutshell is illustrated in Figure 25.4, and descriptions are described below.

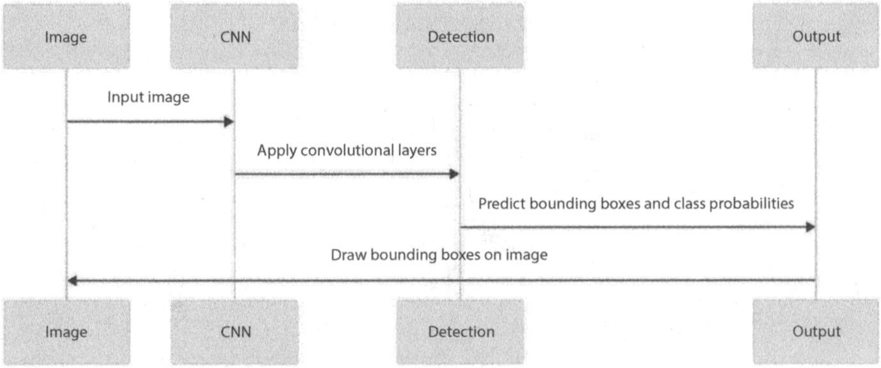

Figure 25.4 Working of YOLO.

- The process starts with an input image fed into the system. This is represented by the participant "Image."
- The image is sent to the CNN, which applies multiple convolutional layers to the image. These layers are responsible for extracting various features from the image, such as edges, textures, and patterns.
- The processed image from the CNN is then sent to the detection phase, represented by the participant "Detection," where the algorithm predicts bounding boxes and class probabilities for objects within the image.
- Bounding boxes are rectangles that surround the detected objects, and class probabilities indicate the likelihood of each detected object belonging to a specific class.
- The detection results are sent to the output phase, depicted as the participant "output," where the output phase draws the predicted bounding boxes on the original image, providing a visual representation of the detected objects.
- The final annotated image, with bounding boxes and labels, is sent back to the "image" participant, completing the process.

In the current work, the development of YOLO model starts with the dataset preparation, which is illustrated in Figure 25.5, whereas Figure 25.6 shows the actual annotated frame of a chili field, where the green box represents the weeds in the frame.

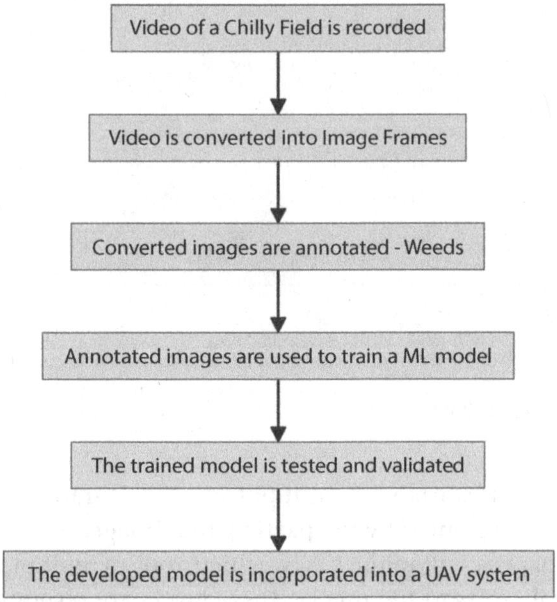

Figure 25.5 Implementation flow of the proposed system.

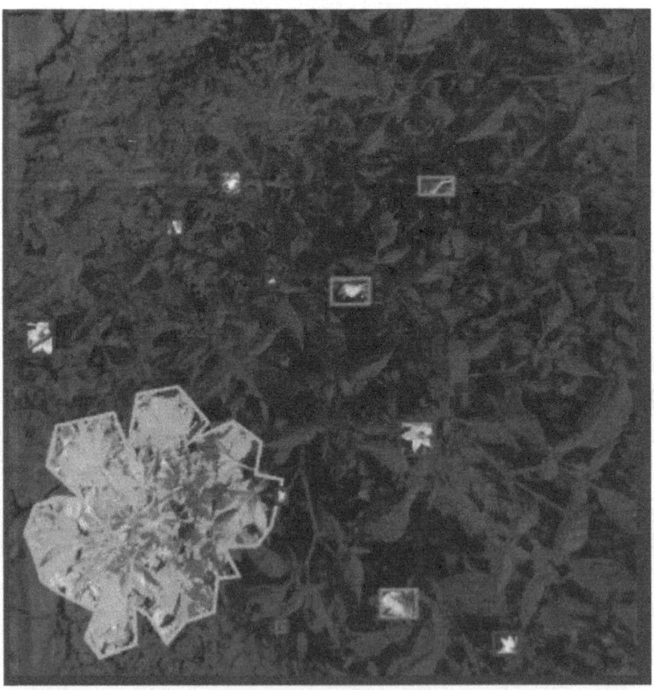

Figure 25.6 Dataset preparation-object annotating.

25.4.1.3 *Publish Data to Google Cloud Using MQTT*

As weed density mapping requires the maps and other technologies to be incorporated, Google's Cloud IoT Core is used as the IoT platform. The platform typically provides basic MQTT and HTTPS data connectivity and in addition provides authentication, visualization, data processing, and alerting. Because the cloud IoT core uses MQTT bridges for telemetry data, the edge device (drone) must connect to the MQTT bridge using the MQTT protocol with the following broker details.

- **MQTT bridge**: mqtt.googleapis.com:8883
- **MQTT topic format**: projects/{project-id}/locations/{region}/registries/{registry-id}/devices/{device-id}

To achieve this, a Python MQTT library such as Paho-MQTT can be used with the MQTT broker URL, port number, client ID, username, and password. This setup allows for seamless communication between the edge device and the cloud platform, enabling real-time data transmission and effective monitoring of weed density across various agricultural fields [14].

25.4.1.4 *Python Code*

The proposed system integrates technologies such as YOLO v8, GPS module, and Google Cloud IoT. First, it initializes a lightweight YOLO v8 model for detecting weeds in video frames captured *via* a camera, counting detected weeds based on confidence scores greater than 0.5. A GPS module (NEO-6M) retrieves latitude and longitude data using serial communication, parsing it from NMEA sentences in GPGGA format. If weeds are detected, the program generates a JSON Web Token (JWT) for secure authentication and publishes the weed count along with GPS coordinates to Google Cloud IoT Core *via* MQTT [15]. The main loop captures video frames, processes them to identify weeds, and triggers data transmission to the cloud while optionally displaying the video feed. This system is particularly useful for precision agriculture, enabling targeted weed management and leveraging IoT for data storage and analysis.

Python code

```
from ultralytics import YOLO
import serial
import jwt
```

```
import datetime
import paho.mqtt.client as mqtt
import json
import cv2

# Initialize YOLO v8 model
def initialize_yolo():
    model = YOLO("yolov8n.pt") # Use a lightweight model for the Raspberry Pi
    return model

# Function to detect weeds using YOLO v8
def detect_weeds(frame, model):
    results = model(frame) # Inference
    weeds_detected = 0
    for result in results[0].boxes:
        if result.conf > 0.5 and result.name == "weed": # Adjust the 'weed' class
name as required
        weeds_detected += 1
    return weeds_detected

# Function to get GPS coordinates from NEO-6M
def get_gps_coordinates():
    gps_serial = serial.Serial("/dev/serial0", baudrate=9600, timeout=1) # /dev/
serial0 maps to GPIO 14 (TX) and 15 (RX)
    while True:
        line = gps_serial.readline().decode("ascii", errors="replace")
        if line.startswith("$GPGGA"): # Parse GPGGA data for latitude and
longitude
    try:
        data = line.split(",")
        if data[2] and data[4]: # Check if latitude and longitude data are available
            latitude = float(data[2]) / 100
            longitude = float(data[4]) / 100
            return latitude, longitude
        except Exception as e:
            print(f"Error parsing GPS data: {e}")
    return None, None

# Function to create JWT for Google Cloud IoT
def create_jwt(project_id, private_key_file, algorithm):
token = {
```

```
        "iat": datetime.datetime.utcnow(),
        "exp": datetime.datetime.utcnow() + datetime.timedelta(minutes=60),
        "aud": project_id,
}
with open(private_key_file, "r") as f:
        private_key = f.read()
return jwt.encode(token, private_key, algorithm=algorithm)

# Function to publish data to Google Cloud IoT
def publish_to_cloud(weeds_count, latitude, longitude):
        project_id = "your-project-id"
        registry_id = "your-registry-id"
        device_id = "your-device-id"
        region = "your-region"
        private_key_file = "path/to/private_key.pem"
        algorithm = "RS256"

        mqtt_bridge_hostname = "mqtt.googleapis.com"
        mqtt_bridge_port = 8883

        client = mqtt.Client(client_id=f"projects/{project_id}/locations/{region}/
registries/{registry_id}/devices/{device_id}")
        client.username_pw_set(username="unused",     password=create_jwt(proj-
ect_id, private_key_file, algorithm))
        client.tls_set() # Secure connection
        client.connect(mqtt_bridge_hostname, mqtt_bridge_port)

        topic = f"/devices/{device_id}/events"
        payload = json.dumps({"weeds_detected": weeds_count, "latitude": latitude,
"longitude": longitude})

        client.publish(topic, payload, qos=1)
        client.disconnect()

# Main loop
def main():
        # Initialize YOLO v8 model and camera
        model = initialize_yolo()
        camera = cv2.VideoCapture(0) # CSI Camera Module

        while True:
```

```
        ret, frame = camera.read()
        if not ret:
            break

        # Detect weeds
        weeds_count = detect_weeds(frame, model)

        if weeds_count > 0:
            # Get GPS coordinates
            lat, lon = get_gps_coordinates()

            if lat is not None and lon is not None:
                # Publish data to cloud
                publish_to_cloud(weeds_count, lat, lon)

        # (Optional) Display the frame
        cv2.imshow("Weed Detection", frame)
        if cv2.waitKey(1) & 0xFF == ord('q'):
            break

    camera.release()
    cv2.destroyAllWindows()

if __name__ == "__main__":
    main()
```

25.4.2 Visualizing Weed Density as a Heat Map at Cloud

Toward the proposed work, the Google's **Cloud IoT Core** service is used, which allows devices to connect securely and send telemetry data. Once the data are in Google Cloud, it is stored, processed, and visualized. The following steps detail the steps to set up the cloud system:

- Create a Google Cloud Project in the Google Cloud Console.
- Enable the **Cloud IoT Core API.**
- Set up a **registry** in IoT Core to manage your devices.
- Register your device (drone) in the registry, providing its unique credentials.
- Once the data reaches the IoT Core, it can be directed to a storage.

- Next, stream the stored data into **BigQuery**, a powerful analytics database.
- Finally, visualize the data using tools such as **Google Data Studio, where** your dashboard is designed with maps (for lat/long) and weed count trends.

Below is a Python script that incorporates an SQL query to interact with Google BigQuery service. The script runs the SQL commands inside the Python program, where the SQL query is written as a string in Python and is passed to BigQuery for execution. Using the Google Cloud BigQuery library, the script authenticates with Google Cloud, submits the SQL query, and retrieves the results. The SQL part (SELECT * FROM ...) defines what data you want to fetch or manipulate, whereas the Python part takes care of connecting to BigQuery, running the query, and processing the results.

Python code

```
from google.cloud import bigquery
def query_bigquery():
    client = bigquery.Client()
    query = """
    SELECT *
    FROM 'your-project-id.dataset.table'
    ORDER BY timestamp DESC
    LIMIT 10
    """
    query_job = client.query(query)
    for row in query_job:
      print(row)
query_bigquery()
```

For an efficient spatial analysis on regional weed count, we can use the grid-based aggregation technique, which groups data into uniform grid cells by rounding latitude and longitude to a fixed decimal place.

SQL code

```
SELECT
    ROUND(Latitude, 2) AS Lat_Rounded,
    ROUND(Longitude, 2) AS Lon_Rounded,
    AVG(Weed_Count) AS Avg_Weed_Count
FROM 'your_project.dataset.table'
```

```
GROUP BY Lat_Rounded, Lon_Rounded
ORDER BY Lat_Rounded, Lon_Rounded;
```

Once the data are simplified, Google Map's API and Folium are used to create a heat map, as shown in Figure 25.7,

Python code

```
import folium
import pandas as pd
# Load aggregated data
data = pd.DataFrame({
    "latitude": [12.9716, 12.9720],
    "longitude": [77.5946, 77.5948],
    "avg_weed_count": [10, 15]
})

# Initialize a map
mymap = folium.Map(location=[12.9716, 77.5946], zoom_start=12)

# Add heatmap data
from folium.plugins import HeatMap
heat_data = [
    [row["latitude"], row["longitude"], row["avg_weed_count"]] for index, row in data.iterrows()
]
HeatMap(heat_data).add_to(mymap)
```

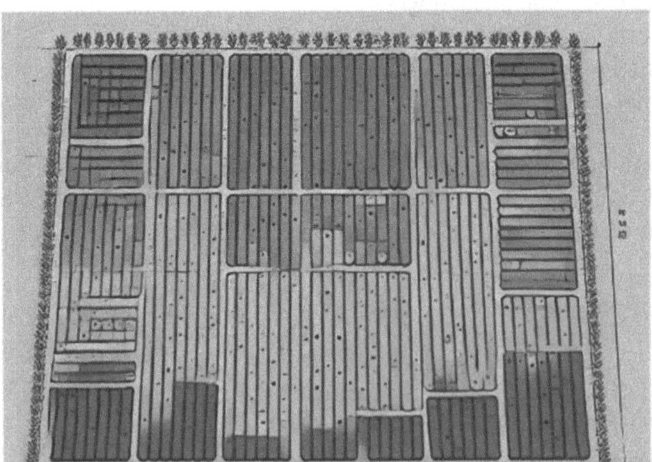

Figure 25.7 Illustration of the detected weed heat map.

```
# Save map
mymap.save("weed_density_map.html")
```

By following these steps, you can effectively identify and analyze the density of weeds in a given area, which can then be used to make data-driven decisions for weed management. In addition, adding filters to view weed data by time, specific zones, or other parameters would give richer insights. Also, combining the weed data with farm boundaries or satellite imagery can facilitate automatic alerts for regions with unusually high weed density.

25.5 Conclusion

This connected UAV-based weed density system is of immense importance due to the growing global food demand and the declining availability of skilled labor in agriculture. Additionally, the system's reduced reliance on chemicals promotes environmental sustainability, contributing to more sustainable agricultural practice. Although YOLO models have shown great promise in weed detection and density mapping, it is important to consider the limitations and challenges associated with their deployment in diverse agricultural settings. Factors such as environmental variability and model robustness need to be addressed to fully harness the potential of these technologies in precision agriculture. On the other hand, the density map can also be used to track changes over time and make informed decisions about weed control measures.

References

1. Thilakarathne, N.N., Bakar, M.S.A., Abas, P.E., Yassin, H., Towards making the fields talks: A real-time cloud enabled IoT crop management platform for smart agriculture. *Front. Plant Sci.*, 13, 1030168, 2023.
2. Elbamby, M.S., Perfecto, C., Liu, C.-F., Park, J., Samarakoon, S., Chen, X., Bennis, M., Wireless edge computing with latency and reliability guarantees. *Proc. IEEE Inst. Electr. Electron. Eng.*, 107, 8, 1717–1737, Aug. 2019.
3. Kumar, S.V., Mary, G.A.A., Mahdal, M., Integrated edge deployable fault diagnostic algorithm for the Internet of Things (IoT): A Methane sensing application. *Sens. (Basel)*, 23, 14, Jul. 2023.
4. Ganesh, Jain, P., Choudhury, A., Dutta, P., Kalita, K., Barsocchi, P., Random forest regression-based machine learning model for accurate estimation of fluid flow in curved pipes. *Processes (Basel)*, 9, 11, 2095, Nov. 2021.

5. Vishnu, S., Mary, A.A.G., Esakki, B., Analyzing the applicability of ML powered microwave sensor for UAV based CH4 sensing. *Int. J. Electr. Electron. Eng. Telecommun.*, 12, 3, 161–170, 2023.
6. Gupta, K.K., Kalita, K., Ghadai, R.K., Ramachandran, M., Gao, X.-Z., Machine learning-based predictive modelling of biodiesel production—A comparative perspective. *Energies (Basel)*, 14, 4, 1122, Feb. 2021.
7. Ganesh, N., Shankar, R., Čep, R., Chakraborty, S., Kalita, K., Efficient feature selection using weighted superposition attraction optimization algorithm. *Appl. Sci. (Basel)*, 13, 5, 3223, Mar. 2023.
8. Ashoka, N.K., Singh, Sunitha, N.H., Saikanth, D.R.K., Singh, O., Sreekumar, G., Singh, B.V., Enhancing agricultural production with digital technologies: A review. *Int. J. Environ. Clim. Change*, 13, 9, 409–422, Jul. 2023.
9. Shanmugasundar, G., Vanitha, M., Čep, R., Kumar, V., Kalita, K., Ramachandran, M., A comparative study of linear, random forest and AdaBoost regressions for modeling non-traditional machining. *Processes (Basel)*, 9, 11, 2015, Nov. 2021.
10. Vercellino, R.B., Hernández, F., Pandolfo, C., Ureta, S., Presotto, A., Agricultural weeds: the contribution of domesticated species to the origin and evolution of feral weeds. *Pest Manag. Sci.*, 79, 3, 922–934, Mar. 2023.
11. Wu, W.-K., Chen, C.-Y., Lee, J.-S., Embedded YOLO, in: *Proceedings of the 2021 International Conference on Multimedia Retrieval*, New York, NY, USA, ACM, Aug. 2021.
12. Agrawal, P., *et al.*, YOLO algorithm implementation for real time object detection and tracking, in: *2022 IEEE Students Conference on Engineering and Systems (SCES)*, IEEE, pp. 1–6, Jul. 2022.
13. Ponika, M., Jahnavi, K., Sridhar, P.S.V.S., Veena, K., Developing a YOLO based Object Detection Application using OpenCV, in: *2023 7th International Conference on Computing Methodologies and Communication (ICCMC)*, IEEE, Feb. 2023.
14. Luthfi, A.M., Karna, N., Mayasari, R., Google maps API implementation on IOT platform for tracking an object using GPS, in: *2019 IEEE Asia Pacific Conference on Wireless and Mobile (APWiMob)*, IEEE, Nov. 2019.
15. Gallo, I., Rehman, A.U., Dehkordi, R.H., Landro, N., La Grassa, R., Boschetti, M., Deep object detection of crop weeds: Performance of YOLOv7 on a real case dataset from UAV images. *Remote Sens. (Basel)*, 15, 2, 539, Jan. 2023.

About the Editors

Kanak Kalita, PhD is an accomplished professor and researcher in the field of Computational Engineering with more than ten years of experience. He has published more than 190 articles and five edited book volumes. His research interests include machine learning, fuzzy decision making, metamodeling, process optimization, the finite element method, and composites.

S. Vishnu Kumar, PhD is an Assistant Professor in the Department of Electronics and Communication Engineering at the Vel Tech Rangarajan Dr. Sagunthala Research and Development Institute of Science and Technology. He has proven his expertise through publication and industrial consultancy projects, including the publication of five scientific research articles, two book chapters, and six research papers presented at international conferences. His research areas include embedded machine learning, Internet of Things, networking, and embedded system design.

M. Niranjanamurthy, PhD is an Assistant Professor in the Department of Artificial Intelligence and Machine Learning at the Bhusanayana Mukundadas Sreenivasaiah Institute of Technology and Management. He has published 25 books and 95 articles in various national and international conferences and journals and filed 30 patents, six of which were granted. His areas of interest are data science, machine learning, e-commerce, and m-commerce.

Index

Also of Interest

Check out these related titles from Scrivener Publishing

Data Driven Modeling, Edited by Arindam Mondal and Souvik Ganguli, ISBN: 9781394287895. Equip yourself with the essentials of informed decision-making with this practical guide to mastering data-driven modeling and extracting actionable, meaningful patterns from the vast sea of modern data.

Quantum-Inspired Approaches for Intelligent Data Processing, Edited by Balamurugan Balusamy, Suman Avdhesh Yadav, S. Ramesh, and M. Vinoth Kumar, ISBN: 9781394336418. Stay ahead of the technological curve with this comprehensive, practical guide that showcases how the fusion of quantum principles and soft computing is delivering transformative solutions across finance, healthcare, and manufacturing.

Supervised and Unsupervised Data Engineering for Multimedia Data, Edited by Suman Kumar Swarnkar, J. P. Patra, Sapna Singh Kshatri, Yogesh Kumar Rathore, and Tien Anh Tran, ISBN: 9781119786344. Explore the cutting-edge realms of data engineering in multimedia with *Supervised and Unsupervised Data Engineering for Multimedia Data*, where expert contributors delve into innovative methodologies, offering invaluable insights to empower both novices and seasoned professionals in mastering the art of manipulating multimedia data with precision and efficiency.

Data Engineering and Data Science: Concepts and Applications, Edited by Kukatlapalli Pradeep Kumar, Aynur Unal, Vinay Jha Pillai, Hari Murthy, and M. Niranjanamurthy, ISBN: 9781119841876. Written and edited by one of the most prolific and well-known experts in the field and his team, this exciting new volume is the "one stop shop" for the concepts and applications of data science and engineering for data scientists across many industries.

Machine Learning and Data Science: Fundamentals and Applications, Edited by Prateek Agrawal, Charu Gupta, Anand Sharma, Vishu Madaan, and Nisheeth Joshi, ISBN: 9781119775614. Written and edited by a team of experts in the field, this collection of papers reflects the most up-to-date and comprehensive current state of machine learning and data science for industry, government, and academia.

DATA WRANGLING: Concepts, Applications, and Tools, Edited by M. Niranjanamurthy, Kavita Sheoran, Geetika Dhand, and Prabhjot Kaurk, ISBN: 9781119879688. Written and edited by some of the world's top experts in the field, this exciting new volume provides state-of-the-art research and latest technological breakthroughs in next-data wrangling, its theoretical concepts, practical applications, and tools for solving everyday problems.

ADVANCES IN DATA SCIENCE AND ANALYTICS, Edited by M. Niranjanamurthy, Hemant Kumar Gianey, and Amir H. Gandomi, ISBN: 9781119791881. Presenting the concepts and advances of data science and analytics, this volume, written and edited by a global team of experts, also goes into the practical applications that can be utilized across multiple disciplines and industries, for both the engineer and the student, focusing on machining learning, big data, business intelligence, and analytics.

CONVERGENCE OF DEEP LEARNING IN CYBER-IOT SYSTEMS AND SECURITY, Edited by Rajdeep Chakraborty, Anupam Ghosh, Jyotsna Kumar Mandal and S. Balamurugan, ISBN: 9781119857211. In-depth analysis of Deep Learning-based cyber-IoT systems and security which will be the industry leader for the next ten years.

MACHINE INTELLIGENCE, BIG DATA ANALYTICS, AND IOT IN IMAGE PROCESSING: Practical Applications, Edited by Ashok Kumar, Megha Bhushan, José A. Galindo, Lalit Garg and Yu-Chen Hu, ISBN: 9781119865049. Discusses both theoretical and practical aspects of how to harness advanced technologies to develop practical applications such as drone-based surveillance, smart transportation, healthcare, farming solutions, and robotics used in automation.

Printed in the USA/Agawam, MA
June 23, 2026

906827.005